BESTSELLING BOOK SERIES

Seagate™ Crystal Reports 7 For Dummies®

The Crystal Reports Toolbar

Button	Function
	Create a new report.
	Open an existing report.
	Save the report.
	Print the report to a printer.
	Preview the report in the Preview Tab.
	Export the report to a file or e-mail.
	Refresh the report data.
	Cut text or an object.
	Copy text or an object.
	Paste text or an object.
	Undo an action.
	Redo an action.
	Insert database, formula, parameter, running totals, and other fields.
	Insert a text object.
	Insert a summary.
	Activate the Report Expert.
	Format any section of the report.
	Activate the Select Expert.
	Set record sort order.
	Insert a graph/chart.
	Insert a map.
	Search for a record on the current report.
100%	Zoom in and out of your report.
	Get context-sensitive help.

Seeing the Data in the Preview Tab

Crystal Reports has two ways to view a report. One is the Design Tab, in which you see the placeholders for the fields, and the other is the Preview Tab, in which real data is inserted into the report from the source database. When you begin creating a new report, only the Design Tab is visible. To see the Preview Tab:

1. **Click the Preview button (or choose File⇨Print Preview).**

   Crystal Reports adds the Preview Tab and shows you a WYSIWIG view of the report: What You See Is What You Get. When you print the report to paper, it should match very closely the Preview Tab layout.

Getting Zoomed!

Zooming in allows you to take a closer look at the formatting of your reports — and to make those teeny-tiny adjustments that make a good report a great one. You can do this in either Design or Preview, but Preview is much more interesting. To take a closer look at your report:

1. **Open the View menu and choose Zoom to get the Magnification Factor dialog box.**
2. **To see more detail, type a number greater than 100 in the Magnification Factor dialog box (you can enter up to 400 as the zoom factor).**

   You have two other choices:

   - Fit Whole Page, which zooms out the view so that you see the entire page at once.
   - Fit One Dimension, which reformats the view so that the entire width of the report is in view.

   To return the view to normal, click the Reset button in this same dialog box.

...For Dummies®: Bestselling Book Series for Beginners

Seagate™ Crystal Reports 7 For Dummies®

The Crystal Reports Format Bar

Button	Function
Arial	Select the font.
14	Select the point size of text.
	Increase the font size of the selected data one point each time you click the button.
	Decrease the font size of the selected data one point each time you click the button.
B	Change the selected data to boldface.
I	Italicize the selected data.
U	Underline the selected data.
	Align the selected data flush left.
	Center the selected data.
	Align the selected data flush right.
$	When a number field is selected, it places a currency symbol with the number.*
,	When a number field is selected, it places a thousands separator in the number.*
%	When a number field is selected, it places a percentage sign with the number.*
	When a number field is selected, adds one decimal place to the number.
	When a number field is selected, subtracts one decimal place from the number.
	Highlight an object.
	Turn group tree on or off.
	Turn supplementary toolbar on or off.

* *Note:* The program refers to your setting in the International section of the Control Panel (Windows 3.*x,* Windows NT) or the Regional section of the Control Panel (Windows 95).

Cheat Sheet $2.95 value. Item 0548-3.
For more information about IDG Books, call 1-800-762-2974.

...For Dummies®: Bestselling Book Series for Beginners

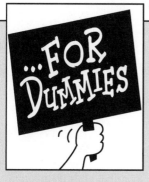

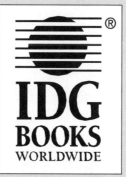

Seagate™ Crystal Reports 7 For Dummies®

by Doug Wolf

IDG Books Worldwide, Inc.
An International Data Group Company

Foster City, CA ◆ Chicago, IL ◆ Indianapolis, IN ◆ New York, NY

Seagate™ Crystal Reports 7 For Dummies®

Published by
IDG Books Worldwide, Inc.
An International Data Group Company
919 E. Hillsdale Blvd.
Suite 400
Foster City, CA 94404
www.idgbooks.com (IDG Books Worldwide Web site)
www.dummies.com (Dummies Press Web site)

Library of Congress Catalog Card No.: 99-60722

ISBN: 0-7645-0548-3

Printed in the United States of America

10 9 8 7 6 5 4 3 2 1

1O/TQ/QT/ZZ/IN

Distributed in the United States by IDG Books Worldwide, Inc.

Distributed by CDG Books Canada Inc. for Canada; by Transworld Publishers Limited in the United Kingdom; by IDG Norge Books for Norway; by IDG Sweden Books for Sweden; by IDG Books Australia Publishing Corporation Pty. Ltd. for Australia and New Zealand; by TransQuest Publishers Pte Ltd. for Singapore, Malaysia, Thailand, Indonesia, and Hong Kong; by Gotop Information Inc. for Taiwan; by ICG Muse, Inc. for Japan; by Norma Comunicaciones S.A. for Colombia; by Intersoft for South Africa; by Le Monde en Tique for France; by International Thomson Publishing for Germany, Austria and Switzerland; by Distribuidora Cuspide for Argentina; by Livraria Cultura for Brazil; by Ediciones ZETA S.C.R. Ltda. for Peru; by WS Computer Publishing Corporation, Inc., for the Philippines; by Contemporanea de Ediciones for Venezuela; by Express Computer Distributors for the Caribbean and West Indies; by Micronesia Media Distributor, Inc. for Micronesia; by Grupo Editorial Norma S.A. for Guatemala; by Chips Computadoras S.A. de C.V. for Mexico; by Editorial Norma de Panama S.A. for Panama; by American Bookshops for Finland. Authorized Sales Agent: Anthony Rudkin Associates for the Middle East and North Africa.

For general information on IDG Books Worldwide's books in the U.S., please call our Consumer Customer Service department at 800-762-2974. For reseller information, including discounts and premium sales, please call our Reseller Customer Service department at 800-434-3422.

For information on where to purchase IDG Books Worldwide's books outside the U.S., please contact our International Sales department at 317-596-5530 or fax 317-596-5692.

For consumer information on foreign language translations, please contact our Customer Service department at 1-800-434-3422, fax 317-596-5692, or e-mail rights@idgbooks.com.

For information on licensing foreign or domestic rights, please phone +1-650-655-3109.

For sales inquiries and special prices for bulk quantities, please contact our Sales department at 650-655-3200 or write to the address above.

For information on using IDG Books Worldwide's books in the classroom or for ordering examination copies, please contact our Educational Sales department at 800-434-2086 or fax 317-596-5499.

For press review copies, author interviews, or other publicity information, please contact our Public Relations department at 650-655-3000 or fax 650-655-3299.

For authorization to photocopy items for corporate, personal, or educational use, please contact Copyright Clearance Center, 222 Rosewood Drive, Danvers, MA 01923, or fax 978-750-4470.

About the Author

Douglas J. Wolf is the author of over 25 other computer software books, ranging from *Quick and Easy Guide to 123* to *ACT! for Windows.* He is the president of Wolf's Byte Productions, which produces video and CD-ROM training on various software products. He is an ACT! Certified Consultant. For more information, or to contact him, browse his Web site at `www.howtosoftware.com`.

He has also been a political consultant, a radio talk show host, and a Pop Warner football coach, and he plays a mean game of tennis. He collects words in his spare time.

ABOUT IDG BOOKS WORLDWIDE

Welcome to the world of IDG Books Worldwide.

IDG Books Worldwide, Inc., is a subsidiary of International Data Group, the world's largest publisher of computer-related information and the leading global provider of information services on information technology. IDG was founded more than 30 years ago by Patrick J. McGovern and now employs more than 9,000 people worldwide. IDG publishes more than 290 computer publications in over 75 countries. More than 90 million people read one or more IDG publications each month.

Launched in 1990, IDG Books Worldwide is today the #1 publisher of best-selling computer books in the United States. We are proud to have received eight awards from the Computer Press Association in recognition of editorial excellence and three from Computer Currents' First Annual Readers' Choice Awards. Our best-selling *...For Dummies®* series has more than 50 million copies in print with translations in 31 languages. IDG Books Worldwide, through a joint venture with IDG's Hi-Tech Beijing, became the first U.S. publisher to publish a computer book in the People's Republic of China. In record time, IDG Books Worldwide has become the first choice for millions of readers around the world who want to learn how to better manage their businesses.

Our mission is simple: Every one of our books is designed to bring extra value and skill-building instructions to the reader. Our books are written by experts who understand and care about our readers. The knowledge base of our editorial staff comes from years of experience in publishing, education, and journalism — experience we use to produce books to carry us into the new millennium. In short, we care about books, so we attract the best people. We devote special attention to details such as audience, interior design, use of icons, and illustrations. And because we use an efficient process of authoring, editing, and desktop publishing our books electronically, we can spend more time ensuring superior content and less time on the technicalities of making books.

You can count on our commitment to deliver high-quality books at competitive prices on topics you want to read about. At IDG Books Worldwide, we continue in the IDG tradition of delivering quality for more than 30 years. You'll find no better book on a subject than one from IDG Books Worldwide.

John Kilcullen
Chairman and CEO
IDG Books Worldwide, Inc.

Steven Berkowitz
President and Publisher
IDG Books Worldwide, Inc.

Eighth Annual Computer Press Awards 1992

Ninth Annual Computer Press Awards 1993

WINNER

Tenth Annual Computer Press Awards 1994

Eleventh Annual Computer Press Awards 1995

IDG is the world's leading IT media, research and exposition company. Founded in 1964, IDG had 1997 revenues of $2.05 billion and has more than 9,000 employees worldwide. IDG offers the widest range of media options that reach IT buyers in 75 countries representing 95% of worldwide IT spending. IDG's diverse product and services portfolio spans six key areas including print publishing, online publishing, expositions and conferences, market research, education and training, and global marketing services. More than 90 million people read one or more of IDG's 290 magazines and newspapers, including IDG's leading global brands — Computerworld, PC World, Network World, Macworld and the Channel World family of publications. IDG Books Worldwide is one of the fastest-growing computer book publishers in the world, with more than 700 titles in 36 languages. The "...For Dummies®" series alone has more than 50 million copies in print. IDG offers online users the largest network of technology-specific Web sites around the world through IDG.net (http://www.idg.net), which comprises more than 225 targeted Web sites in 55 countries worldwide. International Data Corporation (IDC) is the world's largest provider of information technology data, analysis and consulting, with research centers in over 41 countries and more than 400 research analysts worldwide. IDG World Expo is a leading producer of more than 168 globally branded conferences and expositions in 35 countries including E3 (Electronic Entertainment Expo), Macworld Expo, ComNet, Windows World Expo, ICE (Internet Commerce Expo), Agenda, DEMO, and Spotlight. IDG's training subsidiary, ExecuTrain, is the world's largest computer training company, with more than 230 locations worldwide and 785 training courses. IDG Marketing Services helps industry-leading IT companies build international brand recognition by developing global integrated marketing programs via IDG's print, online and exposition products worldwide. Further information about the company can be found at www.idg.com.

1/24/99

Dedication

I want to dedicate the hard work of creating this book to my lovely and talented and oh so sensuous wife, Gloria. She made this book possible by writing some and editing most.

Author's Acknowledgments

Let me begin by acknowledging the folks at Seagate Software who got this book off the ground: Julia Elkins and Ian Galbraith. Next the technical people who patiently read this tome for errors: Kathryn Hunt and Mike Lerch. Finally thanks to Keith Thompson for his brilliant insights when I called for help.

Thanks to the IDG Books team: Joyce Pepple, Mary Corder, Kelly Oliver, Becky Whitney, and Suzanne Thomas.

All of the people involved were indispensable members of the project, and I am sincerely grateful for their involvement.

Publisher's Acknowledgments

We're proud of this book; please register your comments through our IDG Books Worldwide Online Registration Form located at `http://my2cents.dummies.com`.

Some of the people who helped bring this book to market include the following:

Acquisitions, Editorial, and Media Development

Project Editors: Kelly Oliver, Becky Whitney

Acquisitions Editor: Joyce Pepple

Technical Editors: Michael Lerch, Kathryn Hunt

Editorial Manager: Mary P. Corder

Editorial Assistant: Paul E. Kuzmic

Production

Associate Project Coordinator: Maridee Ennis

Layout and Graphics: Angela F. Hunckler, Brent Savage, Jacque Schneider, Kathie Schutte, Janet Seib, Kate Snell, Michael A. Sullivan, Brian Torwelle

Proofreaders: Christine Berman, Kelli Botta, Vickie Broyles, Ethel M. Winslow, Janet M. Withers

Indexer: Sharon Hilgenberg

Special Help

Suzanne Thomas, Valery Bourke

General and Administrative

IDG Books Worldwide, Inc: John Kilcullen, CEO; Steven Berkowitz, President and Publisher

IDG Books Technology Publishing: Brenda McLaughlin, Senior Vice President and Group Pubisher

Dummies Technology Press and Dummies Editorial: Diane Graves Steele, Vice President and Associate Publisher; Mary Bednarek, Director of Acquisitions and Product Development; Kristin A. Cocks, Editorial Director

Dummies Trade Press: Kathleen A. Welton, Vice President and Publisher; Kevin Thornton, Acquisitions Manager

IDG Books Production for Dummies Press: Michael R. Britton, Vice President of Production and Creative Services; Cindy L. Phipps, Manager of Project Coordination, Production Proofreading, and Indexing; Shelley Lea, Supervisor of Graphics and Design; Debbie J. Gates, Production Systems Specialist; Robert Springer, Supervisor of Proofreading; Debbie Stailey, Production Control Manager; Tony Augsburger, Supervisor of Reprints and Bluelines

Dummies Packaging and Book Design: Patty Page, Manager, Promotions Marketing

◆

The publisher would like to give special thanks to Patrick J. McGovern, without whom this book would not have been possible.

◆

Contents at a Glance

Cartoons at a Glance

By Rich Tennant

The 5th Wave
By Rich Tennant
COMPUTER SCIENCES LAB

"I'm sure there will be a good job market when I graduate. I created a virus that will go off that year."

page 367

The 5th Wave
By Rich Tennant

SO POORLY DOCUMENTED IS THE SOFTWARE THAT ROY IS BETA TESTING THAT HE FAILS TO NOTICE THAT THE GAME RULES TO "TWISTER" HAVE ACCIDENTALLY BEEN INCLUDED.

page 7

The 5th Wave
By Rich Tennant

"The new technology has really helped me get organized. I keep my project reports under the PC, budgets under my laptop and memos under my pager."

page 319

The 5th Wave
By Rich Tennant
LARRY MAKES HIS LAST BIG BUSINESS DECISION.
LARRYS HOUSE OF SOFTWARE
MAGNETS 'R US
Yeah, I'm gonna buy out the guy next door and combine the two operations.
HOME AND INDUSTRIAL USE
POWERFUL!

page 115

The 5th Wave
By Rich Tennant
THUD SOFTWARE

"GENTLEMEN, I SAY RATHER THAN FIX THE 'BUGS', WE CHANGE THE DOCUMENTATION AND CALL THEM 'FEATURES'."

page 71

The 5th Wave
By Rich Tennant
WELL, THERE'S YOUR DRAWING SCANNED INTO YOUR BOOK REPORT. I JUST CAN'T FIGURE OUT WHAT THAT GREY FUZZY THING IS ALONG THE EDGE.

page 269

The 5th Wave
By Rich Tennant

"It's a ten-step word-processing program. It comes with a spell-checker, grammar-checker, cliché-checker, whine-checker, passive/aggressive-checker, politically correct-checker, hissy-fit-checker, pretentious pontificating-checker, boring anecdote-checker and a Freudian reference-checker."

page 207

***Fax:* 978-546-7747 • *E-mail:* the5wave@tiac.net**

Table of Contents

Introduction

Welcome to *Seagate Crystal Reports 7 For Dummies.* This book is about one of the best-kept software secrets. Seagate Crystal Reports has been bundled with a wide variety of other software products for several years, and therefore you have not seen it on the software best-seller list. Yet it is a best-seller. If you have used Visual Basic or an accounting package, you have probably seen the product and wondered how to get it to work.

This book covers what you need to know to begin creating reports that not only look good but actually have data that make sense to the person reading them. The good news is that it is not difficult. In fact, creating reports is quite easy after you understand a few basic concepts, such as how a report is laid out and where you insert the records, summaries, totals, and headings.

About This Book

I have written more than 25 books on computer software and have been an ACT! consultant for many years. One constant in my experience is the lack of an easy way to generate reports from the data in databases. Crystal Reports solves that problem.

But most folks do not use a report writer every day. At the end of the month or quarter, all of a sudden you or the boss needs a report on sales activity of a product or sales force, and you are in crunch time trying to figure out how to get the report you want without that creeping feeling of desperation. So I have designed this book to allow you to easily turn to the page you need to find the necessary steps for success. Therefore, the book is targeted to beginners and intermediate users. You do not have to read this book cover to cover; just grab the chapter or subject you require, and read that. The structure is such that if you are a true beginner, you can start with the first few chapters and get a report out the door. If you have written your own database application, you can go to Chapter 7 (which is about formulas) and discover the elements necessary to convert your data to a format Crystal Reports can use.

You need not be a database expert to use Crystal Reports. If you understand how to start programs in Windows 95 and know what data you want to use in reports, you should be in great shape!

Foolish Assumptions

I have made a few assumptions. First, that you are familiar with the rudiments of using a computer and Windows 95 — like that a mouse is not an animal and that Windows has nothing to do with panes (although *pains* may be accurate). Second, that you have, or someone has, installed Crystal Reports and that you have worked with some sort of database program from which you want to garner reports. I do not assume that you understand how databases are constructed — I cover that in Chapter 1. Last, I trust that you have discovered that a computer is stupid — that is, it does only what you ask it to do, and on top of that, it requires that you learn a special language to communicate with it. That is why the phrase "user-friendly" ranks up there with "the check is in the mail" on the list of oft-quoted fibs.

How This Book Is Organized

In this book, I try to present the steps to creating reports and then adding enhancements in the sequence most new users would want. You may find other ideas as to the topics you want to approach and in what order, so glance through the following chapter descriptions and empower yourself.

Note: The screenshots in this book show the Crystal Reports screen as you would see if you are using Windows 95 or Windows NT 4. If you are using a different version of Windows, your screen may look slightly different (for example, Windows 95 and Windows NT show a check mark when a check box is turned on whereas other versions of Windows show an x). Don't worry about this; you follow the same steps in any and all versions of Windows unless otherwise noted.

Part I: What You Need to Know to Survive

Chapter 1: Setting the Table

Not everyone comes to the report-creation process skilled at using and understanding databases. So read this chapter if you have never had to create a database but have only entered data into one. This chapter gives you an idea of how the information is stored and why it is done that way.

Chapter 2: Creating a Simple Report

This chapter takes you through the beginning stages of creating a report, including how to determine the type of report you want and how to start inserting database information into a report. I also give you an introduction to an easy way to generate reports with the Reports Experts.

Chapter 3: Crystal Reports: Basic Skills

The text in a report refers to the stuff you may add that is separate from the database information, such as headings, titles, and footers. A report is only as good as the information it conveys, and the text objects make the report more easily understood.

Part II: Manipulating Records

Chapter 4: Selecting Records

When you access a database, you may want all the records that are in the database or just a certain type of record. This chapter shows you how to pick the ones you want.

Chapter 5: Sorting and Grouping Records

You can manipulate database records in a number of ways. This chapter covers changing the sort order and creating groups.

Part III: Formatting and Formulas for Success

Chapter 6: Graphing and Mapping Data

This chapter shows you more on how to add pizzazz to your reports to make them more readable — and the information more accessible. Plus, you can generate a map of your reports based on the records.

Chapter 7: Using the Crystal Formula Language

Formulas are the way to convert data, combine data from different tables, and perform calculations on data in tables. After you understand the concept of how to construct and insert formulas into a report, you reach a higher plane of reporting. Seagate also has included numerous example formulas, shown in Chapter 7.

Chapter 8: Using Conditional Formatting

Want a record (such as those that are negative numbers or in a group) formatted depending on the information contained in the record? This chapter is where you find the steps to use conditional formatting.

Chapter 9: Creating a Subreport

Find out how to insert one report (a subreport) into another report (a primary report). And find out how beneficial a subreport can be.

Part IV: Putting On Some Finishing Touches

Chapter 10: Formatting Sections of a Report

This chapter offers a further look at applying formatting based on the information in a report section, making it easy to highlight good news — or downplay bad news.

Chapter 11: Creating Presentation-Quality Reports

How about adding pictures, logos, and OLE objects to the report? Find out how in this chapter.

Part V: Creating Specific Types of Reports

Chapter 12: Creating a Cross-Tab Report

A cross-tabulation report allows you an entirely different look at your database information. It's used frequently in market research as adjunct to survey data. A cross tabulation can deliver new insights to your customers and prospects. Crystal Reports makes the process of creating a cross tabulation easy.

Chapter 13: Creating a Summary Report

A summary report prints or displays only the summary information developed by the report process. In other words, when the boss wants only the bottom line, Crystal Reports can deliver. This chapter shows you how to create such a report.

Chapter 14: Linking to Other Databases

Links are a way of combining information from a variety of tables, in a variety of ways. In this chapter, I explain the best ways to join data from different tables.

Part VI: Disseminating Reports without a Hitch

Chapter 15: Distributing Reports

This chapter covers compiling, mailing, and exporting your reports, including posting a report to a Web site.

Chapter 16: Setting Your File Options

Each time you create a report, you can change some automatic settings that determine the size of text, where files are saved, and so on. Each of the settings can be customized to give you complete control of the look of your reports.

Part VII: The Part of Tens

Chapter 17: Ten Questions to Ask Before You Create a Report

Revel in ten questions that — if asked — make creating any report easier.

Chapter 18: Ten Tricks to Enhance Reports

Shine with ten proven means of adding appeal to a report.

Conventions Used in This Book

Taking a leap, I have ignored the Geneva Convention, so often invoked on *Hogan's Heroes,* and have employed the following:

When the instructions say to choose File⇨Save, it means that you are to use your mouse to click (using the left mouse button) the File menu name and then, from the menu that appears, select the Save option. The underlined letter is another means of making the choice. For example, pressing the Alt key and holding it down while pressing the F key also opens the menu.

Occasionally, you are asked to type text or a number to make an example work. Whenever that's the case, the text you are to enter appears in **bold type.**

When you read "select the text," that means you are to click and hold the left mouse button and drag it over the text until it is highlighted, and then release the mouse button.

Sometimes you are asked to select an option that is not a menu item but is a choice that must be clicked with the left mouse button. The selection is displayed in the following typestyle: `equal to, sum`.

At no point do I ask you to refer to the Crystal Reports user's guide. The manual is very comprehensive, if a bit dry. When you get the reporting basics down, you can peruse it for the advanced topics that I don't cover.

Icons Used in This Book

To help you quickly find the information you want to read, or at least to make that information a little more memorable, I've strategically strewn icons throughout this book. Here is the lowdown on the little pictures:

The information beside this icon is a good piece of information to know: Save time, avoid delays, get ahead, and prosper with these tidbits.

Not that Crystal Reports is dangerous or anything (unless you drop the official User's Guide on your foot), but this icon can warn you about things that keep you out of trouble.

If you are interested in the technical and advanced stuff, this icon is the place to go for such information. But you shouldn't need a Ph.D. from MIT to follow along.

This icon reminds you to remember information that it signals. Keep this stuff somewhere in memory or at least written down on the back of envelopes in the top-right drawer of your desk.

If you want to appreciate what Crystal Reports can do, this icon points out the features for you. Some things may seem like magic.

The information beside this icon is considered basic, common knowledge to have in order to function within Crystal Reports. Sort of like the time in fifth grade when you were forced to memorize all the provinces of Canada or the 50 U.S. state capitals so that you could function in life. Basic, common knowledge.

Where to Go from Here

With a cloud of dust and a hearty "Hi-ho, Silver — away!" you are on your journey to go where no report writer has gone before. I promise to make it an easy journey, with few delays and much productivity.

Part I

What You Need to Know to Survive

The 5th Wave
By Rich Tennant
SO POORLY DOCUMENTED IS THE SOFTWARE THAT ROY IS BETA TESTING THAT HE FAILS TO NOTICE THAT THE GAME RULES TO "TWISTER" HAVE ACCIDENTALLY BEEN INCLUDED.

In this part . . .

You know that sooner or later you're going to have to finish the report that your boss asked for. This part shows you how to get something in the boss's hands pretty quickly. Really. It's pretty easy to use Seagate Crystal Reports even though the MIS department bought the program and dropped it in your lap with a slight sneer. Open a report and pop in a few fields, and you're in business. Add a couple of titles, and people will think you are an undiscovered genius. I'm not kidding. It happened to a friend of a relative of a guy that my brother knows. He started creating reports with Crystal Reports and he got a good-paying-annual-raise-three-weeks-off-dental-care-plan-never-get-fired government job. You could be next!

Chapter 1

Setting the Table

In This Chapter

- A look at database construction
- What a database table is
- How a report writer uses database tables

What is life without reports? Every business has a database of some sort, and from those databases, people expect reports. The problem is, most of the products, such as Paradox, Access, ACT!, dBASE, and Peachtree, to name a few, have report-creating capabilities that are limited and clumsy. In addition, corporate users want to create reports on databases that may be in SQL (Structured Query Language), ORACLE, or another mainframe database.

Seagate Crystal Reports can create terrific-looking reports from the data in almost any format you have. Before starting the program, I want to show you how data is stored in products such as Access, Paradox, or FoxPro so that you have an understanding of how Crystal Reports works with your data.

In the Beginning, There Was a Table

When you create a database in virtually any program, the program creates a *table* into which you enter data. This is true whether you enter data into a *form screen* (which is a screen resembling an invoice or other paper type form) or into tabular fields (which is like a spreadsheet with rows and columns).

What do you see when you look at a real-world table? Food! Me too. But in a computer, a table is a structure for storing information. You view the table you sit down to at Thanksgiving from above. You see the turkey, mashed potatoes, gravy, and so on as individual items *on* the table.

Not so with a database table. You look at computer tables from the *side*. So, across the top of the table is a list of fields, and underneath the table top are legs (usually more than the four that a dinner table has). Figure 1-1 shows a computer table.

Figure 1-1: A computer table.

Record	Turkey	Mashed Potatoes	Pie
Alex	6	10	6
Ilsa	2	2	1
Gloria	1	3	3

Because the view is from the side, the top of the table has the column headings, which in Figure 1-1 are Record, Turkey, Mashed Potatoes, and Pie. In a computer database, these would be the *field names* that are in the database.

The names on the left are the individual names (or *records,* in database terms): Alex, Ilsa, and Gloria. In some databases, this column would hold a unique identifier number such as the record number or a person's Social Security number.

A Thanksgiving table is held up by legs of some sort. In a computer database, the table legs separate the individual pieces of data. In Figure 1-1, the number of servings of turkey eaten by Alex (6) is separated by the table leg from the number of servings of mashed potatoes (10) and the number of pieces of pie (6).

A database record consists of the individual pieces of data that run from left to right across and underneath the table top. So, Alex, Ilsa, and Gloria are individual records.

The field names in your database are more likely to be First Name, (Fname), Last Name, (Lname), Address 1, (Add1), Address 2, (Add2), City, State, and Zip, as shown in Figure 1-2. The names are shortened for simplicity, although if you do not know what the abbreviations stand for, things are actually more confusing.

Figure 1-2: A sample database table.

Record#	Fname	Lname	Add1	Add2	City	State	Zip
1	Doug	Wolf	1st	Street	NY	NY	10025
2	Gloria	Lenares	2nd	Place	SF	CA	90024

Form Follows Function

As I mentioned previously, the database you work with may resemble a form. Figure 1-3 shows a database program into which you enter records into the table via a form. Each of the fields in this form are the same as the table headings.

No matter how you enter data into a database, all the information ends up in a table. That is where Crystal Reports comes in.

After you enter thousands of records, any database makes finding and editing one or several an easy task. You can even sort the records by postal code. But, suppose that you want to send a direct mail piece to each of your customers, using bulk mail. The Post Office has strict rules about how the mail is sorted and grouped. Crystal Reports can easily sort and compile a report that shows you how many customers you have in each postal code and sort them in the proper order. In other words, Crystal Reports starts where the reports built in to whatever program you are using as a database leave off.

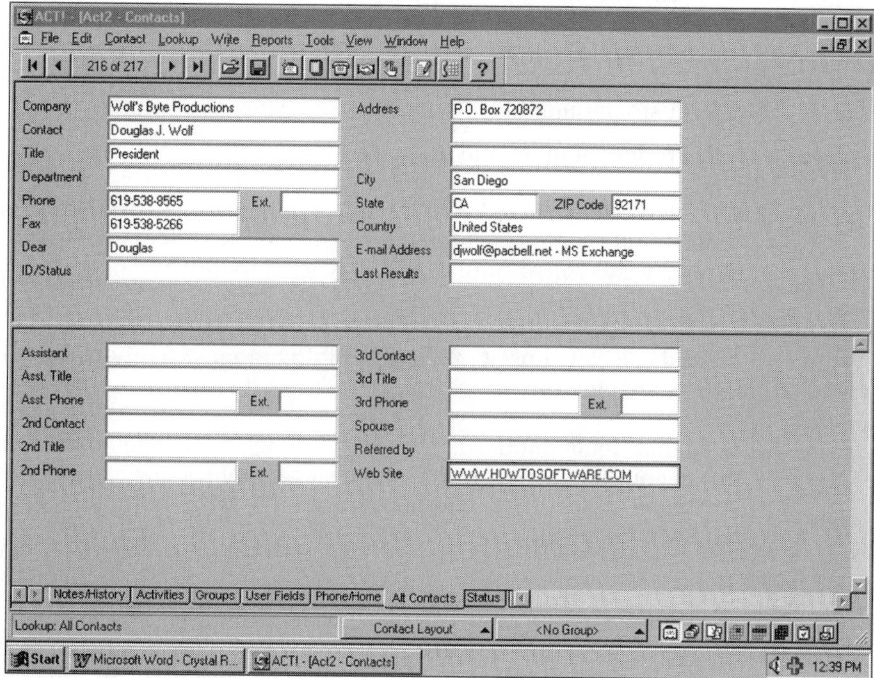

Figure 1-3: Form view of a database.

Table for . . . One or More?

Now consider how a real computer database is constituted. Suppose that your company has products with repeat sales. That is, you sell the same things over and over to the same customer base. If you were the architect of the company's electronic database (in computer lingo, a *systems design engineer,* harumph), sooner or later you would notice that every time the customer orders, essentially the same data is needed to fill the order. Retyping the customer name, address, and so on with every order would be a great waste of time, not to mention re-entering the product information such as price. The solution: Use several tables to hold the data.

1. Customer information
2. Product Information
3. Order information

In the customer information table, you have the specifics of where to ship, where to bill, and so on. You assign each customer a unique customer number. Next, you create a product table that has each product listed by name and number including the price so that the database calculates the cost. Last, you create the order table when the customer places an order. In the order table, you are going to enter:

1. Customer number
2. Product number and quantity

If you have constructed your database properly, the correct customer and product information is entered for you, and the order is complete. This scenario is very typical. Your report may need to involve several tables or a single table from a database. So remember this:

A database can consist of a single table but most likely consists of several interconnected tables.

Keep this fact in mind while working through the examples in the text throughout this book. I begin with a single table, show off the Crystal Reports attributes as best I can, and then move onto using multiple tables to make a report in Chapter 13.

If you are working on standard PC-type databases (such as dBASE, FoxPro, and Paradox), each table is a separate file stored on a local or network drive. Therefore, each time you need a table for you report, you add another physical file — a .dbf file for a dBASE database, for example. But think again about that pesky SQL and a related term — relational databases. A *relational database* is a database designed on the relational model and contains many tables within one database. To obtain information from these tables, an application uses or "talks" SQL. Examples of common relational databases are ORACLE, Sybase, and DB2. The interface to SQL or relational databases from Crystal Reports is ODBC.

Planning the Report

The first thing you need to do before starting Crystal Reports is to sit down with a piece of paper and decide what you want in the report. Admittedly, at this point, visualizing the exact layout of the report may be difficult, but you or the Dilbert-like person demanding that the report be on his desk by Friday should have a clear idea of what you want to appear in the report. Keep in mind that Crystal Reports allows for the creation of myriad mathematical formulas — from simple totals, averages, and maximum and minimums to expressions that Einstein would have admired. You can include graphs, footers, headers, and so on. So, if you anticipate computational needs instead of adding them after the report is constructed, you will save time — and that is the stuff life is made of.

If you are creating a complex report — one that will involve several tables — determine which fields from each table you will be using and how they will be linked. In Chapter 13, I show you a terrific Crystal Reports tool for linking disparate tables.

The other benefits of Crystal Reports, such as the nifty formatting of numbers or text or adding your company logo, can be added at any time — so no need to worry about planning those enhancements right now.

What makes a report?

When you look at a professionally prepared paper report, it usually has a report header, page headings, the details of the individual page, and a report footer.

So does Crystal Reports. Every report that you create has standard layout sections. The trick to understanding how Crystal Reports transfers the paper world to your computer desktop is to think this way: *All the parts of a paper report are represented in the Crystal Reports report window.* In other words, Crystal Reports layers the parts of a paper report onto the computer window so that you can see all the parts at the same time — from title section to summary section.

The origin of Crystal Reports (from the book of Relation, Chapter 1, Verse 1)

Now in that time, a mighty tribe of Programmers known as dBASE nerds existed. They dwelt in the land of Southern California, known for its fine beaches and beautiful weather. But the dBASE nerds did not surf, nor did they spend much time in the Eden-like climate. Verily, the dBASE nerds were mighty storers of information, creating databases that only the high priests of the tribe could understand. And the people cried out, "You dBASE nerds have created these mighty storehouses of data, but we cry for reports! Reports with cross tabs and graphs and lots of fancy fonts." The Programmer High Priests were sore afraid, and asked themselves, "What can we do? We have the knowledge of getting data in, but we cannot get it out! We shall be broken into 16 and even 32 bits! Is no one among us able to satisfy the thirst for reports?"

And much lamenting and wailing occurred about their lack of reports. But they knew not what to do. So in this time a small tribe in the northern lands known as Canada had a tribe of Programmers, too. They were known as the Crystals. These Crystals were skilled in the ways of the database and had the secret knowledge of reports. And lo and behold, from them sprang forth code that took data to a place it had never been. The code created reports so easily that the people were amazed, and their e-mail and faxes chattered with the news. Verily they asked the Crystals for a name for this stupendous code. The wise men of Crystal gathered in council and thought long and hard; much pasta and hops were consumed. Then, after their deliberation, they drew their tribe unto them and declared: "We hereby exclaim the name of our code to be CRYSTAL REPORTS! Go forth from this place and spread the word that a new way of creating reports now exists among us. Truly we have been blessed! And a book shall be struck, so that all the unwashed, known as *Dummies,* shall come to have knowledge of Crystal Reports and the world shall be made good. We have said it; so it shall be."

Crystal Reports uses the information in existing databases. It does not create new databases, nor does it affect the data in the source database itself. If you are working on a large database such as a mainframe ORACLE database with 200,000 records, Crystal Reports is designed to let you access the records you need to create the report outline, and then when the design is finished, you can broaden the selection of records to include more records and more data.

Report distribution

The point of creating reports is distribution of the information. Not only can you print, fax, or e-mail a report, but Crystal Reports also provides a way for you to create a report file that anyone can run on her computer, enabling her to examine the report in detail.

Chapter 2

Creating a Simple Report

In This Chapter

- Starting Crystal Reports
- Accessing a database
- Inserting fields
- Previewing a report
- Moving objects
- Using guidelines
- Using Crystal Reports Experts

In this chapter, you plumb the depths of opening a database and inserting its fields into a report. You also look at the way Seagate Crystal Reports allows you to easily see what your report looks like by using the Preview feature.

Starting Crystal Reports

When you install Crystal Reports on your computer, it adds the Crystal Report Designer to a Crystal Reports program group. Now, how you start Crystal Reports depends on what "flavor" of Microsoft Windows you are using. Are you using Windows 95, Windows NT 3.51 or 4.0, Windows for Workgroups, or just plain old Windows?

If your computer is running Windows 95 or Windows NT 4.0, to start Crystal Reports just do the following:

1. **Click the Start menu.**
2. **Select Programs.**

   Windows 95 displays a list of programs installed on your computer.

3. **Click Seagate Crystal Reports.**

   A sub-menu appears.

4. **Click 16- or 32-bit Crystal Report Designer.**

Don't forget that the screenshots in this book show Crystal Reports in Windows 95.

If you are using any other version of Windows (Windows for Workgroups, Windows NT 3.51, or Windows 3.1), your original computer screen has the Crystal Reports program group visible in the Program Manager. Just do the following:

1. **If the Crystal Reports program group is not already maximized (if you can see a bunch of icons/pictures within the program group, it is maximized), double-click it to make it maximized.**
2. **Double-click the 16- or 32-bit Crystal Report Designer icon.**

Creating a New Report

When you start the Crystal Report Designer, a Welcome dialog box opens that gives you several choices. You can start creating a New Report, Open an existing Report, or Cancel. You can turn off the Welcome dialog box if you would rather not see it. To do so, click in the box next to Show Welcome Dialog at Startup, so that no check mark appears. Just because you turn it off doesn't mean you've worn out your welcome; you simply have to use the File menu to get going. (To turn it back on, choose Help⇨Welcome Dialog.) The Welcome dialog box appears in Figure 2-1.

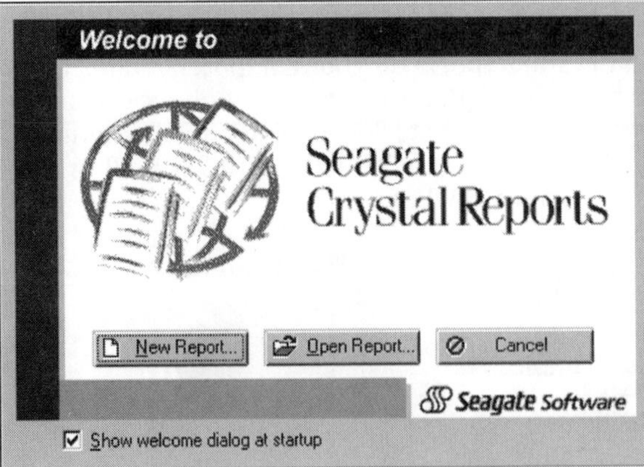

Figure 2-1: The Crystal Reports startup dialog box greets you.

For the example that I want to use, the choice is New Report.

1. **Click the New Report button.**

   The next dialog box is the Report Gallery, as shown in Figure 2-2. The Report Gallery is a collection of report formats from which you can choose to begin creating a report.

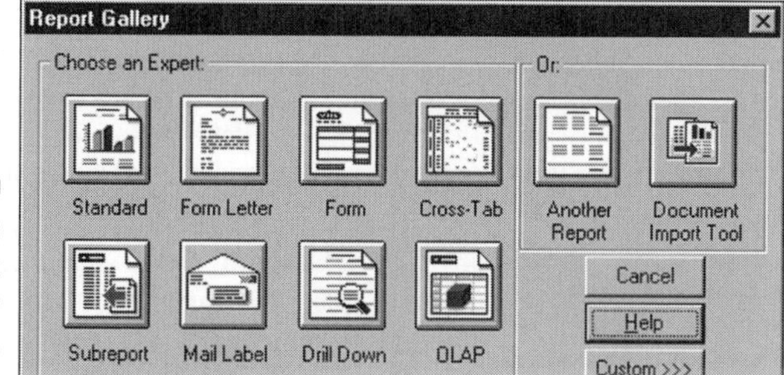

Figure 2-2: The Report Gallery dialog box.

The Report Gallery offers you the opportunity to begin creating a specific type of report right away. To learn more about the various types and how to use the Report Gallery, see "Using the Report Gallery Experts," later in this chapter.

2. **Go ahead and click the Custom button.**

   This button reveals a further set of reports from which to choose, as you see in Figure 2-3.

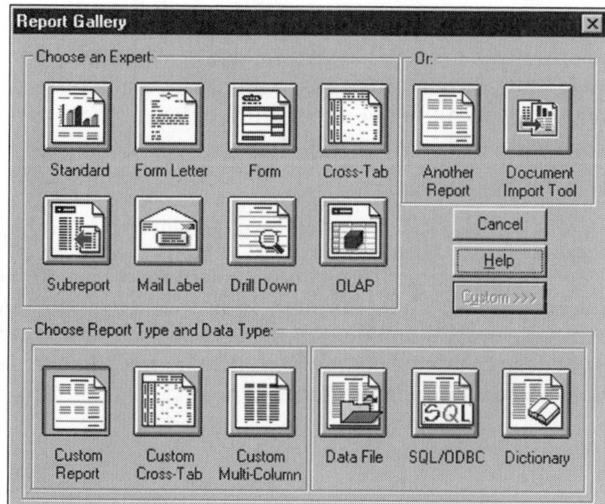

Figure 2-3: The Report Gallery dialog box with the Custom Report exposed.

Report creating options

In Crystal Reports, you have four options when creating reports: Experts, Another Report, which includes importing an existing text document, Custom, or the Document Import tool.

Experts: Ah, it's an oxymoron; you don't have to be an expert to use an Expert. Experts are similar to Microsoft's Wizards. The Expert walks you through each step in the report creation process. It's quick, it's easy, and it's foolproof — you won't forget any major steps. Business users love Experts and usually use Experts to quickly start a report that they can then fine-tune. Power users still use Experts because they're quick, and then the power users just go from there. See "Using the Report Gallery Experts" at the end of this chapter for more information on working with Experts.

Another Report: Ever opened up a word-processing document, started to modify it with the intention of saving it under a different name, and then forgot? Oops. The Another Report option makes sure this never happens. You get a "new, clean" version of the original report and never have to worry about overwriting or ruining the original.

Document Import tool: New to Version 7 is the ability to create a report from a text file that is an existing report. In other words, if you create a report that exists in a text file format from another application, you can import that report into Crystal Reports and use it as the basis for a new Crystal Report.

Custom: With this option, you can build the report from the ground up — you don't have to use the Wizard at all. It gives you a ton of control — you do what you want, when you want. It's normally used by people who like to build the report from the ground up. And working with the Custom option is a great way to learn about Crystal Reports. See where I'm going with this? I use the Custom option through the majority of this book to teach you all the fun, juicy stuff.

At this point, you have a choice. The example report in this chapter uses a database that was created for general use. If you have a specific database from which you want to create a report, you can open it instead. The Data File button allows you to open the database you want — and the one I want, so that is your next step.

3. **Click the Data File button.**

   Crystal Reports opens the Choose Database File dialog box.

   Crystal Reports can open virtually any type of database. Remember that a database can consist of one or many tables. The example database I am using has several tables, but my report has only one to start. It's a Microsoft Access database named Extreme. Figure 2-4 shows the Extreme database as it looks in Access.

Ah, what button, what button?

Select Custom in the Report Gallery dialog box to see the following buttons:

Data File: Use this option when you want to use a standard PC type database in your report (for example, MS Access, FoxPro, or dBASE).

SQL/ODBC: Use this option when you want to use a Structured Query Language database in your report (MS SQL Server, ORACLE, Sybase). And you also click this button if you are using any data that is accessed via Open Database Connectivity (ODBC). Some examples are Informix, DB2/2, Lotus Notes, and Excel.

Dictionary: When you think of Dictionary, you probably think of the Webster's version that translates unknown words. A Crystal Dictionary translates what can be very complicated data in a way the average Joe can understand. If a dictionary exists for you to use (and someone has to have created it for you), you use this option.

Okay, but what if you read all this and still don't know what button to hit on your computer? There are two ways you can solve this mystery:

- If a technical person or another Crystal Reports user is in your organization, he may be able to help you — if you ask him nicely. It may even be worth a café latté.
- If you need to solve this problem on your own, refer to the Data Source chapter of the Crystal Reports User's Guide or search on "Data Sources and Databases Index" in the Crystal Reports online Help. Look up the database you're working with and voilà — problem solved.

4. **To open the database you want, click the drop-down arrow in the List Files of Type box. Select the kind of database you want to open (you have to know the name of the database).**

   You may have to switch to a different file folder and/or drive to locate your database. Or you may have to click the Network button to locate the database on a network drive.

   You are probably thinking, "I thought Windows 95 did away with those short, cryptic file names." Gotcha! When you name a file, the name can be in recognizable English, but Windows 95 waves a magic wand and creates an underlying filename in the old DOS 8.3 (eight characters, a period, and three more characters) format, such as BILGATES.MDB or KINGBILL.HRH.

5. **Double-click the file named xtreme.**

   The Select Tables dialog box appears. This is an advanced feature of Crystal Reports that I cover in Chapter 13.

Customer ID	Customer Credit ID	Customer Name	Contact First N	Contact Last Na	Conta
1	1	City Cyclists	Chris	Christianson	Mr.
2	2	Pathfinders	Christine	Manley	Miss
3	3	Bike-A-Holics Anor	Gary	Jannis	Mr.
4	4	Psycho-Cycle	Alexander	Mast	Mr.
5	5	Sporting Wheels In	Patrick	Reyess	Mr.
6	6	Rockshocks for Jo	Heather	Davis	Ms.
7	7	Poser Cycles	Alex	Smith	Mr.
8	8	Spokes 'N Wheels	Kristina	Chester	Miss
9	9	Trail Blazer's Place	Alexandra	Burris	Mrs.
10	10	Rowdy Rims Comp	Anthony	Shoemaker	Dr.
11	11	Clean Air Transport	Bill	Carter	Mr.
12	12	Hooked on Helmet	Gerry	Wade	Mr.
13	13	C-Gate Cycle Shop	Matthew	Banks	Mr.
14	14	Alley Cat Cycles	Rick	Pratt	Mr.
15	15	The Bike Cellar	Christopher	Carmine	Mr.
16	16	Craze Cycle	Hanna	Hopkins	Ms.
17	17	Hercules Mountain	James	Sergent	Mr.
18	18	Whistler Rentals	Will	Castillo	Mr.

Figure 2-4: The Extreme database, Customer table, in Access.

6. **For the moment, skip this advanced stuff by clicking Customer, and then click OK.**

   Crystal Reports opens the Design tab and the Insert Fields dialog box, as shown in Figure 2-5, and displays the individual field names from the Customer table.

Examples used in this book

In this book, most of the time, I am going to use the sample data that comes with Crystal Reports. It is a Microsoft Access database called Extreme. It contains all the information that the Extreme Mountain Bike Company wants to track for its customers, orders, suppliers, and so on. Even if you have not ridden a bicycle since the second grade, this data should be easy enough to relate to. Many customers need to track and report on data of this type.

Within the table are the field names — Customer ID, Customer Credit ID, Customer Name, and so on (the field names go further across to the right than the screen can show). These are the field names that Crystal Reports finds when you open this database table.

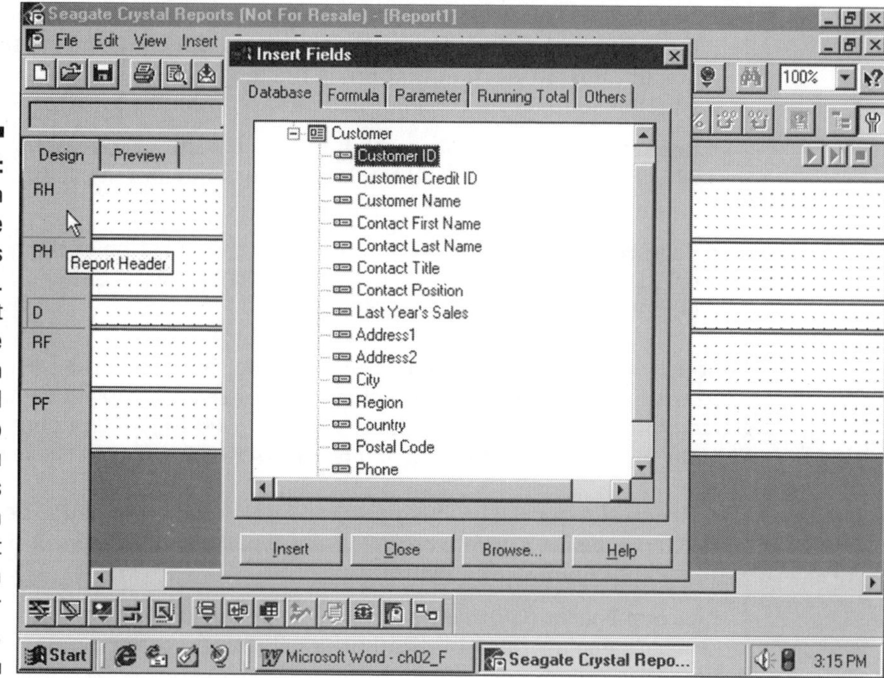

Figure 2-5: The Design tab with the Insert Fields dialog box. Note that the mouse pointer is on the left, and a pop-up menu describes the section of the report on which the pointer rests.

Before going further, think about what you've done and what you are going to do. You have opened an Access database that consists of several tables. You selected a table to use. Crystal Reports then opens the Insert Fields dialog box to list the field names of the Customer table in the Design tab. At this point, you can select the field names and place them in your report. When you do so, Crystal Reports knows that you want to use the data from the records in the Customer table to create your report.

Using the Design Tab

You are on the brink of creating your first report. Before inserting field names, a trip around the Design tab is in order. Remember, Crystal Reports is an electronic version of a paper report and therefore has the same basic components. So look at the report sections in Figure 2-6.

- **Report Header (RH):** This section represents the title or front page of the report. In this section, you insert a title, perhaps a graph, and maybe even a company logo. This section prints once at the beginning of the report.
- **Page Header (PH):** This section represents the header that appears at the top of every page of the report. Typically, it also contains the field names for the columns of data in the body of the report.

- **Details (D):** This section represents the portion of the report that has the individual records from the database. It appears small in the Design tab, but it is the section that holds the most data. This section prints one time for every record in the database.
- **Report Footer (RF):** This section represents the portion of the report in which you can print grand totals and cross-tabulations. It appears once, at the end of the report.
- **Page Footer (PF):** This section represents the portion of the report that prints at the bottom of every page. Typically, it can contain page numbers, the report name, and so on.

Although you cannot see initially the following sections in the Design tab, Crystal Reports adds two more sections if you create groups of data. After you get comfortable with simple reports, you may want to add grouping (see Chapter 5) to your arsenal. A group is a subset of the records in the report.

- **Group Header (GH):** This section contains the group name field, and you can insert a graph, cross-tabulations, and summaries. It prints once at the beginning of each group.
- **Group Footer (GF):** This section is a special footer that contains a summary value for the group and prints at the end of each group (and can contain other information).

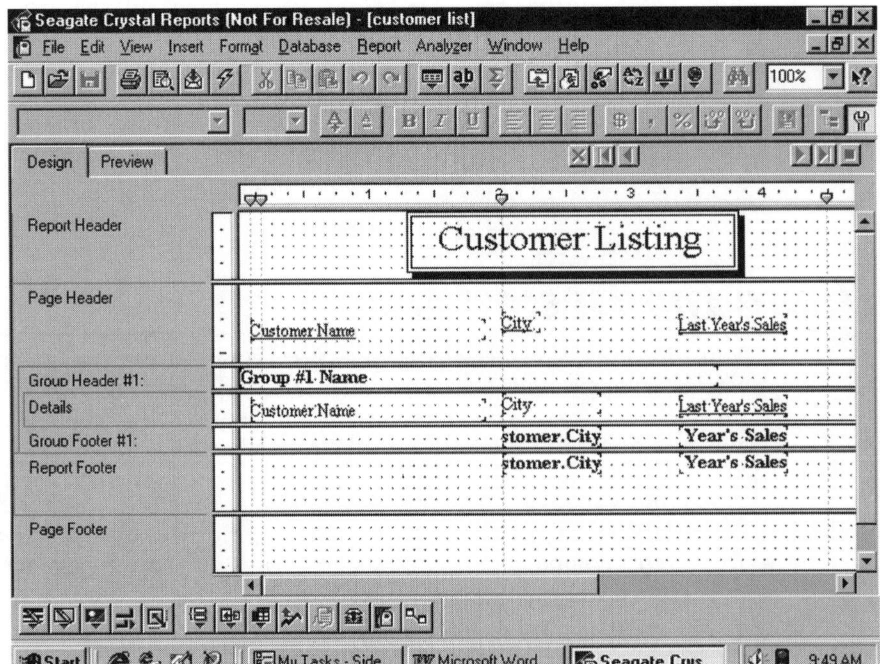

Figure 2-6: The various sections in the Design tab.

I've tried to give you some examples of what you can place in various sections, but you can be quite creative. For example, Crystal Reports puts the Group Name in the Group Header and the group totals in the Group Footer, but you can do just the opposite.

Inserting Data Fields

Every table consists of fields. Those fields contain the information about which you want to report. Crystal Reports needs to have you pick the fields that you want in your report and then place them on the Design tab. In this example report, you may want to include the business name of the customer, the city in which the customer is located, the state, and the total of last year's sales — in all, a total of four fields. The steps to insert fields are the same with every report:

1. **After you start Crystal Reports, select the database that you want to use for the report.**
2. **From the Select Tables dialog box, select a table to use in the report.**

   The Insert Fields dialog box opens.
3. **From the Insert Fields dialog box, select the field you want to use.**
4. **Click the Insert button.**
5. **Move the pointer to the section of the report where you want the field to appear.**
6. **Click the mouse button.**

   The field is inserted at that point.

If you followed the set of steps in the previous section, you opened the Extreme Mountain Bikes database (xtreme), and double-clicked the Customer table, which revealed the list of field names. That table should still be open on your screen. If you didn't follow that set of steps, open the Customer table in the Extreme database.

To insert the Customer Name field into the Design tab:

1. **Click the field name Customer Name.**

   At the bottom of the dialog box, the Insert and Browse buttons become active. More on the Browse button in the section "Browsing Data" later in this chapter.
2. **Click the Insert button.**

   Note: Depending upon your screen resolution and the number of fields in the table, you may not be able to see the buttons at the bottom of the dialog box. Not to worry, simply double-click the field you want to insert!

Or, you can move the mouse pointer to a corner of the dialog box and, when the two-headed arrow replaces the pointer, you can re-size the dialog box.

A funny thing happens! The mouse pointer becomes the international sign for stop — a circle with a line drawn through it. You have not violated any international treaty! Crystal Reports is simply telling you that you have a field attached to the pointer and it is ready for insertion but not in the section where the mouse is currently positioned (your next step).

3. **Drag the pointer toward the top of the screen.**

   When the pointer is positioned over the Design layout, the pointer once again transforms. This time, the pointer becomes an arrow with a long rectangle attached, meaning that the field is ready to be inserted, as shown in Figure 2-7.

4. **Position the rectangle in the Details section of the Design tab as it is in Figure 2-7.**

5. **Click the mouse button to finish the insertion.**

   The result appears in Figure 2-8.

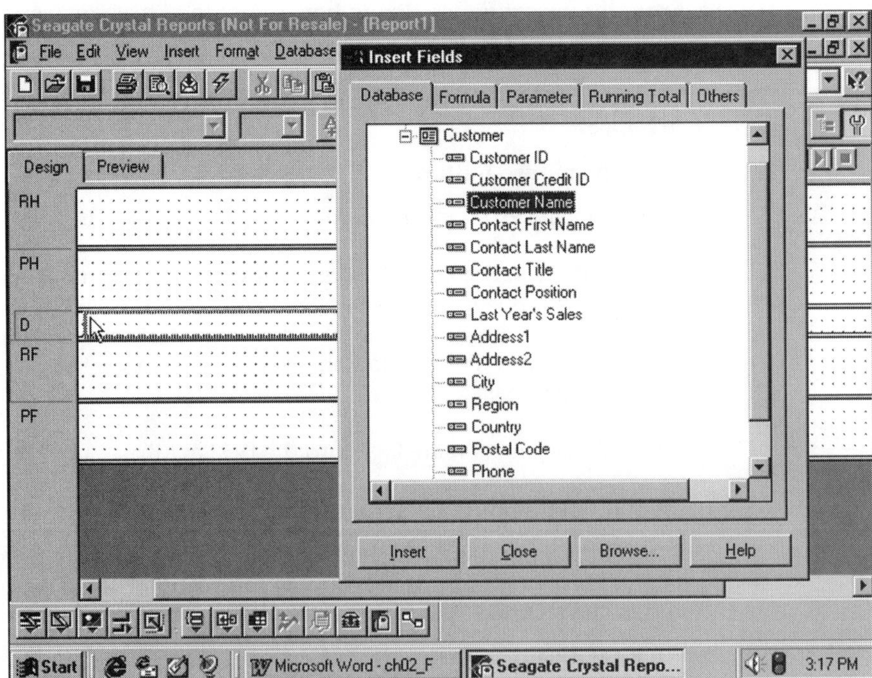

Figure 2-7: Inserting a field.

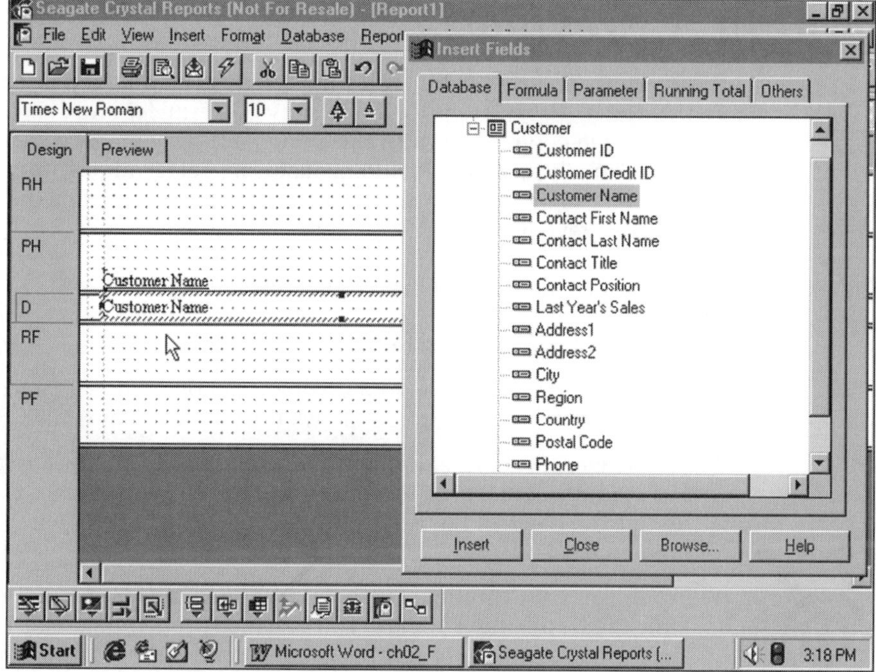

Figure 2-8: The Customer field inserted in the Details section.

After you insert a field, the length of the field is represented by a rectangle. The length of the box alerts you to the length of the field you have inserted. The length of the field comes from the database field, not from Crystal. So a single field can go all the way across from left to right. (I show you how to shorten a long field in a moment.)

Control and shift to select multiple fields at once

If you want to quickly place a couple of fields on the report in one step:

1. **Click the first field in the Insert Fields dialog box to select it.**
2. **Ctrl+click the second and subsequent fields to select them as well.**

If you want to quickly insert a number of adjacent fields:

1. **Click the first field in the Insert Fields dialog box to select it.**
2. **Shift+click the last field you want to insert.**

Notice how all fields between the two selected fields are now highlighted. Now when you insert, you will be inserting all highlighted fields.

The fields are placed in order (top to bottom) into the report as left to right.

Taking a Preview

After you have inserted fields, you want to see the result of placing the fields into the design. Crystal Reports has a very powerful feature called Preview, which works in conjunction with the Design tab. As you make changes in the report of virtually any kind, including inserting fields, adding formatting or formulas, and so on, you can see the effect of the change immediately by going to the Preview tab.

To preview a change in a report, do the following:

1. **Click the Print Preview button.**

   The Print Preview button looks like a sheet of paper with a magnifying glass over the top. Figure 2-9 shows the preview that results.

   As you can see, Crystal Reports has opened the Preview tab and inserted the actual data from the Customer Name field into the report, adding the name of the field to the top of the list of customer names as a column heading.

   When you start creating a new report, the Preview tab is not displayed. Only the Design tab appears. You must first generate a report by using the Print Preview button. After you generate it the first time, you can access it by simply clicking the Preview tab.

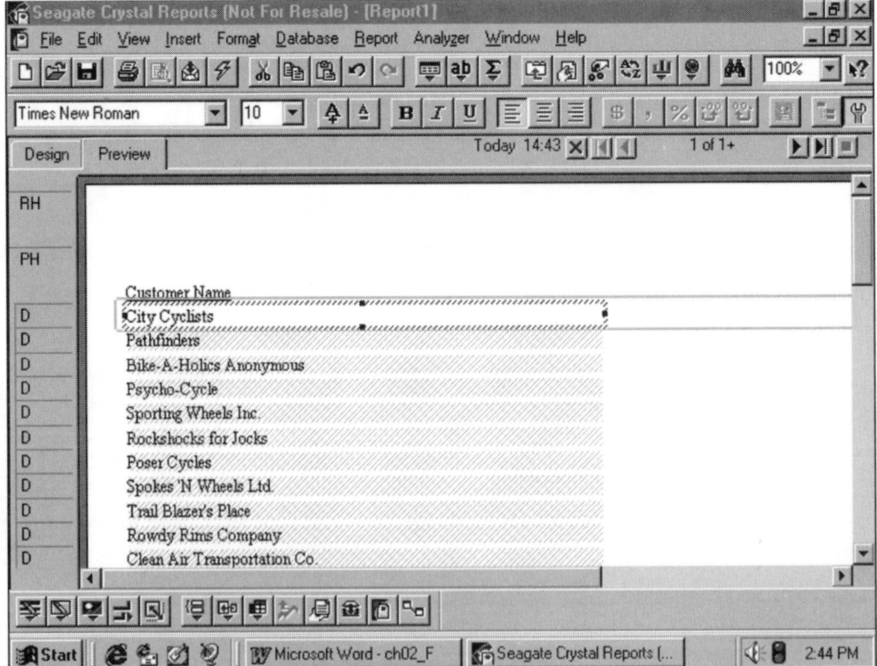

Figure 2-9: A preview of the first field you inserted.

2. **Now that you have seen the preview of the report, switch back to the Design tab. Click the Design tab at the top of the window.**

   Voilà, back in the Design tab.

You need to understand this concept: In the Design tab, you are working with placeholders for the data; in the Preview tab, you are working with actual data itself.

This two-window view of a report, the Design tab and the Preview tab, is what sets Crystal Reports apart from many other report writers. By switching back and forth between the two, you can build a report exactly as you want it because you can see the changes as quickly as you make them!

One other point to make is that when you are working in the Preview tab, the response time of your computer may slow because you are using real data. As you make changes, the actual field data has to be inserted into the report from the table. But you can choose to use old data if you want faster results.

Inserting a Second Field

Adding a second field follows the same procedure as inserting the initial field, except that you have to position the field in the Details section in a different location. If you click the Design tab, you see that Crystal Reports assumes that you are going to continue to add fields to the report, so the Insert Fields dialog box is still open.

If you closed the dialog box accidentally, click the Insert Fields button.

In this report, the plan is to include the customer name, the city in which the customer is located, the state, and the total of last year's sales. To this point, you have inserted the customer name. The next field to insert is the City field:

1. **Click and hold the mouse button on the City field name in the Insert Fields dialog box.**
2. **Drag the mouse pointer into the Detail section of the report and position the rectangle to the right of the placeholder for the Customer Name.**
3. **Release the mouse button.**

   The second field is inserted into the report, as shown in Figure 2-10.
4. **Preview the new object by clicking the Preview tab.**

   The report preview appears, as shown in Figure 2-11.

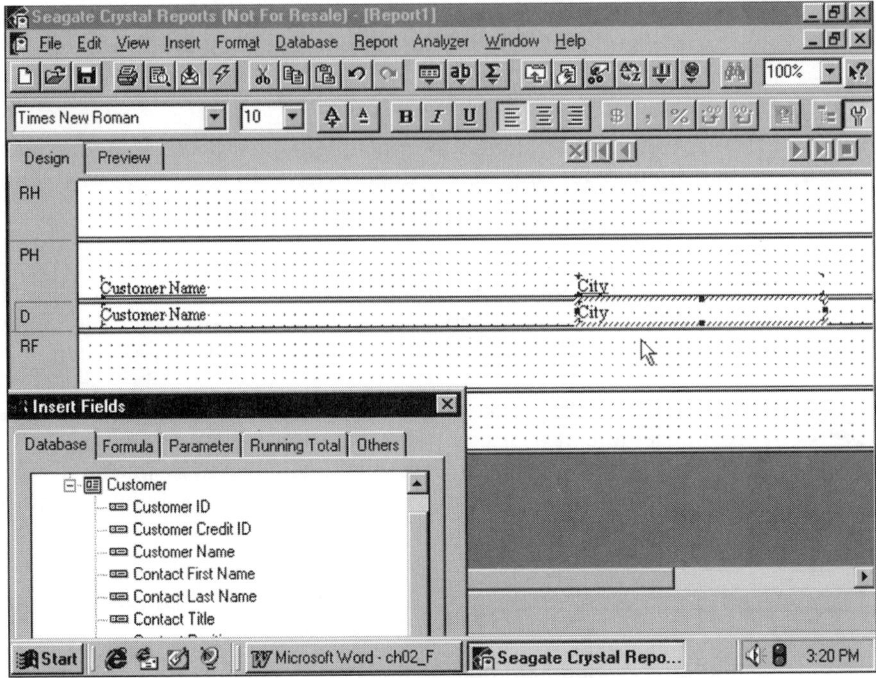

Figure 2-10: The second field, City, is inserted into the Design tab.

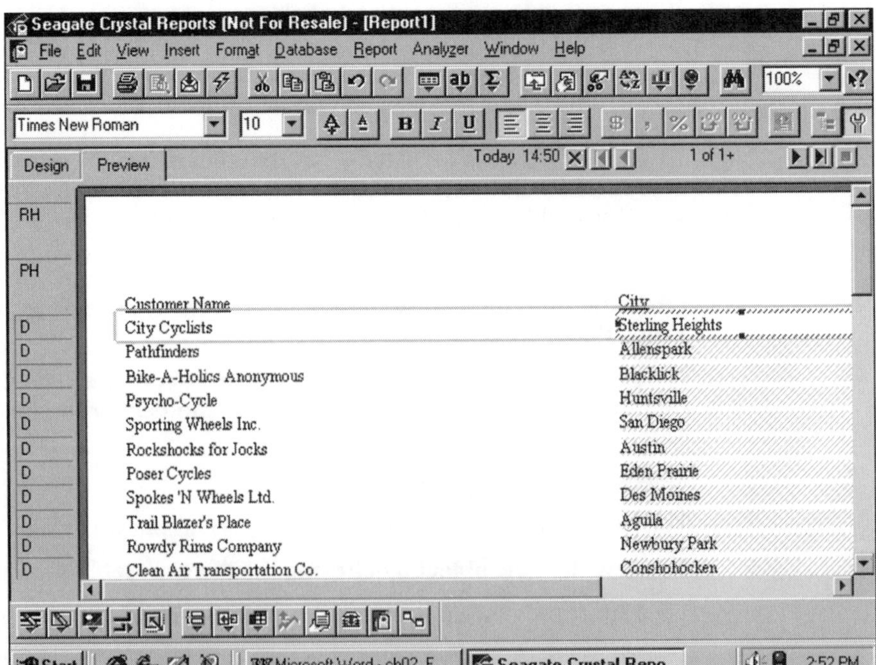

Figure 2-11: The preview of a report with a second field inserted.

Everything you place on a report, from fields to text to graphics, is referred to as objects, in Crystal Reports terminology. So this report has several objects, including the Customer Name field and the City field.

Browsing Data

Many databases have multiple tables and multiple fields. In that situation, you can't be expected to remember exactly which table has the field you need to complete a report.

Before inserting a field into a report, you can look at a sampling of the data in the field and see whether it is the correct data and whether it is of a format that will work properly.

When you use Browse Field Data, you get a sampling of data. You see the first 500 unique values for the field you are browsing. "Unique" meaning that if you are browsing on a City field, you would see Vancouver only once, even if there were 100 records from Vancouver. It is considered a sampling because Crystal Reports is not showing you all the data, just a sampling. Would you really want to see the Order Number for a million records?

To browse field data, do the following:

1. **Open the Insert fields dialog box.**
2. **In the Insert Fields dialog box, click the field name that you want to view.**
3. **Click the Browse button.**

   Note: If you can't see the buttons at the bottom of the dialog box, you can resize the dialog box by first clicking on a corner of the dialog box, and, when the two-headed arrow appears, dragging the cursor toward the outside corner of the screen. Or, you can right-click the field and choose Browse Field Data from the pop-up menu.

   Crystal Reports opens a dialog box showing you the actual data from the field and listing the type of data it is. An example appears in Figure 2-12.

At the top of the dialog box, Crystal Reports tells you that the type is `string` and that the field length is `15`. Of course, this information means nothing to you if you have not worked with data types. The "Type" and "Length" sections that follow may be helpful to you if this is the case.

Type

A data type that is *string* means that it is a character field. A character field has nothing to do with personal values. Rather, it is a field where you can enter *letters* or *numbers.* So a character field may have 12345 or ABCDE and be a valid entry. This property is important because you cannot calculate a total for a character field (you can summarize a string, but you can't sum). Now, you may be thinking, "If the field can have numbers, why can't I get a total?" The answer goes back to the type, which allows you to *mix* numbers and letters. The database designer decided that this field would be allowed to have either numbers or letters in the field. If the designer had designated the field as being Number, instead of String, you could perform calculations because no letters would have been allowed into the field.

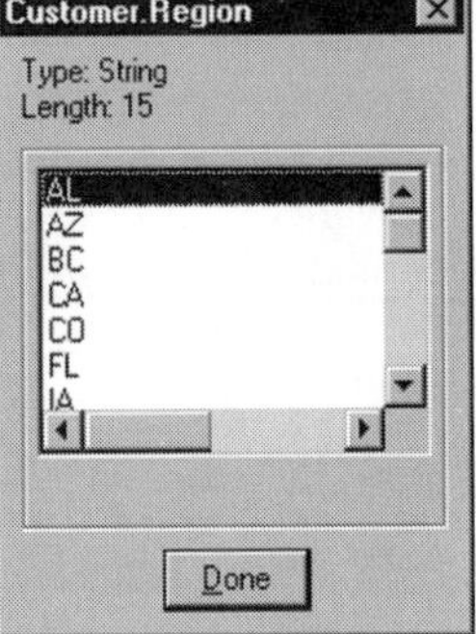

Figure 2-12: The dialog box that appears after you click the Browse button.

Length

The second piece of information that the Browse process yields is the *length* of the field. Again, this length has been determined by the designer of the database, not by Crystal Reports. In the example I used in the previous set of steps, the length is 15 characters, which means 15 letters or numbers or a mixture of the two can be entered into the field. So in that example, when you insert the field name Customer Name into the Details section of the report, Crystal Reports inserts a rectangle 15 characters in length as a visual indicator of how much space it is allowing for the field information. This allocation does not mean that the data in the field *is* that long — only that the designer of the database allowed that much space. So you may find as you construct reports that the length allowed for the field is too much for the report. You can shorten the space allowed.

Changing the field length in the Design tab

Often the length of the field in the database is a waste of space. That is, the data is never long enough to warrant the space allowed. A good example is the Region field shown in Figure 2-12. Scrolling through the data, you can see that all the record entries were two characters. In this case, the designer was using Region as the name for a field that most Americans would name State. However, some countries may have a longer name to indicate region — therefore the extra 13 characters. Because you can see that none of the records in this database have an entry longer than two characters, you can safely shorten the field.

Here's how to change the length of a field after it is selected:

1. **In the Design tab, position the mouse pointer on the far right side of the placeholder that you want to change.**

   The mouse pointer changes to a small (tiny, even) two-headed arrow, pointing left and right. This transformed pointer indicates that you can change the size of the rectangle along the horizontal.

2. **Hold down the mouse button and drag the mouse to the left.**

   The rectangle shrinks in size as you do this. (If the whole rectangle moves, the pointer switched to a four-headed arrow, and you moved the entire field. Drag the mouse back to where it was and try again.)

3. **Release the mouse button after you have resized the field to your liking.**

   In Figure 2-13, the City field has been resized to a much shorter length.

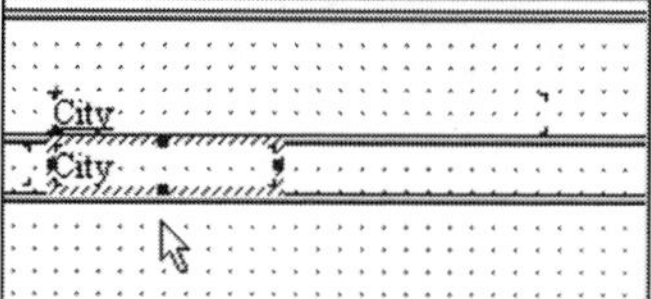

Figure 2-13: The City field resized.

4. **Click the Print Preview button, or the Preview tab, to see the result of resizing.**

When you're resizing a field, click the field and then hold down the Ctrl key as you click the heading, and then adjust the size. By selecting both fields, you can resize both the field and the heading in one step.

In the example report, the City field, although shortened, is still a long way to the right of the Customer Name field. To add more fields to the report, having the two fields closer together would be better (refer to Figure 2-11).

Changing field length in the Preview tab

As you look at the report in the Preview tab, how to change the length of a field is not as readily apparent as in the Design tab. You can do it — you only have to click in the field.

To change a field length from the Preview tab, do the following:

1. **Click the field.**

   Crystal Reports displays the report outline, as shown in Figure 2-14. The outline of the field length appears.

2. **Move the mouse pointer to the right side of the rectangle so that the pointer becomes an arrow pointing left and right.**
3. **Drag the pointer to the left until the field is reduced to the desired length.**
4. **Release the mouse button.**

   If the whole rectangle moves, the pointer switched to a four-headed arrow, and you moved the entire field. Drag the rectangle back to where it was, and try again.

In Figure 2-15, see the Customer Name field at a reduced size, from the Preview tab.

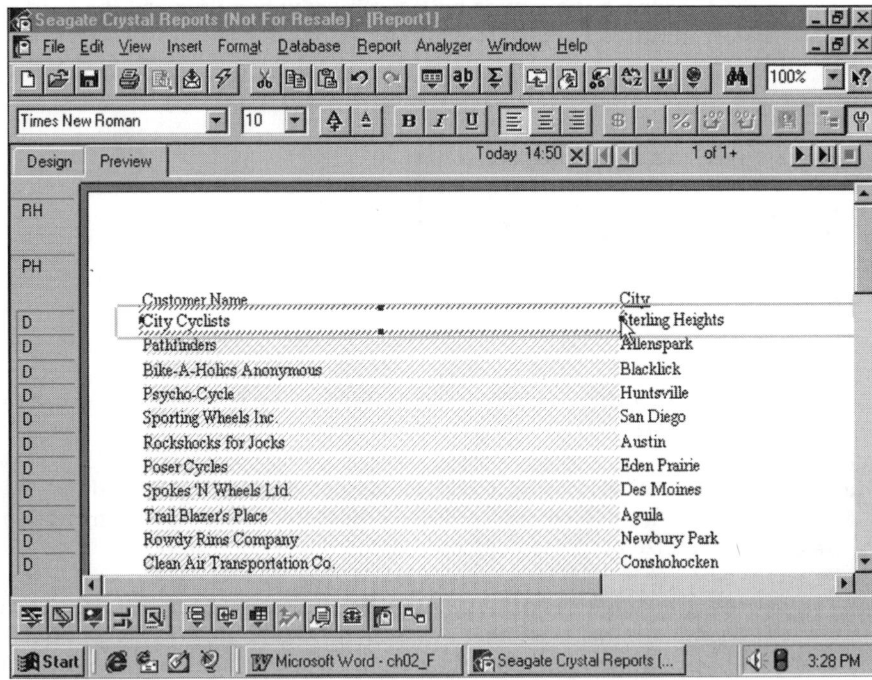

Figure 2-14: You can see design features in the Preview tab, too.

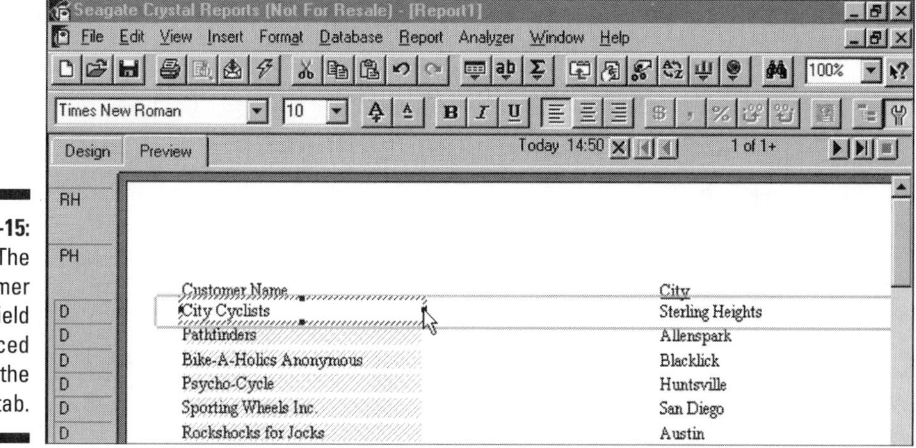

Figure 2-15: The Customer Name field reduced in the Preview tab.

Moving a Field in the Preview Tab

When you resize fields, you may create unnecessary blank space. In this section, I discuss moving an entire field to close up space.

The Preview tab accurately reflects what you will see on paper when the report is printed. If you have many fields in the report, besides reducing the length of individual fields, you can also change the print orientation to *landscape,* which means the report prints along the 11-inch edge of a piece of paper as opposed to the standard 8½-inch edge. As you work with a report, you may want to change the page orientation or even the page size. You can do this at any point by selecting File⇨Printer Setup and changing the paper size, page orientation, or even the printer used.

To move a field in the Preview tab, do the following:

1. **Click the field.**

   When you place the cursor over the field, Crystal Reports displays the formatting outline, as shown in Figure 2-16. In this example, I am moving the City field.

2. **Hold down the mouse button and drag the field to a new position in the report.**

   In this example, the City field is being moved to the left.

3. **Release the mouse pointer after the field is positioned correctly.**

   Figure 2-17 shows the City field moved to the left.

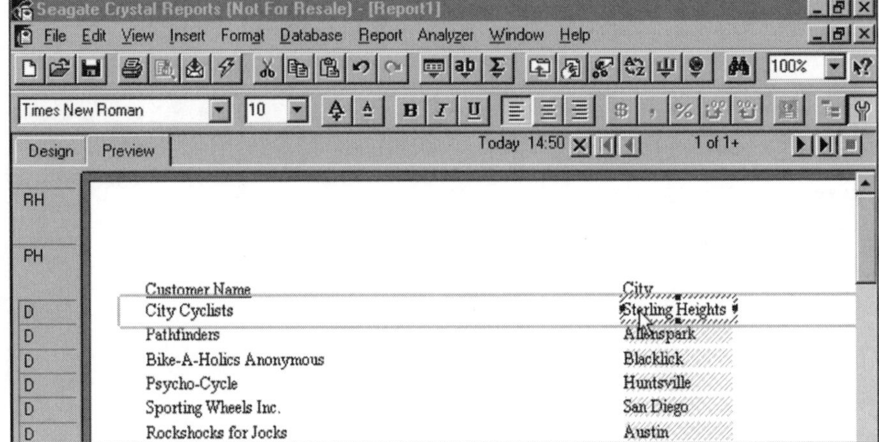

Figure 2-16: The Field format outlined.

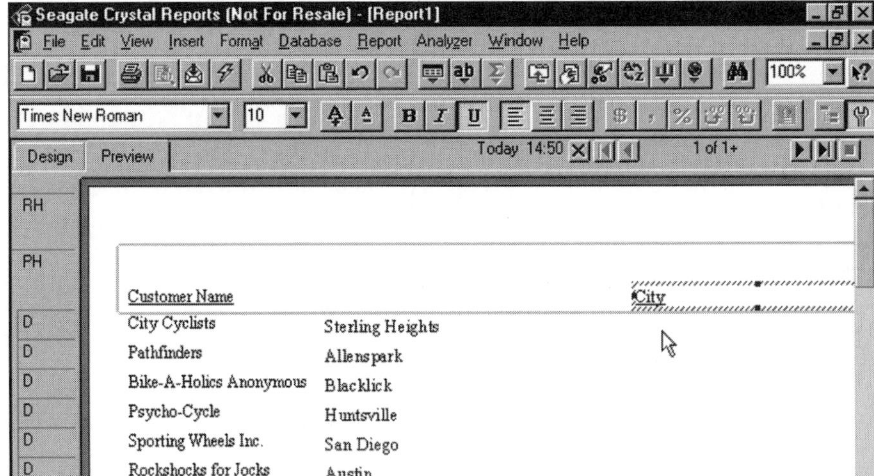

Figure 2-17: The City field, moved to the left.

Well, the field has moved all right, but the column header (in this example, City) has not. The reason is that when you insert a field into a report, Crystal Reports assumes that you want to use the field name as the column header in the report. So it inserts the name, too. You can move the header name, either in Design or Preview mode. Because you can change the name, it is not directly connected to the field itself. So it doesn't move with the field, either. To see the way this works, try the following:

1. **Click the Design tab.**
2. **Click the text object in the Page Header section.**

   In this case, click the City text object.

In Figure 2-18, you can't tell that the name of the column is a separate object! Because it a separate object, you can edit and manipulate it separately from the field itself.

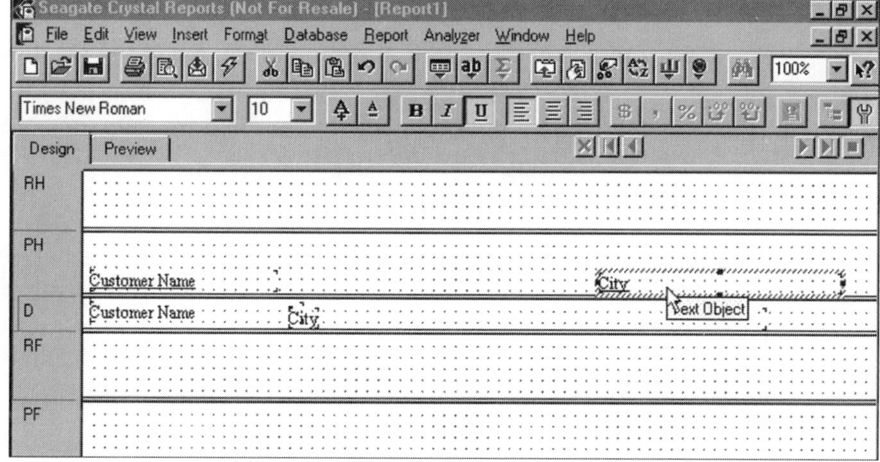

Figure 2-18: The City text object selected in the Design tab.

You can move a field and its heading separately. Seems like a lot of work, doesn't it? You can save yourself a step by clicking the field, Ctrl+clicking the column heading, and then moving them both at once.

Using Guidelines and Rulers to Position Objects

Crystal Reports gives you a pair of tools to line up the field header with the field. The two tools are the rulers, at the top and the left of the report window, and guidelines. The guidelines are vertical lines that run from the ruler down the report. The guidelines help you align objects in the report because the left edge of the objects attaches itself to the guideline. The first step to using these tools is to make sure that they are visible. By default, the rulers and guidelines should be on. If you have upgraded from a previous version of Crystal Reports, they may not be. Take a moment to make sure.

1. **Right-click a blank area anywhere in the report.**

   A menu appears.

   There are four settings that should have a checkmark. They are Show Guidelines in Design, Show Guidelines in Preview, Show Rulers in Design, and Show Rulers in Preview.

2. **Click anywhere in the report to close the menu.**

   A visible vertical line appears at the left edge of the first field already in the report and at the far right of the last field.

To use the guideline to move objects:

1. **Click the guideline end in the ruler at the top of the window in the ruler (it's the little upside-down triangle).**
2. **Hold the left mouse button down and drag the guideline to the desired position on the ruler, in this example to the 2-inch mark.**
3. **Release the mouse button.**

A funny thing about a guideline is that objects that are attached to the guideline line themselves up to it. In other words, you can use the guideline to arrange and align a series of objects in a report.

To attach an object to a guideline, do the following:

1. **In the Design tab, click the object you want to align.**
2. **Hold the mouse button down and drag the object so that its left edge is bumping against the guideline.**
3. **Release the mouse button.**

You observe no changes in the object itself when it is attached to the line. To see whether an object is attached, click the guideline end and drag it to the right or left. The object should move with the line. If an object is attached to a guideline, red markers appear at the corners that are attached to the guideline.

Using Guidelines in Preview

The reason for using guidelines in the Preview tab is the same as in the Design tab — to line up objects. Remember, Crystal Reports allows you to arrange the report layout in either Design or Preview mode. The difference is that in Preview, you are working with real data and not placeholders. (So the performance of your computer may be diminished. In other words, stuff takes longer to happen in Preview than it does in Design, but in Preview you can see the actual report.)

To turn on guidelines in the Preview tab, do the following:

1. **Right-click anywhere in the report.**
2. **From the pop-up menu that appears, select the Show Guidelines in Preview option.**

   The menu appears, as shown in Figure 2-19.

3. **Click anywhere outside of the pop-up menu to close the menu.**

Not too hard, is it? Back in Preview, you can see whether the change has taken effect. Click the text object. The guidelines should appear.

Figure 2-19: The pop-up menu.

Using Grids

A *grid* is a cross section of horizontal and vertical lines. (In fact, the term *gridiron* as a synonym for a football field comes from the fact that at one time, the football field had vertical *and* horizontal lines.) Crystal Reports has a grid, too, which can aid in the placement of objects in the report. In fact, the gridlines have a property known as Snap to Grid, which means that when objects are placed, they snap into alignment vertically and horizontally. This feature is terrific for those reports that require many objects beyond simple text headers and fields. The switch for turning this property off and on is in the pop-up menu that appears when you right-click in the report. By default — that is, automatically — the grid is on in Design tab.

Here's how to turn on the display of the grid:

1. **Right-click anywhere in the white space of the report.**
2. **From the pop-up menu, select Turn on Show Grid in Either Design or Preview.**

   The grid appears, as in Figure 2-20.

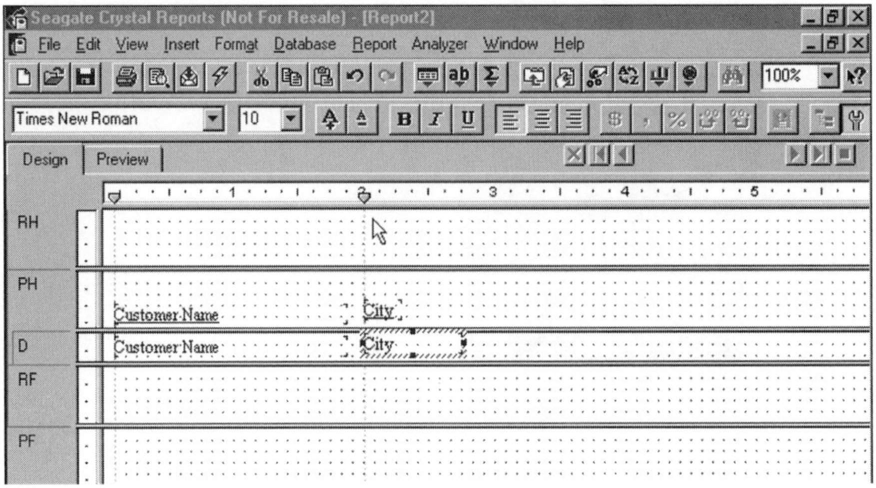

Figure 2-20: The Show Grid feature in the Design tab.

Using the Report Gallery Experts

As you start creating new reports, you have two broad options. After you select the File⇨New option, you can choose a Report Expert or the Custom option from the Report Gallery dialog box. The Custom option assumes that you know something about creating reports and do not need the guidance of the Experts or that you prefer the control of creating your own reports from the ground up.

Looking at the Report Gallery

You must also have some knowledge of Crystal Reports if you choose the Custom Report, Custom Cross-tab, and the Custom Multi-Column reports. However, what if you know the type of report you want but need help? Crystal Reports provides an "expert" to guide you through the steps needed to create the report. Thus, the second path is to use the Crystal Reports built-in Experts! Users new to Crystal Reports love the Report Creation Experts because, within a few minutes, they can create very powerful reports. Even techies sometimes start their reports using a Report Expert.

Take a look at the Report Gallery.

1. **Close any reports you have open (by selecting File⇨Close).** 
2. **Choose File⇨New (or click the New Report button).**

   The Report Gallery dialog box appears.

At the beginning of this chapter, you use the Custom option and then you choose Data File to create a report from scratch. Now take a different path. The Report Experts are available on the following report types, and here is a brief explanation of each type:

- **Standard:** Clicking this button takes you through the steps to create a standard report. You will see the steps in a moment.
- **Form Letter:** Form letters are a common task that people want to create using their database information. Crystal Reports helps you insert the fields you want in the form letter — for example, the address fields and perhaps a field that has an amount due for a bill, a start date for a project, or whatever is appropriate for your business. Then you can import a text file as the body of the letter.
- **Form:** Do you have a form that you use all the time, and it would be much better if it were computerized? Use this expert to create a computer version of your paper form.
- **Cross-Tab:** A Cross-Tab is a report that reveals information in your database in a *by* manner. An example is tabulating sales for a product *by* store. These have a spreadsheet-like look. Chapter 11 covers Cross-Tabs in detail.
- **Subreport:** A subreport is a report that runs inside a master report. The concept of a subreport is that the subreport can be using entirely unrelated database information from the master report. So it can be a graph that shows the total sales for the company. The master report shows the sales for a specific division.
- **Mail Label:** Generally, getting names to align properly on labels from a database is very tricky. Creating a mailing label from the names in your database is the task of this expert.
- **Drill Down:** A drill-down report is a technique for finding detailed information behind a number. For example, if you have a total in your report, the total can be drilled down to show the individual values that compose the total.

Stepping Out with an Expert: A Standard Report

The advantage of using the Report Experts is that you cannot miss a step accidentally. That is, Crystal Reports walks you through the correct process necessary to creating the report. I expand upon these reports and their steps in subsequent chapters. Because these types of reports have some aspects in common and some specific to the type of report, I derive the following sequence from the Standard Report Expert.

From the Report Gallery dialog box, if you click the Standard button, the Standard Report Expert dialog box appears, as shown in Figure 2-21.

A series of tabs are at the top of this dialog box. You can select a tab at any time if you know you want to jump ahead to that tab. Otherwise, the Expert steps you through each tab in order.

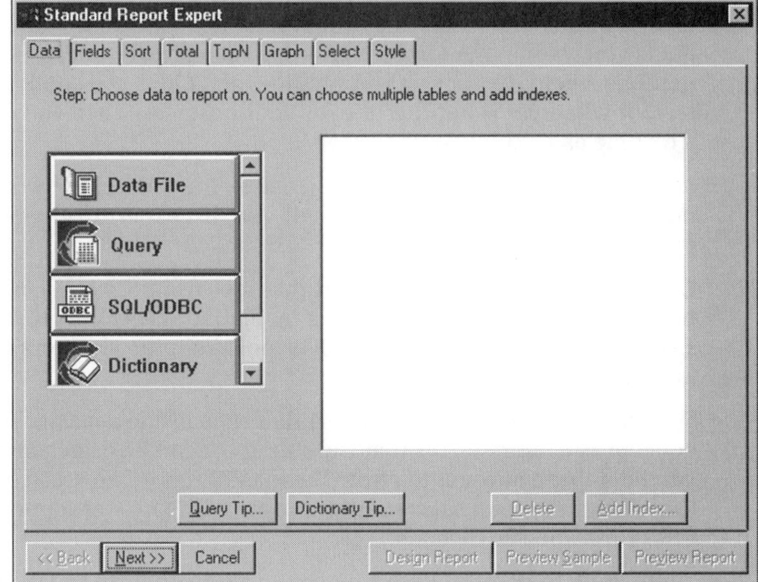

Figure 2-21: The Standard Report Expert dialog box with the Data tab selected.

Data

The initial tab in this dialog box is the Data tab. This tab is used to select the database from which you are going to create the report. The options for selecting a database source are listed in the dialog box. The steps to select a database table are covered earlier in this chapter.

After selecting a database file, Crystal Reports gives you the opportunity to add another database table to the report. This option is for those instances in which the report will include data from unique database files.

Links

The next tab is the Links tab. This tab only appears when you have selected several unique tables. The Visual Linking Expert appears, allowing you to create the necessary links between and among the tables. Linking tables is covered in detail in Chapter 14.

Fields

At this point, you select the individual fields you want in the report. This subject is also covered earlier in this chapter (see "Inserting Data Fields").

Sort

After adding the fields to your report, the next tab is Sort. Crystal Reports is offering you the opportunity to sort the report records by the field of your choice. This tab allows you to also group the records, such as by state or by product. Sorting and grouping records are the subjects of Chapter 5.

Total

Next, Crystal Reports assumes that you want some subtotals, summaries, and grand totals included in the report. So if you have selected a field such as Sales, you can create a subtotal for that field, particularly if you have grouped the sales field by state or product. Adding subtotals is covered in this chapter and in Chapter 7.

TopN

The TopN tab provides a tool for determining which groups have the top five sales numbers, the top ten salespeople, or any other top number you need (you must have a group with a subtotal for this to work). If you were Casey Kasem, you would want the top ten hit songs for the past week listed. You can bypass this tab if your report does not use the TopN feature. Chapter 5 deals with TopN Sorts and other types of sorting and grouping.

Graph

Inserting a graph into your report is available via the Graph tab. Crystal Reports has its own graph editor; therefore you can create virtually any type of graph and annotate to fit your needs and then insert it directly into your report, as I brilliantly describe in Chapter 6. If you don't require a graph in the report, simply skip this tab.

Select

The Select tab is next, and this is an important aspect of Crystal Reports. As you design your report, you may not want all the records in the source database to be part of the report. You may want only records of last month's sales or only the records of sales of ski boots. The Select tab allows you to use only the records you want, as I detail in Chapter 4.

Style

The Standard Report Expert concludes with a choice of report formats, selected from the Style tab. That is, taking all the choices you have made to this point, Crystal Reports includes several handy layouts for formatting the report data. You can take a look at each of the layouts in the dialog box. After choosing a Style, you can then proceed to preview the report, which is a WYSIWYG (what you see is what you get) view of the report. I cover using a variety of formatting techniques in Chapters 8 and 10.

Why you should use an Expert

Not all the Experts arrive at the report in the same manner, but I would advise using them for the reason I stated previously: They lead you step-by-step through the process, thereby eliminating any worry about forgetting a step. Not that you wouldn't get a report without using an Expert, but, on your own, you may not get the exact report you want.

In addition, now you can return to the Report Expert to modify reports. After you preview your report, how do you go about fine-tuning it? After the Report Expert creates the report, you can manually modify it using what you read in this book. For example, you can modify the record selection or insert another field onto the report.

But you may find it quicker to return to the Report Expert and make your changes there. To do this, simply click the Report Expert button or select the Report Expert command from the Report menu.

Chapter 3

Crystal Reports: Basic Skills

In This Chapter

- Opening a saved report
- Inserting text objects
- Formatting text objects
- Moving among pages in a report
- Magnifying the report window

After inserting fields, the next natural step is to add text to define and enhance your report. Text objects, as they are called in Seagate Crystal Reports, can be formatted in a number of ways, so I take a look at that, too. Finally, on my agenda for this chapter is a quick tour of how to move from page to page in a report.

Opening a Saved Report

In Chapter 2, I create a report into which I insert two fields. I then save the report with the brilliant and unique name, ch2. To follow along in this chapter, you can use any of the example reports that Crystal Reports provides. If you happened to follow the steps in Chapter 2, you can continue using that report. Here's how to open a saved report, using my report as an example:

1. **Open Crystal Reports.**

   The Welcome dialog box appears, as shown in Figure 3-1. (If you have clicked off the Show Welcome Dialog Box at Startup box, you do not see this — see separate steps that apply to you, later in this section.)

Figure 3-1: The Welcome dialog box in Crystal Reports.

2. **Click the Open Report button.**

   Crystal Reports opens the aptly named Open dialog box, shown in Figure 3-2. (You can see my saved report — ch2 — in the lower-left corner.) You also see a series of other example reports that you can open to follow the rest of this chapter's examples.

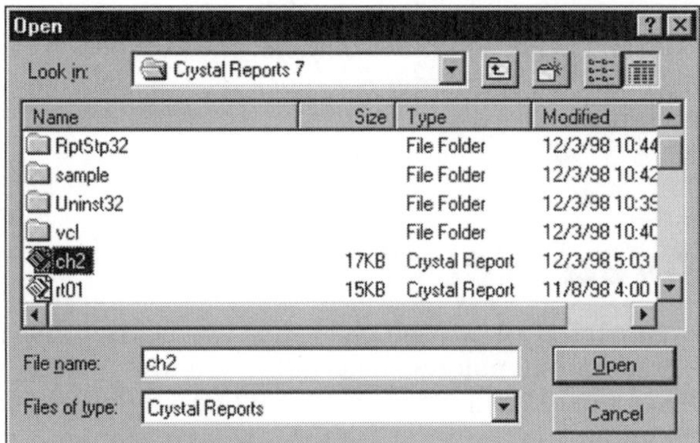

Figure 3-2: The Open dialog box.

3. **Select (by clicking) the report that you want.**

   I click ch2, of course.

4. **Click Open.**

   The ch2 report appears, as shown in Figure 3-3.

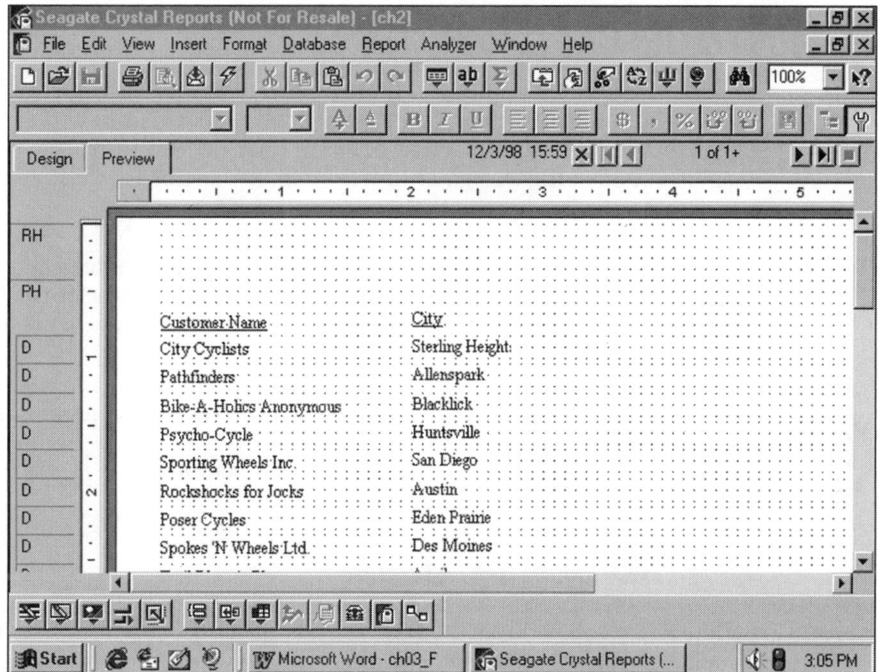

Figure 3-3: Doug's ch2 report opened.

If you have problems opening a saved file, make sure that the Files of Type box in the Open dialog box lists Crystal Reports. Second, make sure that you click the report name so that the name appears in the File Name field *before* you click the Open button. One other possibility is that you saved the report in a folder other than the CRW folder, and you have to locate the report by checking other folders.

If you have shut off the Welcome dialog box, open a saved report this way:

1. **After starting Crystal Reports, click the File menu.**
2. **From the File menu, select Open.**

   The Open dialog box appears.
3. **Click the name of the report you want.**
4. **Click Open.**

Inserting Text Objects

A *text object* is a type of object that you can insert into a report to describe what is in the report, to highlight a particular record, or to add a description. The most common use of a text object is the title for the report. Text objects can be added in the Design or Preview tab. My advice is to add text objects in the Design tab for reasons that soon become obvious.

When you insert fields from a database table, Crystal Reports automatically adds the field name as the header for the column. The header is a text object; therefore, you can modify it by clicking it and typing a new name or by changing its font style.

With Windows 95, 98, or NT, you can add more text to the names of the reports you create, and Crystal Reports also provides a means to add descriptive text to a report, as I describe in Chapter 17.

Adding a text object

Adding a text object from the Design tab is easier because of the layout guides available, including the ability to see exactly to which section of the report the text object is being added. In Preview, the program slows considerably because you are working with live data. So all you need to do is click the Design tab (which appears in Figure 3-4).

The title for a typical report normally appears on the first page of that report. The Report Header section is where you place objects that you want to appear on the title page of the report, because this section of the report is designed to print once. Remember that everything that is part of a report is considered an *object*.

Figure 3-4: The Design tab view of the report.

To insert a text object in the Report Header section of a report:

1. **Click the Insert menu.**
2. **Click Text Object.**

   The mouse pointer has a rectangle outline attached, as shown in Figure 3-5.
3. **Move the rectangle until it is positioned where you want the left edge of the title object to begin.**

   Simply click the left mouse button, causing Crystal Reports to open the text box and ruler guide.

   In Figure 3-6, I have clicked the mouse button. Crystal Reports opens the text ruler above the text box. But you don't have to worry about getting the size exactly correct, because Crystal Reports is intelligent and resizes the text box for you as you type!

   If you decide not to insert a text object, press the Escape (Esc) key.
4. **The insert text cursor is flashing in the text box. Type the text you want for your title.**

   For me, the title is **Doug's Brilliant Report.**

   If you have been creating the text object along with me, notice that the text box expands automatically to accommodate the length of the text being entered.
5. **To finish a text object entry, simply click another part of the report.**

   Do not press Enter; doing so adds an unnecessary additional line.

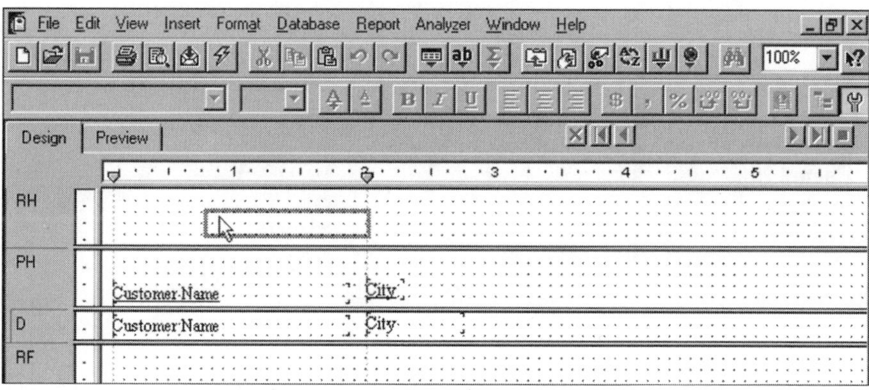

Figure 3-5: A rectangle attached to the pointer.

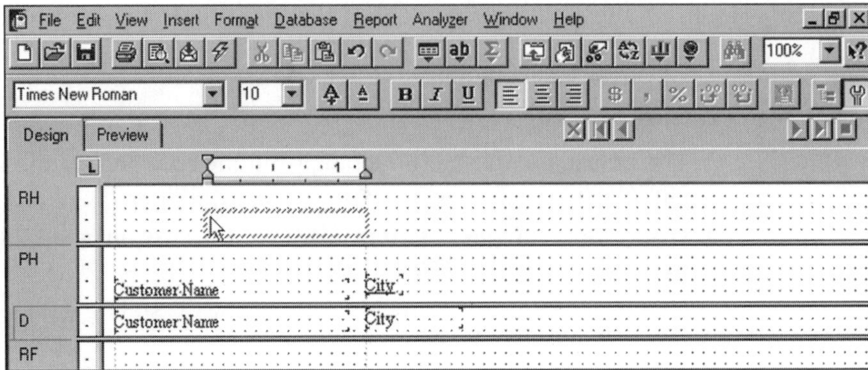

Figure 3-6: A text box ready for text, with a ruler line above it.

Previewing the text object

After you insert a text object, click the Preview tab to see how the text object looks in relation to your report (something like Figure 3-7). The Preview tab gives you an accurate view of how any change to the report actually looks when printed. If you'd like to turn off the grid background, right-click in a blank space of the report. From the pop-up menu that appears, deselect the Grid option.

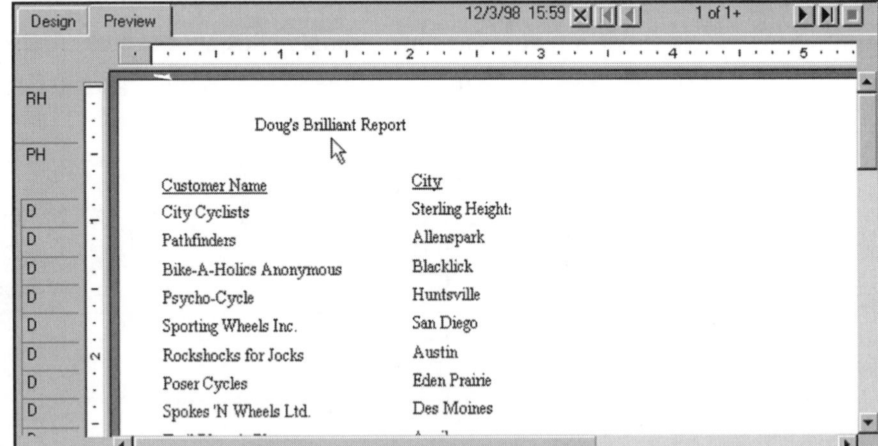

Figure 3-7: The title text object in the Preview tab.

The title may be great, but it's too small for this or any report. Crystal Reports uses a 10-point font by default, so the next logical step is to increase the size of the title. Check Chapter 16 (on file options), which shows you how to set the default sizes and styles of Crystal Reports objects.

Editing a text object

You can make changes to a text object in the Design tab or Preview tab. But the Design tab offers more layout guides, and I recommend using it.

To modify a text object:

1. **Click the Design tab.**
2. **Click the text object that you want to modify.**
3. **Right-click that object.**

   The menu appears, as shown in Figure 3-8.

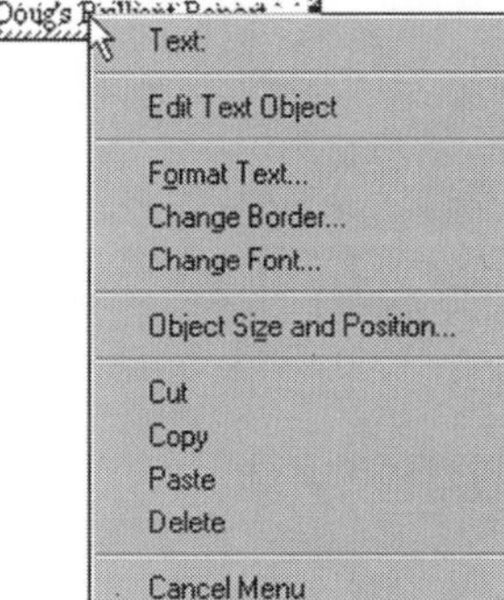

Figure 3-8: The text object format menu.

You can right-click to open a similar menu for other types of objects, too.

The top of the menu tells you which kind of object you have selected — in this case, text. Under that is a list of options from which you can select. Edit Text Object puts the insertion point into the text field and re-opens the ruler, as Figure 3-6 shows.

4. **Select the Format Text choice, which opens the Format Editor dialog box, shown in Figure 3-9.**

   This dialog box has a myriad of options, which I touch upon as needed. At the top of the dialog box are the tabs for different format options. In this example, I want to change the font of the title.

5. **Click the Font tab.**

   The dialog box changes to reflect your selection, as shown in Figure 3-10. Table 3-1 outlines the various elements of the dialog box.

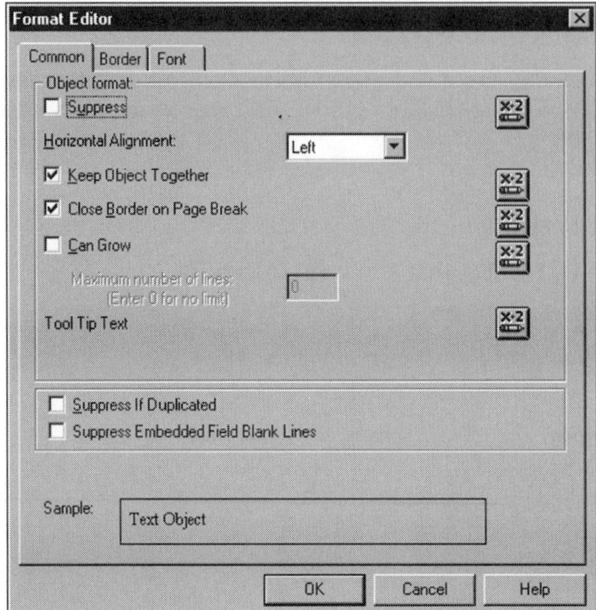

Figure 3-9: The Format Editor dialog box.

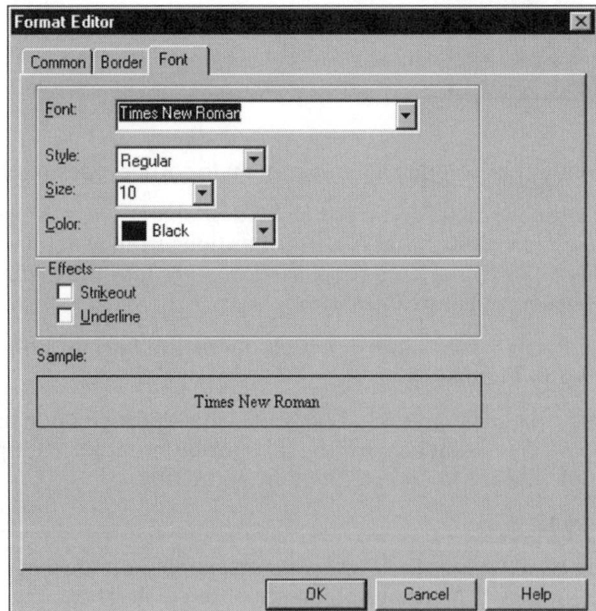

Figure 3-10: The Font tab selected in the Format Editor dialog box.

Table 3-1 Fields That Can Change the Appearance of Your Text

Feature Name	*What It Does*
Font	To select a font, click the down arrow and click the font style you want. Crystal Reports shows you the selection in the Sample field at the bottom of the dialog box. The fonts from which you can choose are determined by the fonts installed on your system.
Style	Click the down arrow in the style menu to select Bold, Italic, Bold Italic, or Regular.
Size	This option interests me most at this point. I want the title to be bigger. You have two options: You can type in the point size you desire, or you can click the down arrow and select a value from the list. In this example, I enter 20 as the point size.
Color	Click the down arrow to select a color for the text.
Strikeout	Check the box for strikeout.
Underline	Check the box for underline.

6. **To modify the text, check the selection(s) you want.**
7. **Click OK.**

In my example, I simply changed the point size to 20. You can see the change in the Design tab, but click the Preview tab for a better look, as shown in Figure 3-11. In order to see the text, I had to expand the text box by clicking the object and dragging a handle away from the text.

Note that in Figure 3-11, several outlines appear, one around the title and another across the top of the page. The outline around the title defines the area of the text object, and the outline across the top of the page defines the Report Header section.

Adding a border and drop shadow to the title

In addition to simply changing the size of the text, you can modify the look of the text object. In this example, I show you how to add a border and then a drop shadow to the title, giving a 3-D effect. I am working in the Preview tab.

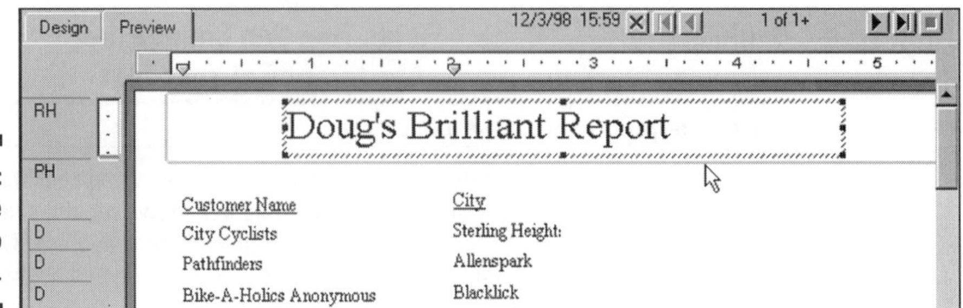

Figure 3-11: The title size changed to 20 points.

To add a border to a text object:

1. **Right-click the text object.**
2. **From the menu, select the Change Border option.**

   The Border tab appears in the Format Editor dialog box, shown in Figure 3-12.

   Most of the time, you want the border completely around the text object, but not always. So Crystal Reports gives you the option of picking which of the sides of the rectangle to include in the border. If you really get fanciful, you can combine different fonts and type sizes with one or more borders for a variety of effects.

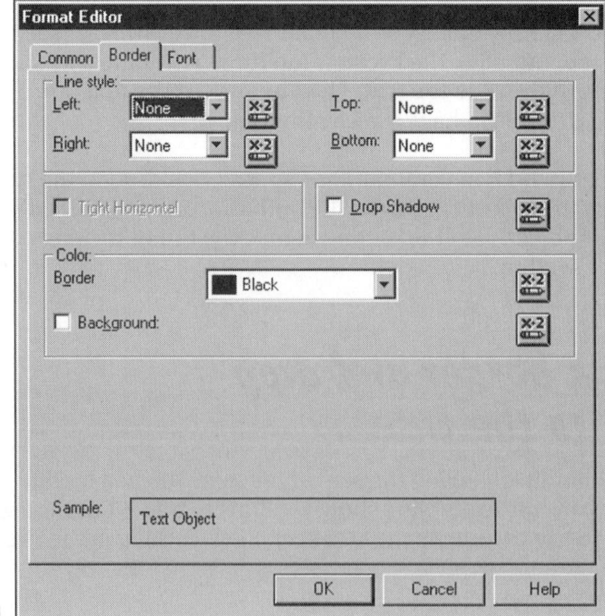

Figure 3-12: The Format Editor dialog box, with the Border tab selected — ready to add a border of your choosing.

In Chapter 8, I show you how to use another option in this dialog box. The small icon that has an X+2 on it is a *conditional formatting tool,* meaning that you can have Crystal Reports execute a formula that determines whether or not the particular border is visible. The practical aspect of this tool is that a report's title can be easily identified by formatting that causes it to appear when printed. For example, if the report shows a net loss in the number of products sold, the border can be printed in a special color (red comes to mind) and with double-lined borders.

3. **Click the pull-down arrow next to the rectangle side that you want to be visible (Left, Right, Top, or Bottom), and select the type of border that you want to appear.**

   Crystal Reports previews the border change at the bottom of the dialog box.

4. **If you want a drop shadow, with or without any border, click in the Drop Shadow check box.**

5. **Click OK.**

   The results appear in Figure 3-13.

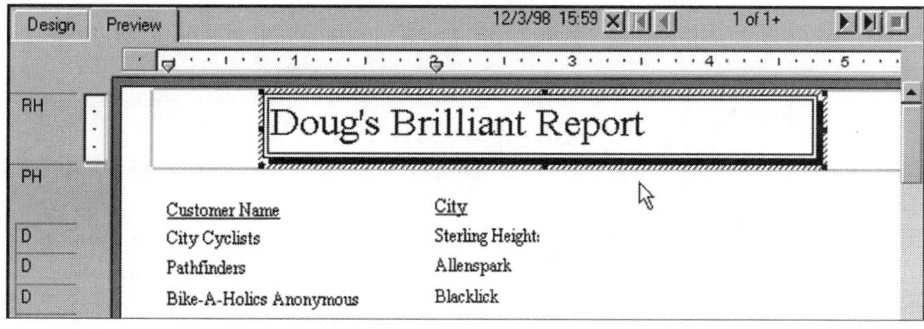

Figure 3-13: A double-lined border with a drop shadow added to my title object.

Adding other fields

To this point, the database fields that I have inserted into the report have been text objects. (After being inserted into the report, they become objects.) To add another layer to a report, find out how to add a field with numbers in "Adding a Number Field," later in this chapter. The process is identical in either case, but numeric fields can be formatted in a number of ways that text database fields cannot. In addition, the Customer table has a Region field that you can use to group the records, as I describe in Chapter 5, so I show you how to add that field, too.

Moving a field in a report

Consider the current layout of the report. At present, the Customer Name field precedes the City field. In the database, you also have a Region field, which is a larger area than the City. So putting the Region field the farthest to the left makes sense, followed by the City and then the Customer Name field.

To move a field in a report:

1. **Click the Design tab.**
2. **Click the field name in the Page Header — in this case, Customer Name.**
3. **Press and hold the Ctrl key.**
4. **Click the database field in the Details section, directly underneath the column heading.**

   Because you press the Ctrl key after you select an object, Crystal Reports assumes that you want to select several objects. So both the column header and column records are selected and can be moved at the same time. Figure 3-14 shows both objects selected.

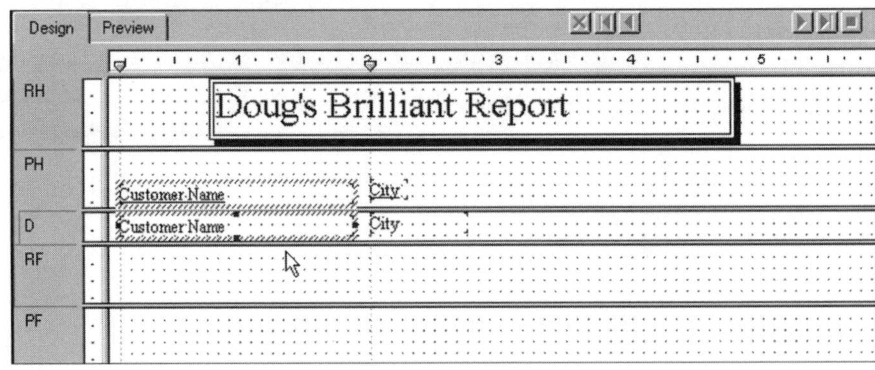

Figure 3-14: The column head and column details both selected.

5. **Click and hold either of the objects already selected. You can release the Ctrl key at this point.**
6. **Drag the mouse to the right.**

   As you do, you see an outline of the objects moving with the mouse pointer.
7. **After they are moved to the position you want, release the mouse button.**

   In Figure 3-15, the two objects that represent the column head of Customer Name and the details have been moved to the right of the City field.

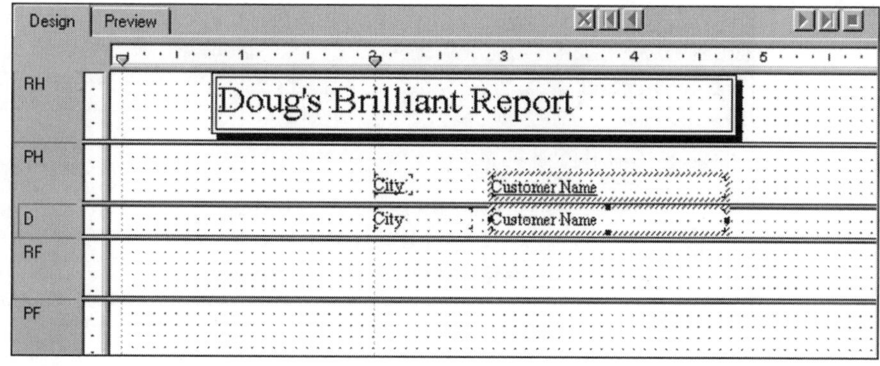

Figure 3-15: The Customer Name field moved to the right of the City field.

You can also move a field text object and the field object at the same time with the ruler line, if the line was inserted by Crystal Reports when you inserted the field into the report. Any subsequent ruler lines will not bind to the object.

Now I want to add the Region field and insert it where the Customer Name field was.

To add a field to a report:

1. **If you are in the Preview tab, click the Design tab.**

2. **Click the Insert Fields button.**

   The Insert Fields dialog box appears.

3. **Click the field name you want to insert.**

   In this case, it's the Region field.

4. **Click Insert.**

5. **Position the mouse pointer so that the field outline is right next to the left margin of the report.**

   You know that you have reached the left margin when Crystal Reports does not let you drag the object any farther.

6. **Click the mouse button.**

   Figure 3-16 shows the results.

Figure 3-16: The Region field added to report.

Adding a Number Field

No difference exists between adding a number field and adding a text field. I just thought that the topic of adding a number field deserves its own section in this book. In this example, I add the field named Last Year's Sales to the Design tab. This particular field consists of numbers, formatted as currency.

1. **If the Insert Fields dialog box is not already open, click the Insert Fields button.**
2. **Scroll the list to locate the Last Year's Sales field name.**

   Note that the fields are not listed in alphabetical order; rather, they are listed in the order they occur in the database.
3. **Click the Last Year's Sales field name and then click Insert.**
4. **Position the field outline so that the field is inserted at the far right of the report.**

Any field in the report can be identified by positioning the mouse pointer on the field in either Design or Preview. When you do so, a pop-up text box appears to tell you the name of the table the field is from, the field name, and the type of field, as shown in Figure 3-17.

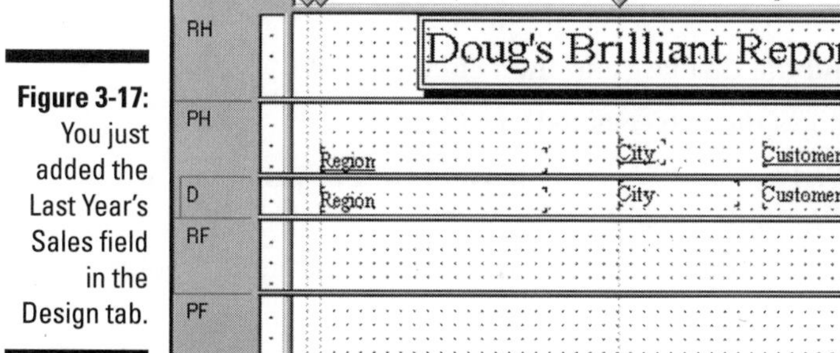

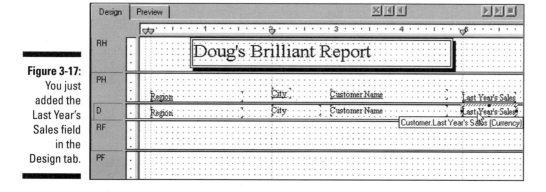

Figure 3-17: You just added the Last Year's Sales field in the Design tab.

As you can see in Figure 3-17, the field is identified as Customer.Last Year's Sales (Currency) via a pop-up menu.

To check the look of the report and see how the printed report will look, click the Preview tab. The new report appears, as shown in Figure 3-18.

Design | Preview | Today 15:46 | 1 of 1+

Doug's Brilliant Report

Region	City	Customer Name	Last Year's Sales
MI	Sterling Height:	City Cyclists	$19,426.76
CO	Allenspark	Pathfinders	$42,601.14
OH	Blacklick	Bike-A-Holics Anonymous	$18,708.52
AL	Huntsville	Psycho-Cycle	$66,791.39
CA	San Diego	Sporting Wheels Inc.	$61,767.84
TX	Austin	Rockshocks for Jocks	$41,443.97
MN	Eden Prairie	Poser Cycles	$21,812.40
IA	Des Moines	Spokes 'N Wheels Ltd.	$23,979.11

Figure 3-18: A preview of the report with new fields added.

Aligning Columns and Headers

This formatting change is easier to execute in the Preview tab than in Design because it is easier to see the results in Preview. You can select the column head and the field containing the records, and thereby align the two objects so that the column head is *centered* over the records.

To align a column header with the records below it:

1. **Select the column header by clicking it.**
2. **Press and hold the Ctrl key and then click the field.**

   Figure 3-19 shows the two selected together.
3. **Release the Ctrl key and open the Format menu (which you see in Figure 3-20) by right-clicking the records.**

   Note that the top of the menu indicates that this is a multiple object selection.

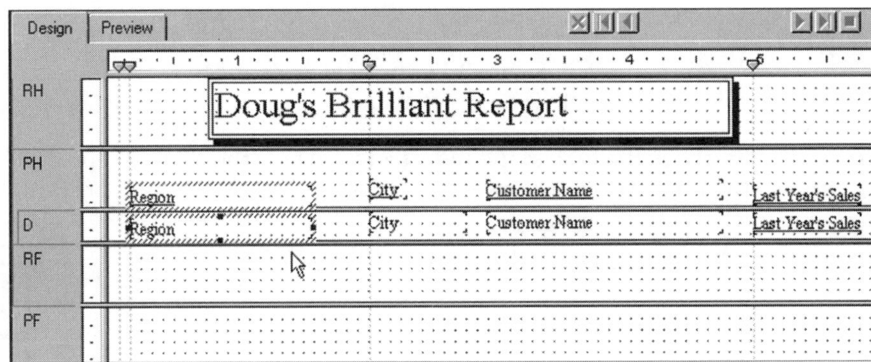

Figure 3-19: Two objects selected, ready for alignment.

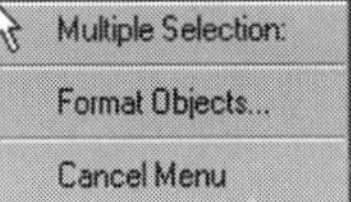

Figure 3-20: The Format menu.

4. **Click the Format Objects option.**

   The Format Editor dialog box appears, as shown in Figure 3-21. (If the Common tab is not on top, click it.) The procedure you want — centering the column — is considered a Horizontal alignment.
5. **Click the down arrow in the Horizontal Alignment box.**
6. **Select the Centered option.**
7. **Click OK.**

   Figure 3-22 shows the results of the change in Preview mode.

You have to admit that it looks much better this way. When you become a little cocky, you can hold down the Ctrl key and select all the column headers and all the records and center them all at once! Crystal Reports recognizes each of the individual headers and columns and aligns them properly.

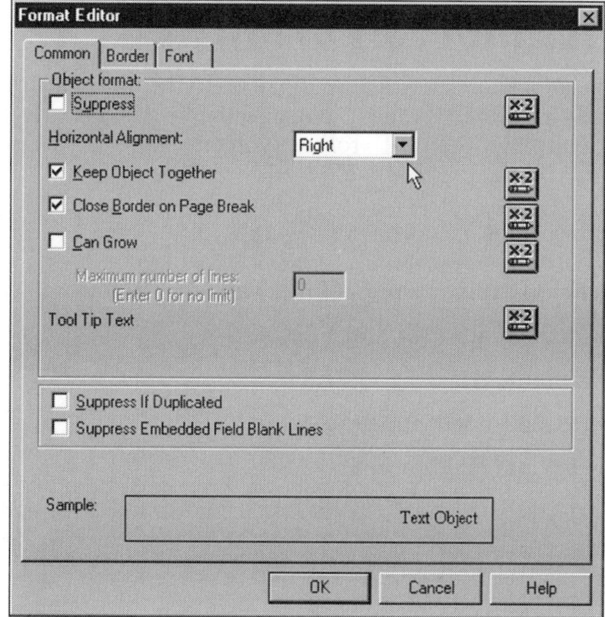

Figure 3-21: The Format Editor dialog box helps you with horizontal alignment.

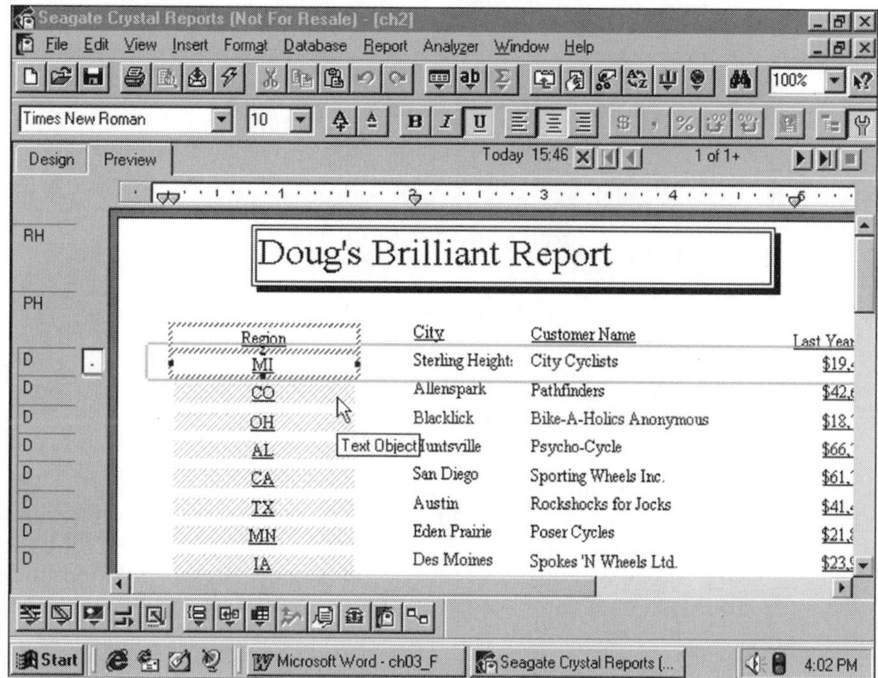

Figure 3-22: The Region column header centered over the records.

Getting the Numbers Formatted

With the text in good shape, it's time to move on to the newly inserted number field (it's actually a CURRENCY field). Because the field is numeric, the formatting choices are broader than with text, as you may expect. This procedure is easiest to execute in the Preview tab because you are using live data.

To format number fields, click the Preview tab.

1. **Click the field in the number column you want to format.**

   In this example, that's Last Year's Sales.

2. **Right-click the field.**

   The menu in Figure 3-23 appears.

3. **Select the Format Field option.**

   The Format Editor dialog box appears, as shown in Figure 3-24.

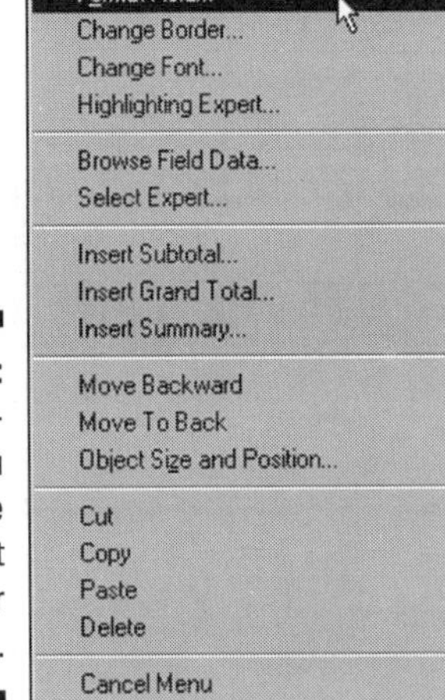

Figure 3-23: With a right-click, you have the Format menu for numbers.

For this example, I am concerned only with a single setting, which is the number of Decimals printed. Currently, the column of numbers includes two decimal places, which are unnecessary clutter. Also note that if the check box next to Use Windows Default Format is checked, those Windows defaults about printing numbers are at work in Crystal Reports. Making a change, though, is easy.

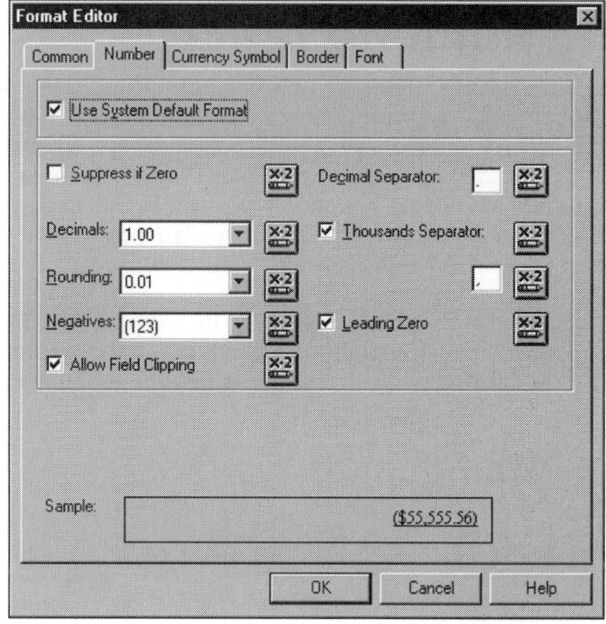

Figure 3-24: The Format Editor dialog box for number fields.

To change the number of decimal places displayed and printed:

1. **Click the down arrow in the Decimals field.**
2. **Click the 1 value, indicating that no decimals follow each numeral.**
3. **Click OK.**

   Figure 3-25 shows the reformatted numbers.

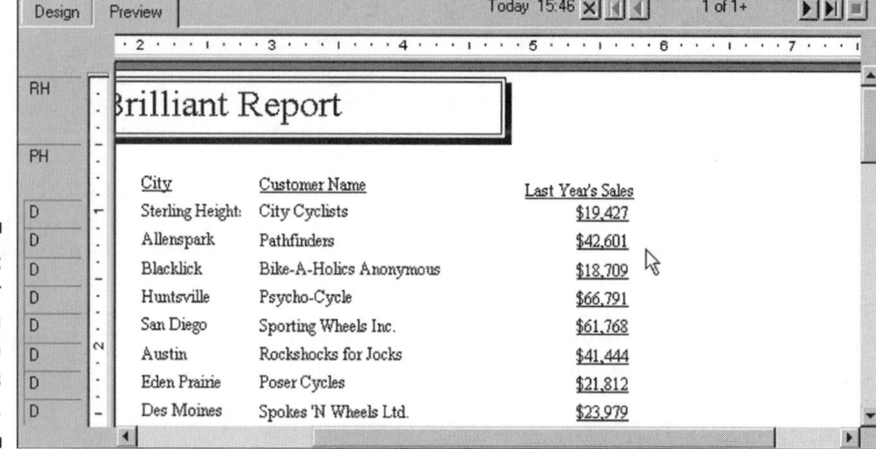

Figure 3-25: The number column with zero decimals displayed.

Using the Highlighting Expert

In previous versions of Crystal Reports, adding formatting based on the number being displayed wasn't easy. For example, in the field Last Year's Sales, it would be useful to a reader if numbers that exceed a set amount or are below a predetermined amount were displayed (and, if you have a color printer, subsequently printed) in a unique color. But in the earlier version, because you had to create a formula to do so, many novice users decided that it was easier to print the report and use a highlighting pen!

All that has changed with Version 7. One of the items that appears on the pop-up menu for numbers is Highlighting Expert. Display it, as shown in Figure 3-26, by right-clicking while the mouse is positioned on a number field.

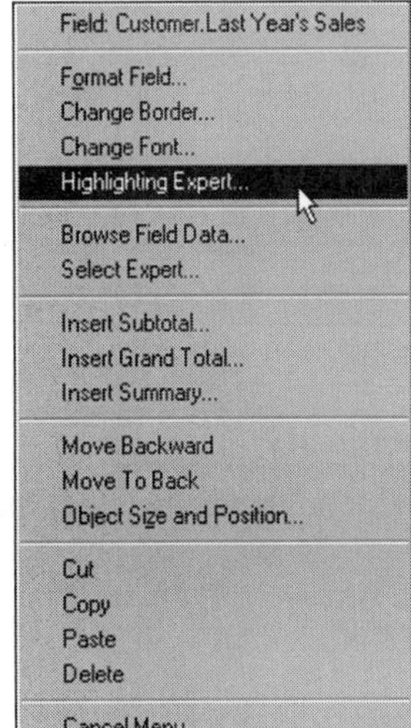

Figure 3-26: The number column with the menu displayed.

By selecting Highlighting Expert, you get the Highlighting Expert dialog box . This dialog box provides a simple way to have Crystal Reports automatically apply a specific font or color based on the value of the number.

The first decision is to determine the values that you want highlighted. In this example, I want values that are greater than 49,500 to be shown in red, with the number in a single-line box. To make this formatting happen, follow these steps:

1. **Click the down arrow to the right of the Value Is field to open the pull-down menu.**

2. **Select the type of condition you want.**

   As you can see in Figure 3-27, several conditional statements are available. I want the Greater Than condition, so I click it.

   Crystal Reports provides a sample of the condition at the left of the dialog box. In order to select a specific number, I can open the pull-down menu right below the Value Is field, and Crystal Reports lets me see the numbers from the field in ascending order. Figure 3-28 shows the numbers from the field in the opened list and the sample at left.

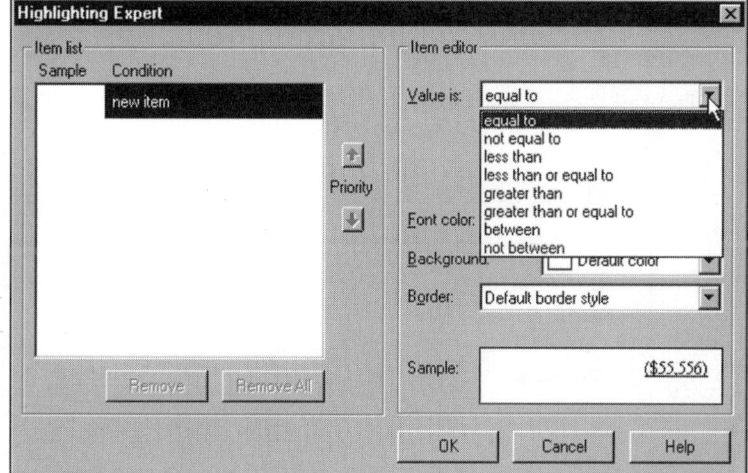

Figure 3-27: The Highlighting Expert dialog box with the Value Is list open.

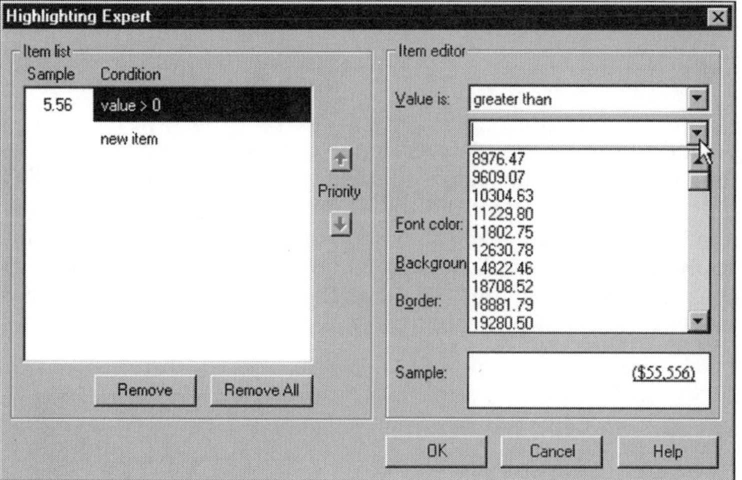

Figure 3-28: The Highlighting Expert dialog box with numbers from the field listed.

3. **Select the number from the list or type the number you want in the field.**

   I select the number 49,524.04 from the list.

4. **Select the color you want for the font.**

   You may also select a background color.

5. **Select the border type.**

   I select a Single box.

   Crystal displays a sample of the styles you select, so you can adjust the settings before applying them.

6. **Click OK.**

   Figure 3-29 reveals the result.

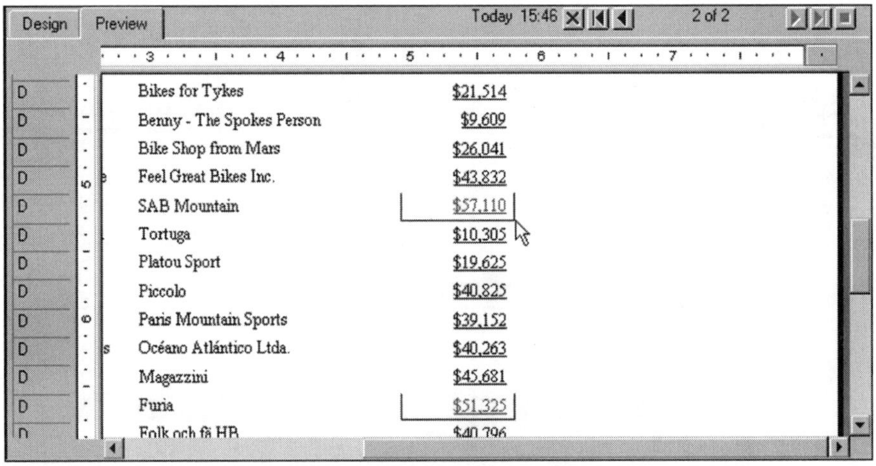

Figure 3-29: A report with formatting applied based on the number.

To add a little more sophistication to the report, you can add a second condition, which highlights values that fall below a certain amount. Following the preceding steps, I select the condition Less Than or Equal To, and I type the number 12000. Figure 3-30 shows the dialog box with both conditions ready to apply. Clicking OK applies the conditions and highlights numbers that meet those conditions. Figure 3-31 shows the report with both types of highlighting.

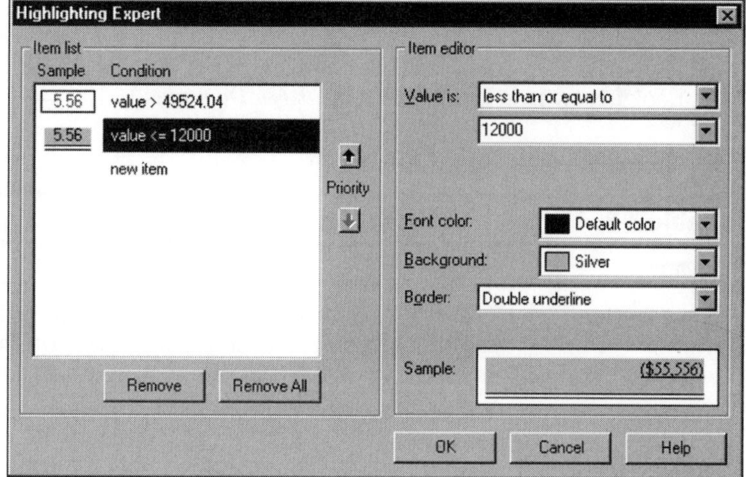

Figure 3-30: Second condition added to the Highlighting Expert dialog box.

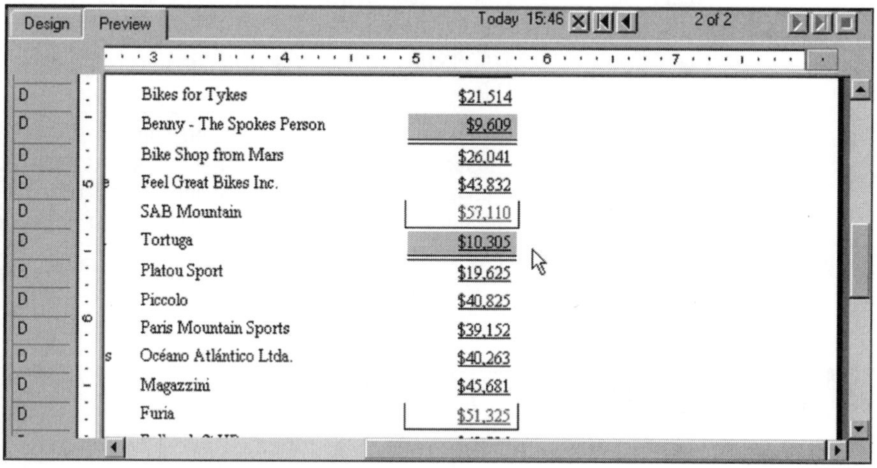

Figure 3-31: A report with two conditions highlighting specified numbers.

Moving from Page to Page in a Report

Frequently, your reports run more than a single page when printed. When you create them in Crystal Reports, you can view a single page at a time. So you need to know how to move from the current page to a previous or following page. The approach is quite easy. At the top-right corner of the Preview tab is a series of three boxes, followed by numbers, and then three more boxes. You can see them in the top right corner of Figure 3-31. The common term for these kinds of buttons is *VCR buttons,* because they imitate the buttons on your VCR to an extent. (By the way, my VCR clock shows the correct time. Look for my next book, *VCR Clocks For Dummies.*)

Table 3-2 tells how these buttons work.

Table 3-2 VCR Buttons in the Preview Tab

Button	*Function*
Close Preview	The first button closes the Preview tab. You may want to close the Preview tab if your system resources (computer memory) are running low and Crystal Reports starts to slow down.
First Page	This button causes Crystal Reports to display the first page of the report.
Previous Page	This button causes Crystal Reports to display the page previous to the current page.
Next Page	This button causes Crystal Reports to display the page following the current page.
Last Page	This button causes Crystal Reports to display the final page in the report.
Stop Transfer	At the far right is a button that only operates when Crystal Reports is reading the database to get or refresh records. If you open the Preview tab and find that it is taking a long time for the report to appear, click this button to stop records from being transferred to the report.

Magnifying the Page

As you add more and more objects to a page, the clutter may overwhelm even the sharpest eye. Or you may have added a combination of objects and need to see them close up before printing. For just these sorts of situations, Crystal Reports gives you a means to *zoom* in on an area of the report.

To zoom your report in or out:

1. **At the right end of the toolbar, click the downward-pointing arrow to view the Zoom Control drop-down list (see Figure 3-32).**

   From this drop-down list, you can select a percentage that will either zoom in on the report (if you choose a percentage greater than 100 percent) or zoom out (if you choose a percentage less than 100 percent).

   Or choose View⇨Zoom.

   The Magnification Factor dialog box appears (see Figure 3-33).

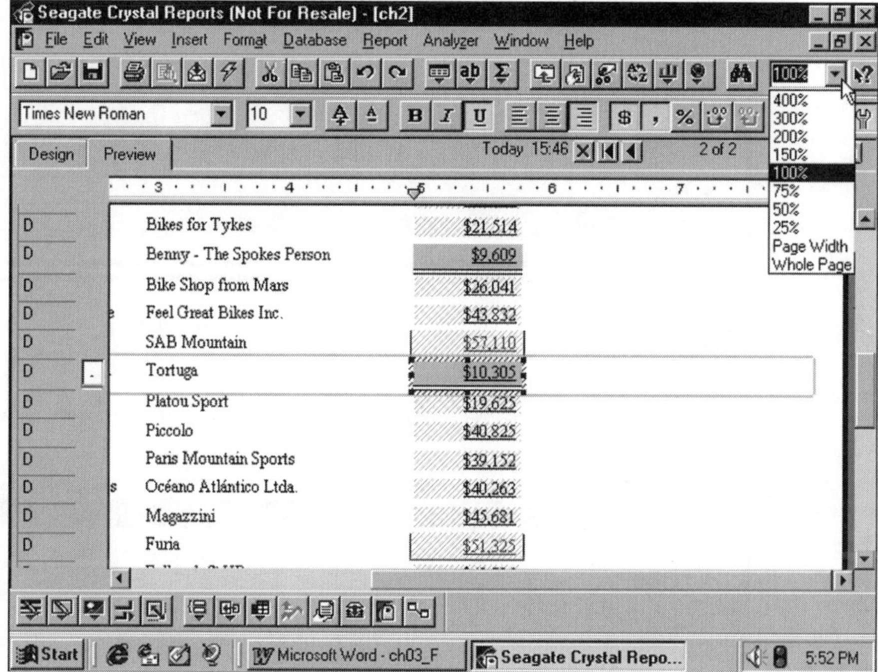

Figure 3-32: Using the Zoom Control drop-down list.

Figure 3-33: Choose View➪Zoom to see the Magnification Factor dialog box for zoooooming.

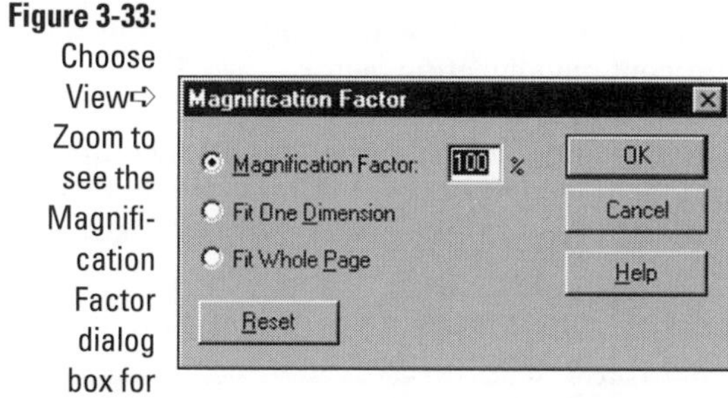

2. **Set the Magnification Factor, either enlarging or shrinking:**

   • To enlarge, type a larger value in the field provided.

     The default value is 100 percent. So if you increase the value, you zoom in on the report. You can enter a number as large as 400. When you do, the report looks like the one in Figure 3-34. It gives you an idea of the ease with which you can see detail using this method.

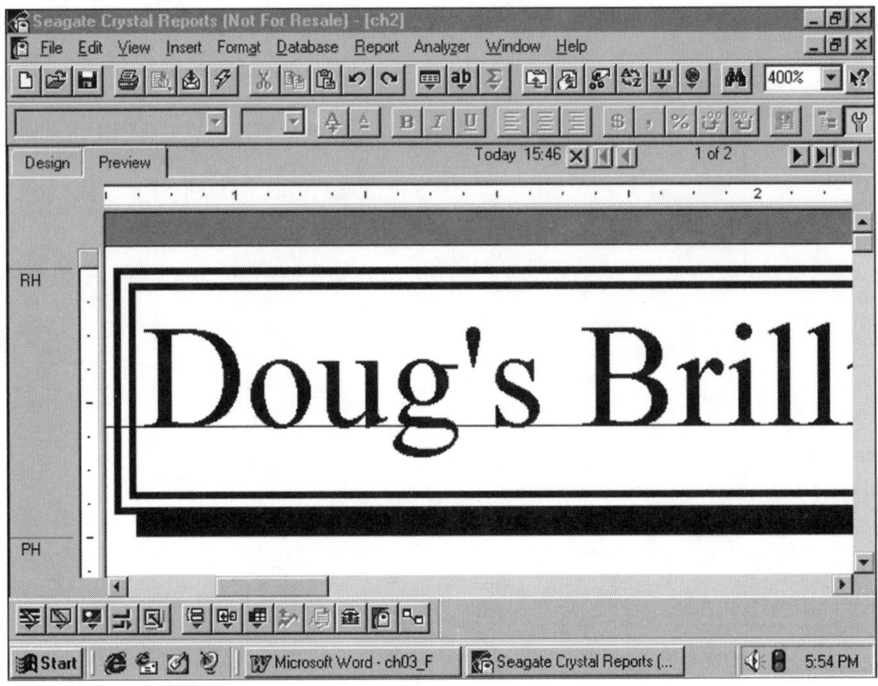

Figure 3-34: Report zooooomed 400 percent.

- To shrink, decrease the number.

  You may do so in order to see the entire page at one time. Figure 3-35 is an example of a 40-percent magnification factor.

The reasons for viewing the entire page are more apparent after you add headers and footers and summary data, which I cover in Chapter 9. Looking at the entire page may save you the chore of printing the report to check the formatting.

Undoing or redoing a format change

If you make a mistake in applying a format when using the Highlighting Expert, you can click the Undo button to remove the last formatting change. The Undo button looks like a curved arrow, pointing left. Click it after applying the format, and the format reverts to the original. After you click the Undo button, the Redo button (with a curved arrow pointing right) is active, allowing you to turn the format back on. These two buttons give you an opportunity to toggle between formats to decide which you want to keep.

In addition, you can always right-click the field and select the Highlight Expert to remove any conditional formatting you have applied.

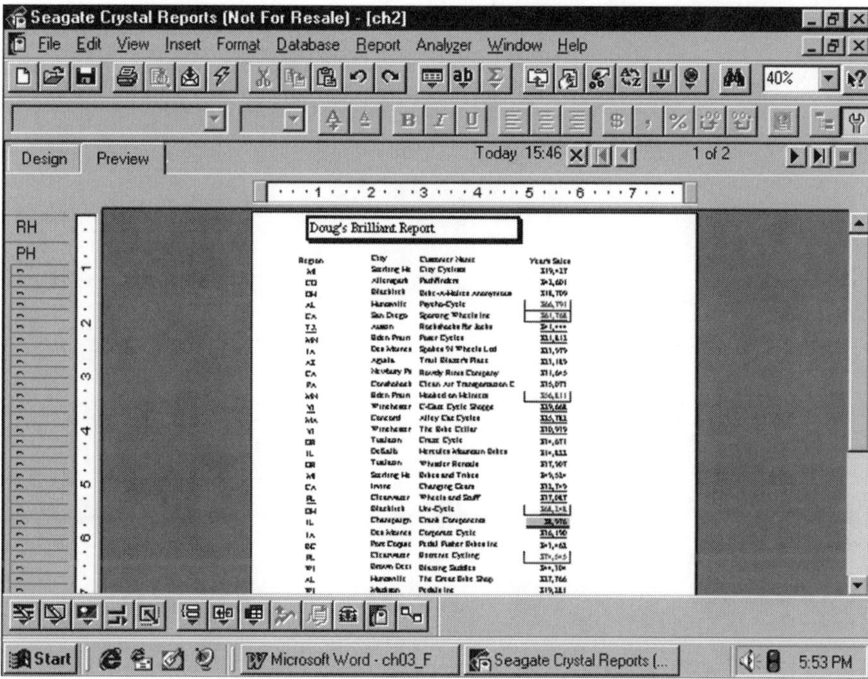

Figure 3-35: Page magnification set at 40 percent.

Part II
Manipulating Records

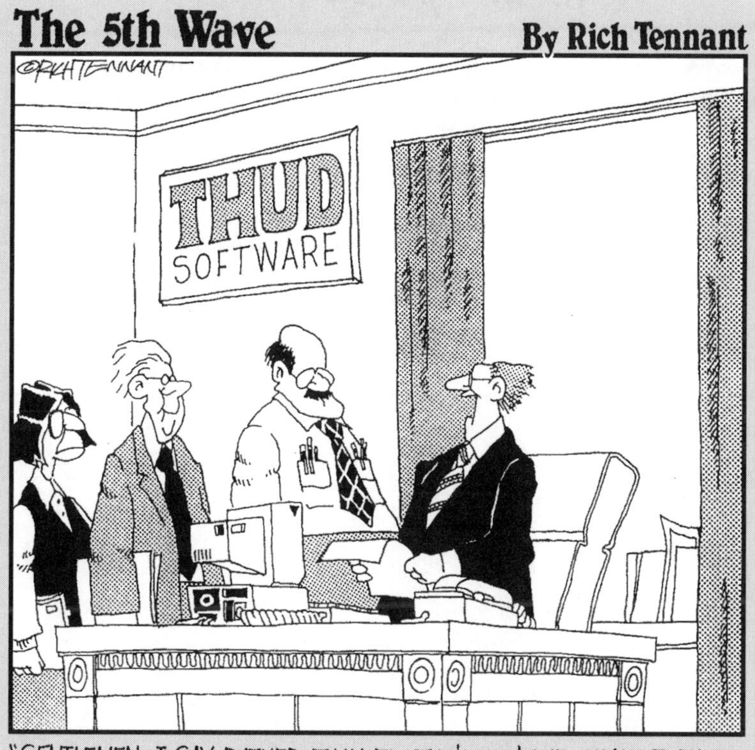

"GENTLEMEN, I SAY RATHER THAN FIX THE 'BUGS', WE CHANGE THE DOCUMENTATION AND CALL THEM 'FEATURES'."

In this part . . .

Stage two, and the whole department is on pins and needles wondering whether your next report is going to discover that the entire West Coast sales division is a bunch of slackers who talk a good game but do not sell anything. Of course, everyone knows that everything loose rolls west, but who would have thought all those salaries were going to pay for hot tubs and Moet and Chandon! Outrageous! Well, this part of the book gives you the power to ferret out the wheat from the chaff, the men from the boys, and the quick from the, er, not so quick.

Chapter 4

Selecting Records

In This Chapter

- Understanding selecting records
- How Crystal Reports handles data requests
- Using the Select Expert
- Working with saved or refreshed data

When you create a report, you may or may not want every record in the database to be in the report. You can limit the number of records, and you can specify which records to include. This chapter gives you the lowdown on selecting records.

What Is Selecting Records?

When you are generating a report, you have to access an existing table in order to create the report. A problem arises when the table consists of thousands of records. You may want a report that consists of records from a specific geographic area, records from a certain sales division, or records only of the products in which you are interested. That is the primary reason to use record selection. This load is not so noticeable in the Design tab, but a large number of records greatly affects performance in the Preview tab. The folks at Seagate Software anticipated your needs and built in a way for you to select only a few records in order to design the report or to have only the records that fit the report criteria.

Using the Select Expert

The Select Expert is a tool that walks you through the process of selecting the records you want to include in the report. Think of the process as filtering the data in the field. If the data is of a certain size, it passes through the filter to be included in the report. If not, it is not included in the report.

Open the Select Expert by clicking the Select Expert button on the toolbar. You can also open the Select Expert by choosing Report➪Select Expert. The Choose Field dialog box then appears, as shown in Figure 4-1.

If you have a database field selected prior to clicking the Select Expert, you bypass the Choose Field dialog box and go directly to the Select Expert by using the field you highlighted.

Notice two things in this dialog box. First, because I have a report open on the screen, Crystal Reports lists the fields that are part of the report as possible candidates for record selection. Second, Crystal Reports also displays field names from the source database table, with good reason. The record selection process is not restricted to the fields in the report. You can use *any* field from the table as the filter. So even though your report may include the fields you want, you can restrict the records included using an entirely different field.

In the following example, I have opened a report that includes a field that has sales numbers. I am going to use that field to restrict which records are included in the report.

To use the Select Expert:

1. **Open the report for which you want to select records.**

2. **Click the Select Expert button, or choose Report➪Select Expert.**

   If you had a database field selected prior to clicking the Select Expert, you bypass the Choose Field database and go directly to the Select Expert by using the field that you highlighted.

3. **In the Choose Field dialog box, click the field you want to use as the record filter. (Click Browse to view the data in the field.)**

   The Select Expert dialog box appears.

4. **Enter the filters you want by using the drop-down boxes.**

5. **Click OK.**

6. **Click Refresh data.**

   Crystal Reports asks you whether you want to use saved data or refreshed data. In most cases, select refreshed data — which means that Crystal Reports rereads the data in the table you are using for the report.

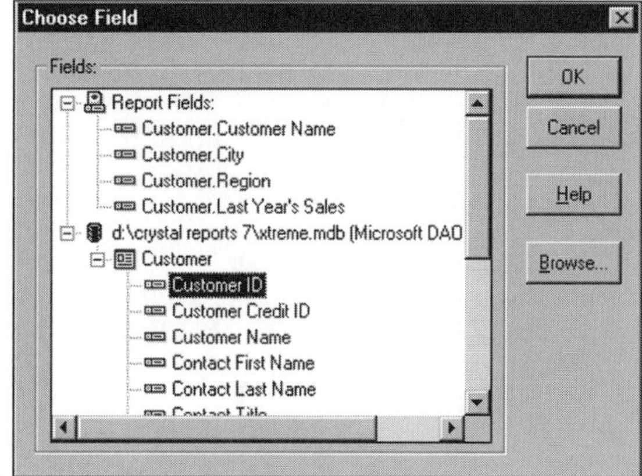

Figure 4-1: The Choose Field dialog box awaits your wise choice.

7. **Click OK.**

Those are the basic steps. Now see what happens to a report when you use the Select Expert. In my report, which includes four fields, one is named Last Year's Sales. Say that you want to restrict the records to those that have a number greater than $50,000 in Last Year's Sales. Here are the steps:

1. **Open the report.**

   In my case, I have opened the report named ch3.

2. **Click the Select Expert button.**
3. **In the Choose Field dialog box, click the Last Year's Sales field.**
4. **Click OK.**

   The Select Expert dialog box opens, as shown in Figure 4-2.

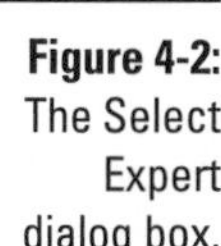

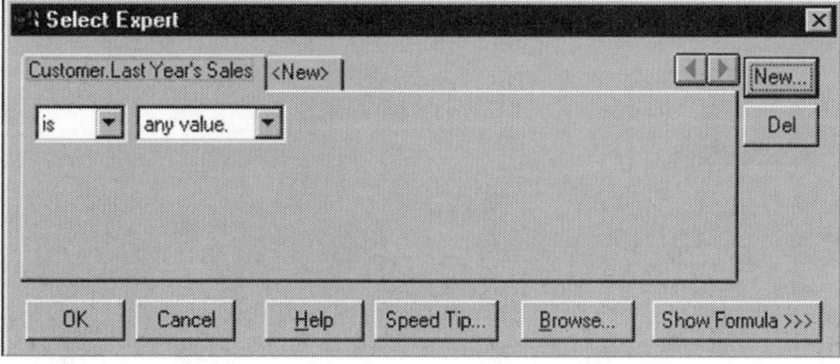

Figure 4-2: The Select Expert dialog box.

5. **To make sure that the field has the data upon which you want to filter, click Browse, as I have done in Figure 4-3.**

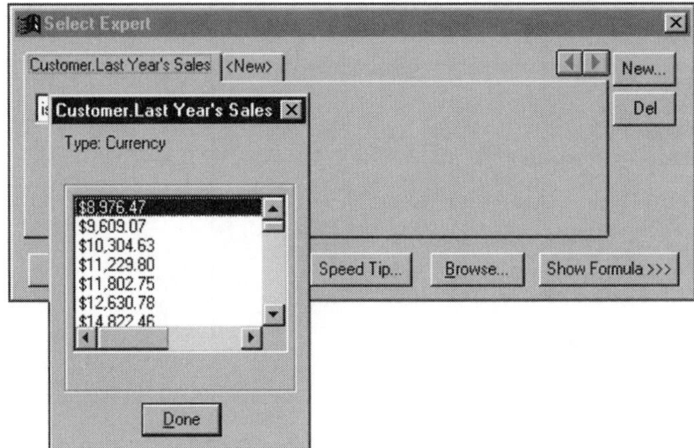

Figure 4-3: Last Year's Sales data browsed.

Browsing data here lets you double-check that this is the field on which you'd like to base your record selection. Click Done when you're finished.

In the next drop-down list, find the option to make the selection work. Figure 4-4 shows the drop-down list opened.

6. **Click the syntax that you want.**

   For this example, you want the records that have sales greater than $50,000, so you click the `greater than` syntax, which is inserted into the field.

   At this point, the criteria reads `LAST YEAR'S SALES IS GREATER THAN`.

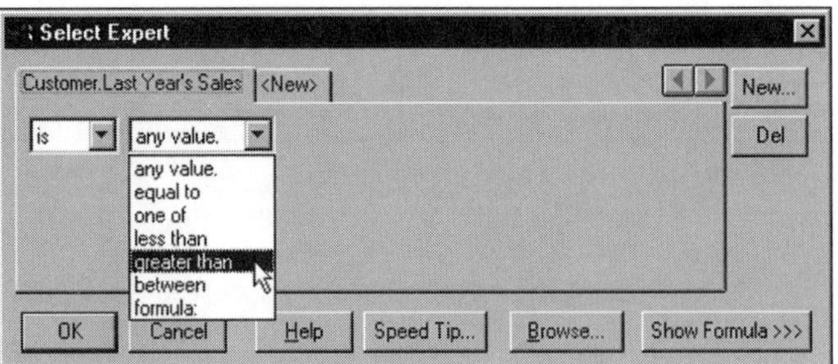

Figure 4-4: The drop-down list is opened in the Select Expert dialog box.

Note: If you select the `greater than` or `less than` option, notice that you get a check box called Or Equal To. When this check box is selected, you also include on your report all records that match the value. In this example, when you turn on the Or Equal To check box, you include on the report records that have Last Year's Sales amount of exactly $50,000 or higher.

So far so good. When you enter the `greater than` syntax, Crystal Reports opens an edit box to the right of the syntax. This box is for entering a number, which completes the criteria. Crystal Reports allows you to take a look at the data again: Click the down arrow at the far right of the edit box. (This method is the alternative way of getting to browse data.) The data appears, as shown in Figure 4-5.

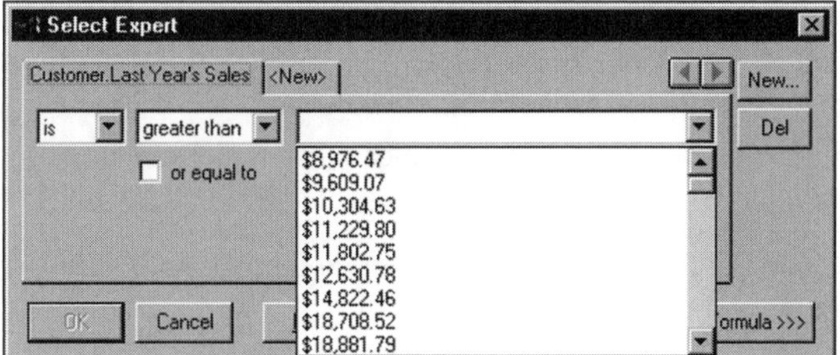

Figure 4-5: The Field data is revealed — you can look at it to decide your criteria.

7. **Simply type the number you want in the box, or reveal the field data by pulling down the arrow at the right of the box and then clicking a number there.**

   In this example, no number is exactly 50,000, so I type the value. In Figure 4-6, I have entered **50000** into the field. Note that you should *not* include a comma as a separator. Crystal Reports does not interpret the comma as part of a number.

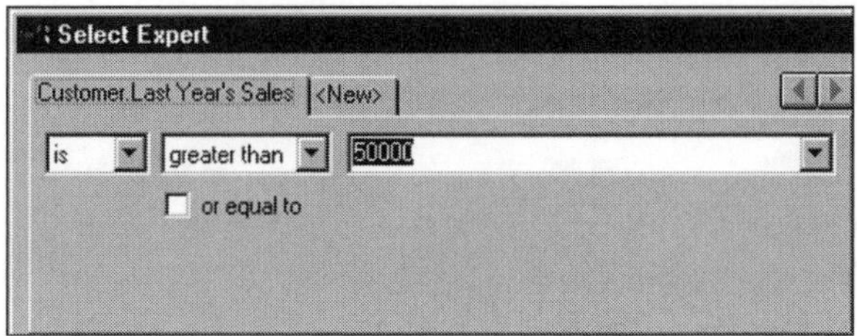

Figure 4-6: 50000 entered into the previously blank field.

   The criteria reads `LAST YEAR'S SALES IS GREATER THAN 50000`. The subject-verb agreement may be suspect, but the criteria syntax is correct.

8. **Click OK.**

   Crystal Reports pops up a dialog box that asks an important question. In a moment, I explain the reason for what I tell you to do here. The dialog box you see asks whether the report should use the current set of saved records or refresh the data. Figure 4-7 shows this dialog box.

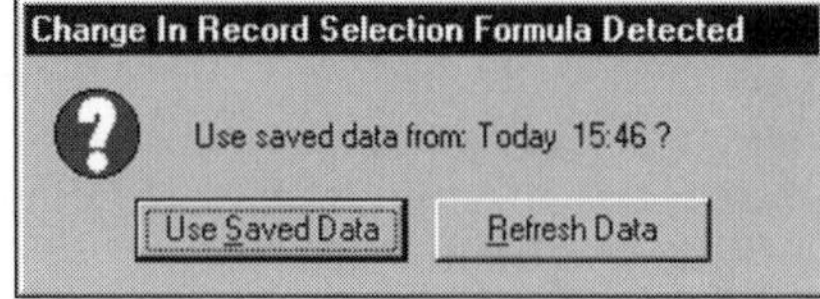

Figure 4-7: Choose saved or refreshed data.

9. **Click Refresh Data, press the F5 key, or click the Refresh button on the toolbar (it has a lightning bolt on it).**

If you are in the Preview tab, you can just click Refresh; Crystal Reports requires no further input from the user. But if you are in the Design tab, Crystal Reports doesn't ask if you want to save or refresh until you ask to go to the Preview tab. Remember: You must be in Preview to see the change. Data is shown only in Preview.

10. **Click the Preview button to see the results.**

Figure 4-8 shows the new, highly filtered report.

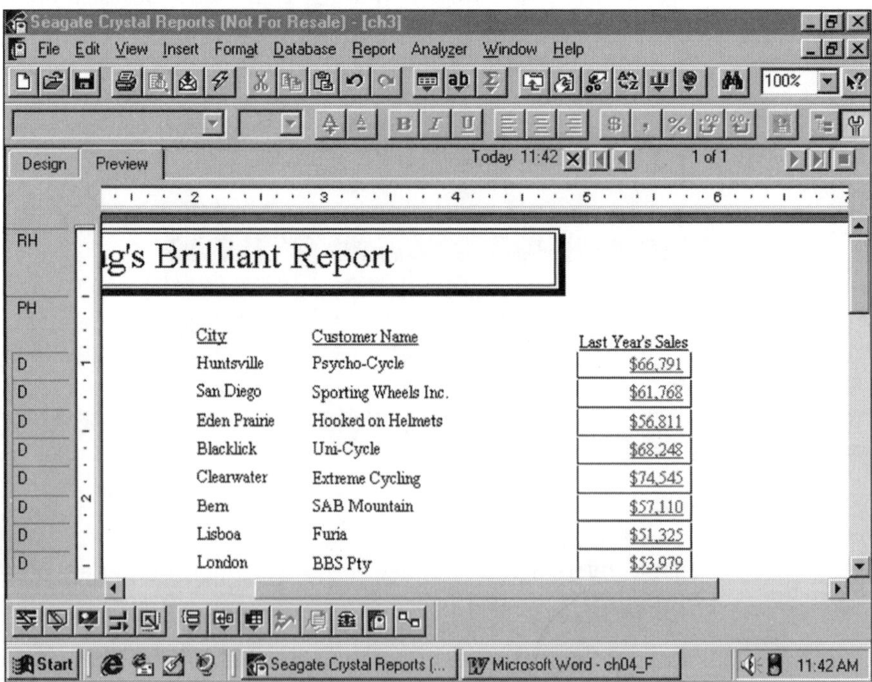

Figure 4-8: A report with filtered records in the Preview tab.

Using saved or refreshed data

In order not to burden the computer system where your data resides and to speed up report creation, Crystal Reports only reads the data from the tables you have included in a report when necessary. Now, on your home computer, you may not think that this feature would be a big deal. It probably is not. However, in a setting in which you are creating reports from a shared database, such as a network with SQL servers, having Crystal Reports reading the shared database at every turn would slow your report-building process.

So why does Crystal Reports sometimes ask the immortal question: Use saved data? Crystal Reports has some built-in smarts and won't bug you for an answer to this question when it knows it is necessary to get more data for the report by going back to the database. Crystal Reports asks you to decide only if it is not sure if rereading the database is necessary. And how do you determine how to answer the question?

If you are narrowing your record selection, click Use Saved Data. For example, perhaps when you first built your record selection, you included all records with sales greater than 0. If you change the record selection to sales greater than 50,000, you can select Use Saved Data because you are narrowing the record selection.

If you are not positive that you are narrowing the record selection, click Refresh Data just to be safe.

Select the Refresh Data on Every Print option by choosing File⇨Options and then clicking the Reporting tab (see Figure 4-9).

Crystal Reports considers printing to be of any kind: print previewing, actual printing to hard copy, or saving the report to a file.

Refreshing the report on demand

Because Crystal Reports saves the records with the report, and time may pass between the time you create the report and the time you plan to use it again, Crystal Reports provides a button to cause it to re-read the records for the report. To refresh report data, do one of the following:

- Click the Refresh button on the toolbar.
- Choose Report⇨Refresh Report Data.
- Press F5.

Crystal Reports provides an indicator for you so that you know exactly when you last refreshed your report data. In Figure 4-10, you can see the numbers that indicate the most recent update.

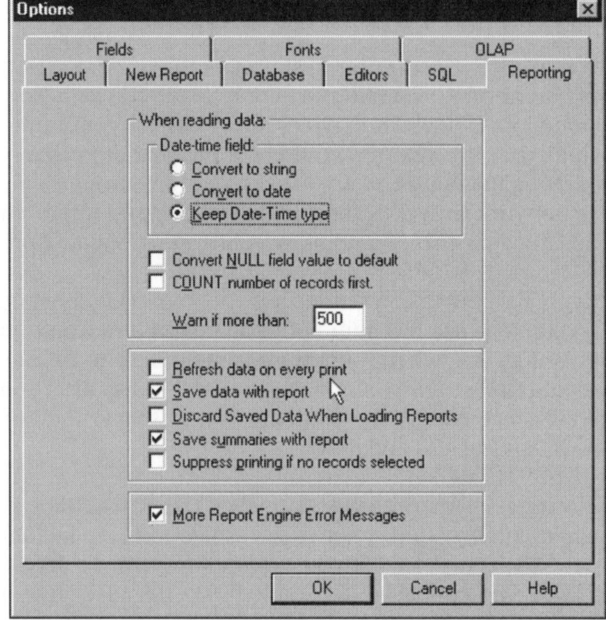

Figure 4-9: Choosing File➪Options and then clicking the Reporting tab allows you to refresh data every time you print.

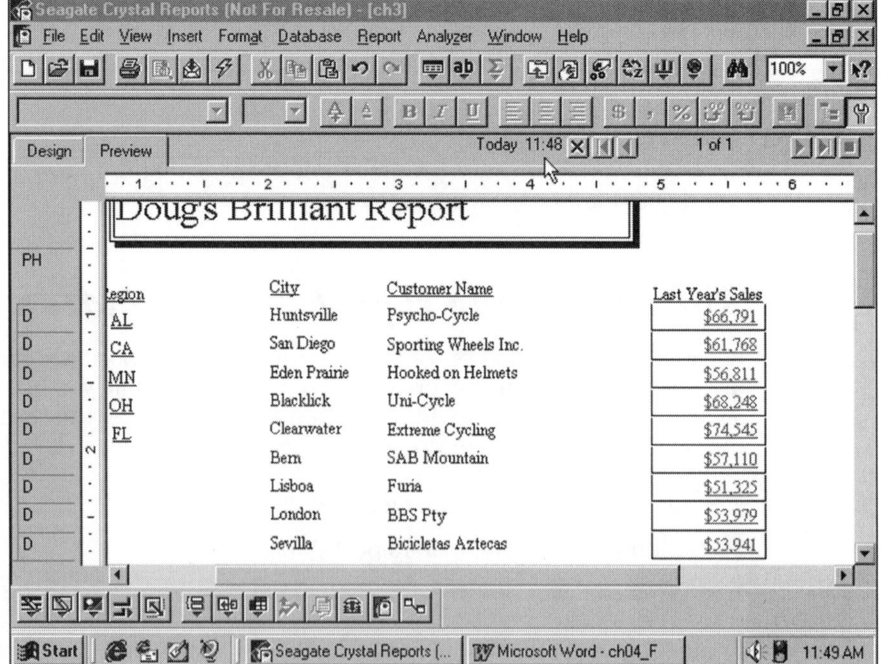

Figure 4-10: The pointer showing you the report date indicator.

Record selection and case sensitivity

Record selection is *case sensitive.* What does this mean for your reports? If the abbreviation for California is entered as CA, ca, or Ca in your database, what records would be included in your report if your record selection is Equal to "CA"? The report would only include those records where the Region is exactly "CA" and won't include any other version (ca, Ca, or cA). This is one reason you may want to use the Browse Field Data button in the Select Expert — to find out how the data is stored.

When working with SQL/ODBC data, you have the ability to select whether or not you want record selection to be case sensitive or insensitive. By default the option is not selected, and your SQL/ODBC record selection is case sensitive. The Case-Insensitive SQL Data option (available under File➪Options➪Database or from File➪Report Options) is where you set whether you want a case-sensitive or case-insensitive record selection. This option is available only when your database server supports case insensitivity.

If the report was refreshed several *weeks* ago, Crystal Reports displays the date and time of the last refresh exactly.

Specifying Select Expert options

Now that you have an idea of how the filtering process works, Table 4-1 presents other ways in which you can filter records. Remember, you do not have to use a field that is in the current report; any field in the database table works.

Table 4-1 Filtering Parameters

Filter	*What It Does*
`is not`	But what if you want to include all records except those where the region is CA? After you choose an option in the second box other than Any Value, you can go back to the first box and change `is` to `is not` (as shown in Figure 4-12). This option is available for any option other than `any value` and `formula`. Remember this; you'll use it at some point.
`any value`	When you see this option, you have no record selection for the field. It's the same as saying, "Give me all records on the report; I don't care about the sales amount."

(continued)

Table 4-1 *(continued)*

Filter	*What It Does*
`equal to`	Filters records so that only an exact match passes through. For example, if you want to see only records that are from California, the field data is equal to CA (assuming the name for California is entered as an abbreviation).
`one of`	Allows you to specify records that match values from a series. So you can enter `one of` **CA, MN,** or **BC.** This filter only allows records that are from CA, MN, or BC to pass through to the report.
`greater than or less than`	Allows you to filter records in which the field value is `less than` a value you choose, or `greater than` a value of your choice. So you can use this filter to cut off records that are at the extremes.
`or equal to`	With either the greater than or less than, you get a check box where you can determine if you want to include the equal to value itself on the report.
`between`	Selects those records that fall into a range that you want. You can enter between 20,000 and 75,000 to get only those records.
`starting with`	Selects records using a text field. So if you want all records that have a field entry beginning with the letter S, this is the filter to use. Furthermore, if you want to find records that begin with SON, you can do so by entering the three characters.
`like`	Although the world now sees computers through Windows 95, in the background are still ways to use tricks that are from the DOS era. For example, the entry D*G (an asterisk) filters records that have any entries in the field that begin with D and end with G. So the words DOG, DOUG, DARING, and DECIDING all pass through this filter. The asterisk is called a *wildcard* character because it matches any character and any number of characters. This works with text data only. Another type of wildcard is the "?" (a question mark). It matches any character, but only one at a time. So, the D?G filter would retrieve records like DOG, DIG. The word DOING would not be retrieved because more than one letter appears between the D and G, not just one.
`formula`	Creates complex filters or filters that do not fit the format of the other filter tools. Chapter 7 is devoted to the Crystal Reports formula language, and the lessons there can be used here to select records. Figure 4-11 shows the formula for a filter. The Formula Editor portion of the dialog box is opened by clicking Show Formula (which then changes to Hide Formula). Even if you have not specified a formula overtly, Crystal Reports creates a formula for every type of record selection that you create. Note in Figure 4-11 that you have a button to access the Formula Editor. In Chapter 7, I explain the concepts of using formulas.

Filter	What It Does
`in the period`	Conducts date range searches. Suppose that you are trying to create a report for a recurring date range. This filter selects records for which the value in the date field falls within the date range specified. When you select this condition, the dialog box displays a scroll list of all Crystal Reports date ranges. Select the range you want from the list. Include all records in which the date falls within the calendar first quarter of the year. Dates from January 1, to April 30 (including January 1 and April 30) are included; all other dates will be excluded. ***Note:*** The `in the period` option always evaluates the record selection relative to your computer's current date. For example, the LastFullMonth option gives you the preceding calendar month. If you preview your report on April 1st, 1997, you see all data for March 1997.

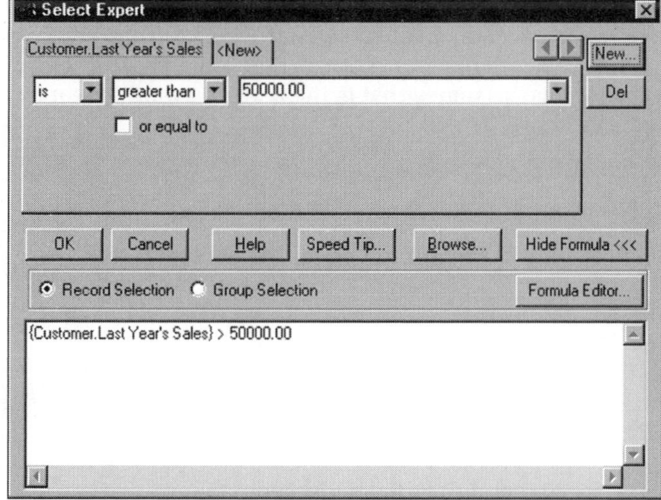

Figure 4-11: A view of the formula that Crystal Reports created automatically exposed in the Select Expert dialog box.

Figure 4-12: `is not` displayed in the Select Expert dialog box. It filters for data that is not CA.

Selecting records on more than one field

With a beginning grasp of the record selection process on a single field, the next question is how to use two or more fields to create a compound record selection. An example is a report that includes only records from a certain region and with sales over a certain amount. You have two ways to approach this type of selection. You can create the first filter and execute it, and then reopen the Select Record Expert and add the second filter. Or you can create both filters in one step. The advantage of the two-step process is that you can check your work step-by-step by previewing the records at each step to make certain that they are what you want.

To create both filters in one step:

1. **In an open report, click the first field you want to use for a filter.**

2. **Click the Select Expert button.**

   The field name already appears in the dialog box.

   Note: You may have noticed that this is a different way of getting to the Select Expert with the field you want to work with. If you have a database field selected on your report when you go to the Select Expert, Crystal Reports assumes that is the field you want to work with. It's a great little shortcut.

3. **Enter the filter criteria.**
4. **Click New at the top of the Select dialog box.**
5. **Select the field you want to use for the second filter.**
6. **Enter the filtering criteria.**
7. **Click OK.**

If you added record selection as I describ in the first section of this chapter, remove the selection to follow this example:

1. **Choose Report and then Select Expert.**
2. **In the Select Expert dialog box, click the Del button.**
3. **Click OK to close the dialog box.**

   Crystal Reports asks if you want to Refresh the report data.

4. **Click No.**

In this example, filter the records so that the report includes only CA (California) with sales from last year greater than 10,000:

1. **In the Design tab, click the Region field.**

2. **Click the Select Expert button.**
3. **In the dialog box, select** `equal to` **and** `CA`**.**
4. **Click New.**

   Crystal Reports opens the Choose Field dialog box, from which you can select a field already in the report or any field from the table.
5. **Select Last Year's Sales, select the** `greater than` **filter, and enter a value of** `10000`**.**

   The completed two-field criteria appear in Figure 4-13.

   In the Select Expert, click the Show Formula button to see the entire record selection. I let Crystal Reports do most of the work. I just drop down a few boxes, and Crystal Reports translates this into a formula your database understands. Sometimes, you want to view this formula to see the Big Picture — how the record selection looks as a whole.

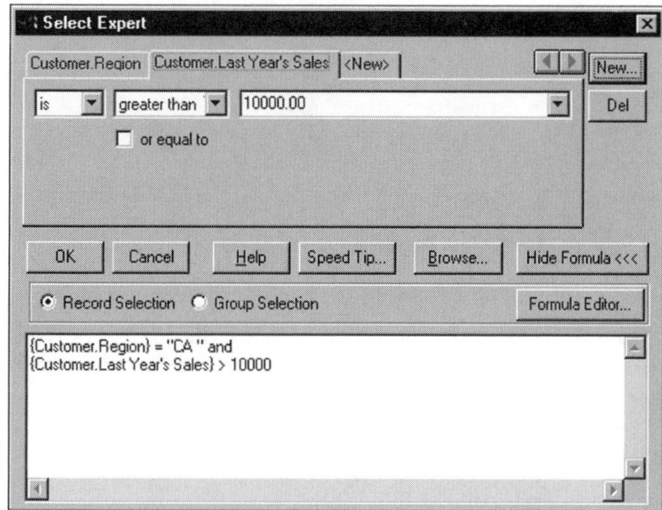

Figure 4-13: Two filters set and ready to go.

6. **Click OK.**

   Crystal Reports filters the records and displays those meeting the criteria in the Preview tab, as shown in Figure 4-14.

This tool is powerful and can be used in many ways to fine-tune the reports you create so that only the records you want are included. Adding a third or fourth filter follows the same procedure as adding a second.

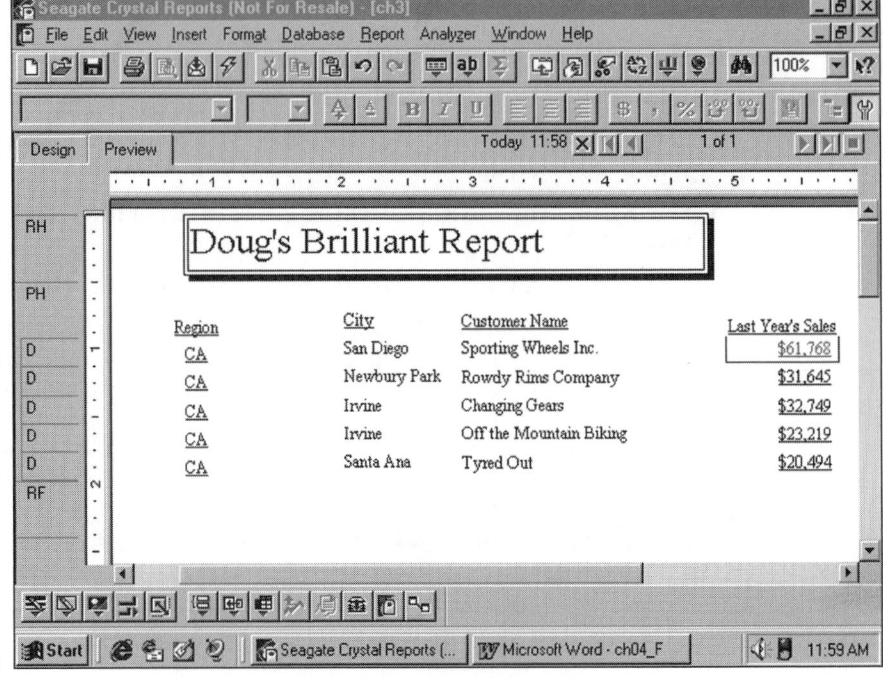

Figure 4-14: Filtering produces a report with California records and sales greater than 10,000.

Removing Record Selection

After selecting records for a specific report, you can save the report or print it. If you want to use the same table to create a different report but need to have access to all the records, you can remove the filter. To remove a Select Expert filter:

1. **Click the Select Expert button.**

   The Select Expert dialog box appears.

2. **Click the filter tab that you want to remove.**
3. **Click the Del button, which deletes that filter.**
4. **Continue deleting filters until the records you want can be part of the report.**
5. **Click OK.**

   Crystal Reports asks you if you want to use saved data or refresh the data.

6. **Click Refresh Data.**

   Crystal Reports re-runs the filter and adds back any records that were previously excluded.

The Select Expert is meant to m
create your record selection. T
you can get more sophisticatec

Using a Parameter

A feature of Crystal Reports th
to add a parameter field to a r
fields automate the process of
a report. In the example about
you can see how to manually
meter field, Crystal Reports p
other words, when you refresl
records you want to include c
having to use the Select Expert to enter a set of reco...
is a terrific tool for helping an inexperienced user correctly create reports.

Imagine that you have a report that you run every month that includes a specific region. In between the monthly report runs, you do all kinds of other reports, so you do not want to use the Select Expert, which would exclude records that you may need. So, you can add a parameter field that allows anyone to select on the fly the records you want included in the report.

To add a parameter field:

1. **Click the Insert Fields button on the Toolbar.**
2. **In the Insert Fields dialog box, click the Parameter tab.**
3. **Click New.**

   The Create Parameter Field dialog box appears, as shown in Figure 4-15.

   Add the name, the prompting text, the value type of the parameter, and any other options you want.

4. **Click OK.**

   The parameter field is saved, and the name you gave it appears in the Insert Fields dialog box. Notice that Crystal Reports adds a "?" before the name.

5. **Click Close.**
6. **If you are working in the Design tab, click the Preview tab.**

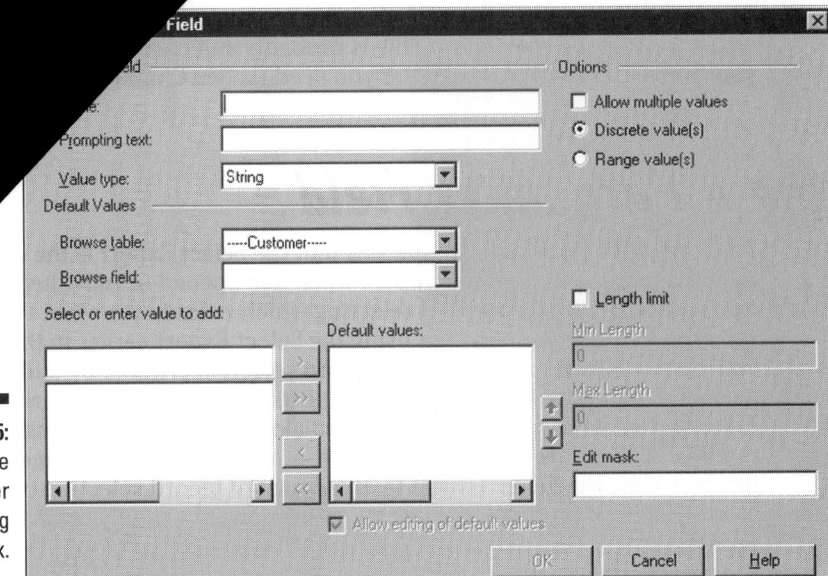

Figure 4-15: The Create Parameter Field dialog box.

7. **Click the Select Expert button.**

   The Choose Field dialog box appears.

   Select the field that relates to the parameter you have selected. If you have created the parameter using Region as the selection criteria, select Region. The Select Expert dialog box appears. Enter the settings as shown in Figure 4-16. Note that the correct settings are `is` and `equal to`.

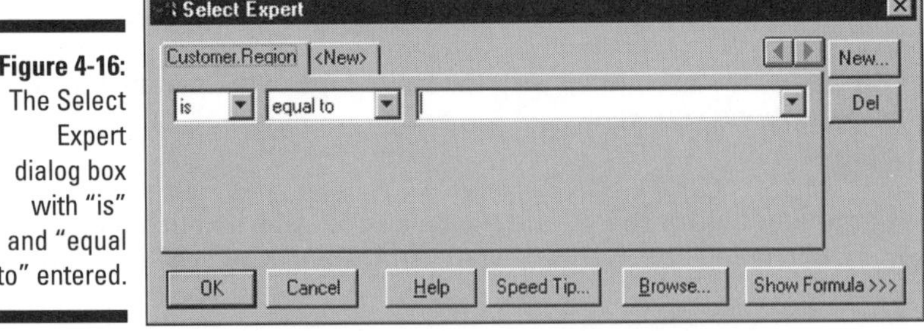

Figure 4-16: The Select Expert dialog box with "is" and "equal to" entered.

8. **Pull down the list for the third field.**

   Figure 4-17 shows the opened field.

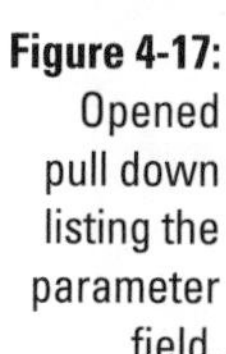

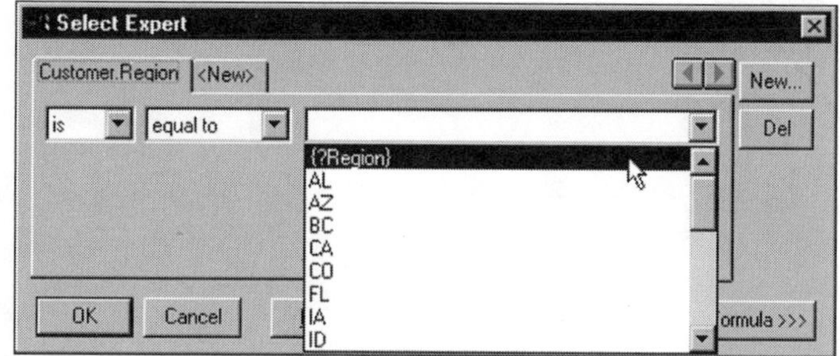

Figure 4-17: Opened pull down listing the parameter field.

At the very top of this list is the parameter field. In this example, the name appears as {?Region}.

9. **Select the parameter field.**
10. **Click OK.**

    Immediately, the dialog box appears and asks you to enter the records you want to select based upon the criteria you have specified. Make the choice as you need. For example, if you were looking at records from just the California region, you could then switch to a new region by entering the region, such as AL for Alabama.

11. **Click OK.**

Parameter field details

After you have added a parameter field to a report, you can generate a report that has the correct set of records without having to know anything about creating selection criteria.

To show you how easy it is, this section takes a detailed look at an example of adding a parameter field. I am using a customer list report that includes the Customer Name, City, and Last Year's Sales fields.

1. **Click the Insert Fields button on the toolbar.**
2. **Click the Parameters tab.**
3. **Click New.**

   The Create Parameter Field dialog box appears, as shown in Figure 4-18.

   The options in the dialog box are explained in Table 4-2.

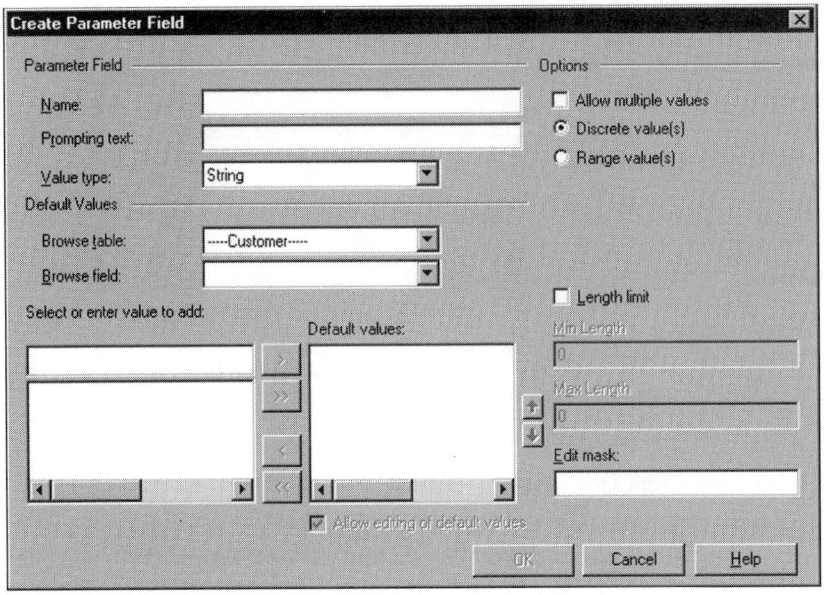

Figure 4-18: The Create Parameter Field dialog box.

Table 4-2	Parameter Field Options
Option	***Description***
Name	This initial entry is easy. Type a name for the parameter field. I used Region to remind me that the region is what the selection is based upon.
Prompting text	This entry determines what text is seen in the dialog box in which you enter the type of records you want included. For example, my text reads `Enter the region you want included in the report.`
Allow Multiple values	Checking this box allows the report creator to enter multiple values as selection criteria. So, if `Region` is the field, allowing multiple values means that more than one region's records can be part of the report.
Discrete values/Range options	These two options work together. A value setting means that each entry in the value field is considered individually. If you want a range, such as a pair of dates or numbers from 1 to 50, or letters from T to W, select the Range option. You cannot choose both Discrete and Range.
Value type	There are several different types of data you can enter as a value for Crystal Reports to find — for example, Boolean, Date, and Date and Time. Crystal Reports helps you make it as fool-proof as possible for the report creator by forcing him to enter a date, text, or whatever you specify in the format you specify. The Crystal Reports online Help explains each of the options in detail.

Option	*Description*
Browse table	Select the table used for developing the report. If the report draws information from several tables, you can select the table that has the field you need to create record selection.
Browse field	After selecting the table to browse, select the field you want to include from that table.
Select or Enter value to add	After you select the table and the field, Crystal Reports generates the list of values from that field. You can then select all or some of the values as defaults.
Length limit	If the report creator is allowed to enter her own values, you can check this box to limit the number.
Allow editing of default values	The default is on, and it should be on unless you must have the value selected from the list you specify.
Edit mask	An edit mask is a way to force the value being entered to conform to a certain style such as XXX-XXX-XXXX. With this mask, only a value such as 555-555-1212 would be accepted as a valid entry.

For this example, the dialog box is complete as shown in Figure 4-19.

With the parameter field complete, the next step is to add it to the report.

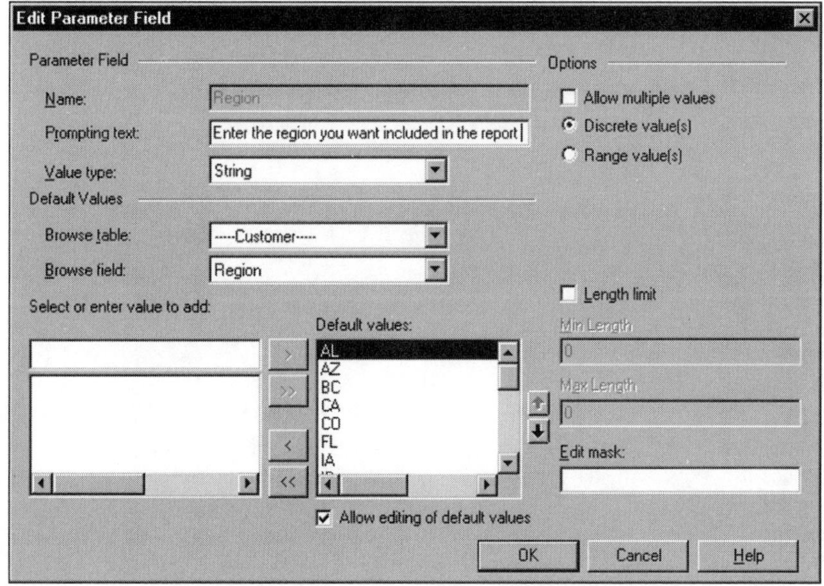

Figure 4-19: The completed dialog box.

4. **Click OK.**
5. **Click Close to close the Insert Fields dialog box.**
6. **Click the Select Expert toolbar button.**

   The Choose Field dialog box appears.
7. **Select the field that matches the one you used to create the parameter field.**

   In this example, I used the Region field.
8. **Click OK.**

   The Select Expert dialog box appears. Because you are using a parameter field, the first entry must be `is` and the second field must be `equal to`. The logic is that the parameter field will contain the variable choices you want for record selection.
9. **Open the drop-down list in the far right field and select the parameter field entry.**

   In this example, I selected the {?Region} entry.
10. **Click OK.**

To see the parameter field in action, click the Refresh button. When you do, the Refresh Report Data dialog box appears. Select the Prompt for New Values option. The Enter Parameter Values dialog box appears, as shown in Figure 4-20. The pull-down list shows you the values from the Region field.

Selecting the first suggested value, AL, creates the report shown in Figure 4-21.

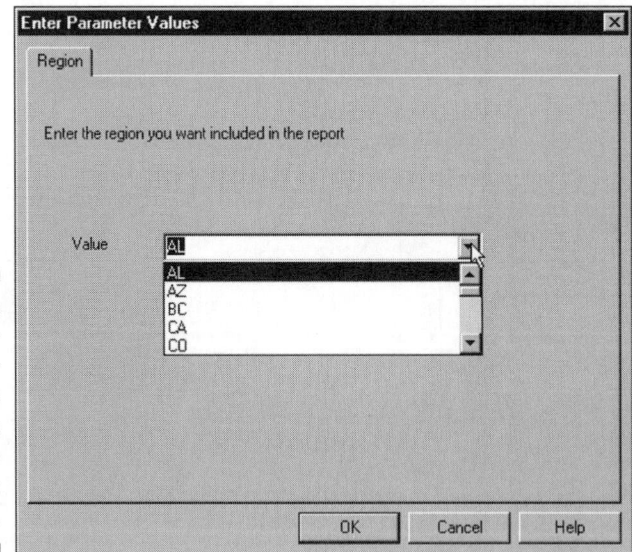

Figure 4-20: The Enter Parameter Values dialog box with the pull-down list.

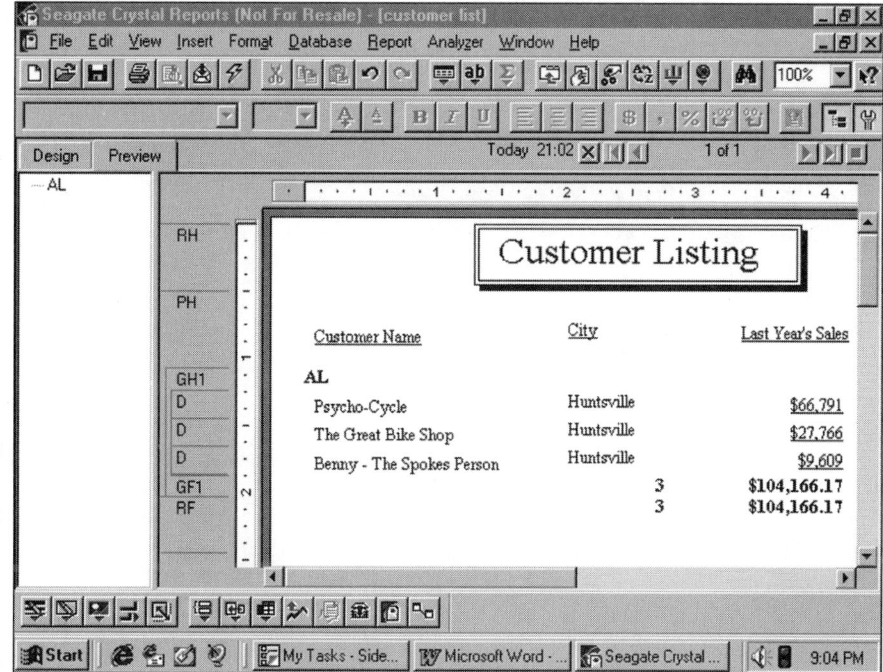

Figure 4-21: A report created using a parameter field.

This feature is a powerful one for automating the report creation process. In this example, I used a single parameter field. However, you can create several more parameter fields and even designate a sort order based on the parameter. By giving you a tool to restrict which records are included in a report, you can design a report and hand it off to a less experienced user confident that the correct records will be included. When anyone tries to open the report or tries to refresh the report data, the parameter field will control which records can be included in the report.

Chapter 5

Sorting and Grouping Records

In This Chapter

- Sorting records
- Inserting groups
- Inserting summaries or subtotals
- Inserting a grand total
- Modifying a group
- Doing a Top N Sort

With an existing report, you may want to sort the records by one or several fields, such as by state or by salesperson. Or you may want to group the records. Suppose that you are creating a sales report and want to group the records by sales region. Within that region, you also want to sort by the amount of sales and calculate subtotals for each region. In this chapter, you discover the steps to sort and group.

In Figure 5-1, you see a typical report that has a series of records, as yet without any grouping or any discernible sort order. The process of sorting and grouping is best accomplished in the Preview tab. So, change to that mode by clicking the Preview tab, or click the Preview button. You can also click the Refresh button or press F5.

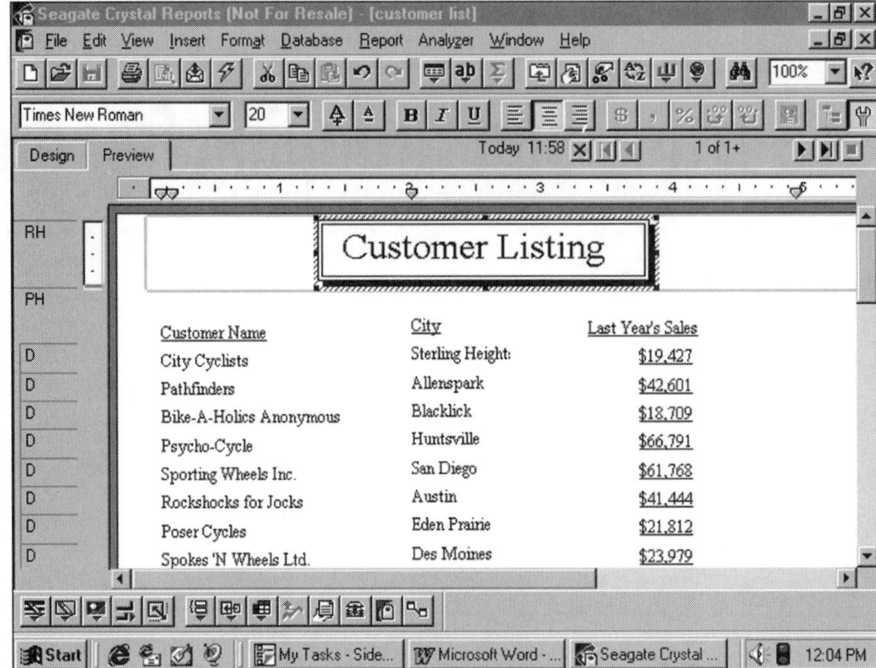

Figure 5-1: A typical report without any sorting or groups, in the Preview tab.

Sorting Records

The first thing you can do with any set of records is to add a sort order. In any report, the steps to change the sort order are as follows:

1. **Choose Report⇨Sort Records (or click the Sort Order button on the toolbar).**

   The Record Sort Order dialog box opens, as shown in Figure 5-2.

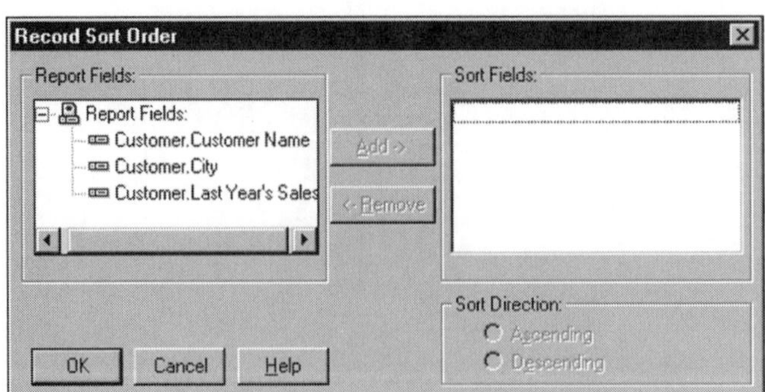

Figure 5-2: The Record Sort Order dialog box.

On the left side of the dialog box, Crystal Reports lists the fields in the report that can be used to perform a sort. In this example, four fields are available: three on the left and one on the right. Your report may have more or fewer fields available for sorting.

2. **Select a field to use for the sort, and then click Add.**
3. **Select the sort order: Ascending or Descending.**
4. **Click OK.**

For a sort to work, the field *must* be included in the report.

The number of sorts you can perform is limited only by the number of fields and the sense it makes. If you do too much sorting, you become, well, out of sorts.

If you perform a sort but then want to return to the previous sort order, click the Undo button on the toolbar.

Breaking Ties

If you have several records that have identical values in the field upon which you have sorted, you can add a second sort field to break the tie. As an example, if you have a set of records that are sorted primarily by the City field, the possibility exists that several records are from the same city. In the example report, several records have Blacklick as the city. So adding a second sort, Last Year's Sales in descending order, shows the records sorted first by the name of the city and then by the sales volume.

To add a second sort value:

1. **Open the Record Sort Order dialog box by choosing Report⇨Sort Records (or by clicking the Sort Order button).**
2. **Click the field name you want as the second sort value, click Add, and then select Descending as the sort order.**

   In this example, I clicked the Last Year's Sales field.
3. **Click OK.**

   Now the records are sorted at two levels, as you can see in Figure 5-3. The Blacklick records are sorted from the largest sales amount to the least.

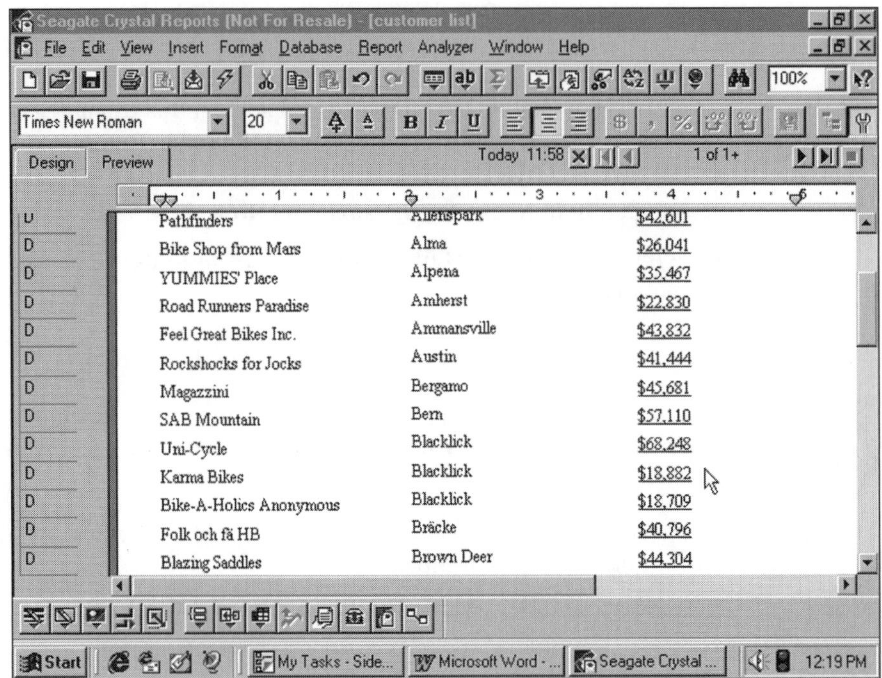

Figure 5-3: Records sorted on two levels — city and sales.

Inserting Groups

Groups provide a handy way to arrange records in a myriad of ways, in order to determine sales strategies, distribution points, under- or over-performing salespeople, and so on. You are probably way ahead of me in thinking of the ways you can create that one report that you used to have to do by hand or wanted to have but could never coax out of your database.

If you change your mind after creating (inserting) a group or decide to use another grouping method, you can easily remove the group and replace it with another. Deleting a group is covered later in this chapter.

In any report, the grouping process follows the same steps:

1. **Choose Insert⇨Group.**
2. **From the Insert Group dialog box, select the field upon which you want the records grouped.**
3. **Select the sort order that you want to occur after the grouping.**

You have two other options, and they deal with how the groups print on paper. The first option, Keep Group Together, keeps grouped records contiguous on the same printed page. Crystal Reports calculates whether the next group can fit on what remains of the current page and, if not, begins printing the group on the page following. Clicking the option, which inserts an X in the box, turns this feature on.

Now you come to another option. Suppose that the group of records is longer than a single printed page? The second option, Repeat Group Header, when turned on, causes Crystal Reports to print the Group Header at the top of each new page.

The best way to use these options is to click OK and see the results of the grouping, and if the records do cover more than a page, decide how to best divide the groups.

If you are unhappy with the results of a grouping and decide, for whatever reason, to remove the group, Crystal Reports cannot undo such a move. You must re-create the group. But at least it warns you!

Group Name Setting

When you insert a group, Crystal Reports may not automatically identify the group for you. There is a setting that determines whether Crystal Reports inserts a space between the records where one group of records ends and another begins, or if the name of the Group appears. So, if you insert a group such as Region (more on this in a moment), and the name of the Region is not inserted anywhere in the report, this may be confusing. I recommend that you check one of the default settings so that the name of the group is always inserted at the same time a group is inserted.

To change a default report option:

1. **Choose File⇨Options.**

   The dialog box is shown in Figure 5-4.

   There are a plethora of choices in this dialog box, but the one you are interested in is in the section labeled Field Options at the lower right.

2. **If it isn't already selected, click the field box in front of Insert Group Name with Group.**

3. **Click OK.**

   Now when you insert a group, the name associated with the group will appear in the space between the groups.

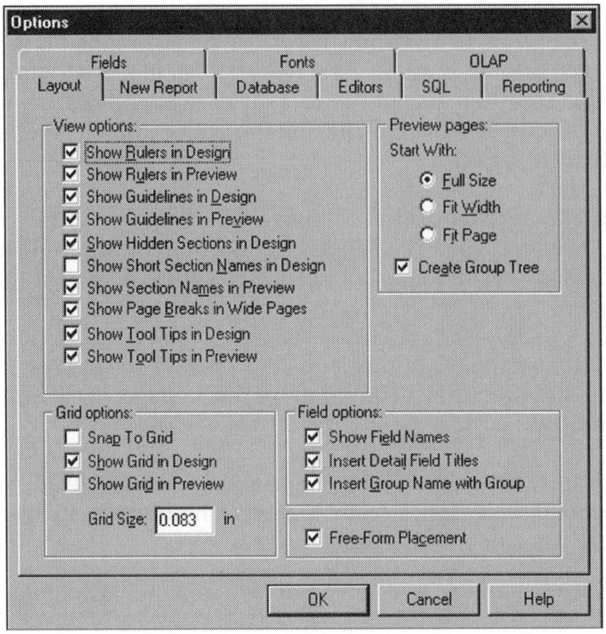

Figure 5-4: The Options dialog box.

In this example, the Customer List report has been opened. In the cold, frozen north, in a far away country known as Canada, *region* is used interchangeably with *state*. So don't let this naming convention throw you. You can use this field to create the group despite the fact that the Customer Region is not part of the *printed* report. The Customer Region is part of the *table* that was accessed to create the report and so is accessible for grouping records in the report.

Here's how to add a group using a field that's not in the report:

1. **Choose Insert⇨Group.**
2. **In the Insert Group dialog box, click the down arrow in the top box to see a list of fields in the tables. Select a field that you want to group but that is not in the report.**

   In this example, I selected the field listed as `Customer.Region`.
3. **Click the down arrow and select the sort order, as shown in Figure 5-5.**

   You can choose a number of ways beyond the standard sorts to arrange the records within a group. For this example, I chose `in ascending order`.

Figure 5-5: Selecting the sort order in the Insert Group dialog box.

4. **Click OK.**

   Figure 5-6 shows the result. You may have to scroll through the list to see the group headers because the first set of records may be not associated with a particular region in your report — particularly if your report includes records from other countries.

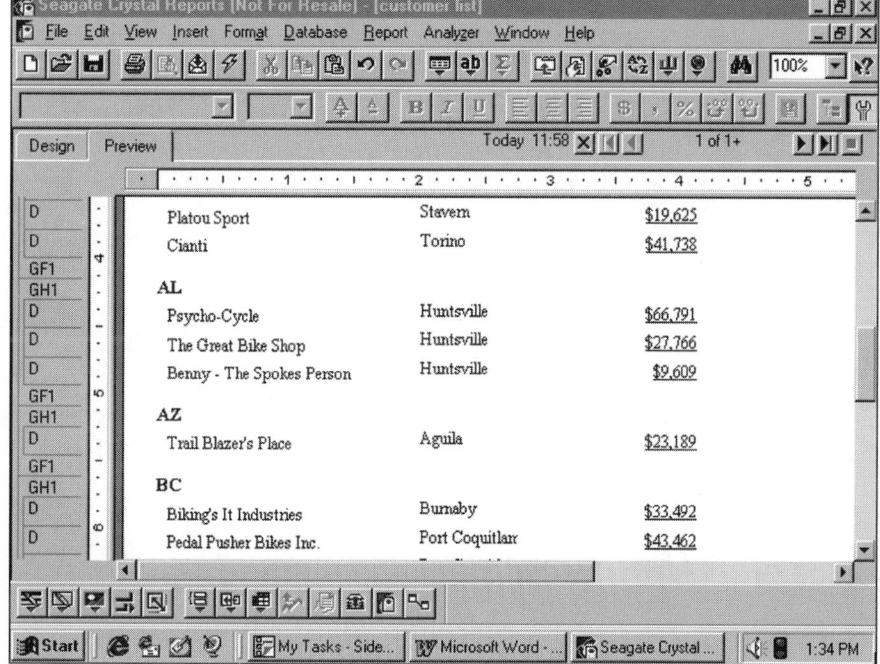

Figure 5-6: Records grouped by the Region field, even though Region field itself doesn't appear in the report.

Crystal Reports always places at the beginning of the report records that do not meet a group definition.

As you can see, the grouping effect is to arrange the records by region, which in this particular database is the same as state. So the first group has AL as its header, which in this case stands for Alabama. The second grouping is headed by AZ (for Arizona), followed by BC for British Columbia. Within each individual group, the records are in data-entry order (the way that they were placed in the database).

Group Tree Options

On the far left side of the Preview tab, you see the list of groups that have been created. This list is called the Group Tree, and it makes moving to the group associated with the records easy. For example, to see the detail records associated with a particular region, you simply click the group name, and the Preview window shows the page that contains those records.

In addition, the Group Tree can be used to create a Drill Down preview window. A Drill Down is a subset of detail records from the report and has its own tab at the top of the Preview window. Click a group name, and then *right-click* to open the shortcut menu. Two choices appear: Hide and Drill Down. Click Drill Down, and the report preview includes a tab with the group name; only the records associated with this group are displayed. You may drill down as many groups as you want. When you print the report, only the main report in Preview prints. To print a Drill Down, you must click the Drill Down tab and then click the Printer icon.

The other option available when you right-click the Group Tree is the Hide option, which closes the Group Tree. You may want to do this if you need more space in the Preview window to see your report columns. To restore a closed Group Tree, choose View⇨Group Tree or click the Group Tree button.

Viewing Groups in the Design Tab

If you have added a group to the report, switch to the Design tab, and take a look at the way adding a group changes the underlying report structure.

Open the pop-up menu so that you can see the effect of the group:

1. **Click the Design tab.**

   On the left edge of the report is the name `Group Header #1`.

2. **Right-click** `Group Header #1`.

   The shortcut menu appears, as shown in Figure 5-7.

   Note that in the Design tab, the Group section surrounds the Details section of the report. This arrangement makes sense because the groups are created by arranging the individual records in the Details section of the report. Also, the menu tells you the name of the file used to make the group and the sort order, A for ascending.

3. **Close the shortcut menu by clicking in the report.**

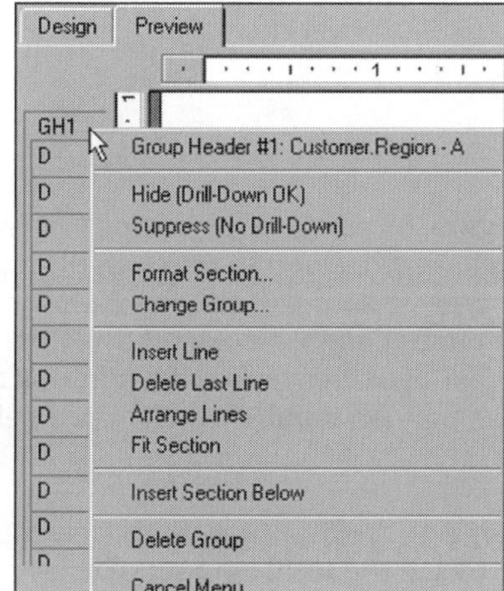

Figure 5-7: The shortcut menu for the Group Header.

Deleting or undoing a group

If the results of a grouping are not what you expected, you can undo the group or delete the group. In the case of undoing, you create a *toggle,* that is, you can undo the group and then turn the group back on without having to go through the steps to create the group.

- To undo a group, choose Edit⇨Undo. You can also press Alt + Backspace or Ctrl + Z.
- To Redo a Group, choose Edit⇨Redo Group. You can also press Ctrl + Y.

If you use any formatting or formula commands after using undo on a group, the toggle is no longer available, because Crystal Reports then assumes you want to undo only the most recent action.

Deleting a group

Deleting a group is a permanent way to remove a group, if the grouping is entirely unsatisfactory.

1. **Choose Edit⇨Delete Group.**

   After you select this option, Crystal Reports pops open an alert box waring you that deleting a group cannot be undone.

2. **Click OK to proceed.**
3. **Click Yes to accept the warning.**

Inserting a Total

With the records separated by region, or whatever grouping you have chosen, you can add calculations for each group in the form of a subtotal and a summary. The difference is the type of data you choose. Numbers can be calculated, whereas text such as names cannot be added together, but they can be counted. Crystal Reports distinguishes between a subtotal and a summary in this way: A subtotal works only on number or currency fields. A summary works on all data types.

A total can be inserted in the Design or Preview tabs. In this example, I add a total to Last Year's Sales in order to see the total amount of sales by region.

To add a total to a number field:

1. **Click the field in Details that has the numbers you want to calculate.**

   For this example, I clicked the Last Year's Sales field.

2. **Choose Insert⇨Summary (or click the Insert Summary button).**
3. **In the Insert Summary dialog box (see Figure 5-8), click the first down arrow to see the types of calculations that can be performed. Choose** `sum`.

   The list necessarily changes based on the type of field selected.

   In the second box, Crystal automatically inserts any grouping you have performed as the sorting and grouping to be used. You can make a change to this sort/group by clicking the down arrow and choosing a new field upon which to sort and/or group.

4. **Make sure that** `Group #1: Customer.Region-A` **appears.**
5. **Click OK.**

   Figure 5-9 shows the result of adding the summary to the Customer List report.

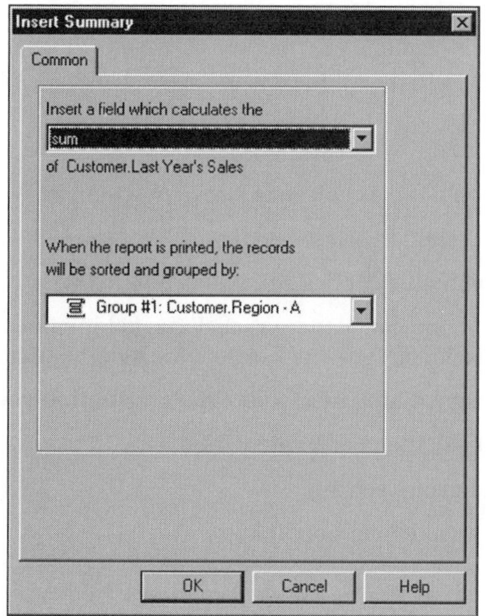

Figure 5-8: The Insert Summary dialog box.

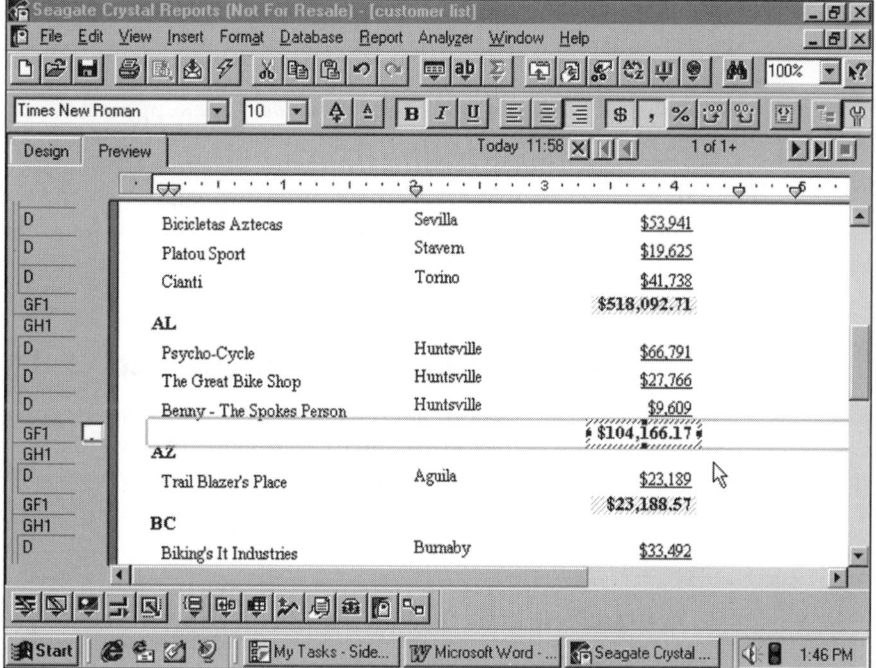

Figure 5-9: The Customer List report with new summary totals.

In this example, the totaling is calculated on a *number* field. Another example of using summary totals is *counting* the number of records in a particular group. This requires that you use a different type of calculation, named *count*.

To count the number of records in a report or by group:

1. **Click a field that you have not already used for a summary.**

   In this example, I selected the City field.

2. **Choose Insert⇨Summary (or click the Insert Summary button).**

   And don't forget that you can also right-click the field to open the Insert Summary dialog box. If you right-click, select the Insert Summary option.

3. **In the Insert Summary dialog box, select the calculation you want.**

   In this example, I chose the `count` calculation.

4. **You can modify the group setting.**

   If you have already created a group, it appears.

5. **Click OK.**

   See my results in Figure 5-10.

In this example, the number of records per group is calculated and the result inserted between the groups. For the second group, AL, you see three records. With a small group such as this, you can count the records yourself. But as your report grows in length, the number of records can become overwhelming, and after all, this work is what *computers* are supposed to do, not people.

In the two previous examples, you discover how to total a series of numbers and to generate a count of records by group. I want to take the example a step further by showing you how to calculate the total of Last Year's Sales for the entire report and a total count of all records in the report.

Inserting a numeric grand total

You can insert the grand total from any page in a report, but you must move to the last page in order to see the total. You do not have to have any other totals, such as by groups, in order for this to process properly, but you must be in the Preview tab to see the result.

To insert a grand total:

1. **In Details, click the field for which you want to create a grand total.**

   Do not select a field for which you have already created a grand total (although it is possible to insert the results of a grand total in more than one place in a report).

   In this example, I selected the Last Year's Sales field.

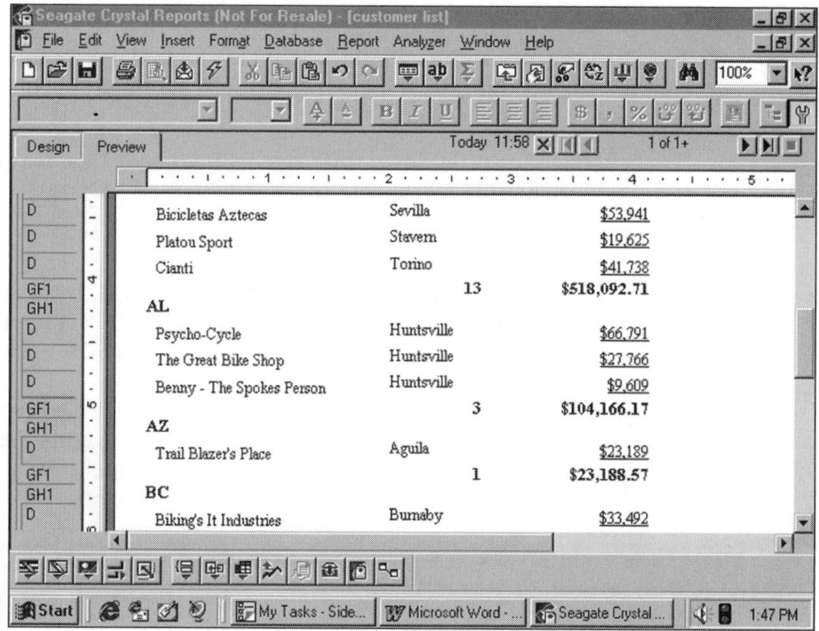

Figure 5-10: Records counted by group.

2. **Right-click on the field you selected in Step 1, and then from the shortcut menu, click Insert Grand Total or choose Insert⇨Insert Grand Total.**

   After you select Insert Grand Total, the Insert Grand Total dialog box opens.

3. **In the dialog box, select the type of calculation.**

   In this example, I selected `sum`, as shown in Figure 5-11.

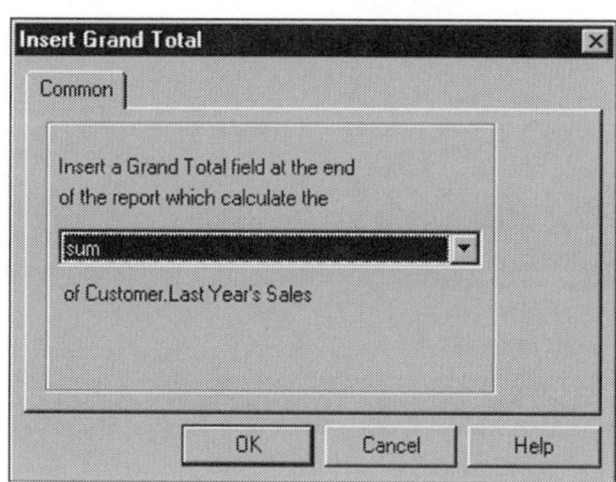

Figure 5-11: The Insert Grand Total dialog box.

4. **Click OK.**

5. **To see the result of the calculation, go to the last page of the report by clicking the far-right page control button (Last Page) in the upper-right part of the window.**

   You may have to scroll down the page, using the vertical scroll bar control on the right side of the window.

   Figure 5-12 shows my results.

To check and see whether the number is correct — that is, whether it calculated the field you chose — move the mouse pointer onto the number. The shortcut menu reveals the definition, as shown in Figure 5-13.

By moving the mouse pointer onto the value for any summing operation, you can verify that the calculation is what you desired. If you right-click the value, the shortcut menu allows you to change the summary operation if desired.

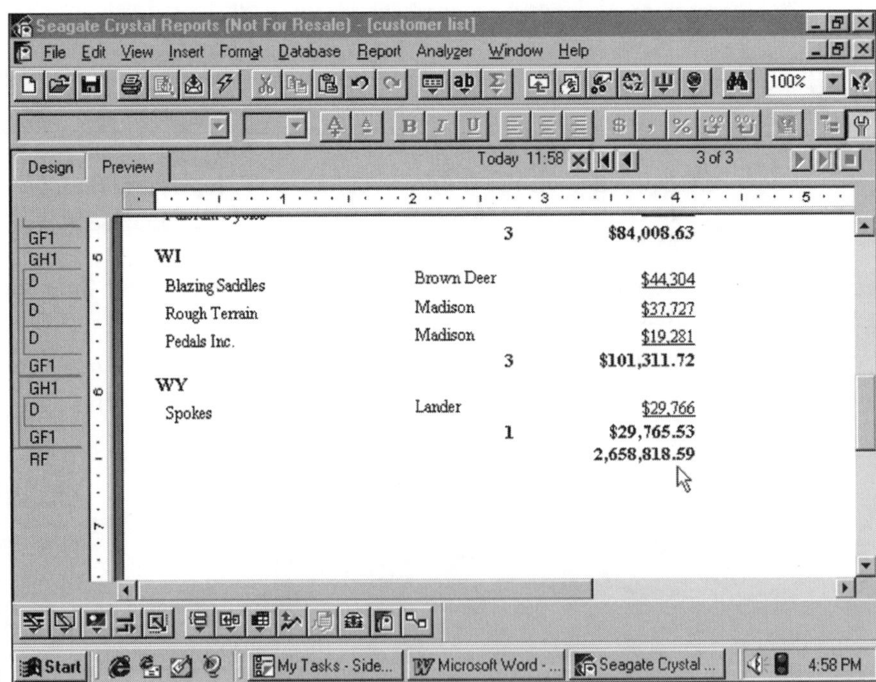

Figure 5-12: A grand total added at the end of the report.

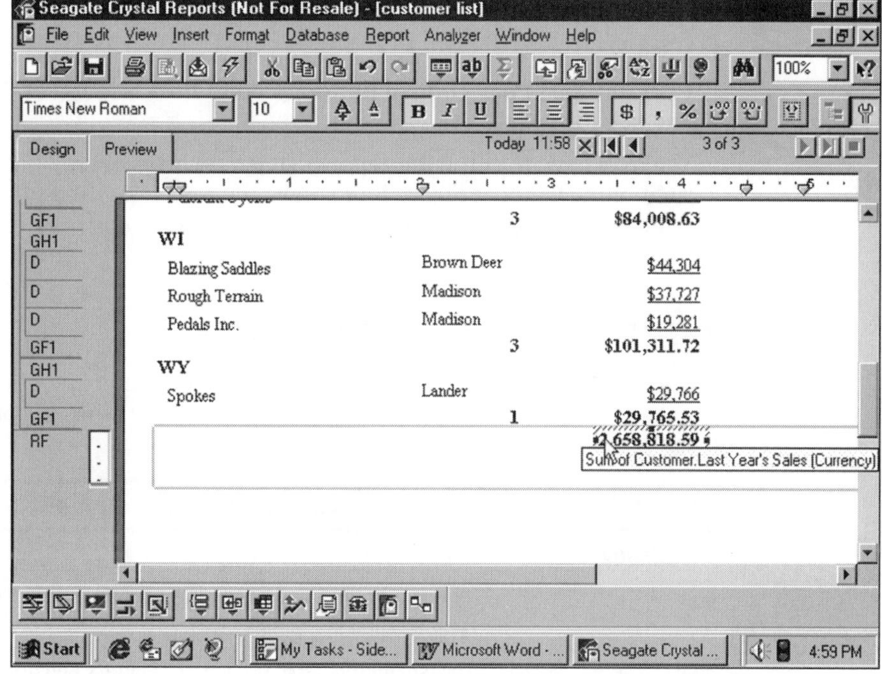

Figure 5-13: The mouse pointer reveals the type of calculation in use.

Inserting a grand total for text

The next total that is useful for any report is a grand total of the number of records in the report. Crystal Reports indicates the number of records in a report in the Preview tab at the bottom right of the window. But it does not automatically *print* the number of records in a report. The grand total usually prints at the end of the report, but you can insert it into the Report Header. You must be in Preview mode to see the result.

To insert the grand total of the number of records in a report:

1. **Click a field in the report that you have not already used to tally a grand total.**

   (Do not suppose that you cannot grand total a field twice, but for this set of steps, use a field without a grand total.)

2. **Right-click, and from the menu that appears, select Insert Grand Total.**

   The Insert Grand Total dialog box appears.

3. **Select** `count` **as the type of calculation you want.**
4. **Click OK.**
5. **Click the Last Page control button to go to the last page of the report and see the result.**

   You may have to scroll the report using the vertical scroll bar at the right of the window. Figure 5-14 shows the result of grand totaling the numbers of records in a report, which in this example is 77 records.

Defining other calculations

The kind of summary operation you can perform depends upon the type of data in the field you have selected. Table 5-1 shows the types of calculations you can perform and their respective uses.

Table 5-1 Calculations You Can Perform on Fields

Calculation	*What It Does*
`maximum`	This summary works on text or numbers and prints the largest value in the field.
`minimum`	This summary works on text or numbers and prints the minimum value in the field.
`count`	This summary works on text or numbers and prints the number of entries in the field.
`distinct count`	This summary works on text or numbers and prints the number of unique records in the field. Ergo, if you have three records that are from Doug's Cycle Shop, Crystal Reports counts them as a single entry.
`sum`	This summary works only on numeric and currency fields and prints the total of the values in the field.
`average`	This summary works only on numeric and currency fields and prints the average of the values in the field.
`sample variance`	This summary works only on numeric and currency fields and prints the sample variance of a series of values.
`sample standard deviation`	This summary works only on numeric and currency fields and prints the standard deviation of the values in the field. If you have grouped data, then the standard deviation is printed by group.
`population variance`	This summary works only on numeric and currency fields and prints the population variance of the data.
`population standard deviation`	This summary works only on numeric and currency fields and prints the population standard deviation.

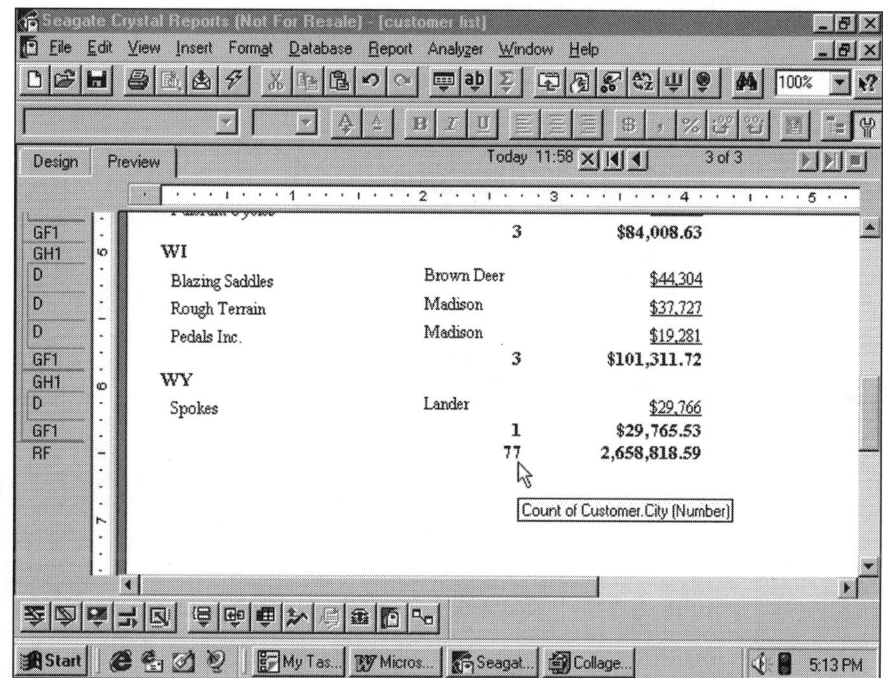

Figure 5-14: The grand total of all records in the report.

I must admit that the last four operations listed in Table 5-1 are out of my scope of knowledge. Consult your statistics textbook for explanations.

Changing a Group

If you have created a group, you can delete the group if you want or you can modify the existing group. A modification is best made in the Design tab, although it can be done in Preview mode. In this example, I show you how to fine-tune an existing group.

To modify an existing group:

1. **Click the Design tab.**
2. **At the left edge of the Design tab, locate the group you want to modify. Right-click the group name.**
3. **From the menu that appears, choose the Change Group option.**

   The Change Group Options dialog box arrives (as shown in Figure 5-15).

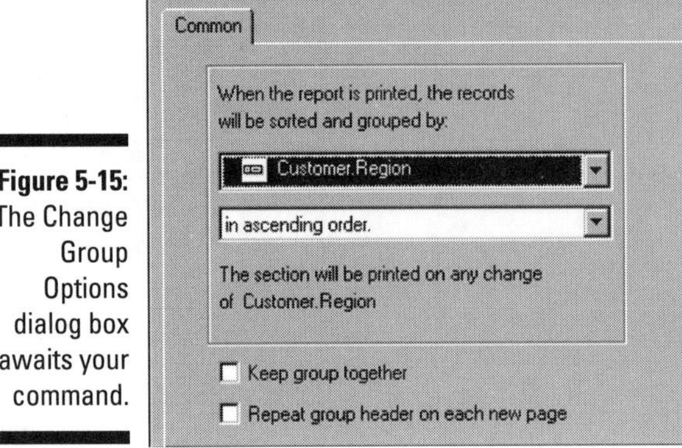

Figure 5-15: The Change Group Options dialog box awaits your command.

At this point, you can change the group by selecting a different field upon which to group and by changing the sort order. Two other options appear, which control the way the report prints. Table 5-2 shows these options.

Table 5-2 Options in the Change Group Options Dialog Box

Option	*What It Does*
`Keep group together`	Selecting this option causes Crystal Reports to print all the records in a group on the same page of the report. So if the group starts printing at the middle of the page and the page is not long enough for all the records to fit, Crystal Reports leaves a blank space at the end of the current page and begins printing the records at the beginning of a new page. A group of records may be longer than a single page. In that case, you can change the font size to reduce the amount of space used. See Chapter 3 for more information on text formatting.
`Repeat group header on each new page`	In the case where the group covers more than a single page or if you want to use the least number of pages for the report but want to be able to easily identify the groups, Crystal Reports prints the heading for the group at the beginning of each new page.

Doing a Top N Sort

A Top N Sort is a way to determine which groups of records are at the top. (A Bottom N Sort does the same for records at the bottom.) For example, if you want to determine which states are the top 5 for sales of your product, you first group the records by state and then add the Top N Sort. The *N* in the heading of this topic refers to any number. Crystal Reports can sort the top 5, the top 10, the top 100, or whatever value you want to use. In the examples earlier in this chapter, the records have been sorted in ascending or descending order, whether as an entire report or within groups. This is a sort of a different kind, but one you will find very useful.

Only fields with numbers are eligible for this type of sort.

To create a Top N Sort:

1. **Choose Report⇨TopN/Sort Group Expert.**

   The Top N/Sort Group Expert opens.

   You can't use the Top N Sort if you have no groups in your report or if the group does not have a summary or subtotal, because you can always sort individual records in ascending or descending order. So the idea is that you have created groups and then want to see how the *groups* sort out in terms of sales or whatever criteria you have in mind.

2. **Enter the type of sort you want by clicking the down arrow.**

   You have three choices Top N, Bottom N, or All. An example is shown in Figure 5-16. In this example, I indicate that I want to see the top 5 as the sort.

   Crystal Reports groups the top 5 or whatever number you designate and throws the remaining records into another Group labeled *Others.* Notice that each of the top 5 groups has its total printed by group, and, if you scroll down, the Others group then has a single total. Be aware that if you have included a grand total in your report for the number of records in the report or the total of a number field, Crystal Reports calculates those numbers based on *all* records in the report, not only the Top N group numbers.

   The other sorting options are `Sort All`, which rearranges all the groups in ascending or descending order, or `Bottom N`, which allows you to arrange the number of groups using the smallest N records as the sort, such as show me the sales regions with the lowest 5 sales amounts.

3. **Select the field upon which you want the sort to occur. (It must be a summary field.)**

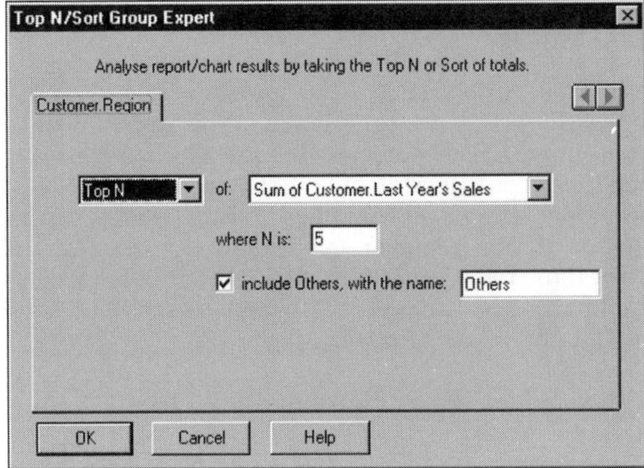

Figure 5-16: The Top N/Sort Group Expert dialog box filled with sort values.

In this example, only one field, Last Year's Sales, has numbers and therefore is the only field upon which Crystal Reports can perform this particular type of sort. You may have a report with several number fields. Figure 5-17 shows the completed dialog box.

4. **Click OK.**

   The report is sorted as shown in Figure 5-17.

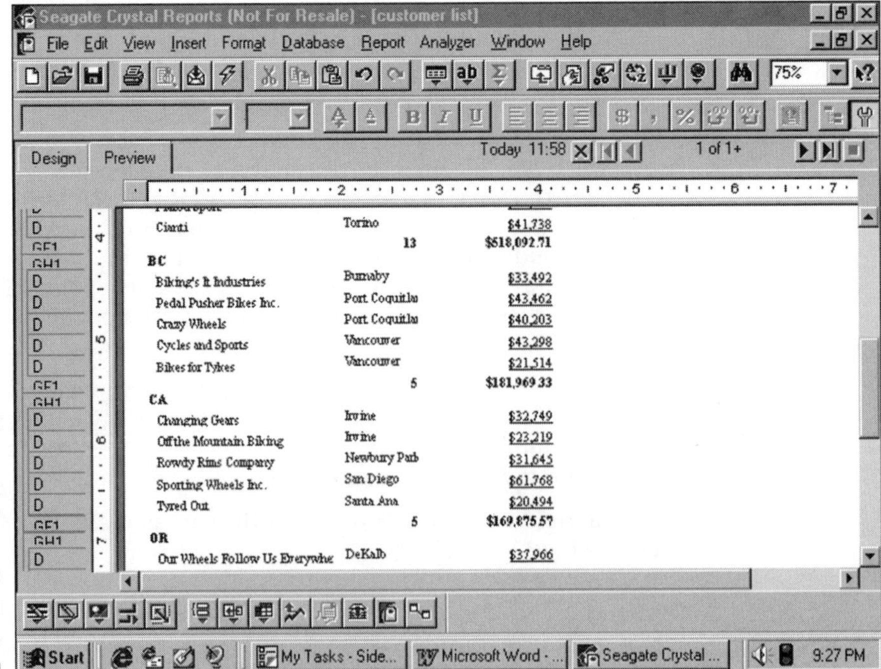

Figure 5-17: A report sorted for the top 5 in each of its Region groups.

Part III

Formatting and Formulas for Success

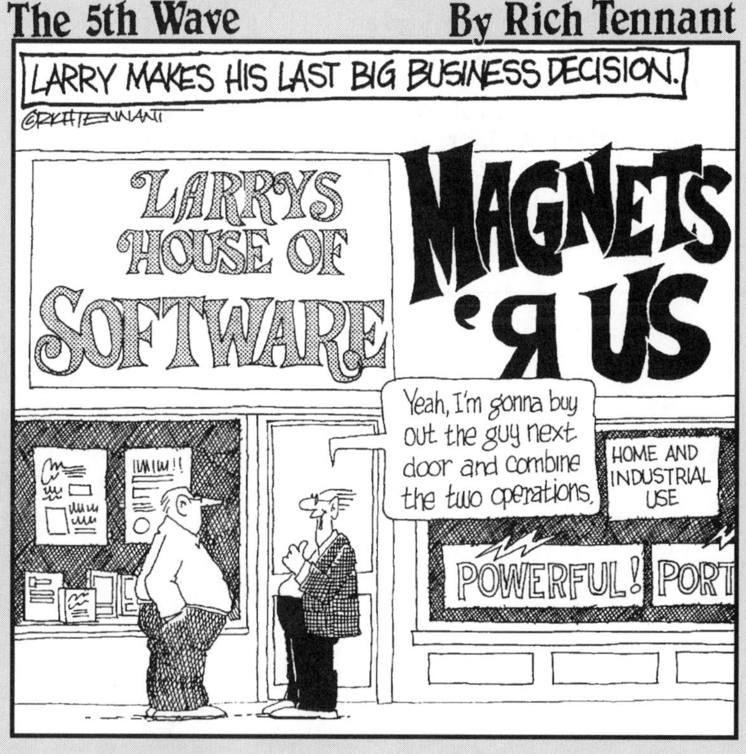

The 5th Wave
By Rich Tennant
LARRY MAKES HIS LAST BIG BUSINESS DECISION.
LARRYS HOUSE OF SOFTWARE
MAGNETS 'R US
Yeah, I'm gonna buy out the guy next door and combine the two operations.
HOME AND INDUSTRIAL USE
POWERFUL!
PORT

In this part . . .

Time to add the dazzle and sizzle. Add a couple of charts, and the boss will look good — and you will look even better. Add the company logo and a picture of the president of the company doing a rumba on the table at the company picnic, and you really have hit the big time! And why not — you can link all kinds of graphics to a report using the techniques in this part. Every department will covet you as the person needed to get their reports just right. No, I am *not* going to repeat that tired cliché about a picture being worth a thousand words. I refuse to stoop so low.

Chapter 6

Graphing and Mapping Data

In This Chapter

- Creating a graph
- Modifying a graph
- Drilling down on a graph
- Changing the graph type
- Using and applying graph templates

With the release of Version 7, Crystal Reports has substantially upgraded its graphing capabilities and, as a bonus, has added a mapping function. I can think of a dozen ways in which a company can use maps in conjunction with reports. For example, the decision for determining where to locate a new distribution hub for a company's products could be based on a report that plots where the focus of its orders originate. In this chapter, I cover both graphing and mapping aspects.

Creating a Map from a Report

I believe in clichés, because the truth is that a cliché almost always has a strong element of truth. So the cliché that a picture is worth a thousand words, to me is true. People can more easily understand relationships among numbers if the numbers are displayed in a graph. With this fact in mind, Seagate Crystal Reports includes a graphing function. Graphs can be drawn for any summary or subtotal field, detail or formula, or cross-tab data. As is true with other aspects of the report, a graph is considered to be an *object* in the report, making it amenable to being moved around.

The graph is dependent on the section of the report in which it is placed. For instance, placing the graph in the Report Header or Footer section means that the data for the entire report is represented. If the graph is in a Group Header or Footer, the data in that group is represented in the graph.

After you decide what to graph, the next decision is which kind of graph to use. Different graph types are better at displaying different kinds of information. For example, a pie graph is the best choice when you want to identify portions of a whole. Column graphs are preferable for representing data over a period of time, as in the amount of sales for a product, month by month over the course of a year.

By trying different graph types on your data, you can discern which graph best conveys the information. Fortunately, Crystal Reports makes creating a graph easy as pie.

Creating and Inserting a Graph

Crystal Reports includes a Chart/Graph Expert to walk you through the process of creating or editing a graph. Here are all the basic steps to inserting a graph into your report:

1. **Choose Insert⇨Chart or click the Insert Chart button on the toolbar.**

   The Chart Expert opens.

2. **In the Type tab, click the graph type you want.**
3. **Click the Data tab and choose the data to be graphed, how many times you want the chart to be shown, and where.**

   With a report containing only one level of grouping, your choice is Once per report, by default. (For details about groups, see Chapter 5.)

4. **Use the On Change Of box to pick the summary or subtotal information to be graphed.**

   Again, this option is where you would select the Detail, Formula or Cross-Tab data if you had selected those graph types.

5. **Click the Options tab to add a legend, show gridlines, show values on risers, direction of the bars, choose a font type, and specify the range of values.**
6. **Click the Text tab to determine what text is going to accompany the graph.**

   You can have a title, a subtitle, footnote, group title, series title, and the X, Y, and Z axis titles. At a minimum, you should probably enter a title.

7. **Click OK.**

   Crystal Reports inserts the graph into the section you indicated in Step 2.

Whew! Those steps are numerous and offer many choices, but the number of choices makes it easy to highly customize your graph. A real-life example is in order.

Crystal Reports graphs

You can graph four types of data with Crystal Reports: Group; Detail, Formula; Cross-Tab; and OLAP.

Group graphs: Use this option when you want to display one summary or subtotal in a graph. For example, when creating a Sales by Region report, you may want to create a Group graph that shows the sales subtotals for each Region and place it at the beginning of your report. The next section of this chapter looks at creating a Group graph.

Detail, Formula: You can use this graph option to display database or formula field data from the detail section on a graph. Perhaps within each region on your sales report you want to show a bar chart of individual sales within the region. You can also use this option if you want to display two or more summaries or subtotals in one graph. Creating this type of graph will not be covered in this chapter; refer to the online Help.

Cross-Tab: This graphing option enables you to show cross-tab data in a graph. This option is available only if you selected an existing cross-tab object on your report before selecting Insert⇨Graph/Chart Expert. This graphing option is not covered in this book.

OLAP: Use this option to chart on an OLAP grid. OLAP data can be used as a basis for this chart, and groups or summary fields are not required. This type of graph is not covered in this book.

Creating a Group Graph

I have opened the Custlist report as my example data. For simplicity in creating a graph, I used the Select Expert to include records from five regions.

If you do not have this report available, quickly create the report using the following instructions. Or you can use a report you have already created as long as it has one group and one subtotal.

1. **Create a new report using the Customer table within the xtreme database.**

   See Chapter 2 for more information.

2. **Insert the following fields into the detail section:**

   - The Customer Name field from the Customer table
   - The City field from the Customer table
   - The Last Year's Sales field from the Customer table

   See "Inserting Fields" in Chapter 2 for more information.

   While inserting fields you may want to resize the fields to make more room on your report.

3. **Only include records on the report from the following regions AL, AZ, BC, CA, and CO.**

   See Chapter 4 if you need further information.

4. **Group on the Region field from the Customer table.**

   See Chapter 5 for more information on creating groups.

5. **Create a total of Last Year's Sales for each Region using the Subtotal feature.**

   See Chapter 5 for more information.

6. **Add the Customer Listing heading, by creating a text object.**

Your report should look similar to the report in Figure 6-1.

A report must have a group and a summary or subtotal for that group in order to create the Group graph. Now for the real-life example of inserting a graph:

1. **Choose Insert⇨Chart (or just click the Insert Chart button).**

   The dialog box appears, as shown in Figure 6-2. Across the top of the dialog box you see the tabs Type, Data, Axes, Options, and Text.

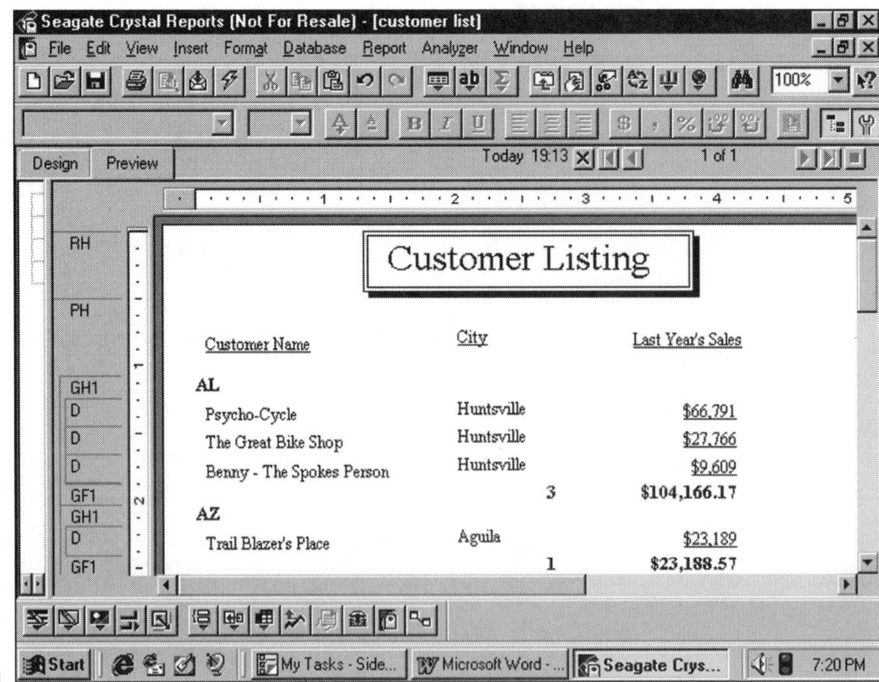

Figure 6-1: Does your sample report look like this?

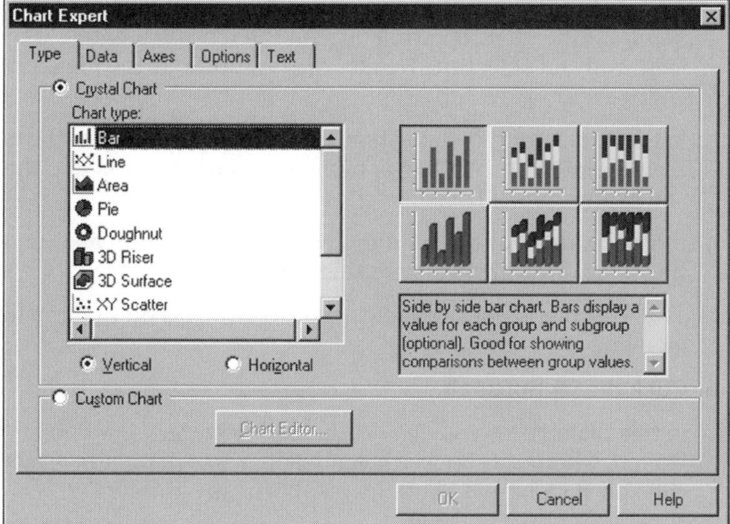

Figure 6-2: The Chart Expert dialog box.

2. **From the Type tab, choose the type of graph you want.**

   In this example, click Pie. There are several different kinds of pie charts to choose from. In this example, I used the default.

3. **Click the Data tab to choose the data you want to graph.**

   You can see the Data tab in Figure 6-3.

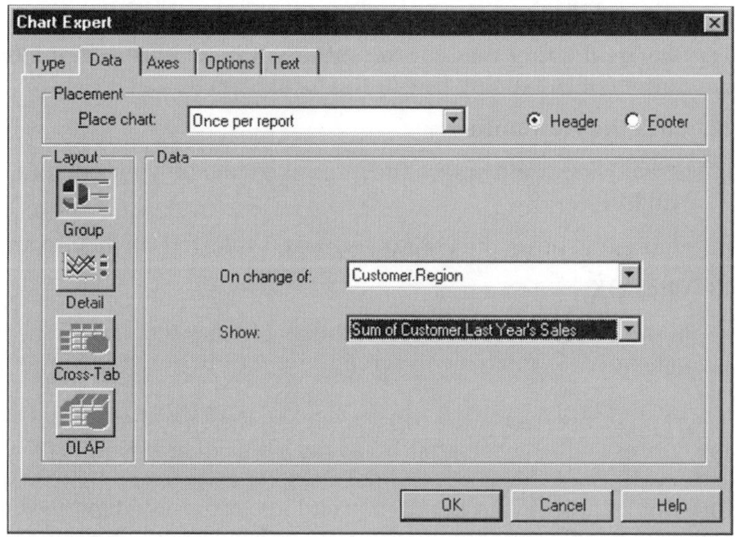

Figure 6-3: The Data tab specifications for a pie.

This dialog tab is very comprehensive. Crystal Reports assumes that you want the chart inserted once in the report as noted in the Placement field. You can select the Header or the Footer as the location for the chart.

In the middle of the dialog box, the Data section shows the values that are generated at the Change of the Customer Region, and the chart shows the Sum of Last Year's Sales.

4. **In this example, I selected the Footer radio button as the location for the chart. I left the other settings as is.**

   The Axes tab is not relevant to a pie chart, so skip that tab for the moment.

5. **Click the Options tab.**

   In this dialog box, you can set the bar color, how data points are displayed, whether there is a legend, and if so, where it is placed. Also, you can specify a bar size and the display of any markers.

6. **Click the Text tab.**

   From this tab, you can enter text to display in the report.

7. **Click the Title field, if the insertion point is not already there.**
8. **For this example, enter** Example Chart **as the title.**

   This text eventually displays centered at the top of the graph.

9. **Click the Subtitle text box.**
10. **For this example, type** Five **Regions as the subtitle.**

    This text displays in a smaller font just below the title.

11. **Change the font type for the subtitle. Click Subtitle in the list at the bottom of the dialog box in the format section.**
12. **Click the Font button.**

    Crystal Reports displays the fonts available on your computer via Windows.

    Figure 6-4 shows the Font dialog box. I selected the Arial Narrow font.

13. **Click OK.**

    In the Design tab, you can see the graph inserted in the report, as shown in Figure 6-5. You have to scroll the report to get to the footer.

The graph is inserted in the top-left edge of the specified section. You can move or resize the graph after it has been placed in the report.

Hint: Don't panic if your graph doesn't look as expected in the Design tab. Check the Preview tab first. Crystal Reports inserts the text titles you specified. It automatically creates a legend that designates a different color for every region, and it inserts the percentage for each region.

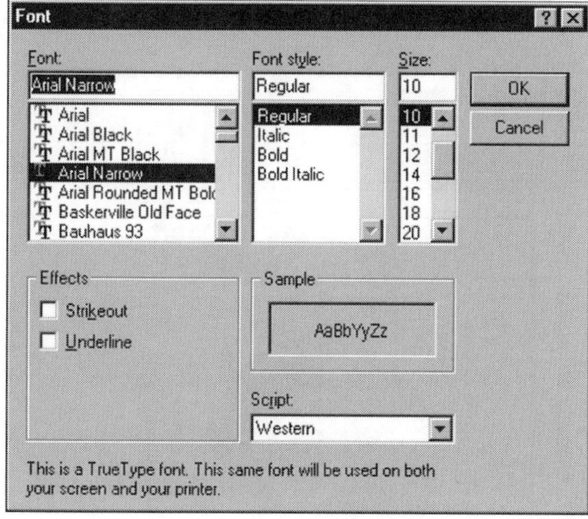

Figure 6.4: The Font dialog box for the subtitle.

To view the graph in the Preview tab, you have to move to the end of the report because the graph is in the Report Footer section.

Figure 6-6 shows how the report looks when you preview it.

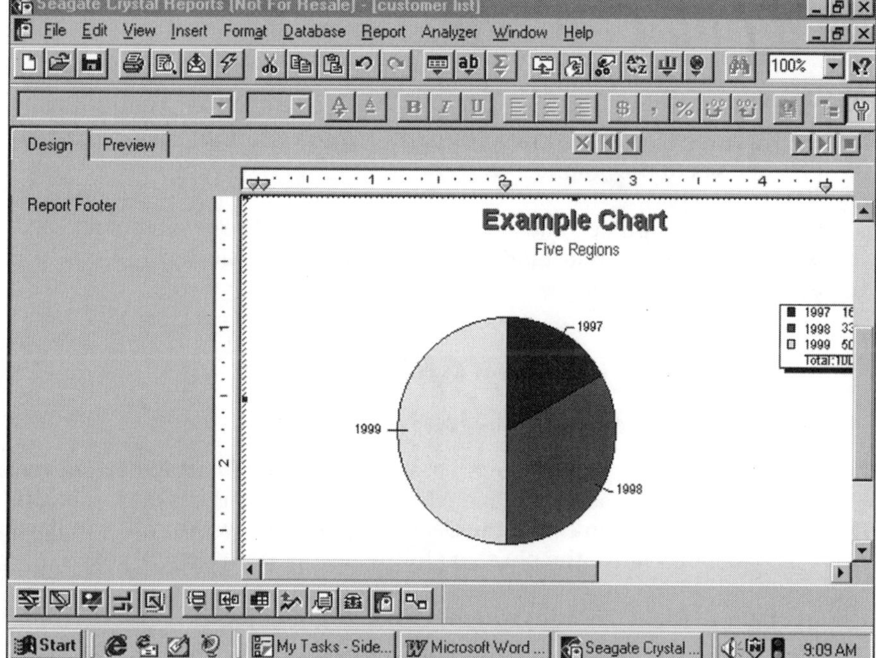

Figure 6-5: A pie chart inserted in the Report Footer as seen in the Design mode.

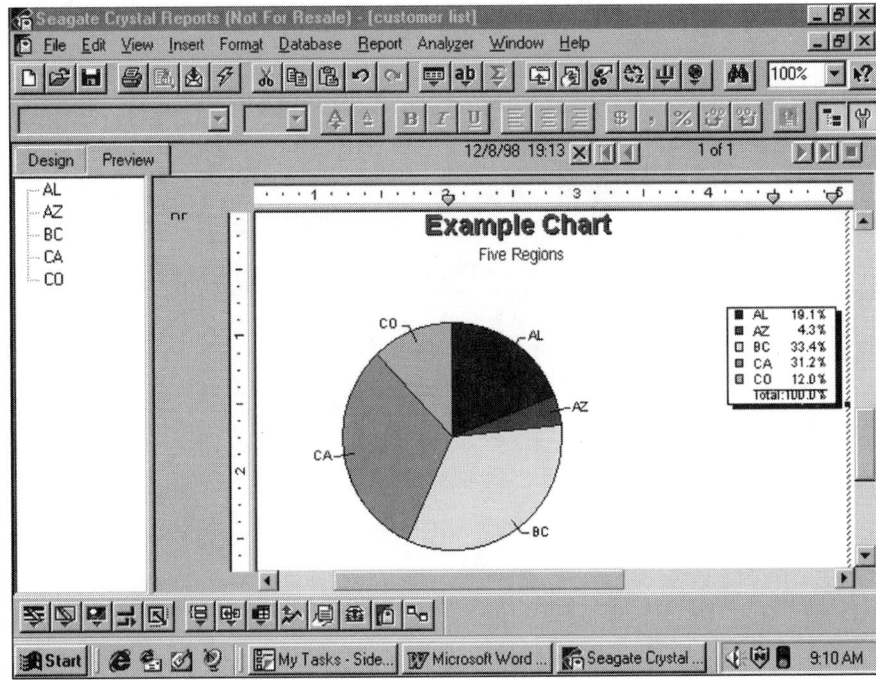

Figure 6-6: Your graph in the Preview tab.

Modifying a Graph

If you decide you want to make adjustments to your graph, you can modify a graph using the editing process. You have full formatting control of every graph element. Using any chart or graph you have inserted, make modifications to the graph.

Each graph becomes an object in a report. The graph object can be moved, resized, and reformatted just like any other object.

Moving the graph to the header (no change)

The easiest way to move a graph is to let the Chart Expert move it for you. Check out your chart and where it displays in the report. Using the Data tab and starting in either the Design or the Preview tab, you can have Crystal Reports move the pie chart to the header or footer for you:

1. **Right-click anywhere on the graph object.**

   The Chart menu displays.

2. **Click Chart Expert.**

   The Chart Expert displays.

3. **Click the Data tab.**
4. **Click the radio button next to** `Header`.

   Doing this tells Crystal Reports to move the graph to the Report Header.

5. **Click OK.**

Crystal Reports returns you to Design or Preview. The chart is now placed in the Report Header. When you preview the graph, you notice that Crystal Reports placed it in the top-left corner of the Report Header, right on top of the title, so you may have to resize or move either the chart or the title to see both.

The next section shows you how to fine-tune the positions of your graphs.

Where you place the chart determines where the chart prints in the report and which data is included in the chart. Use Table 6-1 to determine the best location for your chart.

Table 6-1 Choosing a Location for a Chart

Graph Location	*Prints*	*Includes Data*
Report Header	At the beginning of the report	For the entire report
Group Header	At the beginning of the group	For each group
Group Footer	At the end of the group	For each group
Report Footer	At the end of the report	For the entire report

Moving the chart

If you want to move a graph you have already placed in a report, be assured that it moves just like any other object.

Because the chart is an object, clicking the chart displays the gray border with handles. The gray border shows you the outline of the object. The handles are the square boxes in the corners and in the middle of the lines. When the chart was placed in the header, it covered part of the report title that had been inserted. Move the chart so that the entire title displays:

1. **From the Preview tab, click the chart so that the handles display.**

   While the pointer is over the object border, it turns into a magnifying glass. This pointer indicates that you can move this object.

2. **Click and drag the chart down the page until the top line of the chart is even with the bottom of the title object.**

   You can also move the chart to the right to center it across the page.

3. **Release the mouse button.**

   The chart redraws in the new location, and the entire title is visible. See Figure 6-7.

Note: Even though you moved the chart, it is still in the Report Header section, so it prints in the header of the report.

Resizing a chart

When you click an object, a gray outline and handles appear. You use the handles to resize a chart, or any object, for that matter.

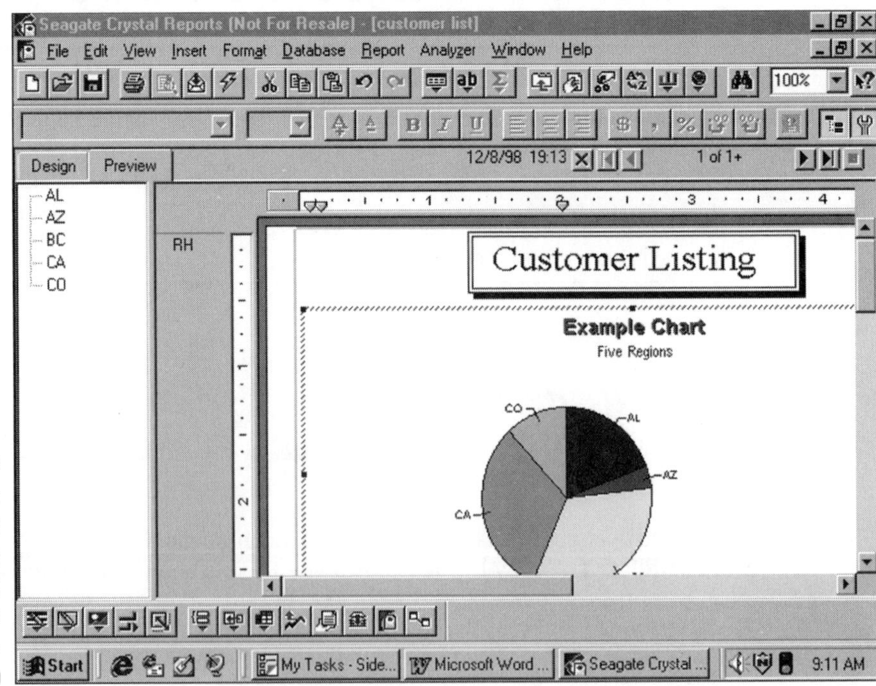

Figure 6-7: The chart has been moved below the title.

1. **Click the chart so that the handles display.**
2. **Move the pointer over a handle until a two-headed arrow displays.**
3. **Click and drag the two-headed arrow until the chart is the size you want.**

   If you click and drag a two-headed arrow in a corner of the object, you change the shape of the object in a diagonal direction. If you click and drag a two-headed arrow on one of the sides of the object, you move that side in or out.

Resizing and moving an object using the handles, the two-headed arrows, and the cross with arrows works the same way with every object.

Resizing with the Chart Expert

Clicking and dragging is the fast way to resize the chart, but if you need added precision, you can specify the exact dimensions of the chart using the Chart Expert.

1. **Right-click the chart.**
2. **From the menu that appears, select Object Size and Position.**

   The Object Size and Position dialog box appears, as shown in Figure 6-8.

Figure 6-8: The Object Size and Position dialog box.

3. **Enter the dimensions you need to make the chart the size you need.**
4. **Click OK to finish.**

   You can click the Undo button if the resizing is not what you expected.

Adding a border

The graph, like any object, can be formatted. You may want to add a border to enhance any graph by following these basic steps.

1. **Right-click the chart.**

   The Chart menu displays.

2. **Click Change Border.**

   The Format Editor dialog box appears, with the Border tab chosen.

3. **Choose the border properties you want to display with the chart and click OK.**

For this example, add a navy single-line border with a drop shadow.

1. **In the Preview tab, right-click anywhere on the chart.**

   The Chart menu displays.

2. **Click Change Border.**

   The Format Editor dialog box appears, with the Border tab chosen, as shown in Figure 6-9.

3. **Click the drop-down arrows to choose single borders for the Left, Right, Top, and Bottom of the chart.**

4. **Click in the check box next to Drop Shadow.**

   If a check already appears in the check box, skip to Step 5.

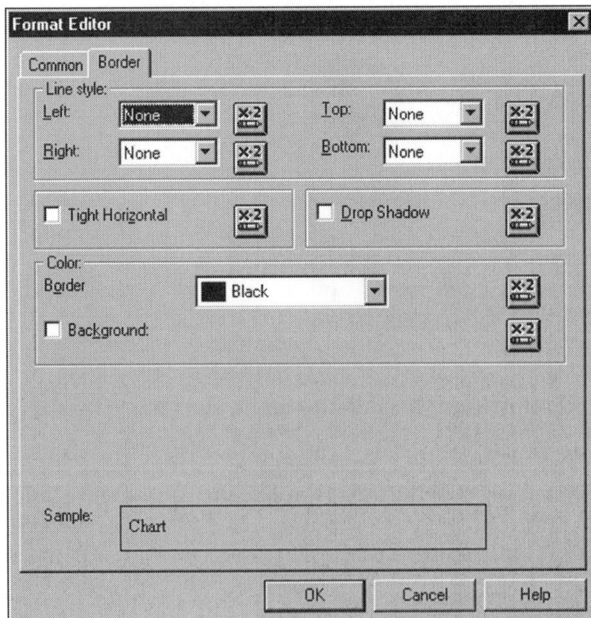

Figure 6-9: The Format Editor dialog box, with the Border tab on top.

5. **Click the drop-down arrow in the Color box and choose** `Navy` **for the border color.**
6. **Click OK.**

   The graph has a border, as shown in Figure 6-10.

Customizing your chart

Suppose that your company and your report have a preferred color scheme. How do you make your chart match that color scheme? Well, using the Chart Expert, you can change the colors of each piece of the pie in the pie chart to make them coordinate.

The Custom option is very powerful. It lets you change colors, select from more than 80 chart styles, and modify almost any component of your chart. The following steps get you to a point where you can make those changes:

1. **Right-click anywhere on the chart.**

   The Chart menu opens.
2. **Click Chart Expert.**

   The Chart Expert appears.

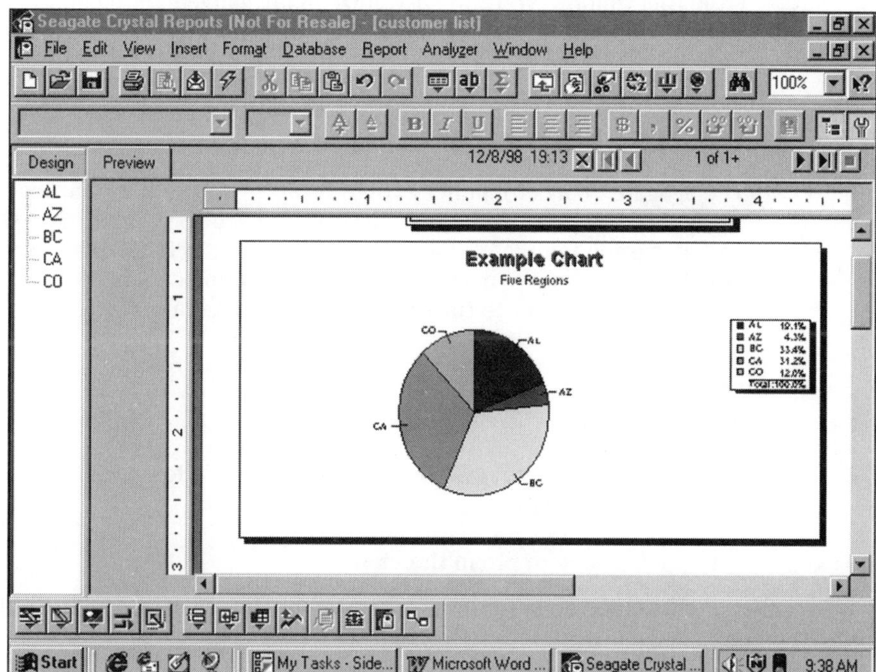

Figure 6-10: The graph with a drop shadow border.

3. **From the Type tab, click the Custom radio button.**
4. **Click the Chart Editor button.**
5. **Click OK.**

   The Seagate Charts window appears, as shown in Figure 6-11.

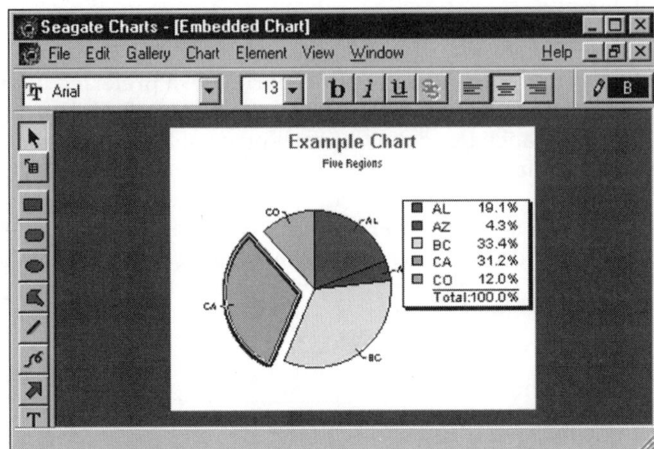

Figure 6-11: Seagate Charts window, opened from within the Chart Expert dialog box.

From this window, you can customize many aspects of the chart. The following sections of this chapter show you a few ways to customize this pie chart.

Using the ChartEditor

The Seagate Charts tool offers you 80 graph types and formatting control of every graph object. A very popular feature of the Seagate Charts window is creating graph templates. I address this topic later in this chapter. In this section, I show you some of the most popular editing capabilities of the Seagate Charts window. Refer to the online Help for more information.

Changing graph colors

Make this a bold-colored pie chart!

With the Seagate Charts window on the screen, follow the steps to change the colors of a slice of pie:

1. **Click a slice of pie in the chart.**

   At the top right of the window, below the menu, are a little pencil icon and a little paintbrush icon with a color block next to it.

Note: If you are working in a 16-bit operating system, the pencil and paintbrush icons may appear in the bottom left of the window.

2. **Click the paintbrush.**

   A multi-colored box opens up just above the icon. On the left of this box are two boxes placed on top of one another. The top box tells you the color you have chosen. The bottom box shows the color where your pointer is located. Each color has a number, so you can identify that same color in any other objects you add to your report.

3. **Click the color you want for that slice of pie.**
4. **Repeat Steps 1 through 3 until you have changed the color for the entire pie.**

With the Seagate Chart window open, click the various objects. The numbers, the callout lines, the title, and subtitle are all small objects within the graph object. From this window, you can change the font, size, color, location, and other characteristics of these objects.

Depending on the company you keep, the numbered color scheme may be very important. I once worked for a company where the company logo had to appear in a particular green (number 86) or black, because that logo represented the company. No other color was acceptable. When a copy of your report displays on a company intranet, be sure that the color of the logo is correct by defining the color number. Then use that number for your logo every time.

Changing a font size

The font size for the numbers that represent the percentage of sales is so small it makes it difficult to read. With a few clicks, you can change the font size of this or any text on the graph. Figure 6-10 shows the small font size for the numbers in the pie chart.

1. **Click the percentage numbers in the chart.**
2. **Look in the box just below the Element menu that shows the number of the font size. Click the down arrow to the right of that number.**

   The current font size is 7 points. A list drops down with various font sizes.

3. **Click 11.**

   All the highlighted numbers change after you make the selection. Notice how Crystal Reports has changed all the percentages to the same size. You can also right-click to open the Number Format dialog box to make changes.

To select multiple objects in the graph, click the first object and then hold down the shift key while selecting the remaining objects.

Detaching a slice of pie

Often you see a piece of pie in a pie chart set apart for recognition. In this example, detach the piece of pie of the highest sales region:

1. **From the Seagate Charts window, click the slice of pie with the highest percentage of sales.**
2. **Choose Chart⇨Detach Slice.**

   From this menu you can make many adjustments to the pie chart for the thickness of the chart, the rotation of the chart, and the size of the chart. After you do, the various detachment options are displayed.
3. **Click Minor.**

   The detached slice of pie appears.

Undoing changes

Oops! You made a big mistake. Say that you have spheres floating in your chart, but you don't want them. If you do something you do not want to do, you can undo the changes.

You must undo directly after doing something. The Charts Expert only remembers one step back. You can't undo a mistake you made three tasks ago. Here's how to undo: After making a change in a chart that you don't like, choose Edit⇨Undo. This action undoes that last action you did.

Saving the pie chart

1. **Select File and Close.**

   You are prompted to save the chart.
2. **Click Yes.**
3. **From the Chart Expert, click OK.**

The changes you have made in the Crystal Chart window are applied to the graph in your Design or Preview tab.

If you don't close and save the Crystal Chart window and then click OK, the changes you have made are not applied to the graph in your report.

Deleting a graph

In Version 7.0 of Crystal Reports, deleting a graph can be undone — but not in previous versions of the software. Use caution when deleting a graph.

1. **Begin in either the Design tab or the Preview tab.**
2. **Click the graph so that the gray border and handles display.**
3. **Press Delete on the keyboard, or right-click the graph and choose Delete from the Chart menu that appears.**
4. **Click Yes to delete the chart. Click No to keep the chart in the report.**

Drilling Down on a Graph

Drill-down is a process that enables you to see the details of summary information in a report. The pie chart I have been working with so far in this chapter holds the summary information of top sales by region. While viewing your graph, you can view the details of the summary information that *gave* you the graphed results.

Drilling down on reports is available from within Crystal Reports only. If you use the Crystal Reports Engine to distribute your reports with your application, the drill down feature is *not* available in those reports. In addition, drilling down is only available for group graphs. For more information on distributing reports, see Chapter 15.

The steps to follow to drill down to see more detailed information are:

1. **Click the Preview tab to open it.**
2. **Move the pointer over a segment of the graph.**

   The pointer becomes a magnifying glass.
3. **Double-click a section of the graph.**

   The details of the summary information are displayed in a drill-down tab. The tab displays at the top of the Report window. Figure 6-12 shows a drill-down tab for the ICA Region.

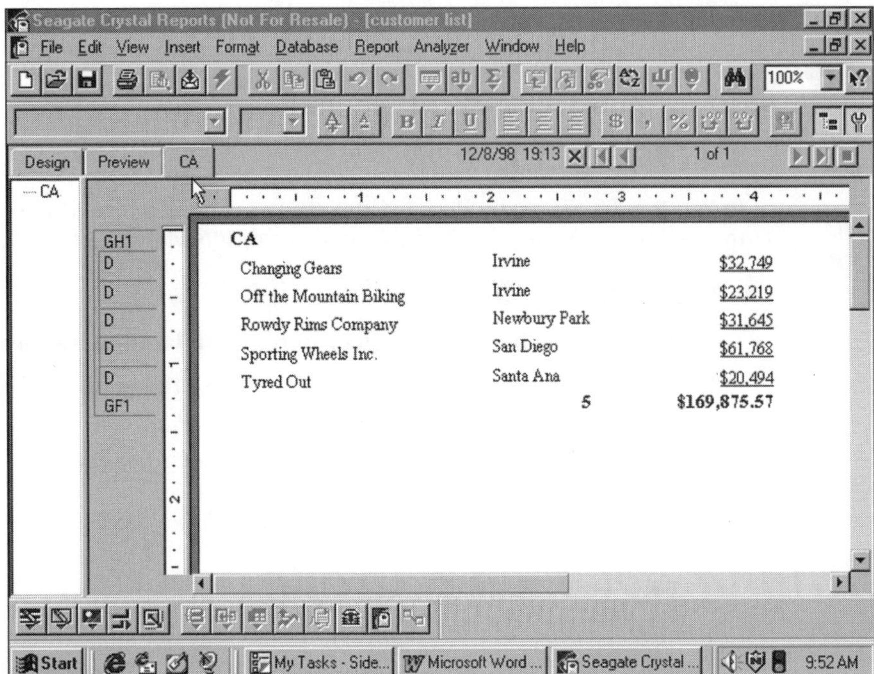

Figure 6-12: Drill-down into California.

4. **To create a drill-down tab for each section, double-click all the sections in turn.**
5. **Close a drill-down tab by clicking the Close Tab button (the red X to the right of the date and time display in the Preview tab).**

   Closing the drill-down tab does not close the report.

Adding a special effect

For a classy finish to any graph, add a special effect. A special effect adds interesting backgrounds making the chart stand out. (You must open Chart Expert, of course, to add an effect. See "Customizing your chart" earlier in this chapter for details.)

1. **Right-click your chart.**
2. **From the menu that appears, click Chart Expert.**
3. **Click the Custom Chart radio button.**

4. **Choose View➪Special Effect Palette, and make certain that the part of the chart you want to change is selected.**

   In this example, I selected the background of the chart.

   The Special Effect dialog box appears.

5. **Click Texture on the right side.**
6. **Click the drop-down button at the top.**
7. **Click** `4 Blues`.
8. **Click Apply.**

   The background of your graph displays the 4 Blues motif.

9. **Click the Close button (the X in the upper-right corner) to close the Special Effect palette.**

   Figure 6-13 shows how the special effect looks with the Special Effect palette still open.

Note: Some of the special effects may look like good backgrounds for reports displayed on the World Wide Web.

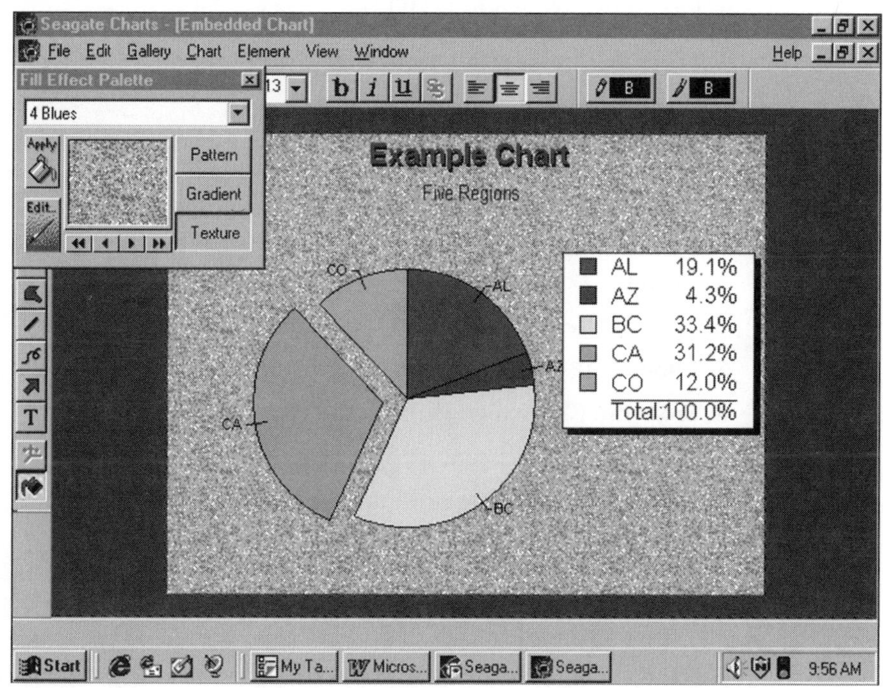

Figure 6-13: The Special Effect palette with applied special effects.

Changing the Graph Type

Some types of data work better with different types of graphs. Earlier in this chapter, in "Creating and Inserting a Graph," you see how effective a pie chart is in showing the top five sales regions. When you are plotting percentages of a whole, pie charts show the proportion of each section to the whole very well. If you want to show monthly sales over the past year, a line graph is effective in showing the highs and lows.

Applying the graph gallery

While in the Seagate Charts window, choose the Gallery menu. Move your pointer to the various menu options. As the menu opens on the right, move your pointer to those options.

Each menu displays a picture of the graph type available on the gallery. Not all chart types work with every set of data.

Now you can experiment with many kinds of charts. Apply the changes to a chart by taking the following steps:

1. **From the Preview tab, right-click the graph.**

   The Chart menu opens.

2. **Choose Chart Expert.**

   The Chart Expert dialog box appears.

3. **Click the Type tab and the Custom Chart radio button.**
4. **Click the Chart Editor button.**

   The Seagate Charts window opens.

5. **Choose the Gallery menu.**
6. **From the Gallery menu, click the type of graph you want.**

   Feel free to experiment with a variety of graphs.

7. **If you don't like how a graph looks, choose Edit⇨Undo.**

Using a Chart Template

A chart template is useful when you want to create a chart that is consistent each time it appears. Each time you create a chart that represents the top five sales, you apply the chart template. Each top five sales chart looks identical to the last, except for the changes in data. You can use this chart month after month, year after year, as a template so your reports have a consistent look.

Saving a chart as a template

With the chart you have created on-screen, stay in the Seagate Charts window.

When you have created the chart to your liking, save the chart.

1. **From the Seagate Charts window, choose File➪Save As.**

   The Save As dialog box appears.

2. **Type the name of the file you want to save.**

   Crystal Reports saves the format of the chart in a separate file that you can reuse.

You should create one template for each chart type you commonly work with. For example, I have one template for bar charts and a separate one for pie charts.

Applying the template

To apply the template, open a completely new report with a pie chart in it. Or create a new pie chart. When you apply a template, the template must be of a similar nature to the chart in the file. Select a bar graph template to apply to a bar graph. Select a histogram template to apply to a histogram graph, and so on.

Open Chart Expert with a new pie chart in it. First open a report (see Chapter 3 for how to open a report), and then open Chart Expert and Custom. With a file open and with a graph in it:

1. **Right-click anywhere on the graph.**
2. **Click Chart Expert.**

   The Chart Expert appears.

3. **Click the Custom Chart button.**
4. **Click the Chart Editor button.**

   The graph displays in the Seagate Charts window.

   Apply the standard template you have created to this graph.

5. **Choose File➪Apply Template.**

   The Apply Template dialog box appears.

6. **Select `Temp01` (or any chart you previously saved).**
7. **Click the Open button.**

   The template you created is applied to the chart in the Crystal Charts window.

The chart now has the same color scheme and the same font size. It takes on the appearance of the applied template.

Underlaying a chart on a report

A chart is more useful if it's visible at the same time as the data it represents. So, Crystal Reports 7 enables you to underlay a chart next to or underneath the details in a report. The feature is not what I would call automatic — that is, you have to tweak the results you get. Using the report that has been the example in this chapter, take a look at what happened when I tried to underlay the chart.

1. **The chart must be in the Report Header section of the report.**

2. **Click the Section Expert toolbar button, or choose Format⇨Section.**

   You have to use this tool to move the chart into a different section of the report. Figure 6-14 shows the Section Expert dialog box.

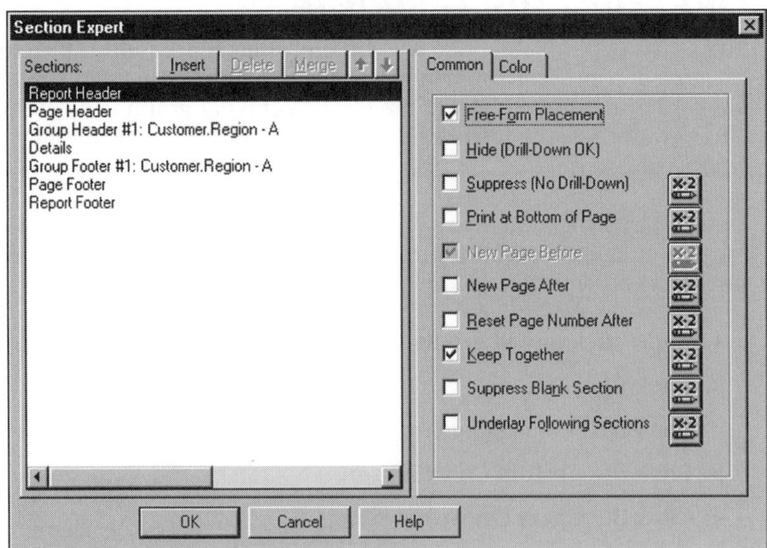

Figure 6-14: The Section Expert dialog box.

3. **In the Sections at the left side of the dialog box, click the Report Header section.**
4. **At the bottom right, click the radio button in front of the option Underlay Following Sections.**
5. **Click OK.**

   Figure 6-15 shows the result of the underlaying of the chart.

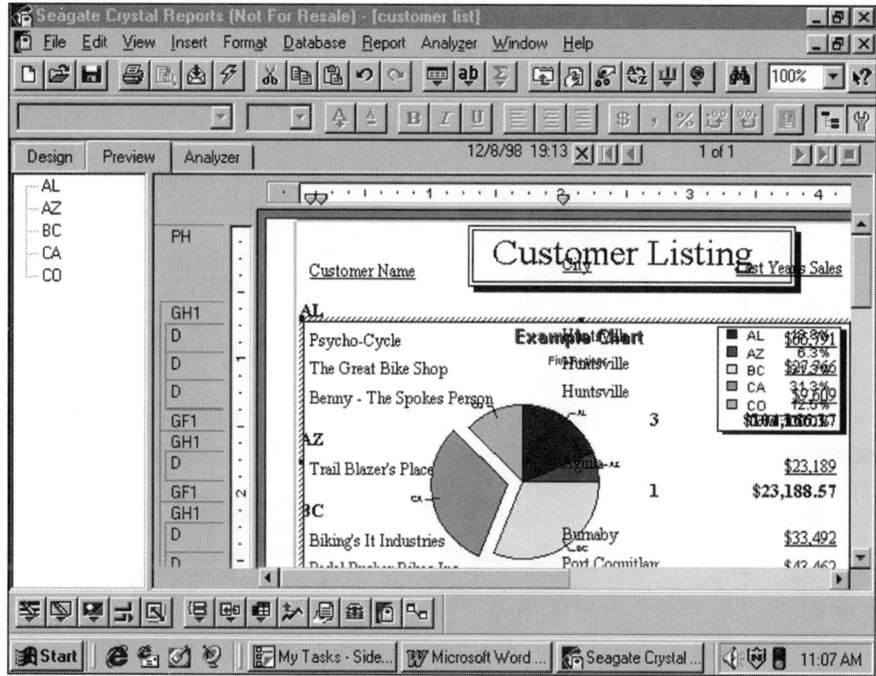

Figure 6-15: The chart underlaying the details section of the report.

As you can see, this action makes it difficult to see anything very clearly. One of the remedies is to move the entire chart to the right.

1. **The remedy is easier to apply in the Design tab. So click it.**
2. **Click the chart, hold your left mouse button down, and drag the chart to the right.**
3. **Click the Preview button.**

   The look of the report improves but is not yet perfect. To make the chart readable, I deleted the title object and returned to the Section Expert and supressed the Page Header section. Then, I resized the chart as described earlier. You can see my results in Figure 6-16, which has been reduced to 75% using the Zoom Control pull-down list.

With these few examples, you can see that Crystal Reports has virtually no limits in terms of the types of charts you can add to a report and the customization of a chart. The charts print gorgeously on a color printer, and they may get you that raise you've been bugging your boss about.

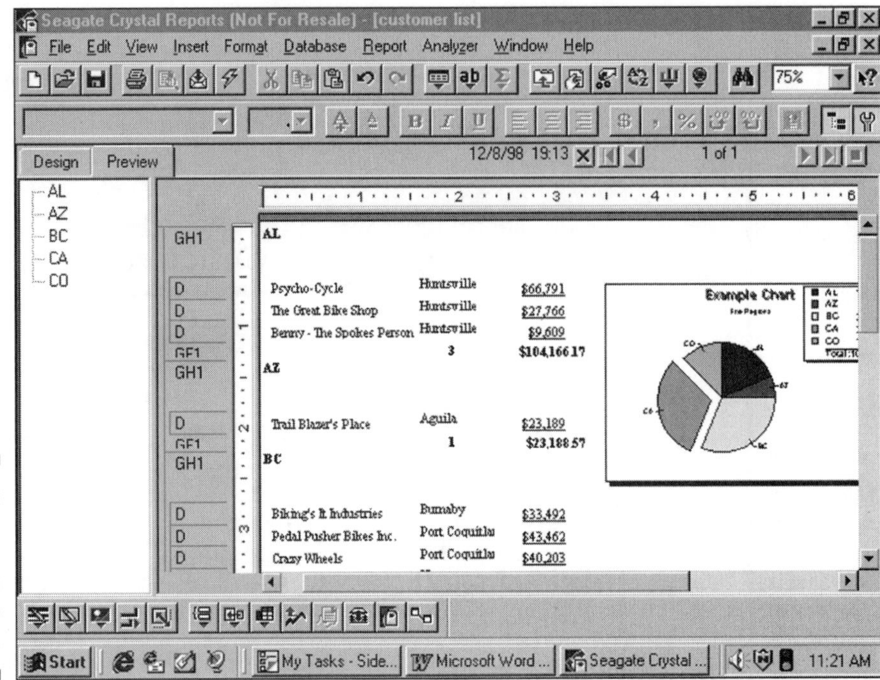

Figure 6-16: A resized chart and some design elements removed.

Mapping a report

New to Version 7.0 is the capability to insert a map that creates a visual representation of different parts of a report. You can create a map that details groups, detail fields, cross-tab summaries, and OLAP data. The procedure to produce a map of your data is similar to creating a chart. When you add a map, you can add it as you do a chart, in the header or footer or in a group header or footer. The distinction is whether the map depicts the entire report or only the data in the specific group.

Brief descriptions of each type of map are outlined in Table 6-2.

Table 6-2 Mapping Options

Map type	*Description*
Ranged	A ranged map has nothing to do with cowboys. Rather, it depicts data by first selecting a range (for example, 1 to 10) and then assigning a color to each range. The ranges can be modified if you want. You can make the range an equal count range, strictly equal ranges, a natural break range, or a standard deviation. For more on how the ranges work, check the online Help. By default, Crystal Reports uses this style of map and equal count as the range type.

Map type	Description
Dot Density	Ever looked at a photograph of the United States from space? If you have, then you have a good idea of what this map illustrates. This map gives impressions rather than hard data analysis. For example, if you were uncertain where to locate a new distribution warehouse, you could use this map to illustrate the location of your dealer network, and then you would have some idea of where your business is generated.
Graduated	Use this type of map to generate a pictorial representation of the relative size of a value. If your report is total sales by store, the marker would increase with the larger number of sales.
Pie Chart	This map displays a pie chart over each geographic area. So, this type map is a chart inside a map. The pie chart is generated by the individual values in the geographic region.
Bar Chart	This map is the same as the pie chart, but not all data is well represented by a pie chart. So, you can try either type and see what looks best.

Inserting a map

After creating a report, you can insert a map. In this example, the Customer Listing report is the source of my map.

1. **Click the Insert Map button on the toolbar, or choose Insert⇨Map.**

   The Map Expert dialog box appears, as shown in Figure 6-17.

2. **Select the Header or Footer for the location of the map.**

   In this example, I selected Footer as location.

   Note that Crystal Reports has intelligently assumed that the map should be based on the change in Customer Region (that is, state) and that the value to be mapped is the total for sales by customer from the previous year. Looks good to me, so on to the next step.

3. **Click OK.**

   Not a very big step, I acknowledge, but important.

   The map is inserted in the footer, as shown in Figure 6-18.

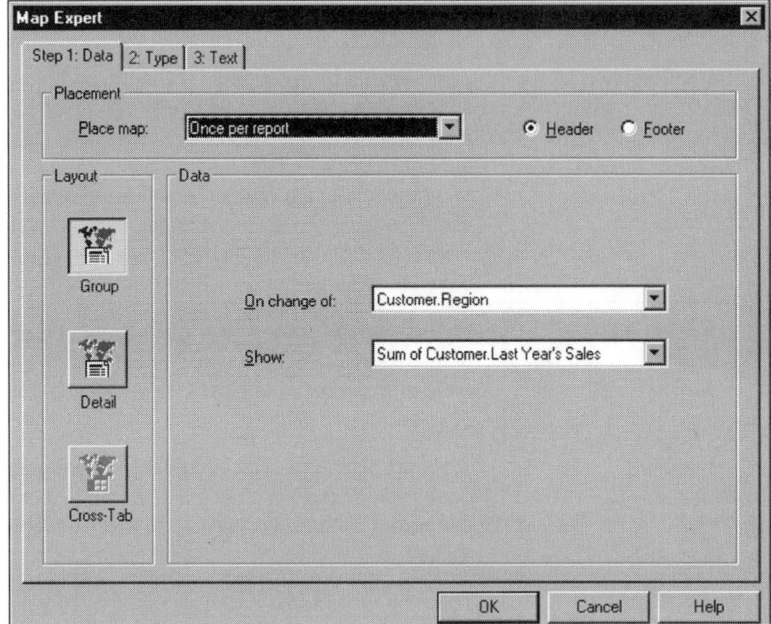

Figure 6-17: The Map Expert dialog box.

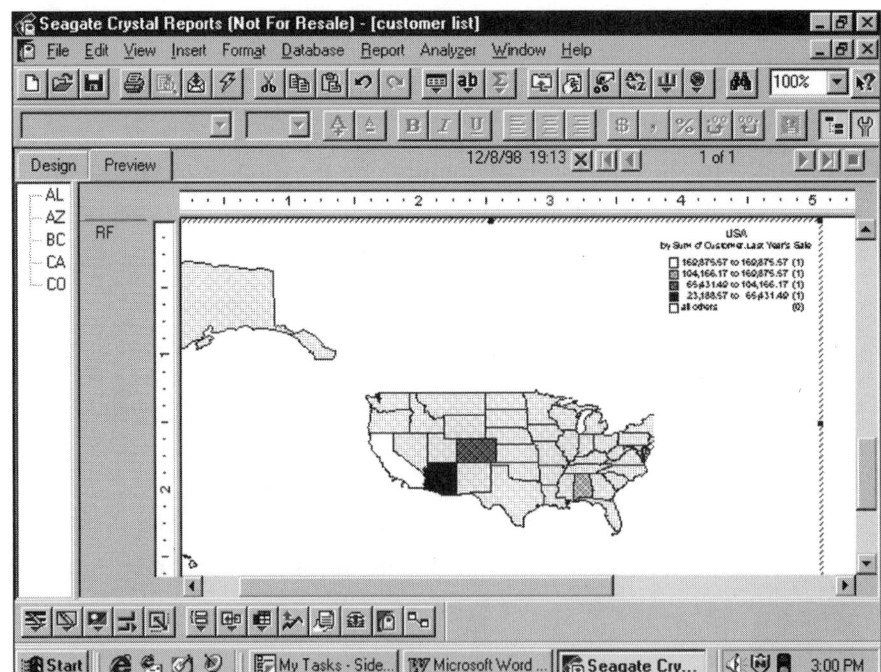

Figure 6-18: A map of the United States in the report footer.

At the upper right is the legend for the map. Crystal Reports has assigned the color white for the region (state) with the highest value of sales, California. The remaining regions have their own colors. Admittedly, seeing the distinctions on-screen is difficult, but printing the report in color yields a better view.

Changing the type of map

You can easily try a different type of map and see if the data is better served.

1. **Right-click the map.**

   The Map menu appears.

2. **Choose Map Expert.**
3. **Click the Type tab.**

   The other map types are available, as shown in Figure 6-19.

4. **Click the Dot Density map type.**
5. **Click OK.**

   The Dot Density map type replaces the existing map, as shown in Figure 6-20.

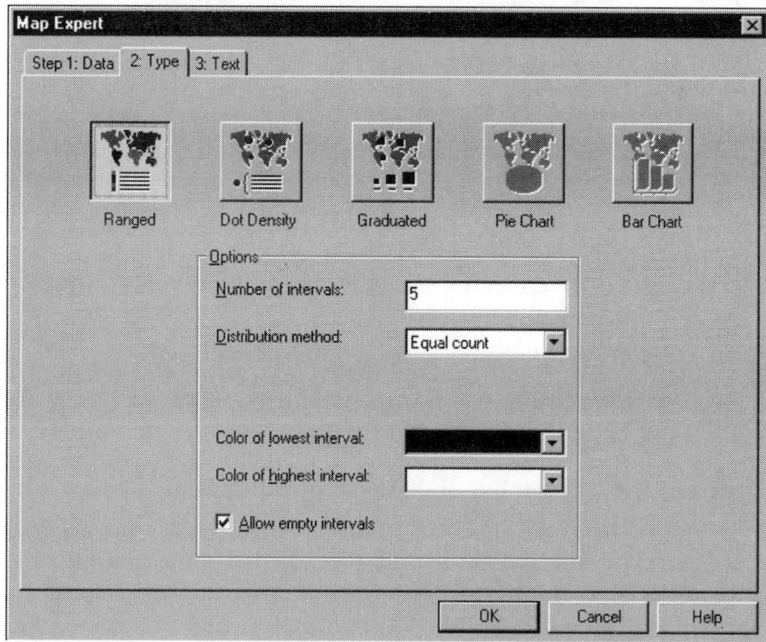

Figure 6-19: The Map Expert dialog box with the Type tab selected.

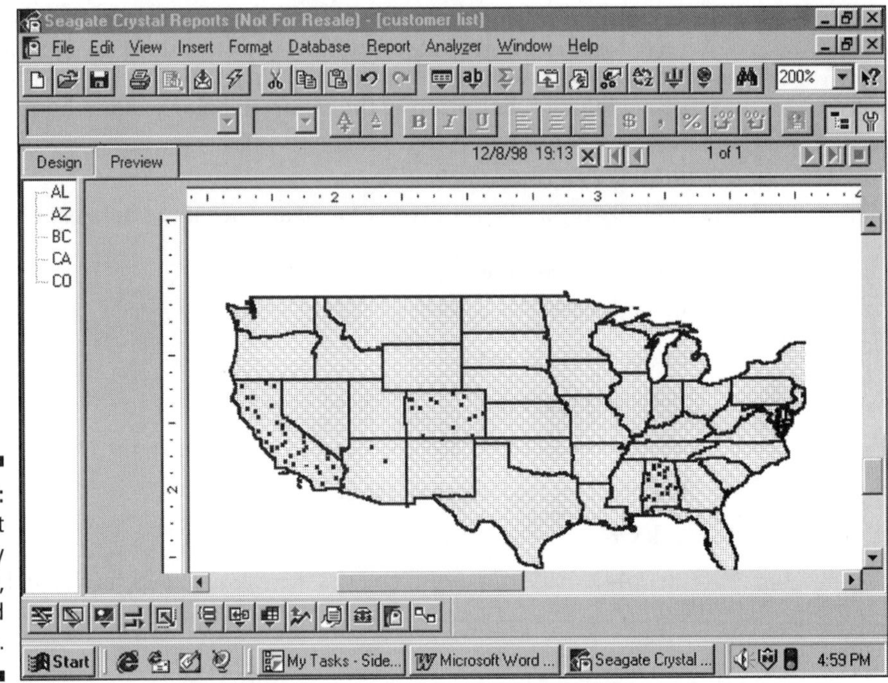

Figure 6-20: A Dot Density map, zoomed 200%.

Mapping on details

Summary maps are easy enough; I found detail mapping to be a little harder in that — uh-oh, you have to think! You must first remove any groups you have created. Skip Steps 1 and 2 if you do not have a group in the report.

1. **Choose Edit⇨Delete Group.**

   Crystal Reports warns you that removing a group cannot be undone. Press ahead!

   Crystal Reports displays the Groups in the report.

2. **Select the Group you want to delete and click OK.**
3. **Click the Insert Map tool button.**
4. **Click the Detail button in the Map Expert dialog box.**

   Several options appear. Because my underlying report is of last year's sales by store, I want to create a map that shows a value for each of the stores by region (state).

   All maps must have a geographic field entry.

5. **In the Available Fields section, click the Customer.Region field.**

6. **Click the arrow that precedes the Geographic field box.**

   Enter the field name **Customer.Region** into the box.

   Then you decide which field to use when changing the map display, that is, what field is a discrete value to be mapped. In this case, the values are by store name, which is the field Customer.Customer Name.

7. **Click that field and then click the arrow that precedes the On Change Of box.**

   So, I have selected the region for the geographic distinction, and as the name of the customer changes, a value is mapped. Now I have to determine the number.

8. **The value to map is the Customer.Last Year's Sales. Click that field and then click the arrow to the left of the Map Values box.**

   Crystal Reports automatically assumes that you want to summarize the values. But because there is only a single value per store, that won't work.

9. **Click Customer.Last Year's Sales in the Map Values box.**

   Underneath the Map Values box, the Don't Summarize Values option becomes active.

10. **Click to insert a check mark in front of Don't Summarize Values.**

    Figure 6-21 shows the correctly completed dialog box.

11. **Click the Type tab.**

12. **Choose Pie Chart as the type of map.**

13. **Click OK.**

14. **To see the map in more detail right-click the map and choose Analyzer.**

    Doing so opens another tab in the report with the map shown by itself, as shown in Figure 6-22.

Analyzing a map

With the map shown in an Analyzer tab, you can easily zoom in or out or pan the map.

1. **Right-click the map.**

2. **Select Zoom In.**

   The mouse pointer becomes a magnifying glass shape, with a plus sign (+).

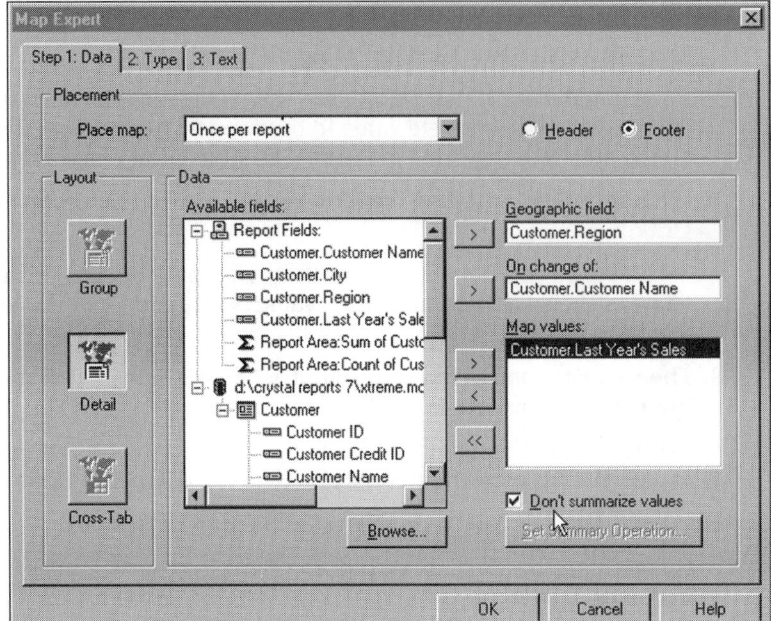

Figure 6-21: Fields properly entered for mapping report details.

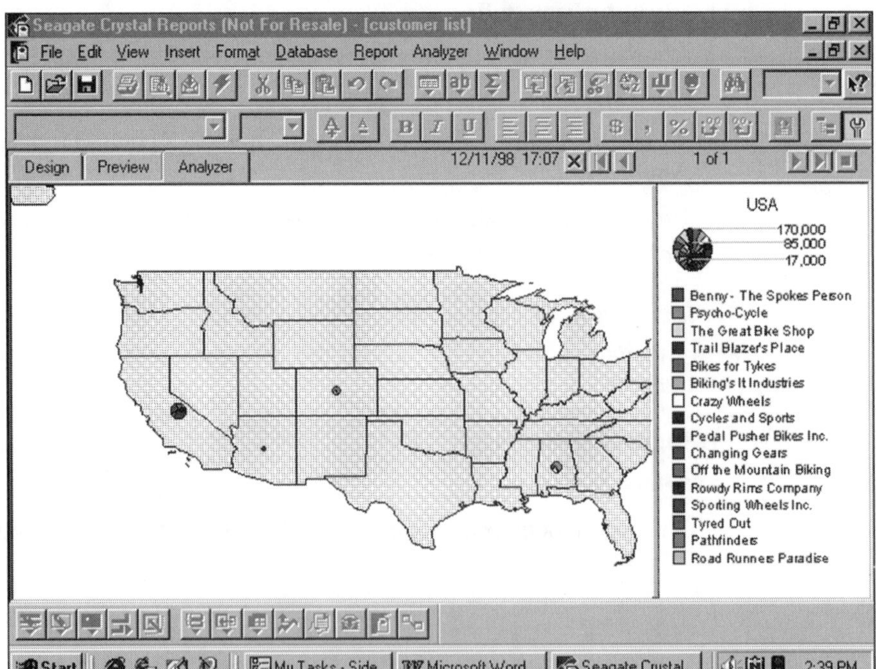

Figure 6-22: A detail map with the pie charts for each region in the Analyzer tab.

From this point, every time you click the left mouse button, the view of the map is zoomed in, showing greater detail. Conversely, you can right-click and select Zoom Out and the magnifying glass will have a minus sign (-), and each click reveals more of the big picture. Selecting Pan from the menu enables you to easily scroll the map in several directions.

Close the Map Analyzer tab by clicking the red X near the report date and time stamp.

Underlaying a map

As with a chart, a map can underlay the following sections of a report. To underlay the map, move the map to the report header, and use the Section Expert.

The ability to add a map to your reports is truly remarkable. It enables you to see reports in a context that is more readably available to the human mind. If you are an alien with an inhuman mind, looking at the map to plan an invasion, be aware that the real U.S. looks like a "boot" from high in the sky.

Chapter 7

Using the Crystal Formula Language

In This Chapter

- Inserting formulas in a report
- Discovering basic calculations and summary operations
- Manipulating strings
- Creating date calculations
- Creating if-then-else calculations
- Creating Boolean formulas
- Accessing ready-to-use formulas

If you hated algebra and dreaded calculus, do not skip this chapter because you think that math is what Seagate Crystal Reports formulas are. You can do many easy calculations without becoming a Hawking or a Newton.

What Is a Formula?

A formula is simply a *symbolic statement* that manipulates the data in your report. That is all it is. The tricky part is getting the formula to work with your data the way you want. But that tricky part is why you bought this book, isn't it? So you can have me show you how to get these things to work. Let's give it a whirl.

Chapter 4 helps you understand how to insert predefined summary calculations into a report using the built-in subtotal and *summary* operations. You do not have to type the particulars to make that happen; only indicate to Crystal Reports where and what field you want totaled and the total happens. In this chapter, you can see how to create mathematical and other calculations to suit your specifications.

A basic idea for a formula is to calculate the gross profit of products sold by your company. So to figure that number, you subtract the cost of the product from the sales price. A little more complicated formula is one that calculates the time elapsed between two dates. You may use this formula to determine whether a client is past due on a bill. This type of report is known as an *aging report.* Or suppose that the database has stored numbers as string values. In other words, the entries in the field look like numbers, but the database has designated the field as characters. Crystal Reports cannot perform a numeric calculation until you convert the characters to numeric, something you can do with formulas.

A really cool formula is a branching, or conditional formula, also known as an *if-then-else formula.* An example is a calculation that says that *if* the total amount owed is more than $1,000, *then* call your lawyer, or *else* call the client yourself. So the formula branches in two directions, depending upon the number generated. You do this kind of calculation every day while shopping. Computers are not as smart as you, and you have to create a precise formula for them to calculate what you do intuitively.

Acquainting Yourself with the Parts of a Formula

A formula consists of several distinct parts. First, you have to have database fields upon which the calculations are performed. Second, you have operators that perform calculations, and third, you have functions that are hybrid operators — meaning that a function performs an operation beyond simple + and – calculations.

Opening the Formula Editor

You can insert a formula into a report at any time when you want to perform a calculation beyond a simple sum on a field in your database. Before opening the database, these are the general steps that you undertake to insert a formula:

1. **Open the report into which you want to insert a formula.**
2. **Choose Insert⇨Formula Field.**
3. **The Insert Fields dialog box appears, as shown in Figure 7-1.**

   If any formulas already exist in the report, they appear in the dialog box.

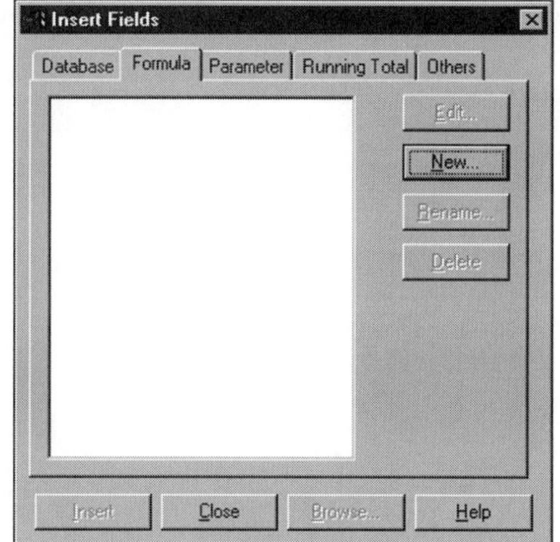

Figure 7-1: The Insert Fields dialog box, with the Formula tab selected.

4. **Click New.**
5. **In the Formula Name dialog box, enter a name for the formula.**

   This point is important because Crystal Reports uses the formula name as the field header in the report. It can contain spaces and special characters — and can contain as much text as you can fit in the text box. The name should be descriptive enough so that you can interpret what the formula does. In this example, I name the formula **TEST**.
6. **Click OK.**

   The Formula Editor dialog box appears, as shown in Figure 7-2.

In order to see more details in this dialog box, you can grab the border and expand the dialog box, and you can expand the size of each individual list box by positioning the pointer on the frames between the lists and dragging left or right.

This dialog box may be a little intimidating, but it is very approachable. At the left is the list of the Fields in the database that is open. In the middle is the list of Functions, and at the far right are the Operators.

The formula process consists of picking from each list, just like a menu, except you have no limits! That is, you could select six Fields, two Functions, and ten Operators — if you want.

Figure 7-2: The Formula Editor dialog box.

The Fields box

All fields in the table(s) used in the report are listed in the Fields box. If you have already inserted fields into the report, they are listed at the top of the list under the heading `Report Fields` (rather than `Database Fields` you see in Figure 7-2). Those fields are listed with the table name preceding them so that you can always tell where the fields are located. So if you have a report with fields from unique tables, you can identify the source of each field. Any formulas that have been inserted into the report have an @ sign preceding them, and parameter fields have a ? sign.

One of the new features of Version 7 is the pop-up description text that appears when you move the mouse pointer over a formula or a long field name that cannot be seen in its entirety in the Fields box. If you move the mouse pointer over one of the formula fields that are shown in Figure 7-2, which have been visually truncated because of the amount of white space available to display the name, a pop-up box appears showing the entire name.

You may notice that some fields appear in both the Reports field and the Database field section of the Fields box. Crystal Reports assumes that if you place a field on your report, you are likely to want to use it elsewhere in your report and includes it under Report Fields to make it easy to find. All fields are listed under Database Fields.

Table names are listed, too, and you can double-click the table name to see each of the individual fields in the table. A second double-click closes the list. This feature allows you to easily surf the database for the table you want and then, in turn, surf the table for the exact field that you may need to create the formula. If you have created any groups, they, too, are listed and can be used in formulas.

If you have groups on your report, all the information regarding the group (the Group Name field and any subtotals or summaries for the group) is also listed in the fields box below report fields. If you want to reference this information within a formula, highlight it and select to save yourself time.

The Functions box

Functions are those exotic creatures that are *pre-built* formulas of a sort. Functions are hybrids in that they contain mathematical operations that are difficult for an average person to build, such as calculating the Quick Ratios for a business report. In other words, these are tools that exist for you to use instead of you having to build them yourself.

You'll notice if you scroll through the functions box that there is a ton of information. How do you find what you're looking for? The functions are organized to make your life easier. The first category of functions is Arithmetic; double-click it to see the functions to work with numbers. The next category is a Strings category that you can use to find functions when working with text or number fields. The remainder of the functions list is organized in the same manner.

The Operators box

Some of the arithmetic operators may be more familiar to you in that the symbols are mathematical symbols such as addition, subtraction, and so on. There are also other categories of operators for use against other data types or in other situations. Double-click to see individual formulas, and note that Crystal Reports shows you the correct way to use the operator by including an X and a Y as substitutes for the values.

The Formula text box

This is where you can do the work and create the formula. After you select a Field, Function, or Operator, it is inserted into the Formula text box. That way, you can see exactly what you are building as you go.

The Check button

After laboring mightily on a formula, have Crystal Reports check it for you. Simply click the Check button, which has the X-2 and a check mark on it, and the formula is examined for any syntax problems. No, *syntax* is not a form of taxation on liquor or cigarettes (that is a *sin tax*), but rather the proper placement of the parts of the formula. If a mistake is found, Crystal Reports moves the cursor to the area of the formula that it thinks is incorrect and prompts you with a dialog box message.

If you are working on a long or complicated formula, you can check it at any point. Simply click the Check button, and Crystal Reports makes sure it can understand what you have done to that point in the formula. You can then continue with the rest of the formula — confident that it's correct.

The Save button

Click the Save button after you have created the formula, had Crystal Reports check it for you, and been given an okay. By the way, if you did not execute a check before clicking the Save button, Crystal Reports does it anyway. If it finds a mistake, it gives you the option to correct the formula.

The Browse Field Data button — for accuracy

When you select a field that you think is the correct one for your formula, you can be sure that it is correct:

1. **Highlight the field name.**
2. **Click the Browse Field Data button to see the actual data in the field.**

Browsing also tells you the length of the field and the data type.

Syntax 101

What follows is a table of syntax that you use when creating formulas to make them as easy as possible. Table 7-1 lists them and explains their uses.

Table 7-1 Tools for Creating a Formula

Tool	*What It Does*
//	These two forward slashes can add a comment to the formula. Use comments to document your formulas and what the formula does — it will make modifying reports in the future much easier. So in any formula, you can type **//**; the text after // is not treated as part of the formula nor does it print.
()	The parentheses denote the arguments following a function. When you use a function in a formula, it may need information inside the parentheses in order to work. An example is the Trim(str) function. If you insert the Trim function in a formula, it has to have something inside the brackets to act upon.
{}	These are French braces, Oo La La! Not to get excited, they simply indicate that the information enclosed is a Database field, formula, parameter field, or special field. You see them a lot.
" "	Any kind of character enclosed in quotation marks is called a *literal.* In a formula, a literal is text that you want to print at a certain point in the report. For example, if your formula calculates the length of time since your company has been paid by a customer, you can have Crystal Reports print PAST DUE by inserting it into the formula as a literal.

Crystal Reports ignores upper- or lowercase in the formula (except when looking at database values), as well as carriage returns (pressing Enter, for you post-typewriter types). Line breaks, too, are okay, as are spaces. Crystal reads the formula left to right and then top to bottom, regardless.

Going Down the Road to Creating a Formula

The best way to understand how formulas work is to use real data in examples. The remainder of the chapter will add formulas to the Formula report (instruction follows on how to create it). In the following examples, you can create the formula report and follow exactly or try adding individual formulas to reports you may already have created against your own data.

If you'd like to work through the following examples, please take a moment to create the following report. If you need a bit of help, refer back to previous sections of the book as indicated.

1. **Create a new report utilizing all tables within the xtreme database.**

   Use the Smart linking suggested by Crystal Reports. See "Accessing a Database" in Chapter 2 for more information.

2. **Insert the following fields into the detail section:**

   - The Customer Name field from the Customer table
   - The Product Name field from the Product table
   - The Unit Price field from the Orders Detail table
   - The Quantity field from the Orders Detail table

   See Chapter 2 for details on inserting fields.

   While inserting fields, you may want to resize the fields to make more room on your report.

3. **Only include records on the report from California (you would want to base the record selection on the Region field from the Customer table being equal to CA).**

   See Chapter 4 if you need further information.

4. **Group on the Order ID field from the Orders table.**

   See Chapter 5 for more information on creating groups.

5. **Save the report as ch7, if you want to follow along with the examples in this chapter.**

Eliminating Blank Records with a Formula

One of the challenges that occurs with real databases is that you may have a report that includes some data that is useless because it is only partially complete. In situations such as this, you will have to modify your record selection to exclude the partial data. In this situation, I include only records that have a quantity greater than zero.

1. **In the ch7 report, click the Select Expert button.**

   The Select Expert dialog box appears, with the one condition, which is records from California only.

2. **Click the New tab.**

   The Choose Field dialog box opens.

3. **Select the Quantity field by double-clicking it.**

   Because it is part of the report, it is listed at the top of the list under Report Fields.

   The Choose Field dialog box then closes.

4. **Back in the Select Expert dialog box, in the second drop-down box from the left, select the** `Greater than` **criteria.**

5. **In the third drop-down box from the left, type a zero (0).**

   The formula can be viewed by clicking the Show Formula button. The formula extracts only those records in California and with a Quantity greater than 0 (see Figure 7-3).

6. **Click OK to complete the record selection process.**

   Crystal Reports asks if you want to refresh or use saved data.

7. **Select saved data.**

   No records with a zero quantity remain.

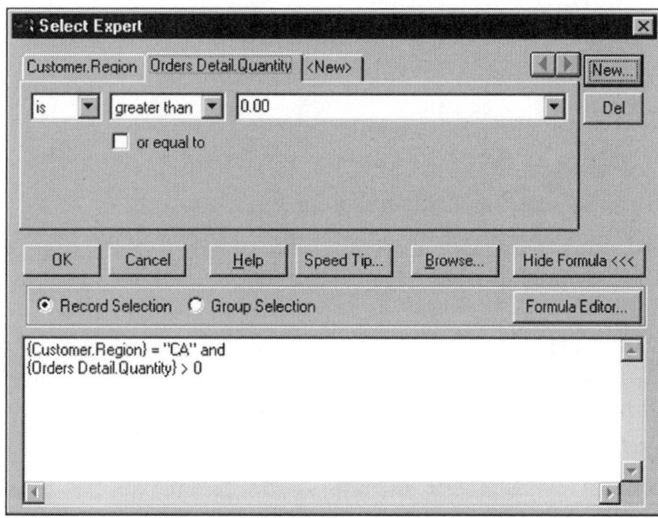

Figure 7-3: Preparing to select records from California that are greater than zero.

Creating a Formula

With the report fields in place, and any records with zero values eliminated, the next step is to create the formula that multiplies the quantity by the number of units. Crystal Reports treats a formula as an object, and wherever you place the formula in the report is where the results of the formula are displayed. You can perform these steps in the Design tab.

To create the price multiplication formula:

1. **Use the ch7 report I suggested you create at the onset of this chapter, or open any report that has two fields that can be multiplied.**

2. **Click Insert Fields on the toolbar.**
3. **Click the Formula tab.**
4. **Click New.**

   Crystal Reports opens the Formula Name dialog box, into which you must enter a name for the formula.

5. **Enter something original, such as** Total.

   Take a look at Figure 7-4 as an example.

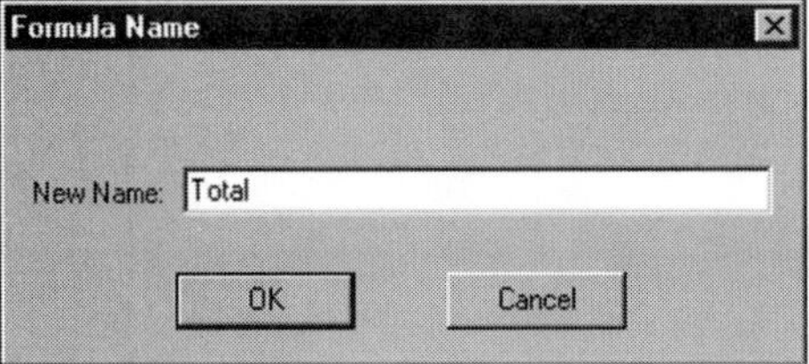

Figure 7-4: The formula with a Total name.

6. **Click OK.**

   The Formula Editor dialog box appears.

   You are on the brink of becoming a *Smarty.* Everything that you have done in this book to this point has been pretty straightforward. Now, greatness has been thrust upon you — carpe diem!

   Your goal is to multiply the unit cost by the quantity. In the Fields list of this dialog box is a list of the fields, formulas, and groups in the report. Your targets are the two fields Unit Price and Quantity.

7. **Double-click the first field you plan to multiply.**

   In this example report, in the Fields list, double-click `Orders Detail.Unit Price`.

   The field name pops into the Formula text box in the bottom half of the dialog box, as you see in Figure 7-5.

   Just in case you have forgotten, the name of the table in which the field is located, is part of the field name — in this case, Orders Detail.Unit Price.

   The next step is to enter the mathematical operator that multiplies the numbers in this field by the numbers in the Quantity field.

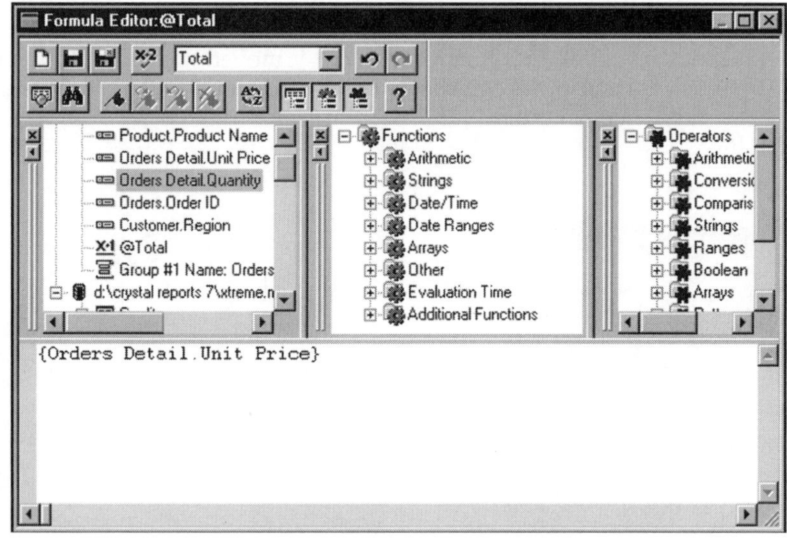

Figure 7-5: The Unit Price field in the Formula text box.

8. **Double-click** `Multiply (x*y).`

   The Operators are in the upper-right box of the dialog box. The Arithmetic operators appear at the top of the list, and one of these is `Multiply (x*y)`, which is the one you want.

   Crystal Reports inserts only the * symbol in the Formula text box, so it may be hard to see.

9. **In the Fields list, double-click the next field in the formula.**

   In this example, I double-clicked `Orders Detail.Quantity`.

   The second field is inserted into the Formula text box and looks like this:

   ```
   {Orders Detail.Unit Price} * {Orders Detail.Quantity}
   ```

Check, please!

Although Crystal Reports checks the formula automatically after you click the Save button or the Save and Close button, clicking Check is a good idea in order to confirm that your formula has the correct syntax.

1. **Click Check.**

   The No Errors alert box appears, as shown in Figure 7-6.

2. **Click OK to close the dialog box.**

   If Crystal Reports found a mistake, it moved the cursor to the portion of the formula it recognized as being erroneous, and a message appears to assist you in the fix.

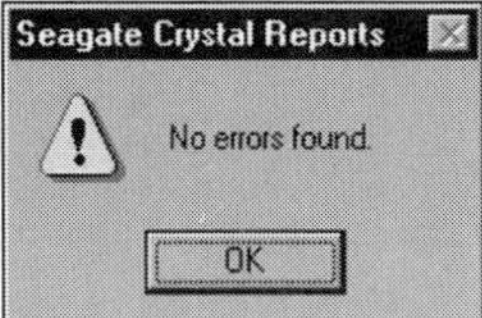

Figure 7-6: Crystal Reports says that the formula checks out!

Saving the Total formula

The final step is to save the formula.

A warning here: Just because Crystal Reports examined the formula and determined that it was properly constructed does not necessarily mean that the formula is correct. In the case of a simple formula such as this one, you can easily feel confident that the results of the formula are correct. But if you create highly intricate formulas, even if they are properly constructed, they can give the wrong results. Understand this difference, and use a common sense approach to the results you get when you check your formula. If you're sure that you're on the right track, continue on the road to completion:

1. **Click the Save and Close button.**

   The Insert Fields dialog box is still open with the newly created formula listed.

2. **Click the formula name.**

   In this example, I clicked Total.

3. **Click Insert.**

4. **In the Design tab, insert the formula to the far right in the Details section of the report by clicking where you want the formula to go.**

   It appears, similar to Figure 7-7.

5. **In the Insert Fields dialog box, click Close.**

6. **Hold onto your hat; this is the moment of truth. Click the Preview tab.**

   If everything went according to plan, your new report looks similar to the one in Figure 7-8.

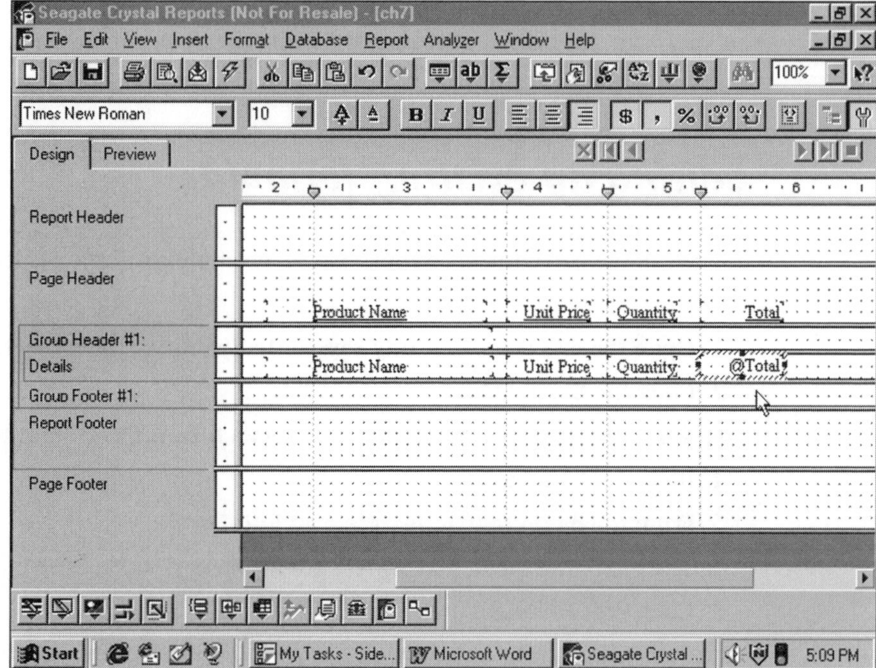

Figure 7-7: The formula name Total inserted into the Details section.

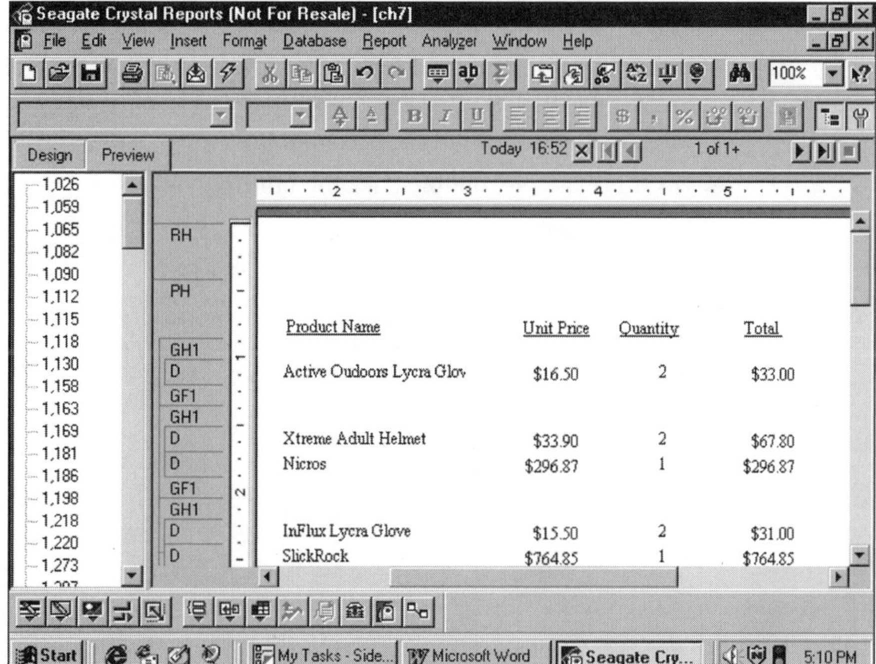

Figure 7-8: A preview of the report with the new formula added.

Pretty exciting, I think! The ability to calculate all kinds of results is limited only by your ingenuity. In the rest of this chapter, I show you other terrific formulas using this same report.

Editing an existing formula

Before moving to a new example formula, take a look at how easily you can edit a formula currently in a report. In this example, you add a calculation to compute the extended sales price *plus tax.*

1. **Open the ch7 report, or any report that you may have created.**
2. **Click the Design tab.**
3. **Click the Total formula field, or select a formula you want to edit.**
4. **Right-click the mouse.**
5. **From the menu that appears, select Edit Formula.**

   The top of the menu that appears reads Field:@Total.
6. **Click Edit Formula.**

   The Formula Editor dialog box appears, with the Total formula (or the formula you have selected to edit) displayed in the Formula text box. The text for the Total formula currently is:

   ```
   {Orders Detail.Unit Price} * {Orders Detail.Quantity}
   ```

   In this example, the sales tax rate is 7 percent. All you need to do is edit the formula to add the percentage.
7. **Click at the far right of the formula.**
8. **For this example, double-click the Multiply operator.**

   The * is inserted.
9. **Type:** 1.07.

   This edit causes Crystal Reports to take the results of the first portion of the formula and multiply that by 1.07, which is equivalent to adding 7 percent. The formula text should now be:

   ```
   {Orders Detail.Unit Price} * {Orders Detail.Quantity} * 1.07
   ```
10. **Click the Save and Close button.**

    The formula should check okay; Crystal Reports displays a small alert box indicating so.

11. **Click OK.**

    You return to the Design tab. Click the Preview tab to see the new values for total that include the sales tax.

Adding a Formula That Totals by Group

With Crystal Reports, you can easily insert Subtotals, Summaries, and Grand Totals into a report automatically with built-in summary operations (see Chapter 5). There may also be times when you want to work with these summaries in the Formula Editor. Perhaps you want to calculate a percentage of total. In this section, I show you how to create these summaries within the formula language. Remember, let Crystal Reports do the work for you if you simply want to place the summary on the report. You only need to create a summary this way when you want to use it within a Formula. The report is grouped by order ID, and say that you have already created a total of the orders including sales tax. Therefore, the steps to create a formula that will total by the orders is as follows:

1. **Using the ch7 report, click the Design tab.**

2. **Click the Insert Fields button on the toolbar and then click the Formula tab.**
3. **In the Formula tab, click New and enter a name, in the Formula Name dialog box, for the formula.**

   A suggestion is **Group Sum.**
4. **Click OK to open the Formula Editor dialog box.**
5. **Start the formula by double-clicking the Sum (fld, condFld) function.**

   You can find Sum (fld, condFld) in the Functions list of the Formula Editor dialog box. Double-click the Arithmetic header to see the formula you need.

   The function is inserted into the Formula text box.
6. **The first field to be summed is the one that gives you the extended price plus the sales tax, which is @Total. Double-click the formula name in the Fields list.**

   The first part of the formula is completed, as shown here:

   ```
   Sum({@Total},)
   ```

   Note that Crystal Reports automatically inserts a pair of French braces to enclose the formula name for you.

Summing up

The two most often used summary functions are Sum (fld) and Sum (fld, condfld). You would use the Sum (fld) when you want to sum a field for the entire report. For example, if you wanted to create a total for Last Year's Sales for the entire report, your formula would be Sum ({Customer.Last Year's Sales}). This is equivalent to letting Crystal Reports automatically create a grand total for you.

You use the Sum (fld, condFld) function when you want to create a total for each group. The fld is the actual field you want to summarize, and the condFld is the group field for which you want a total.

7. **Still in the Formula text box, move your cursor to the right of the comma.**

   You are now ready to enter the group field that will be subtotaled.

8. **Double-click** `Group#1Name:Orders.Order ID` **in the Fields list.**
9. **Delete the text** `Group Name` **in the formula.**

   The completed formula appears here:

   ```
   Sum({@Total},{Orders Detail.Order ID})
   ```

10. **Click the Save and Close button.**
11. **In the Insert Fields dialog box, click** `Group Sum`**.**
12. **Insert the formula in the Group Footer section of the report by moving the pointer to the Group Footer and clicking. (You probably want to insert it below the Total formula.)**

    This placement is important because you want the results to print after every group. Figure 7-9 shows the completed report in the Design tab. The pointer indicates the location of the Group Sum formula.

13. **Click Close in the Insert Fields dialog box.**
14. **Click the Preview tab.**

    Your report looks like the one in Figure 7-10. I have formatted the field so that the results of the formula are shown in bold.

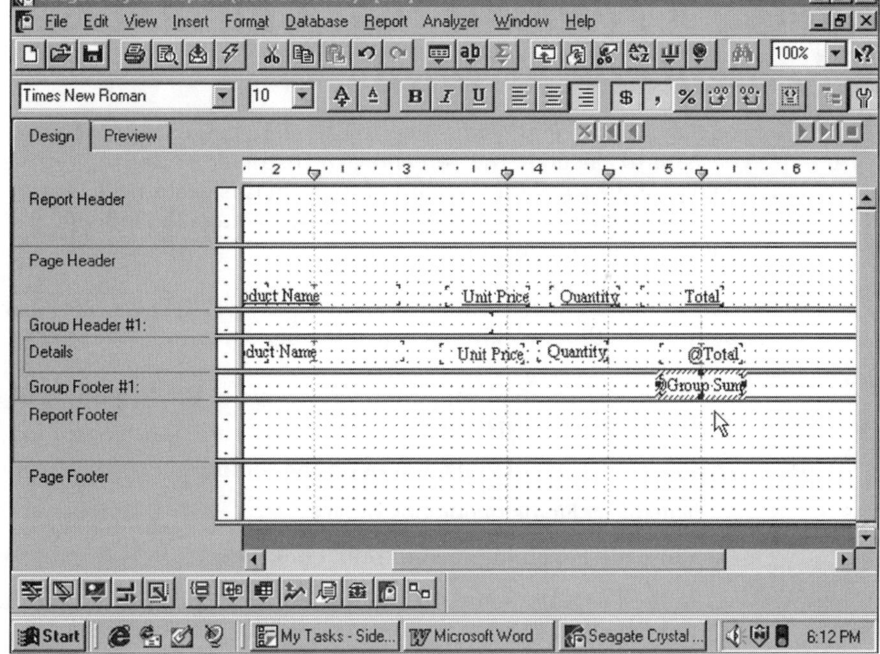

Figure 7-9: The Group Sum formula inserted in the Group Footer section of the report.

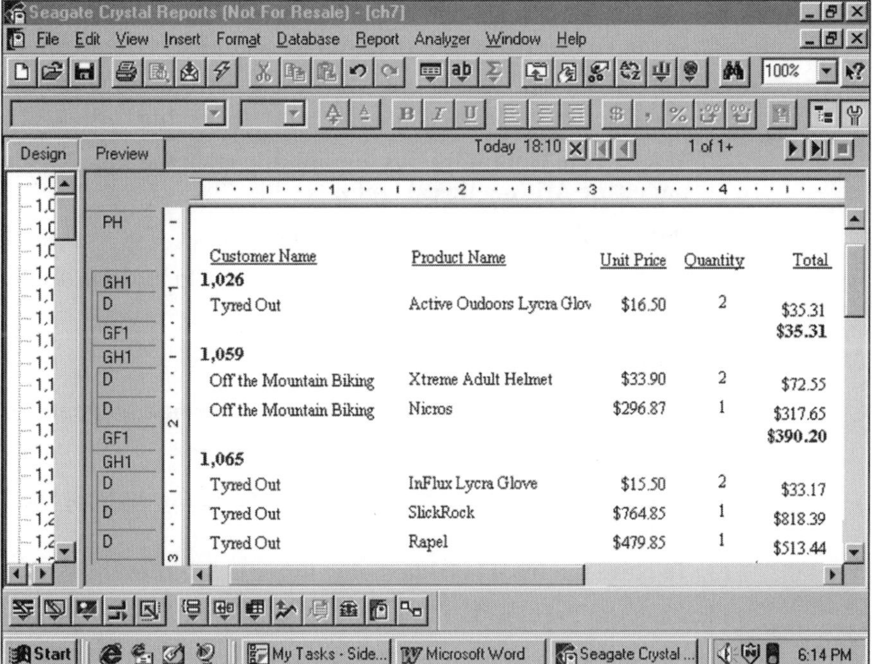

Figure 7-10: The Group Sum formula does its work!

Adding a Formula That Calculates a Percentage of Total

You may want to create formulas to calculate percentage of totals. Perhaps you want to calculate the percentage a customer's sales represents as a percentage of the sales for the entire report. In this example, I show you how to create a calculation to determine what percentage the individual record represents of the total for the order.

When you want to calculate percentages, Crystal Reports has a percentage operator (%) that quickly calculates the percentage.

1. **In the ch7 report I suggested you create at the beginning of the chapter, click the Design tab.**

2. **Click the Insert Fields button on the toolbar.**

   The Insert Fields dialog box opens.

3. **Click the Formula tab, and then click New.**
4. **In the Formula Name dialog box, enter a name for the formula, such as** Percent of Order.
5. **Click OK.**

   The Formula Editor dialog box opens.

6. **In the Fields list, scroll until you locate the** `@Total` **formula and double-click it.**

   The function is inserted into the Formula text box.

7. **Move to the Operators box and double-click the Percent Operator under the Arithmetic category.**
8. **Double-click** `@Group Sum` **in the Fields box.**

   The completed formula in formula text should look like this:

   ```
   {@Total} % {@Group Sum}
   ```

9. **Click Save and Close.**
10. **In the Insert fields dialog box, click the formula** `Percent of Order`.
11. **Click Insert.**
12. **Insert the formula in the Details section to the right of the Total formula.**
13. **To close the Insert Fields dialog box, click Close.**
14. **Click the Preview tab to see the results, as shown in Figure 7-11.**

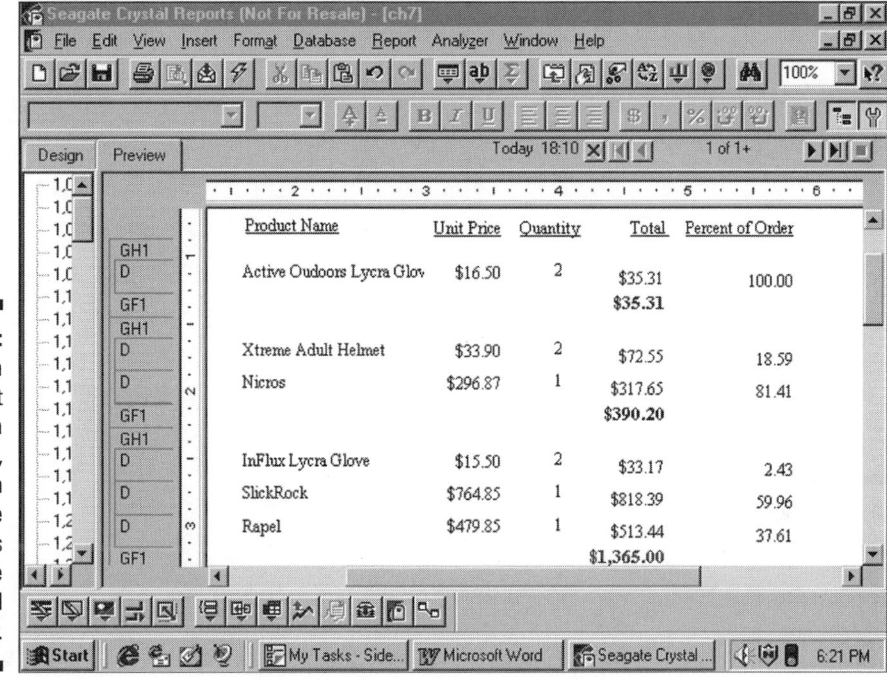

Figure 7-11: With a percent formula inserted, you can easily see each item's percentage of the total order.

Entering a Running Total

In previous versions of Crystal Reports, you had to be facile with the Formula Editor to create a formula that would add the total of the previous record with the current one and then display the total. Because the need for this formula was so widespread and resulted in too many product support calls, Version 7 has the formula built in — sort of. So, you do not have to do a great deal of fancy footwork to get this type of formula to work the way you want.

1. **Using the ch7 report, click the Insert Fields button on the toolbar.**
2. **Select the Running Total tab.**
3. **Click New. When you do, the Running Total Field dialog box appears, as shown in Figure 7-12.**
4. **Enter a name for the formula.**

   For this example, I used Rtotal.

   Okay, now the thinking cap goes on. I want a field that keeps a cumulative total of each of the values by store, including the sales tax. So, I want to use the value that has been derived by the Total formula.

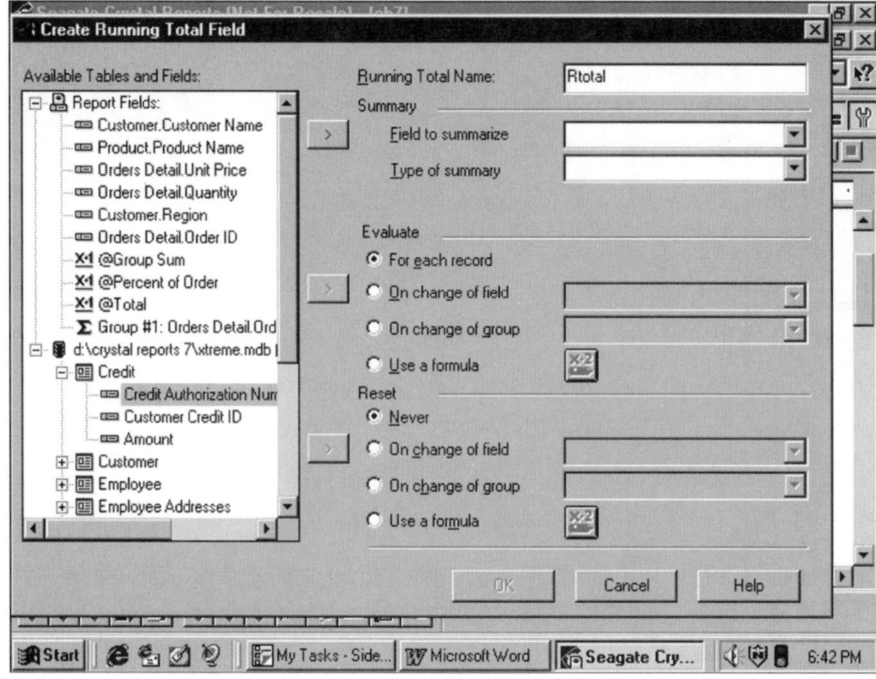

Figure 7-12: The Create Running Total Field dialog box.

5. **Click the @Total formula.**
6. **Click the right-pointing arrow that precedes the box labeled Field to Summarize.**

   The @Total field name is entered.
7. **In the Type of Summary box, click the pull-down arrow to see the wide range of operations that can be performed.**

   For this example, select `sum`.
8. **The next step is to determine at what interval the sum should be calculated. In this case, I want every record to be included in the running total throughout the report. So, click the radio button in front of For Each Record.**
9. **Finally, you can have total reset itself at different intervals.**

   For this example, I want the total to run without being reset. So the choice is Never. You can really get creative and use a formula to determine when the reset should occur, such as when the value in the running total is greater than a pre-determined amount. No need to get that out of hand here — leave it to the real geeks who think they really need it. Figure 7-13 shows the completed dialog box.
10. **Click OK, and then insert the formula.**

    Figure 7-14 shows the running total at the far right of the report.

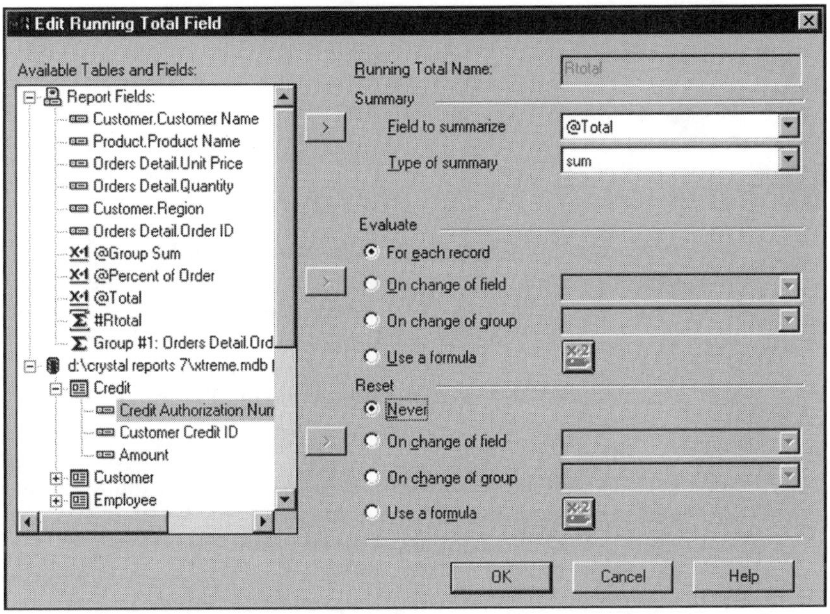

Figure 7-13: The Edit Running Total Field dialog box completed.

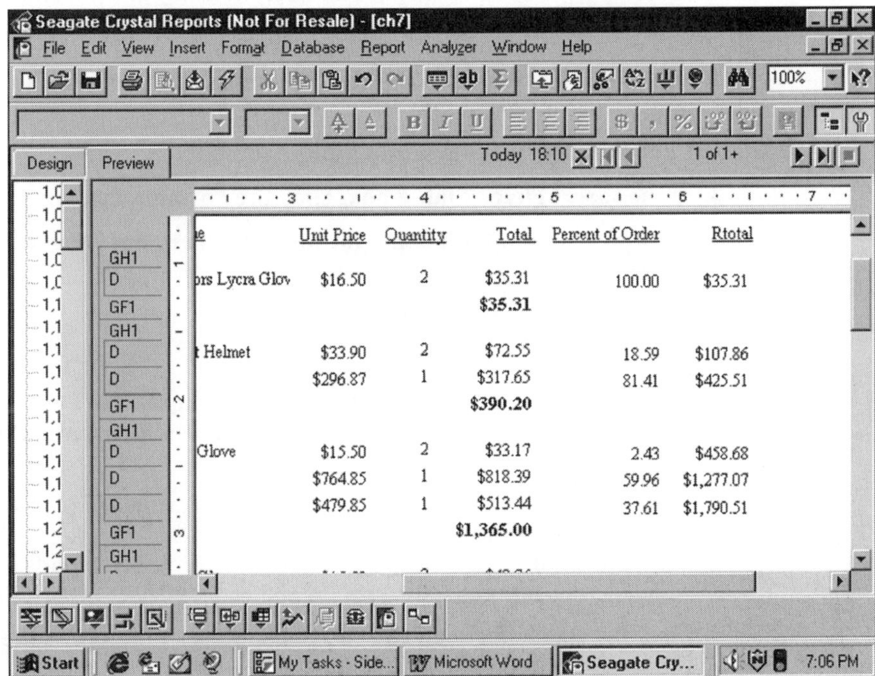

Figure 7-14: A running total added to the report.

The salient idea here is to determine what the running total needs to show. Crystal Reports has a variety of summing formulas built-in, but this type of formula adds a new dimension.

Working with Text Strings

Text strings are characters that can be numbers or letters, but the key is that they are considered to be text *even if* they look like numbers. Text strings can be manipulated to fit a variety of needs. Combining a first and last name in a report when the two pieces of information are in two distinct fields in a table is a common need. For the combination of multiple fields, Text Objects is the easy and powerful way to go (as I describe in Chapter 10).

Even though you use text objects to combine fields, there are certain situations where you need the additional power of the Formula Editor. Perhaps you need to change the case of a name in a field. A formula can be created that reverses the case from upper to lower or lower to upper.

In the xtreme database, one table is named Customer. In that table is a field named First Name. The task is to use a formula to change the case of the letters in the Last Name field. In this example, the entry in the Contact Last Name field is changed with a formula.

1. **Open the ch7 report I suggested you create throughout this chapter, and click the Design tab.**

2. **Click the Insert Fields button on the toolbar.**
3. **In the Insert Fields dialog box, click the Formula tab.**
4. **Click New and enter a name for the formula in the Formula Name dialog box.**

   I suggest **Change case** as the name.
5. **Click OK.**
6. **In the Formula Editor dialog box, click Strings in the Functions box. Scroll the list of string functions until you see Uppercase. Double-click Uppercase.**

   The Uppercase function is inserted into the Formula text box. The way that this function works is that it reads the characters in the field and converts them to uppercase, unless the character is already uppercase, which is then ignored.
7. **Click the space between the two parentheses that follow the Uppercase operator (if it is not already blinking there).**

8. **In the fields box, scroll until you locate the field named Customer.Contact Last Name.**
9. **Double-click the field name, and it is inserted into the formula.**

   The formula reads

   ```
   UpperCase ({Customer.Contact Last Name})
   ```

10. **Click Save and Close.**

    The Formula Editor dialog box closes.

11. **In the Insert Fields dialog box, click the formula name, Change Case. and then click Insert.**
12. **Insert the Change Case formula field in the Details section to the right of Rtotal.**

    Figure 7-15 shows the result of the Change Case formula in the Preview tab.

A text object is the quickest and simplest way to combine multiple fields. You can use text objects to combine a first and last name, but you can also use text objects to combine formula fields with other fields or text, as I describe in Chapter 10.

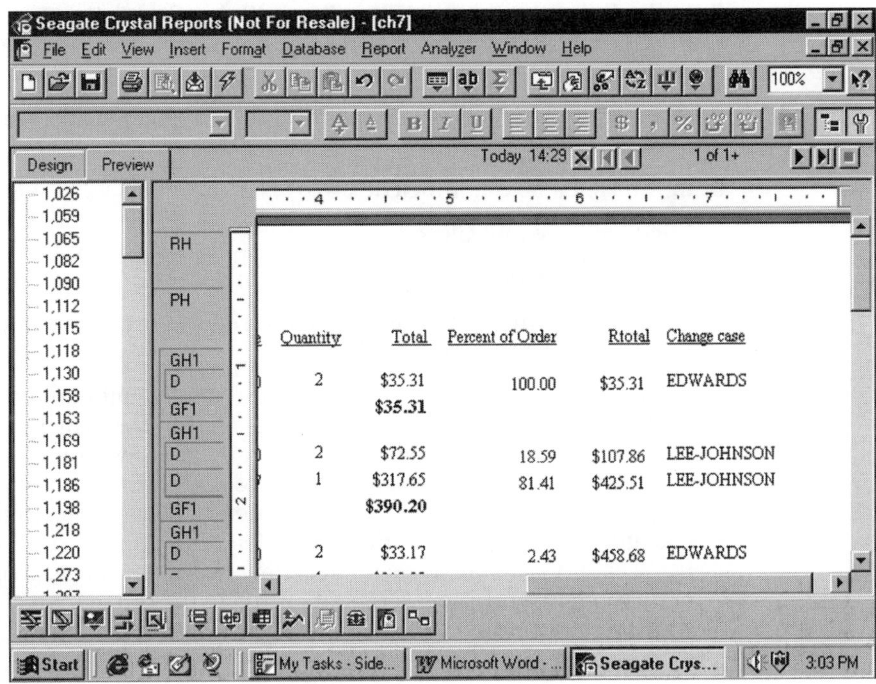

Figure 7-15: The Last Name in all uppercase letters.

Changing Numbers to Words

You may have a report that has numbers in a field that you would prefer to display as words. The most common use of this formula is for check writing. In most checks, both the numbers and the words are included to indicate the amount of the check.

In the ch7 database report, the Total/Tax field serves as the basis for this example of changing numbers to words:

1. **Using the ch7 report, click the Design tab.**

2. **Click the Insert Fields button on the toolbar.**
3. **In the dialog box that opens, click the Formula tab.**
4. **Click New.**
5. **In the Formula Name dialog box, enter a name for the formula.**

   I suggest you use **Words.**
6. **Click OK.**

   The Formula Editor dialog box opens.
7. **In the Functions list, scroll the list until you find `ToWords(x)`. (You find it under the second category of functions — Strings.) Double-click it.**

   The insertion point is inside the parentheses; you are now ready for the next step.
8. **In the Fields box, double-click `@Total`.**
9. **Click the Save and Close button.**
10. **In the Insert Fields dialog box, click `Words`.**
11. **Insert it into the Details section to the right of the Uppercase formula field, as shown in Figure 7-16.**

    You may notice at this point that you are running out of room across your report. You could move and resize fields to try to make enough room for the Words formula. But if you are part way through a report and realize you will need to have more room to work across, you can change the page layout. From the File menu, Select Printer Setup. In this dialog box you can change the page orientation from Portrait to Landscape. Crystal Reports immediately resizes the page, giving you more room to work. Be aware that changing the orientation changes the way the report prints, too.
12. **Click the Preview tab.**

    The report matches Figure 7-17.

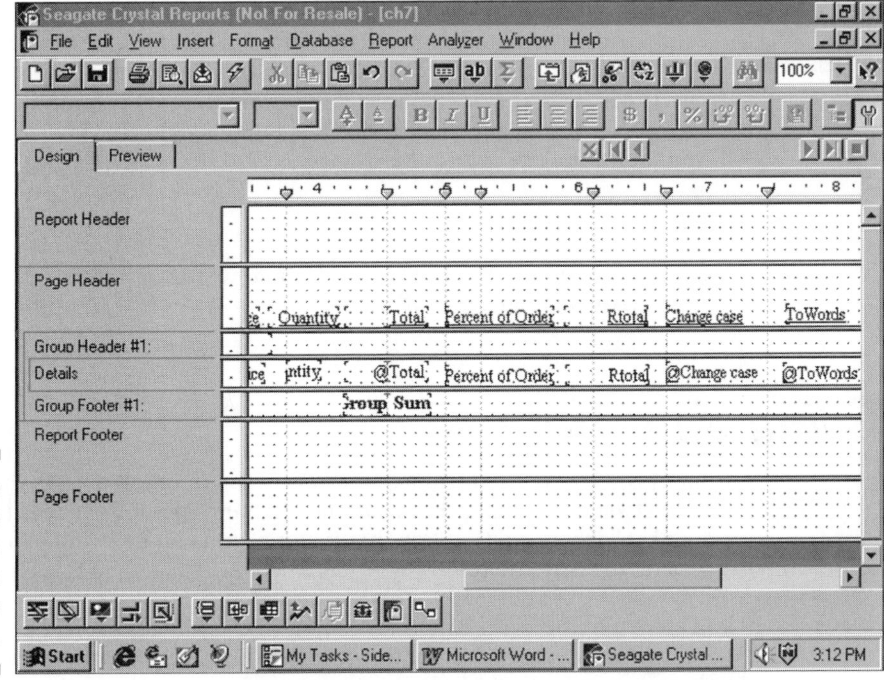

Figure 7-16: The To Words formula inserted into the report.

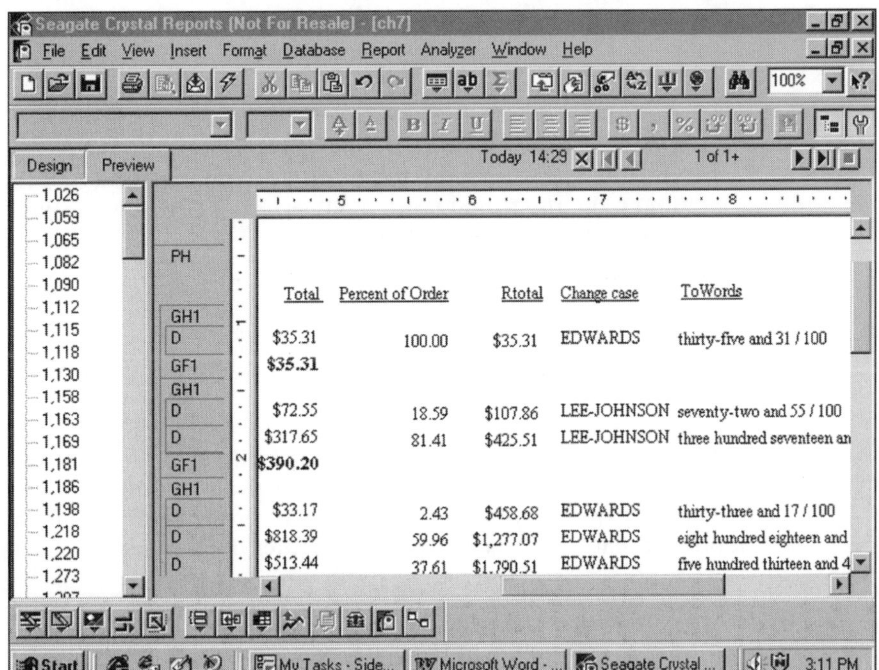

Figure 7-17: Words and numbers written out as words in the report.

You may have noticed that when you created the Words formula it wrote out the Total formula to two decimal places. If you would prefer to control how many decimal places are displayed, you can use the second ToWords option (ToWords, x,#places). For example, if you wanted to convert the Total formula to words but display it with zero decimal places, you would use the following formula:

```
ToWords(({@Total}),0)
```

Crystal Reports converts the Total formula to words and also round and display to zero decimal places.

Going on a Date

Another popular type of formula determines the number of days that have passed between two dates. For example, if your company records the date a product is ordered and the date that it ships, you can determine how long processing the order takes.

If you have a report with date information of this sort, you can use it to create the formula by inserting the date fields into a report or use the ch7 database example report from this chapter. The steps that follow begin by editing the report that has been used to this point in the chapter. You will delete a few fields to give you a little more room to work.

To delete fields and/or field names:

1. **Click the Design tab.**
2. **Click the Quantity field, hold down the Control key, and then click the Total field, the Rtotal field, the Percent of Order field, the Uppercase field, and the ToWords field.**

   Remember to click the column headers, too.
3. **Press the Delete key.**

   Both fields and column headers are deleted from the report.

In this example, you subtract the Order Date from the Shipment Date to determine the number of days it took to place the order. You can simply place the formula that calculates the number of days on the report, but you may want to place the Order.Ship Date and Order.Order Date field on the report so that you can check to see whether the formula is working correctly.

1. **Click the Insert Fields button on the toolbar.**

   The Insert Fields dialog box opens.

2. **Scroll the list until you see the table** `Orders`.
3. **Double-click** `Orders.Order Date`.
4. **Move the pointer to the Details section of the report and click to insert the field to the right of the other fields.**
5. **Repeat Steps 3 through 4 with the field Orders.Ship Date.**
6. **Both fields appear with the date and time. Remove the time from both fields.**
7. **Click the Order Date field, press the Control, key and click the Ship Date field.**
8. **Right-click and select Format Objects from the menu.**

   The Format Editor dialog box appears as shown in Figure 7-18.

9. **Click the Date/Time tab and open the pull-down to select Date.**
10. **Click OK to close the dialog box.**
11. **Click the Formula tab in the Insert Fields dialog box.**
12. **Click New.**

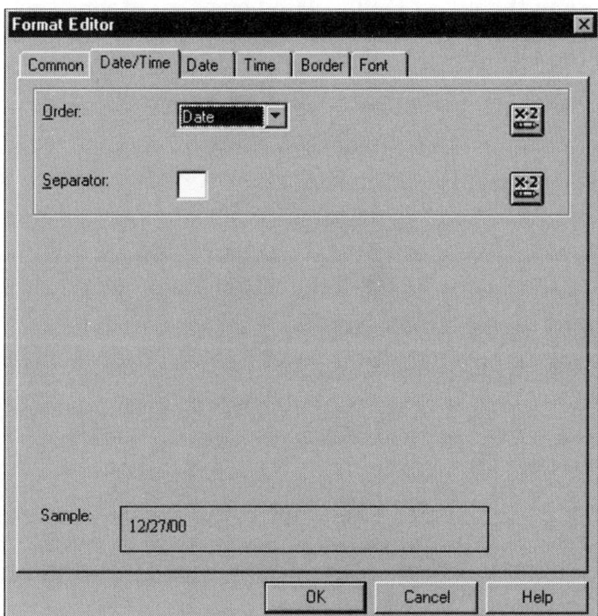

Figure 7-18: The Format Editor dialog box.

13. **When the Formula Name dialog box appears asking for a name, type:** Processing Days.
14. **Click OK.**

    The Formula Editor dialog box appears.
15. **In the Fields list, locate** `Orders.Ship Date` **and double-click it.**

    The field name is inserted into the Formula text box.
16. **Because the formula is a subtraction, in the Operators field, double-click the Subtract operator** `Subtract (x-y)`.
17. **In the Fields box, find** `Orders.Order Date` **and double-click it.**

    The text in the formula text should be:

    `{Orders.Ship Date} - {Orders.Order Date}`
18. **Click the Save and Close button.**

    The Formula Editor dialog box closes.
19. **From the Insert Fields dialog box, click the formula name** `Processing Days`.
20. **Click Insert.**
21. **Click in the Details section to insert the field placeholder of the report to the right of the date fields.**
22. **Click Close in the Insert Fields dialog box.**
23. **Click the Preview tab.**

    The results appear, as shown in Figure 7-19. You can right-click the Processing Days field to format the results to 0 (zero) decimal places. Choose the Format Field option from the shortcut menu and select the number of decimal places you want displayed.

Undoing

Have you ever hit a button and then regretted it? Perhaps you delete a field you actually want to keep on your report. Crystal Reports has an Undo feature that you should remember in just such instances. If you ever want to back up one step, use the Edit⇨Undo option.

Edit Undo will also let you undo multiple steps. So if you ever get into a jam, keep hitting Undo until you get back to where you want to be.

There are some steps that cannot be undone. When you see the confirm command, Crystal Reports is just reminding you to tread carefully — what you're about to do cannot be undone. If you don't want to proceed, simply click the No button.

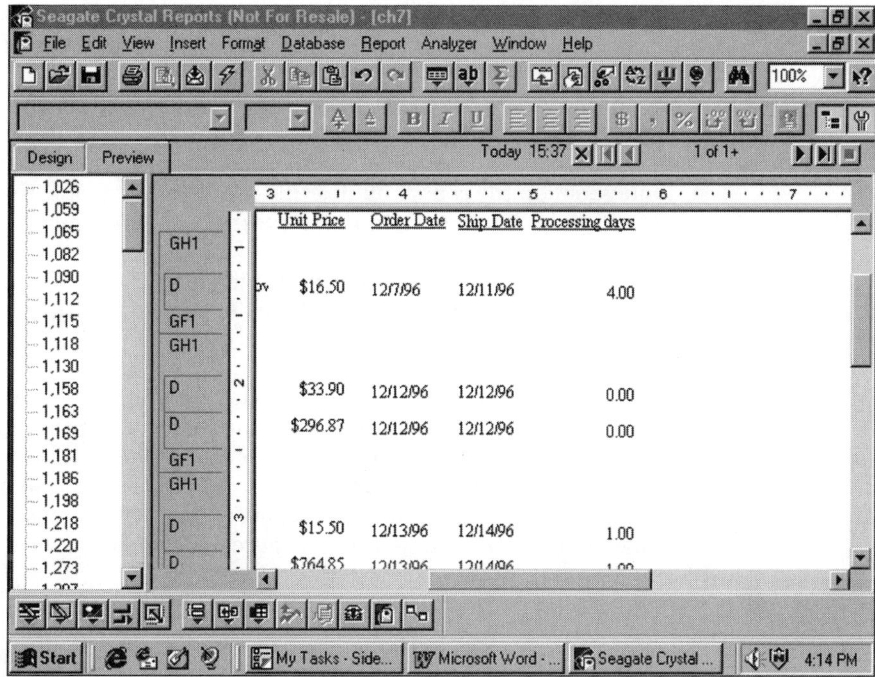

Figure 7-19: Two date fields and the results of subtracting the two.

When you want to change the number of decimal places for a number field, you can use the Increase or Decrease Decimals button from the format bar (see the Cheat Sheet). In this case, simply click the Decrease Decimals button twice with the Processing Days formula selected to remove two decimal places.

Using If-Then-Else Formulas

An *if-then-else formula* is a formula that you use to examine a value and then, depending on the value, execute one or more alternatives. A simple example is the case of someone owing your company money. The formula can look at the date and then either print *30 Days Past Due* or *60 Days Past Due,* depending on how long it has been since the last payment. The current date is the condition that determines the next action.

In Crystal Reports, both actions that may be taken after looking at the condition must be the same *type* of action. In other words, if the result is to print a text string (30 Days Past Due), the other option (60 Days Past Due) must be a text string also.

For those of you with a programming background, you do not have to include an else statement for these formulas to work. If the condition fails the if-then test, 0 is returned for numerics and ""(a blank text string) for text.

In this example, the ch7 report is used with several fields that have been added earlier. If you are using your own database, all you need is a report that has a numeric field. Adjust the conditional values to fit your data.

In order for you to work this example, you want to modify your report a bit.

Make some room on the report by deleting the following fields: the Order Date field, the Ship Date field, and the Processing Days formula.

Then add back the Orders Detail.Quantity Field and the Total formula into the Details section. Your report should look similar to Figure 7-20 before continuing.

Now begin the formula creation process. To become familiar with an if-then-else formula, you are going to create a formula that will display "Excellent" for any record that has a Total amount greater than 750. The formula looks at the value in the record and then prints the appropriate response based on that value. The formula is simple: If the value is less than or equal to a specific number, nothing is printed, but if it is greater than a specified value, the word Excellent is printed.

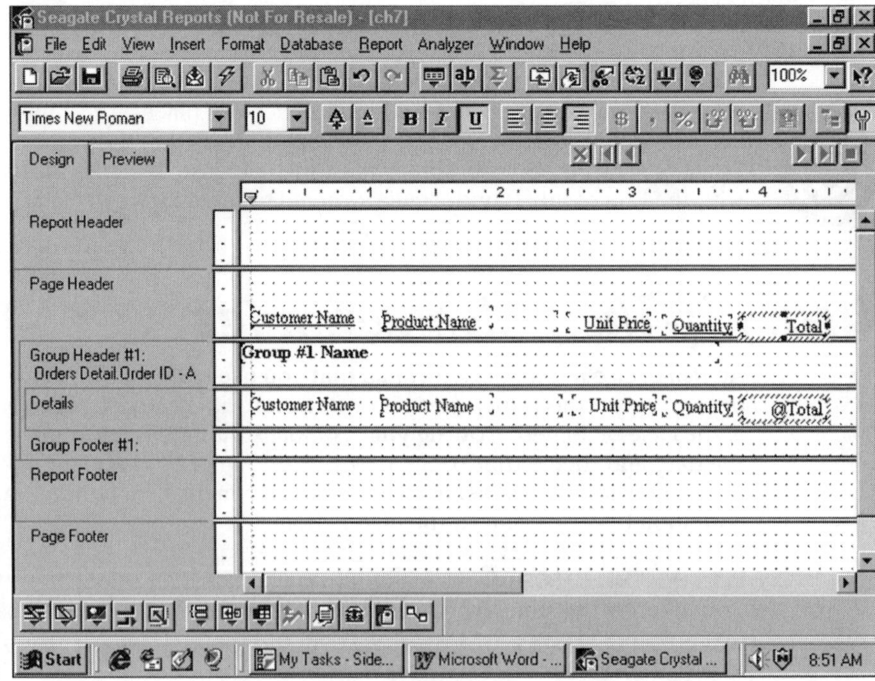

Figure 7-20: Does your report look like this?

1. **Click the Formula tab of the Insert Fields dialog box. If it is not open, click the Insert Fields button.**
2. **Click New.**
3. **In the Formula Name dialog box that appears, type:** Great Sales.
4. **To continue, click OK.**

   The Formula Editor dialog box opens.
5. **Scroll the Operators list until you see the operator that reads** `If x then y else z`**. (You will find it towards the bottom of the operator box under a category called Others.) Double-click the operator.**

   The `if then else` is inserted into the formula text. You will use this to start building a formula. Notice the cursor is positioned between `if` and `then`: This is where you normally start building your formula.
6. **In the Fields list, scroll the list to locate** `@Total`**. Double-click it.**

   The formula name is inserted. It will be inserted at the cursor between `if` and `then`.

   Your formula should appear as:

   ```
   if {@Total} then else
   ```
7. **Locate the greater than operator > in the Operators list by scrolling the list; it reads** `Greater than (x>y)`**. Double-click it.**

   It is under the heading Comparisons.

   The operator is inserted into the formula.
8. **The next step is to add the test,** `Is total greater than 750?`.

   Your formula should now appear as:

   ```
   if {@Total} > 750 then else
   ```

   Okay, 750 is now the condition (the `if`) in this formula. So if the result in the Total field is greater than 750 — then what? Well, you have to add the rest of the formula, that's what.
9. **Position the insertion point between the words** `then` **and** `else`.
10. **Type:** "Excellent".

    You must have quotation marks on either side of the word. With this part of the formula inserted, Crystal Reports prints the word *Excellent* whenever the value in Total/Tax is greater than 750.

    Note: A literal is the portion of a formula that is printed in the report exactly as you type it, depending on the result of the formula.

11. **Delete the word** `else` **by double-clicking on it and pressing the Delete key.**

    You need to do this because only one literal is being printed.

    At this point, the condition is either met or not, and if it is not, then a blank text string (it looks just like nothing) prints in the report. The finished formula looks like this:

    ```
    if {@Total} > 750 then "Excellent"
    ```

12. **Click Save and Close.**

    The Formula Editor dialog box closes.

13. **In the Insert Fields dialog box, click** `Great Sales`**.**

14. **Click Insert.**

15. **Position the pointer in the Details section of the report to the right of the Total field, and click to insert the field.**

16. **Click the Preview tab.**

    This is the big moment. If it works for you, you have passed into the higher ranks of Crystal Report users. Hopefully your report looks like the one in Figure 7-21.

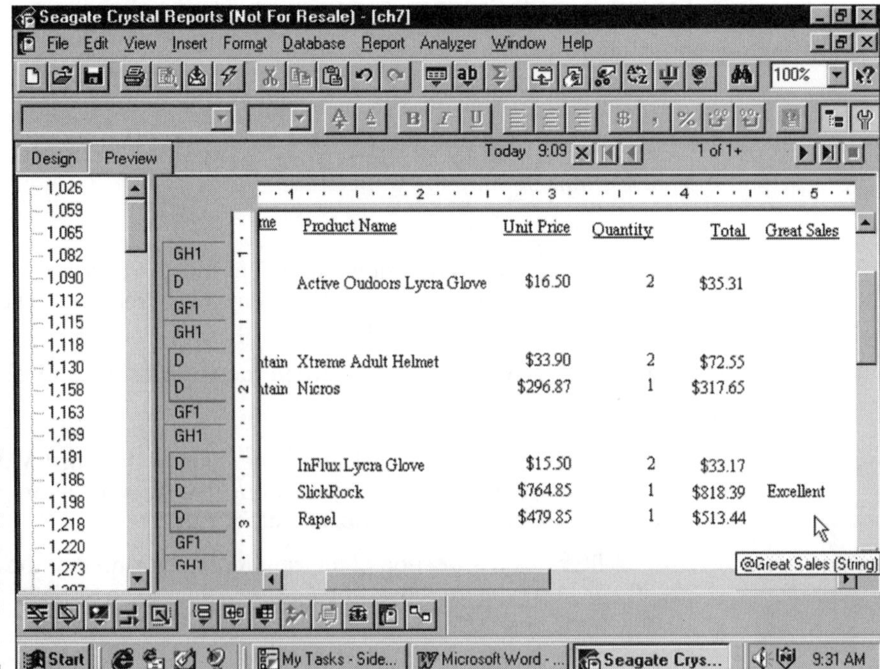

Figure 7-21: An excellent report with a complex if-then-else formula.

Figure 7-21 reveals the work of this formula in that only the records with sales in excess of $750 have any text printed. Although this formula works, it would be better if every record had a notation of some sort. The section "Modifying an if-then-else formula" next in this chapter helps you modify the formula to include several more text options.

In this example, we used an `if then` formula. It told the program what to do if the Total was over 750 and did nothing if the total was not over 750.

But how would you create a formula if you want to display "Excellent" when sales are greater than 750 and "Poor" in all other situations? You would use the following formula:

```
if {@Total} > 750 then "Excellent" else "Poor"
```

The `else "Poor"` tells Crystal to display "Poor" if sales are less than or equal to 750.

Modifying an if-then-else formula

Nothing is particularly tricky about modifying this kind of formula, but it may require a little careful formula building. In the preceding example above, you simply printed "Excellent" if the Total was over 750. This time, you'll get a little more complicated. You still want to display "Excellent" for amounts over 750. But when the amount is over 500, you want to display "Good" and in all other situations — "Stinko".

1. **Click the Design tab.**
2.  **If the Insert Fields dialog box is not already open, click the Insert Fields button on the toolbar.**
3. **In the Insert Fields dialog box, click the Formula tab.**
4. **Click** `Great Sales`.
5. **Click Edit.**
6. **Position the insertion point after** `Excellent`.

   Crystal Reports allows you to type the words needed to make the formula work; you are not required to select them from the Operators list.
7. **Type:** else if.
8. **Enter the formula name @Total by double-clicking it.**
9. **Type the greater than sign:** >.
10. **Type:** 500.
11. **Type:** then.
12. **Type:** "Good".

13. **Type:** else.
14. **Type:** "Stinko".

    The completed three-condition formula text should look like this:

    ```
    if {@Total} > 750 then "Excellent" else if {@Total} > 500
    then "Good" else "Stinko"
    ```

Notice that I've broken the formula over three lines. Crystal does not care where you insert line breaks. Simply place them where it makes sense to you.

To get the three different comments, I used an *if-then-else-if* formula. The first line asks Crystal Reports to check if sales were greater than 750 and if they are to display "Excellent". The next line then tells Crystal Reports when sales were not greater than 750 to continue to check to see if sales were greater than 500 and when they are to display "Good". Think of the else "Stinko" as just saying: If it's not greater than 750 or greater than 500, then display "Stinko".

15. **Click Save and Close.**
16. **Click the Preview tab to see the results in the report, as shown in Figure 7-22.**

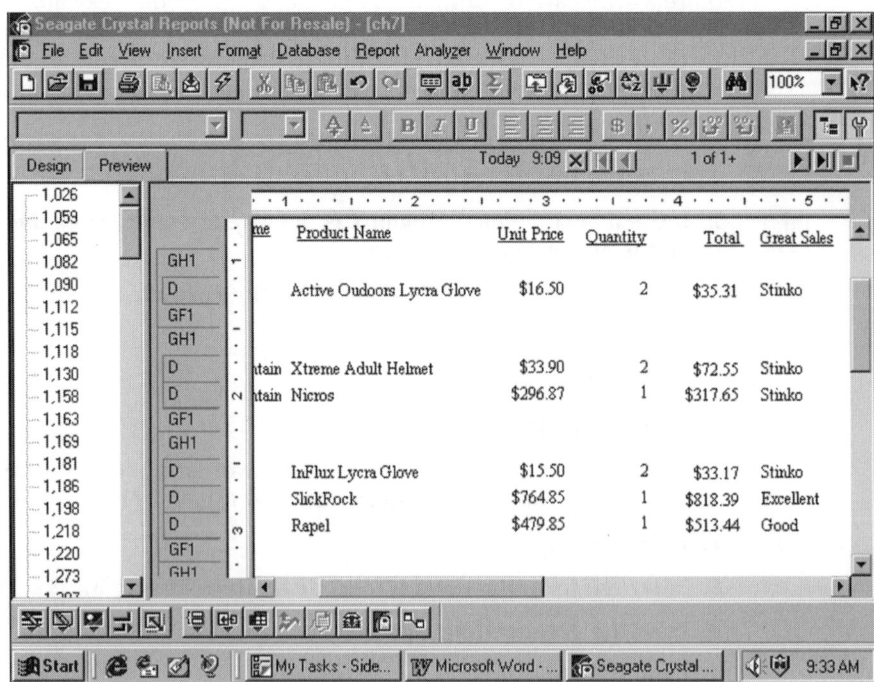

Figure 7-22: A preview of a report and if-then-else-if formula.

Nested if-then-else formulas

You just looked at two variations of working with fairly simple *if-then-else* formulas. If you need to, you can get quite complicated with these types of formulas. You can create very powerful, multi-condition formulas. This procedure is known as *nesting formulas.* A nested if-then-else formula can evaluate two conditions and then print a text string (as in the previous example) or whatever you designate.

This formula looks at the country and the sales amount to determine a discount percentage.

```
if Country = USA then
if Sales > 1000000 then .25
else .20 else if Sales > 1000000 then .15 else .10
```

Now try to work your way through what this formula is showing. First of all, it checks to see which country the record deals with. If it is the USA, it continues to check the amount of that American sale. If the American sale is greater than 1 million, the formula sets the discount rate at 25 percent. If the American sale is not greater than 1 million, the formula sets the discount rate to 20 percent. However, if the country is *not* USA, the formula skips the test completely. It assumes this is a foreign sale. The formula then checks the foreign sale to see if it is greater than 1 million. If it is, the discount rate gets set to 15 percent. Otherwise, it gets set to 10 percent.

Understanding Boolean Formulas

A Boolean formula is not anything esoteric. (Ahh ha! I have not slipped one of these exotic words in lately, have I?! *Esoteric* means knowledge for the highly intelligent or for the privileged.) It is simply a formula that returns one of two possible answers: True or False.

You may use a Boolean formula if you have a field that has numbers in it and you want the formula to print whether or not the numbers meet a condition. Usually, you use Boolean formulas as a basis for another action in Crystal Reports, such as record selection, as I describe in Chapter 4, or conditional formatting, as I describe in Chapter 8.

To get familiar with Boolean formulas, just create a formula that displays True if Total is greater than 500 and False when not. To create a Boolean formula:

1. **In the Design tab, open the Insert Fields dialog box by clicking the Insert Fields button on the toolbar.**

2. **Click the Formula tab.**
3. **Click New, and type a formula name in the Formula Name dialog box.**

   I suggest you use **Boolean.**
4. **Click OK.**

   The Formula Editor dialog box opens.
5. **In the Fields list, double-click** `Total`.

   The formula name is inserted into the Formula text box.
6. **Type a greater than sign:** >.
7. **Type** 500.

   The completed formula reads: `{@Total}> 500.`
8. **Click Save and Close.**
9. **From the Insert Fields dialog box, click the formula name** `Boolean`.
10. **Click Insert.**
11. **Position the pointer to the right of the existing fields in the Details section and click to insert the formula.**

    The result appears, as shown in Figure 7-23. Values greater than $500 are True, and values smaller than $500 are False.

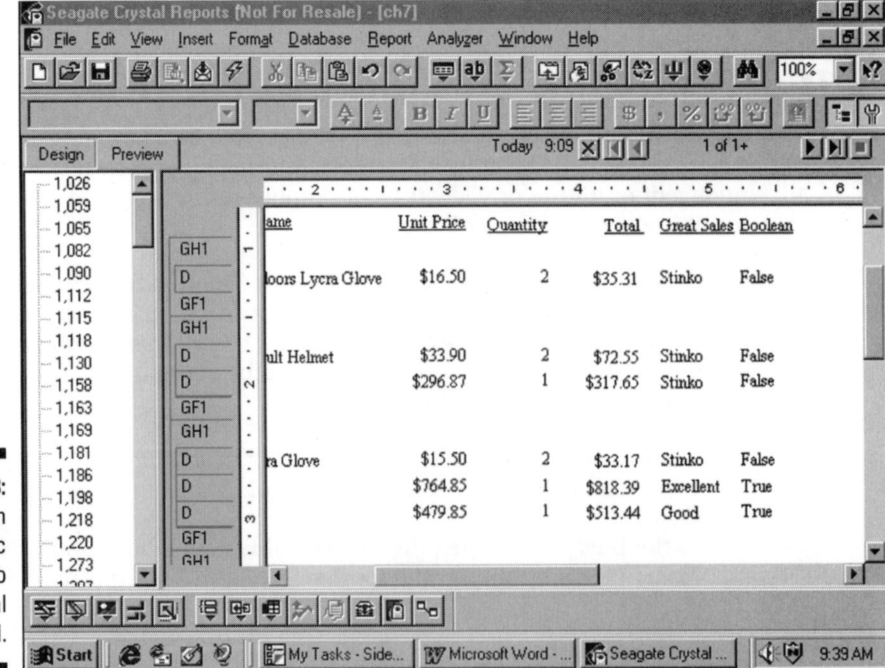

Figure 7-23: Boolean logic applied to the Total field.

Creating a Record Selection Formula

When you select a database and its table to be part of a report, you may want the entire set of records to be included in the report. Many times you will not, and Crystal Reports provides a way to select specific records for the report, as I describe in Chapter 4. Formulas can be incorporated into the selection process to add precision to the selection process. If you are creating a report, you may want to add numeric ranges to capture records in certain sales volumes, transactions occurring in specific date ranges, or records that pertain to a certain area of the country. The simple selection criteria are handled easily via the Select Expert. But, there will come a time when you need more advanced selections to create the report. You can simulate the following example with any database you have that includes state as a field. Otherwise, follow the steps in this example to understand how to create a formula for record selection.

In the example report I use in this chapter, the records were selected by using the Region field and CA as the match. But suppose that the records are entered into the underlying database in an inconsistent manner. Some records are entered with the region as *CA* and some with the region as *ca.* In Crystal Reports, record selection is dependent on the case sensitivity in the source database and must be precise. So any records that have *ca* in them when you indicate that you want records with *CA,* are not included in a report. You can try this potential pitfall yourself with the ch7 report, using Region as the selection field, by replacing `CA` with `ca` in the Select Record dialog box.

To overcome this obstacle and to make certain that all records are included in the selection, uppercase or not, you can create a Record Selection formula using Boolean logic.

Use the Select Expert as much as possible to get Crystal Reports to create your record selection easily. In the Select Expert, you simply use the drop-down boxes to build a record selection criteria. Crystal Reports, behind the scenes, creates a Boolean formula given what you have entered. It compares the Boolean formula against each record in the report, and when it returns True, the record will be included. If it returns False, the record will not be included in your report.

Keep this in mind when modifying the Record Selection formula. You need to ensure you are creating a Boolean formula that returns True when you want to include the record in the report. To show you how this works, assume that the Region field can be stored as ca, CA, Ca or cA. You want to include all occurrences of ca in the report, regardless of what case they are in. To do this, we convert the text in the Region field to uppercase and then search for an uppercase CA.

1. **Click the Select Expert button.**

   The Select Expert dialog box appears. In this example ch7 report, the previous selection criteria, *Region equal to CA and Quantity greater than 0,* is still in effect. If you are using your own database, the Choose Field dialog box opens first. Choose state as the field upon which to make the selection (assuming that you have state as a field in your database); the Select Expert dialog box then appears. Click the down arrow in the second box from the left, and select the *equal to* setting. Next, a third box opens to the right, and in that box enter the state from which you want records. At this point, you can follow the remaining steps.

2. **Click Show Formula.**

   The underlying formula for record selection appears at the bottom of the dialog box, as shown in Figure 7-24.

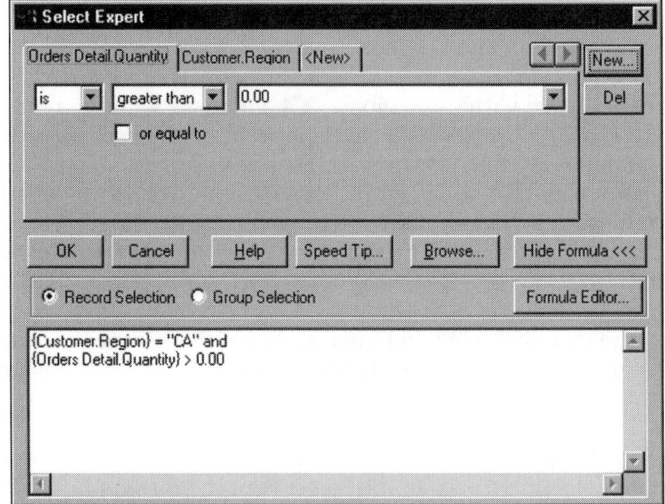

Figure 7-24: The Select Expert dialog box with the formula exposed.

   Remember, you added Quantity greater than 0 to exclude records with only partial data.

3. **Click Formula Editor.**

   The Formula Editor dialog box opens.

4. **Place your cursor before the {Customer.Region} field.**

   This is where you want to insert the UpperCase function.

5. **In the Functions list, double-click** `UpperCase ()`**, which is listed under the String heading.**

Headings are listed within the Functions list that designate what kind of function follows. This feature makes finding the function easier for you.

Crystal Reports inserts the formula, but the close parenthesis (the one on the right) is not enclosing the Customer.Region portion of the formula.

6. **Delete the close parenthesis at its current location, and type it after** `Customer.Region` **and before the =.**

7. **Click Save and Close.**

   The completed formula now appears in the Select Expert dialog box. Your formula should look like this:

```
UpperCase ({Customer.Region}) = "CA" and
{Orders Detail.Quantity} > 0.00
```

8. **Click OK to close the Select Expert dialog box.**

To see the changes, if any, click the Preview tab. After you do, Crystal Reports asks if you want to use saved or refreshed data. Currently the saved records are only records that have CA as region, so click Refresh Data. Crystal Reports seeks out the database tables and finds any records that meet the new criteria.

See Chapter 4 for a full description of Saved versus Refresh data.

In this chapter, you have scratched the surface of what Crystal Reports can do with formulas. A complete listing of every function and operator is found in the Seagate Crystal Reports User's Guide.

If you are trying to create a report from a database such as ACT!, you may encounter a problem when you try to access a field which in ACT! is supposed to be a currency or number field. To use Crystal Reports properly with ACT! you need to have Version 3.08 or greater of ACT! and have updated registry files from Seagate Software. You can also get them from my website, WWW.HOWTOSOFTWARE.COM.

If you're not sure if your field is coming into Crystal Reports as a currency or number, just choose Browse Field Data — on that field. The Browse dialog box will show you what Crystal Reports believes it is seeing for a datatype.

More Formulas to Try

My goal in this chapter is to give you an idea of the possibilities, not exhaust them — an impossible feat. If you have read the whole chapter, you now have an idea about how to create your own formulas — and frankly, only the surface has been scratched as to the number and types of formulas that can be created.

Seagate provides a bunch of tested formulas that fit most situations. The formulas are indexed and then explained in a step-by-step way. Follow these steps to find out where this treasure trove is hiding.

1. **Click the Help menu and choose the Search option.**

   The Help Topics dialog box opens.

2. **Click the Index tab.**

   The index of topics appears, as shown in Figure 7-25.

3. **Type the topic on which you want to see more information.**

   In this example, type **formulas**.

4. **The topic you want is listed as Formulas in Action Index.**

5. **Click the Formulas in Action Index, and then click the Display button.**

   Figure 7-26 shows the result.

There are 17 formulas for you to look at and adapt to your particular need. Take a look at the detail of one formula so that you can see how it can work for you.

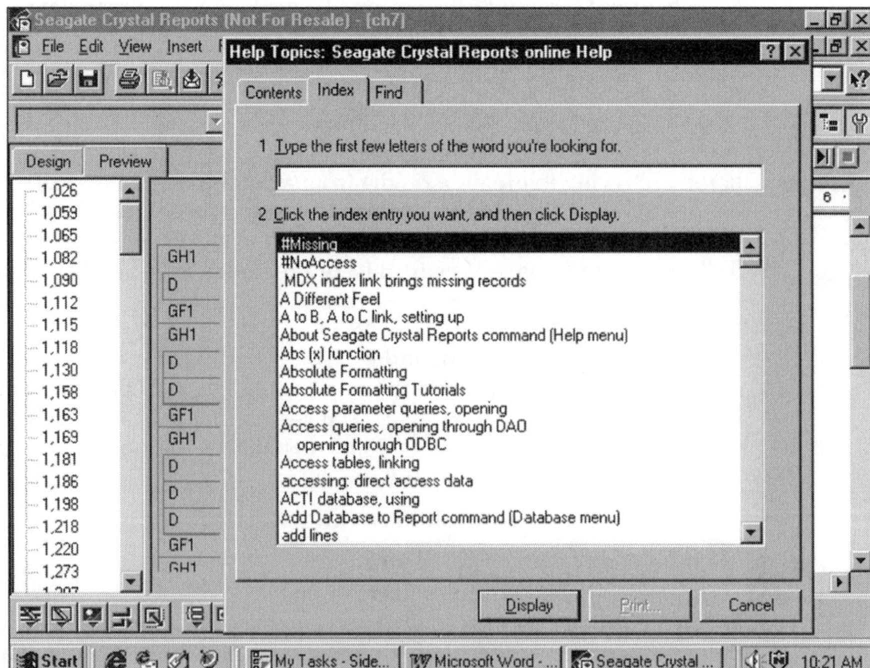

Figure 7-25: The Help Topics, Index tab.

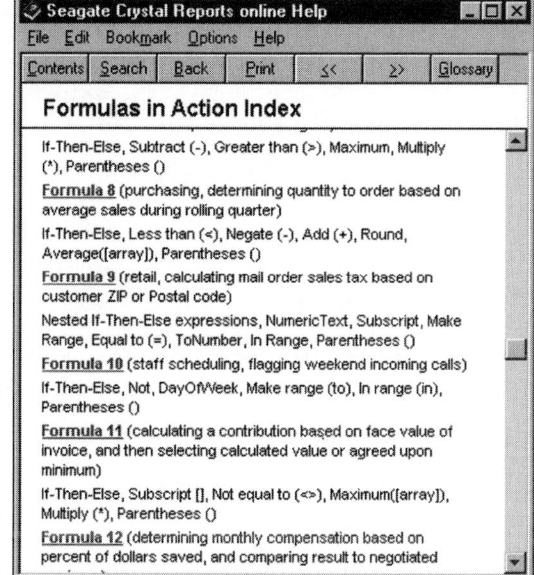

Figure 7-26: The Formulas in Action Index page.

1. **Scroll through the list of formulas until you see Formula 9.**
2. **Click the Formula 9 hyperlink.**

   The link is identified by the underline and the fact that when you move the mouse pointer to the words Formula 9, the pointer changes to a hand.

   Figure 7-27 shows the detailed look at the formula.

I suggest that when you find a formula that is close to what you need, print the topic, which makes it easier to follow. In addition, you can cut and paste the sample formula syntax into the Formula Editor directly from the Help window.

1. **Use the Help, Search, and Formulas in Action index to locate the formula you want to use.**
2. **Click and drag to select the formula text.**
3. **Right-click the mouse and select the Copy command.**
4. **Open the Formula Editor by selecting the Insert button on the Toolbar.**
5. **From the dialog box, select Formula.**

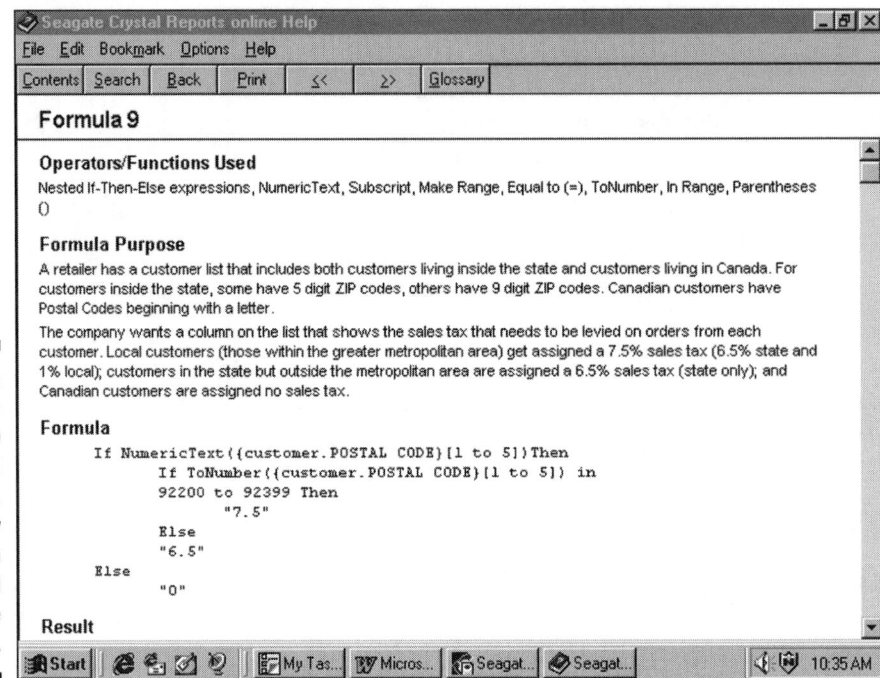

Figure 7-27: The Formula 9 detailed explanation. The window has been enlarged to the maximum.

6. **Click New and enter a name for the formula.**

   The Formula Editor dialog box opens with the insertion point in the Formula Editor box.

7. **Right-click and choose Paste from the menu.**

   The sample formula syntax is inserted for you.

At this point, you can add the numbers, functions, or whatever you need to adapt the formula to fit your report, as shown in Figure 7-28.

More Help on Formulas

If the example formulas include operators and/or functions that look like Greek, Crystal Reports has help for that problem. The Help section includes a reference section that describes and explains the intricacies of using the individual components.

To get a detailed explanation on a particular operator or function:

1. **Open the Help menu and choose Seagate Crystal Reports Help.**
2. **From the next window, select the Reference hypertext link.**

3. Select either the Functions index or Operators index.

Figure 7-29 shows the opening page of the Functions Index page.

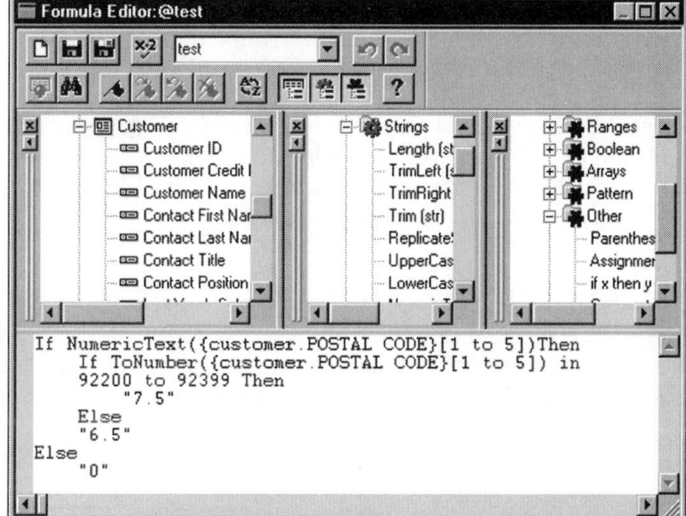

Figure 7-28: The Formula Editor dialog box with a sample formula from the Help pasted into it.

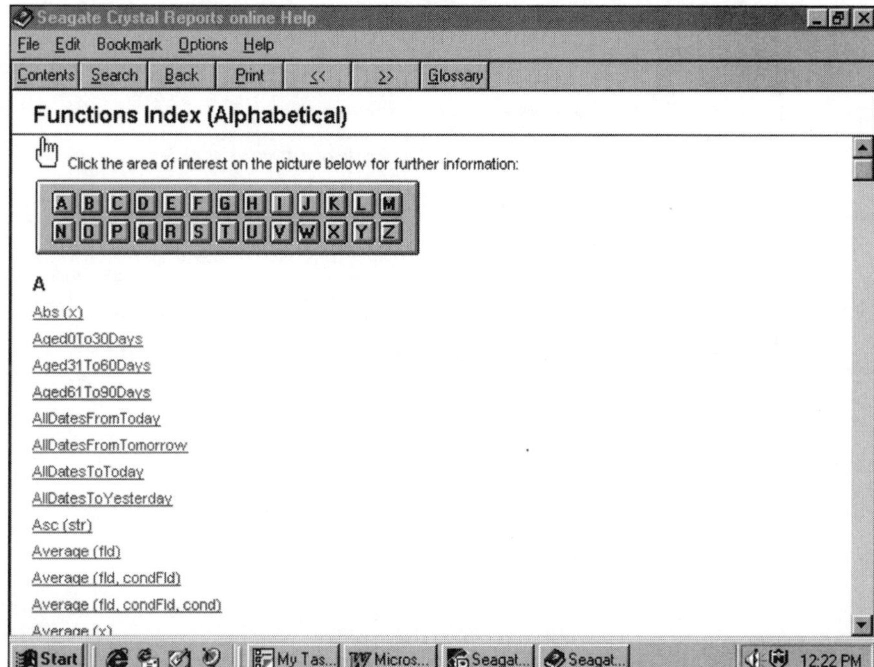

Figure 7-29: The Functions Index page.

4. **At the top of this page is an alphabet. Click the letter that is the first in the name of the function you want — if you know it. If not, you can scroll the list to see the names of the individual functions/operators.**
5. **Locate the function you think you want to use, and click the name.**

   A detailed explanation of the use and implementation of the function is displayed. Figure 7-30 shows such an example.

If all else fails, you can send an e-mail to the technical support folks at Seagate Software, and they will answer back. Open the Help menu and select Seagate Software on the Web. From the submenu, select Online Support. Your Web browser will crank up and dial directly to the Seagate Software Web site.

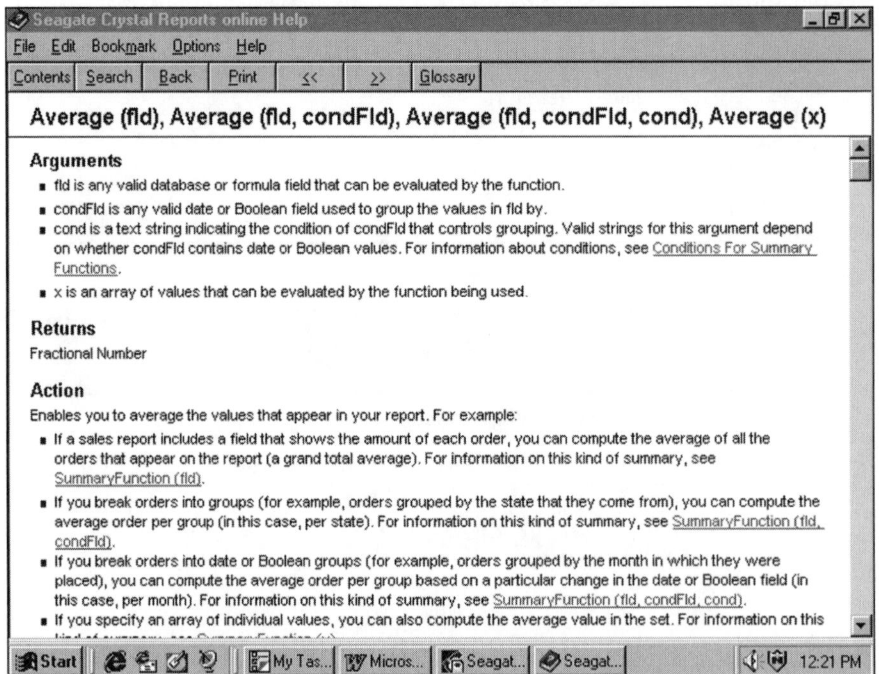

Figure 7-30: A function explained in detail.

Chapter 8

Using Conditional Formatting

In This Chapter

- Absolute versus conditional formatting
- Setting a conditional format for fields and objects

The idea of *conditional formatting* is that objects such as numbers are displayed a certain way if the number is of certain value. So, you can create formulas that determine the format of your report depending on the data within the report. The same idea applies to sections of a report. You will probably get much more out of this chapter if you read Chapter 7 on formulas first.

Absolute versus Conditional Formatting

When you add a format to an object in Crystal Reports (see Chapter 10 for more on formatting), whether it be a text object or a field of numbers, that object is displayed and printed per your formatting. This type of formatting is considered to be *absolute* in that it stays the same despite what numbers or values are being printed.

But, if you want to add intelligence to your report, Crystal Reports can evaluate the field and, based on the value, print the field in different formats. A simple example is to print every negative number in red ink. Or you can have Crystal Reports look at a text string, and if that string matches a string that you designate, Crystal Reports can then execute an action for you.

Another idea is to add conditional formatting to your company invoices. Suppose a customer has not paid his invoice for 90 days. By printing in red the amount owed, overdue invoices would be easy to identify in a report.

Using On or Off Properties

An on or off property is identical to a formula that returns True or False. Either the condition is met, or it is not — and if it is, the format is turned on. Simple enough.

Using Attribute Properties

Attribute Properties are identical to if-then-else formulas in that several types of formatting can occur depending on the result of the formula you have created. For example, the Attribute Property can print a number in red if the value is equal to or less than 0 (zero), or print in black if the value is greater than 100, and print in blue if the value is greater than 500. See Chapter 7 on formulas for more information on this technique.

Crystal Reports tests each record and determines which format should be used, per your formula. A good start on learning conditional formatting is printing numbers in red if they are zero.

Figure 8-1 is a report that shows sales figures for a series of stores.

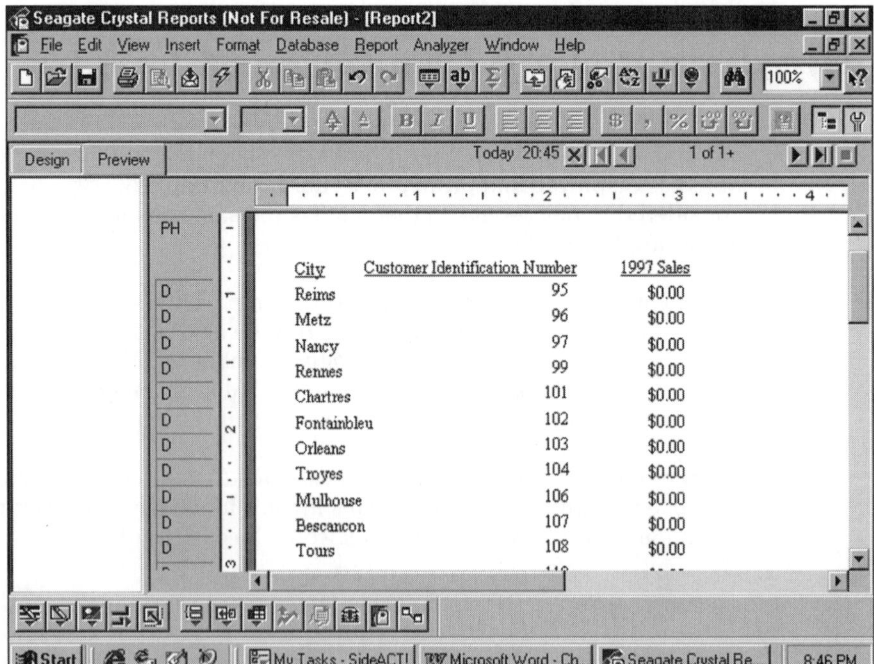

Figure 8-1: A sample report with records with zero values.

The report includes several figures that are zero numbers. Identifying the zero numbers would be much easier if they were more prominent in the report. Granted, it is easy to identify the zeroes if you simply sort the report using the 1997 Sales field in ascending order. But, if you want any other type of grouping, the zeroes may get lost in the list. You can use the following steps to add conditional formatting to any report:

1. **Right-click the field that you want to format.**

   A menu appears, as shown in Figure 8-2.

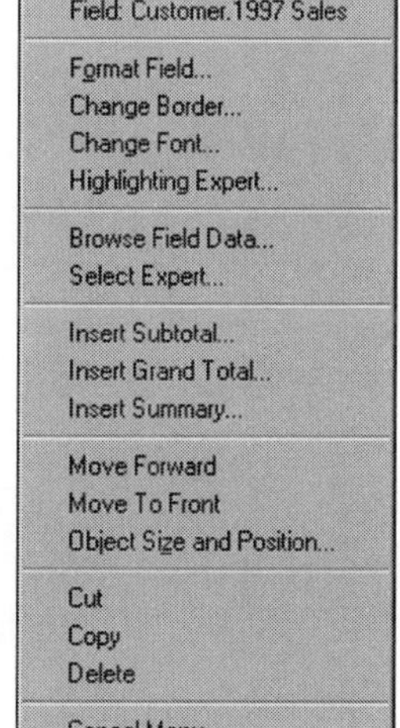

Figure 8-2: The shortcut menu for a field.

2. **Click the Format Field option.**

   The Format Editor dialog box appears, as shown in Figure 8-3.

   Because the mouse pointer was on a number field when you right-clicked, Crystal Reports assumes that you want to modify the number format. Not quite!

3. **Click the Font tab at the top of the dialog box.**

   Figure 8-4 shows the dialog box that is displayed.

4. **Click the Conditional Formatting button.**

   When you click this button, the Format Formula Editor dialog box opens, as shown in Figure 8-5.

   Wherever you see the Conditional Formatting button (X+2), you have the opportunity to add conditions to that particular portion of the report.

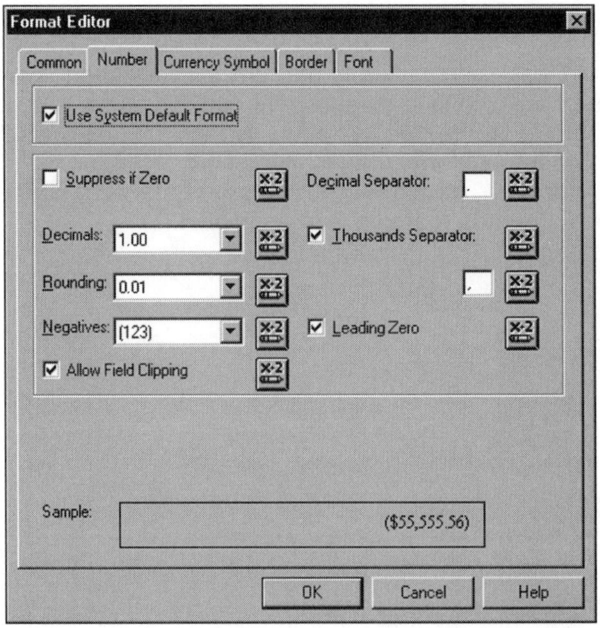

Figure 8-3: The Format Editor dialog box.

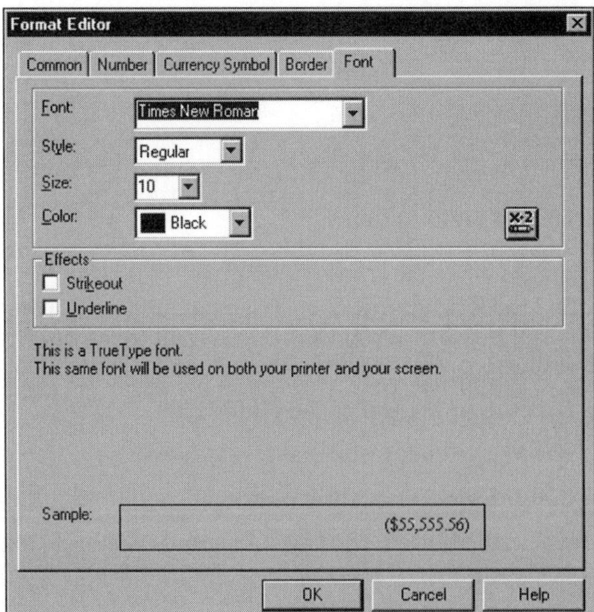

Figure 8-4: The Font tab clicked in the Format Editor dialog box.

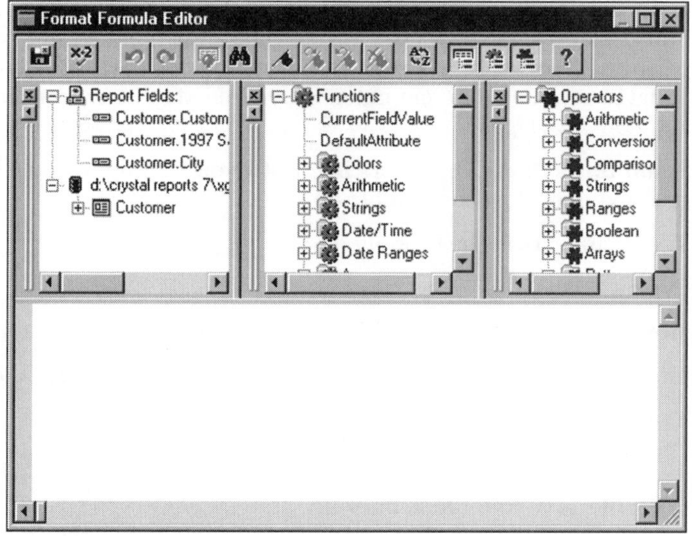

Figure 8-5: The Format Formula Editor dialog box.

This dialog box has four main components:

- The Fields box, which lists the fields in the report, the Groups, formulas, and report source database tables.
- The Functions that are prebuilt formulas that perform specific calculations.
- The last box has arithmetic operators and is named Operators.
- The final box is the Formula text box in which the actual formula is created.

5. **Because this formula requires two variables, you need to use an if-then-else formula.**

   To do so, scroll the Operators to find the `if x then y else z` operator. It's located under the Other heading. To see the entire list, click the plus sign in front of Other. Double-click the operator. The `if then else` operator is inserted into the Formula text box.

   Note that the blinking insertion point is located inside the current formula, between the `if` and `then`, right where it should be.

6. **Double-click the field to which you want to apply conditional formatting.**

   The formula name is inserted into the Field text box, like in this example formula:

   ```
   if {Customer.Last Year's Sales} then else
   ```

The insertion point moves to the end of the field name outside the bracket. The next step is to indicate the calculation Crystal Reports is to perform. In this case, you want to format values that are less than or equal to zero in a different color. So, you need to insert the less than (<) and equal (=) signs.

7. **Scroll through the Operators box until you find the Less or Equal (x < = y) operator, and double-click it.**

   The =< appears in the formula.

8. **Type a zero:** 0.

9. **Move the insertion point so that it is after the word** `then` **and type** Red.

10. **Move the insertion point after the word** `else` **and type** Black.

    The completed example formula appears as:

    ```
    if {Customer.Last Year's Sales} < = 0 then Red else Black
    ```

11. **Click the Save and Close button.**

    If the formula contains any errors, Crystal Reports does not accept it and displays a dialog box with a warning and the most likely cause of the error.

Because this is an exercise that uses color to define the output, I can't show you how it looks in this black-and-white book. You can see the effect of the red color if you have entered the formula on your reports, provided they contain negative numbers. If you have a color printer, you can share this wonderful format with your colleagues.

Another conditional format

When you create a report, you often want to print a Report Footer that gives the name of the author, tells the report date, or describes what is contained in the report. But you may want the front page of the report to be free of any footer. You may want a page number to print on every page except the first, for example. To accomplish this task, you must add a conditional format after inserting the field into the Page Footer section, as follows:

1. **In the Design window, choose Insert⇨Special Fields.**

   The Insert Fields dialog box appears, as shown in Figure 8-6.

2. **Select the special field you want to insert.**

   In this case, the choice is Page Number. When you make the selection, the pointer changes to a grayed box, allowing you to insert the Page Number field anywhere in the report.

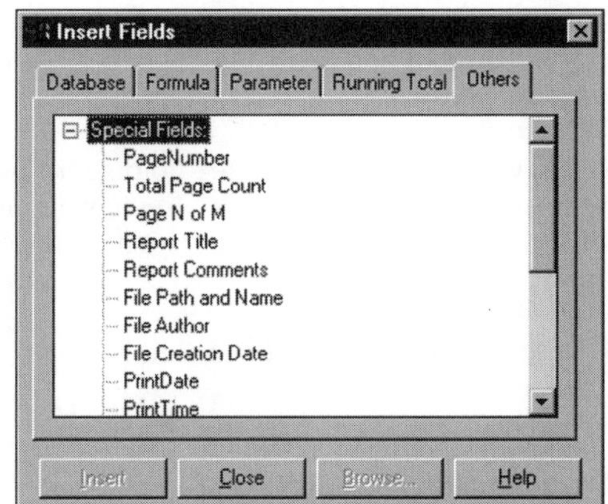

Figure 8-6: The Insert Fields dialog box with the Others tab open.

3. **Move the mouse pointer to the Page Footer section of the report.**

   Be careful that you position the field in the Page Footer section — it appears beneath the Report Footer, and so it can be confusing.

4. **Click the mouse button to insert the field, and then click the Close button in the Insert Fields dialog box.**
5. **Right-click the inserted field and choose Format Field.**

   The Format Editor dialog box appears.

6. **Click the Common tab.**
7. **Click the Suppress box so that a check mark is inserted.**

8. **Click the Conditional Formatting button.**

   The Format Formula Editor dialog box appears.

9. **Scroll through the Function box until you see the function named PageNumber. (It's listed under the Other heading.) Click the plus sign (+) to see the functions.**
10. **Double-click the PageNumber Function.**
11. **After the function, type** = 1.

    The completed PageNumber formula thus appears in the Formula text box:

    ```
    PageNumber = 1
    ```

12. **Click the Save and Close button.**
13. **Click OK to close the Format Editor dialog box.**

So, what this formula is telling Crystal Reports is to Suppress the Page Number only if the number is equal to one, which is the first page of the report.

You are looking at the Design window and should see no discernible changes. The only way to see if the formula worked is to go to Preview and look at the first page of the report, at the bottom, and then go to the next page and see if the page number has printed.

More information on this kind of formatting is covered in Chapter 10.

Deleting a conditional format

The only way to delete a conditional format — unless you want to erase the field or object, too — is to erase the text in the Formula text box in the Formula Editor. The following steps show you how to delete a conditional font format.

1. **Right-click the field upon which you have applied a conditional font format.**
2. **Click Format Field from the shortcut menu that appears.**

   The Format Editor dialog box appears.
3. **Click the Font tab.**
4. **Click the Conditional Formatting button.**
5. **The Format Formula Editor dialog box appears.**
6. **Click the formula, and drag the mouse over it until the formula is completely highlighted.**
7. **Press the Delete key, or right-click and choose Cut.**
8. **Click the Save and Close button.**

Other conditional formats must be removed by selecting the object that is affected and opening the Format Editor dialog box to select the attribute to which you have applied a formula. Open the Format Formula Editor and delete the formula, then click the Save and Close button.

Conditional formatting is a tool that can be exploited throughout a report. Anywhere you see the Conditional Formatting button is a place where you can tweak your report to get it just right. And if you are an obsessive-compulsive when it comes to perfecting reports, keep your Valium handy.

Chapter 9

Creating a Subreport

In This Chapter . . .

- Figuring out when to use a subreport
- Adding a subreport
- Viewing a linked subreport

A subreport enables you to insert one report into another report. Suppose that you have created two separate reports, and for some reason you want to include one of the reports in the other report in order to illustrate something. You would use a subreport to do that. However, as with many features of Crystal Reports, subreports can be quite complicated — so pay attention!

First of all, you have to start by understanding the terminology. The report into which you are going to insert a report is the *primary report.* The report you are going to insert into the primary report is the *subreport.*

A subreport has many of the same characteristics as a regular report, but there are a few subtle differences. For example, a subreport is inserted as an object in a primary report. That means you can't edit a subreport from the primary report.

Another characteristic of a subreport is that it can be placed in any section of a primary report. The entire subreport prints in the section in which you place it.

The third main difference between a report and a subreport is that you can't place a subreport in a report if it also has a subreport. No double-dipping on subreports, folks!

When Do I Add a Subreport?

At what point might you want to add a subreport? Well, you can add one anytime you want to combine two unrelated reports into a single report. You can also use a subreport to connect data that cannot be linked in another manner. You may want to add a subreport when you want to look at the same data two different ways in the same report. Or, you can use a subreport if you are performing a one-to-many lookup from a field that is not indexed on the lookup field.

A *one-to-many relationship* is one you may run into in a relational database. What it means is that for every record in one table, you may have more than one matching record in a linked table. For example, although sometimes one customer purchases only one product, most often that *one* customer purchases *many* products. In this case, the data for the two records are usually connected using a lookup table. One of the fields in the lookup table may not be indexed. If this is the case, you may be able to improve report generation performance if you link the tables via a subreport.

Creating a Scenario

To help demonstrate when you would want to use a subreport, I'm going to create a scenario in this section. Say that you are the head of marketing for Xtreme Mountain Bike, Inc. You have a fleet of sales representatives, but the vice president doesn't know all of them because they are dispersed around the globe. You plan to present a short report to the vice president using the quarterly sales report you have already created. This report is called the empsales report in the Xtreme folder.

You intend to jog the memory of the vice president to find out which of your sales representatives is truly outstanding for this quarter. To do this, add that person's employee profile to the report. You have already created the employee profile report, so you can conveniently just add that small bit of information to the quarterly sales report. You can find the employee profile report under the name empprof in the Xtreme folder.

Before you get started, you have to understand that the employee sales (empsales) report was created using a parameter. That means that when you open the employee sales report, you type the name of the employee for which you want to see sales. A report that is unique to that person appears. When you add the subreport, only the employee profile for that named person displays. This makes sense, as you would not want every employee profile to display in the quarterly sales report. In this example, you just want to show off the top person!

With Crystal Reports open, go ahead and open the report that you are going to use for the primary report, in this example.

1. **Click the Open button.**
2. **Navigate to and then double-click the Xtreme folder.**
3. **Click the empsales report and then click the Open button.**

   The employee sales report opens in the Design window.
4. **Click the Print Preview button.**

   The Enter Parameter values window displays. From this window, you select the name of the sales person whose unique sales report you want to see.
5. **In this case, select the report for Anne Dodsworth and then click OK.**

   The preview of the report for Ms. Dodsworth prints to the screen.

Adding the Subreport

If you followed the instructions in the last section, you should have the unique report designed just for Ms. Dodsworth on the screen. It is easier to control the location of the subreport if you are in the Design window, so click the Design tab to move back to the Design window.

There are two ways to insert a subreport. You can select the Insert menu and then select subreport, or you can click the Subreport button on the supplementary toolbar. I prefer the one-step approach.

1. **Click the Subreport button on the supplementary toolbar.**

   The Insert Subreport dialog box displays with two tabs. You are in the Subreport tab. On this tab you have two options. You can create a report on-the-fly by clicking the Create a Subreport radio button. The other option is to select a report that is already created. The report you want to use is already created, so . . .
2. **Click the Choose a Report radio button.**

   When you click this button, the browse option is activated.
3. **Click Browse and then click the empprof report in the Xtreme folder.**
4. **Click Open.**

   The path to the empprof report displays in the Report File Name box. Figure 9-1 shows how your Subreport tab should look at this point.
5. **Click the Link tab in the Insert Subreport dialog box.**

   In this particular example, you want only the employee profile of Ms. Dodsworth to display with the report, not the profile of every employee. Therefore, you have to link these two reports. This means that you will help Crystal Reports find some common field between the two reports in order to find a perfect match. The list of available fields in the container report is listed on the left of the dialog box. (Notice that the terminology has suddenly shifted. The *container report* is the primary report.)

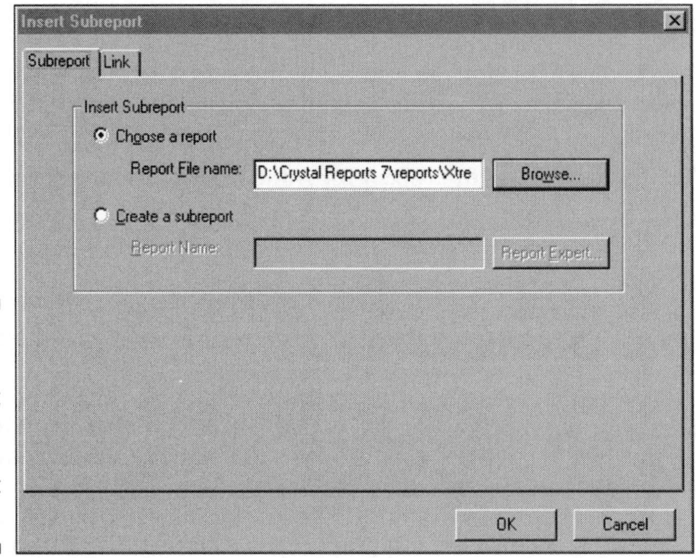

Figure 9-1: The Subreport tab of the Insert a Subreport dialog box.

6. **Highlight the name of the field you are going to use to connect the two reports.**

   In this example, highlight Employee.LastName.

7. **Click Employee.LastName and then click the right-facing arrow.**

   Employee.LastName moves over to the right box. Now select only the data in the subreport that matches the data you enter on the parameter field when you view the employee sales quarterly report.

8. **Click OK.**

   When you click OK, a gray box displays with your mouse pointer. You are now ready to place the subreport in your primary report.

9. **Click one time to place the subreport in the area you want.**

   In this example, place the subreport in the Report Header A section by moving the mouse pointer to the Report Header A section and clicking one time. A rectangle appears in the Report Header A section, as you see in Figure 9-2.

Figure 9-2: The Subreport rectangle inserted in the Report Header A section.

Viewing the Linked Subreport

You have placed the subreport on the design window. View the subreport in the primary report by previewing the report.

1. **Click the Print Preview button on the toolbar.**

   The Enter Parameter Values dialog box opens. Make sure Anne Dodsworth's name appears in the Value box.

2. **Click OK.**

   You now see the preview of the subreport in the primary report, as shown in Figure 9-3.

As you can see, the employee profile for Anne Dodsworth displays just below the report header. You can also see that there are two logos. You may want to clean this report up a bit by removing the logo from the primary report. You can't edit the subreport from the primary report Design window.

Notice that an additional tab is now at the top of the report window. The usual tabs, Design and Preview, are there. In addition, the empprof.rpt tab is there. This tab links you to the employee profile subreport. Because this is a linked report, you can edit the subreport from this tab. Beware! Any changes you make here also affect the original report.

Figure 9-3: The Subreport in the primary report.

Options for Subreports

As with most features in Crystal Reports, a myriad of subreport options are available for the user. In the previous sections, I tell you how to add a subreport from one perspective. In this example, the subreport is linked to the report. You can add a subreport that is not linked. An unlinked subreport does not necessarily have any field that is associated with any field in the primary report.

Another option is creating a subreport on the fly. Choosing this option opens a Design tab for the subreport you are creating. From one window, you can click a tab to design the primary report and then click the subreport tab to design the subreport. You can add more than one subreport to a primary report. You simply open the primary report and then repeat the steps for inserting a subreport for each subreports you want in the primary report. You can place subreports in separate sections in the report or side-by-side in one section.

Part IV

Putting On Some Finishing Touches

"It's a ten-step word-processing program. It comes with a spell-checker, grammar-checker, cliché-checker, whine-checker, passive/aggressive-checker, politically correct-checker, hissy-fit-checker, pretentious pontificating-checker, boring anecdote-checker and a Freudian reference-checker."

In this part . . .

Many great artists are not recognized as such in their lifetimes. In this part, you cannot be ignored. Great honors await those who read this part. Your reports will show the talents known only to a gifted few — at least until this book arrived. Polish the chrome, a slight adjustment of the carburetor, and your report is ready for the Indy 500. As they say, 10 percent of the job takes 90 percent of the time. Well, with the information in this part, you will be taking a long lunch and heading home early — while everyone is convinced that you slaved for hours over your reports. Ha! If only they knew your secret!

Chapter 10

Formatting Sections of a Report

In This Chapter

- Resizing a section
- Formatting sections with the Section Expert

The way a report prints is highly dependent upon the format of the individual sections in a report. This chapter deals with making your report look just right. (Chapter 11 shows you how you can add real pizzazz by combining the section formatting with other objects.)

In this chapter, I am going to show you how to change the layout of sections of the report. These techniques make reading your reports and highlighting certain aspects of the report much easier.

Changing the Size of a Section

Each report you create in Crystal Reports has a minimum of five sections: the Report Header, the Page Header, the Details, the Report Footer, and the Page Footer. Crystal Reports allocates space for each section. You can modify the space for any and all sections; however, judging what adjustments may be necessary to the different sections is difficult until you print the report. The Preview tab gives an excellent representation of what the printed report will look like, but with the huge number of printers, each with its own quirks, the best way to test your formatting is to actually make a hard copy.

The Design tab is the place to be if you want to make changes in the size of a section. On the left side of the window, in the gray area, each of the sections is labeled. Between the section labels are thin horizontal lines, representing the boundaries between the sections. The lines are the key to eyeball adjustments in that you can move your pointer to a line, click and hold the left mouse button, and drag the line to adjust the height of the section. A simple example follows.

To change the height of a section:

1. **In any report, click the Design tab.**

   A typical report appears in Figure 10-1.

2. **Click the line dividing the section and hold down the left mouse button.**

   Click in the design area, not in the left margin. When you do, the mouse pointer changes to a double-horizontal line. You will be resizing the section above the mouse pointer.

3. **Drag the line up or down.**

   The entire line moves with your pointer.

4. **Release the mouse button where you want the line to be redrawn.**

In Figure 10-2, the Report Footer line has been dragged up to decrease the size of the Report Footer.

To see what effect the changing of a Report Footer has (or any other change you make), click the Preview tab, as shown in Figure 10-3.

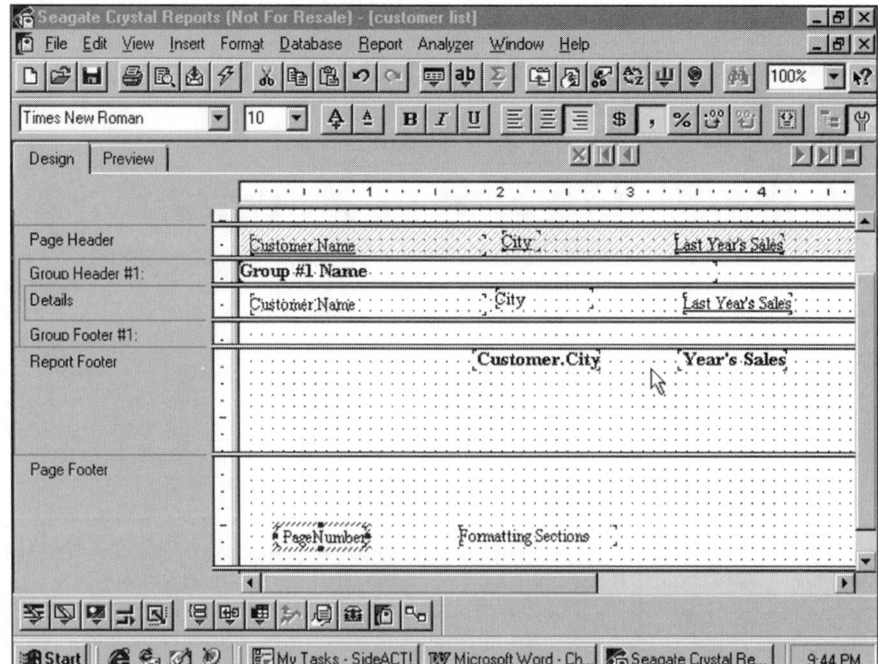

Figure 10-1: A typical report from the Design point of view.

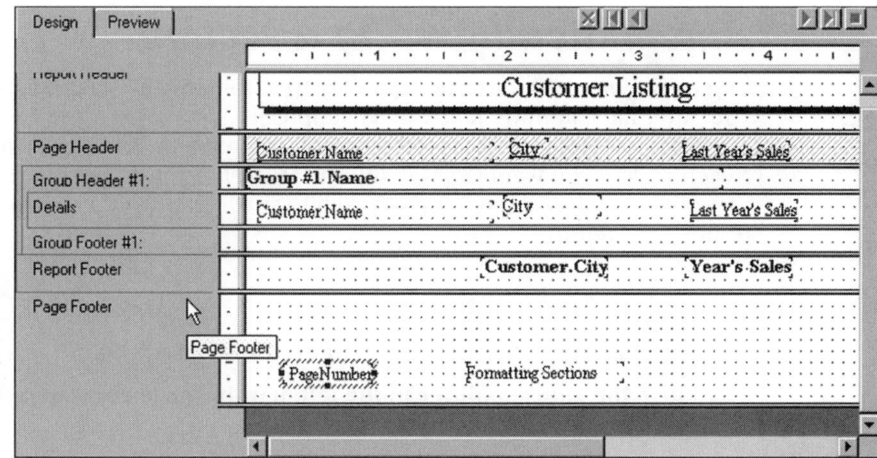

Figure 10-2: The Report Footer border is now resized.

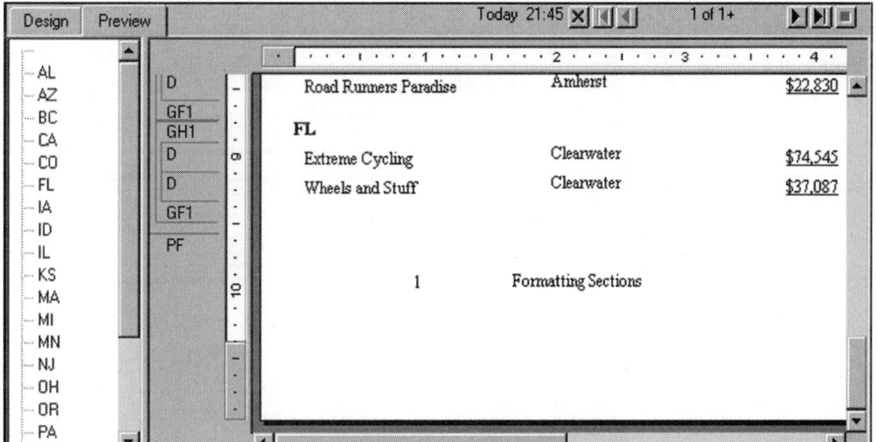

Figure 10-3: The Page Footer is higher up on the page in the Preview tab.

You can also squeeze the Report Footer to a smaller size. First, drag the Page Footer line down the page; then, drag the line that indicates the bottom of the page itself up. Crystal Reports does not allow you to draw the line so closely that any object inserted into a section will be hidden. In Figure 10-4, the Page Footer is reduced to a very small size.

Click the Preview tab to see the results, as shown in Figure 10-5.

By clicking near the bottom of the page, the outline of the Page Footer appears.

Automatically sizing a section

Crystal Reports includes the capability to automatically size a section for you. After all, computer software is supposed to make your job easier. Suppose that you have inserted a text object, a graph, and a Special field into a section, and you want Crystal Reports to best fit the objects to the section. Crystal Reports also eliminates any white space that would be wasted when printing the report.

To automatically size a section:

1. **Insert as many objects as you want in a section.**
2. **Move the mouse pointer to the left margin space corresponding to the section you want to modify.**

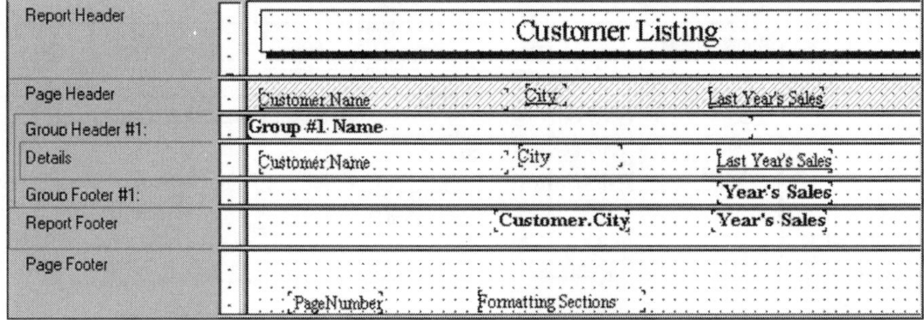

Figure 10-4: The Page Footer section is squeezed to a small space.

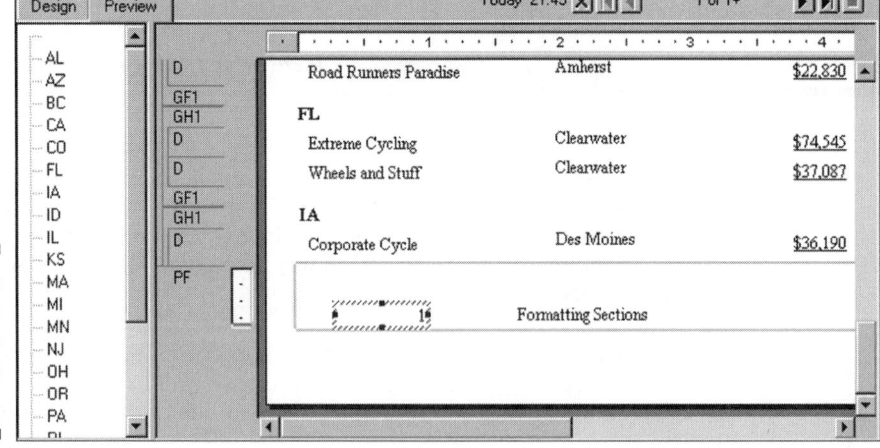

Figure 10-5: The reduced size of Page Footer in Preview tab.

3. **Right-click in the margin.**

   A menu appears, as shown in Figure 10-6.

   In this example, the space for the Page Footer has been increased and several objects are present.

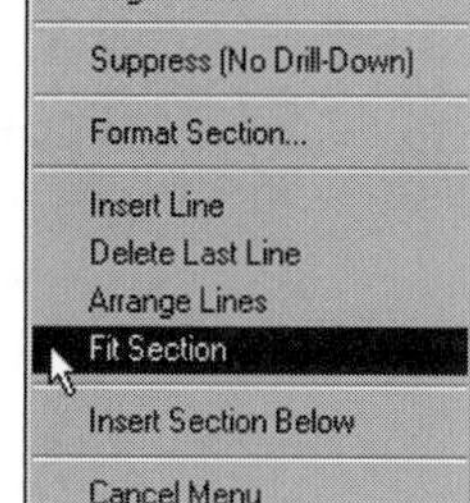

Figure 10-6: The section shortcut menu.

4. **Click the Fit Section option.**

   Figure 10-7 shows that the bottom of the page line has been drawn up against the text object, `Making a Section Fit`, so as to eliminate any unneeded space in the printed report.

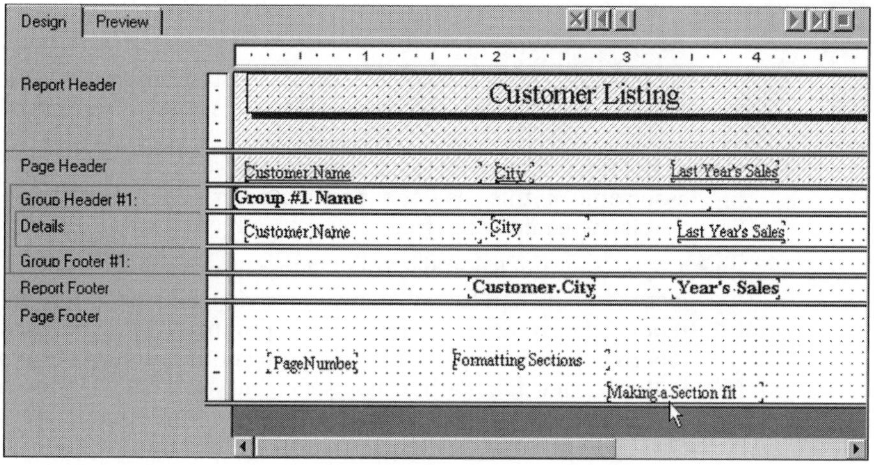

Figure 10-7: The Page Footer is resized automatically to make the best use of the available space.

Looking at the shortcut menu

If you follow the steps in the previous section, you click the right mouse button on the left margin of the Design tab. When you do that, a menu appears that lists, among other things, the Fit Section option, which automatically arranges the size of a section with several objects. But you need to know about several other options in that menu. Figure 10-8 shows the opened menu.

If you are ever in doubt about what you can do to or on a particular object in Crystal Reports, just right-click the object. A shortcut menu comes up with a concise list of what you are able to do.

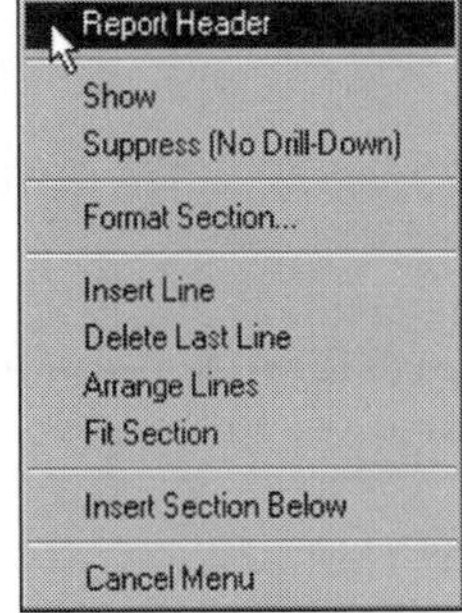

Figure 10-8: The shortcut menu appears when right-clicking the margin in the Design tab.

The key point of a shortcut menu is the fact that it provides a quick list of relevant actions available for the object or objects currently selected.

- At the top of the menu is the name of the section with which the menu is associated. In this case, the mouse pointer was on the Report Header, so that is the name at the top.
- The next option listed has to do with drill-downs. A *drill-down* is simply a means to hide and then display underlying information, as required, on a report. For example, if your report is grouped by Region, you can see the record details for a particular region by double-clicking the Group Name in the Preview tab. Rather than seeing all the detailed information, you can hide the detail and just see the summary information for the region. Crystal Reports adds a tab at the top of the Report window indicating the individual group (see Figure 10-9). You can also drill-down on a graph, as I describe in Chapter 6.
- If you do not want the drill-down capability available for a particular section, right-click that section, and you have two options. You can hide the section so that it does not print but can be drilled-down, or you can suppress the section so that it is hidden from print and cannot be drilled-down.

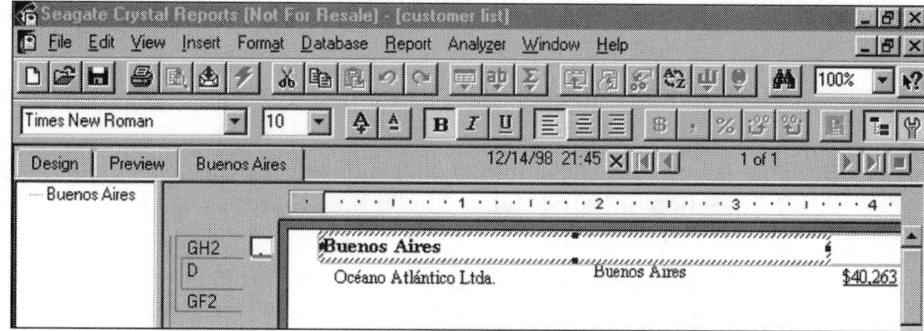

Figure: 10-9: The drill-down beside the Preview tab.

For example, you may use this capability if you are doing a report on salaries. You can do the summary calculations, but the report won't print the underlying contents of the section, thus preserving confidentiality.

Drill-down is not available at run-time in either case.

- When you hide or suppress a section in the Design tab, the left margin changes to reflect the new format. In Figure 10-10, the Report Header has been suppressed and therefore is no longer listed in the margin.

Drill-down is not available in run-time versions of reports, as I describe in Chapter 15.

- The next item on the list, after the Format Section option, which opens the dialog box, is the Insert Line option. This option works in conjunction with the next two options, Delete Last Line and Arrange Lines. Crystal Reports includes line formatting options to enable you to precisely size the sections in the report. You already know how to click and drag the sections to resize them, but with the line-by-line format, you can get the sections just right. Notice that red marks indicate that an object is attached to a guideline.

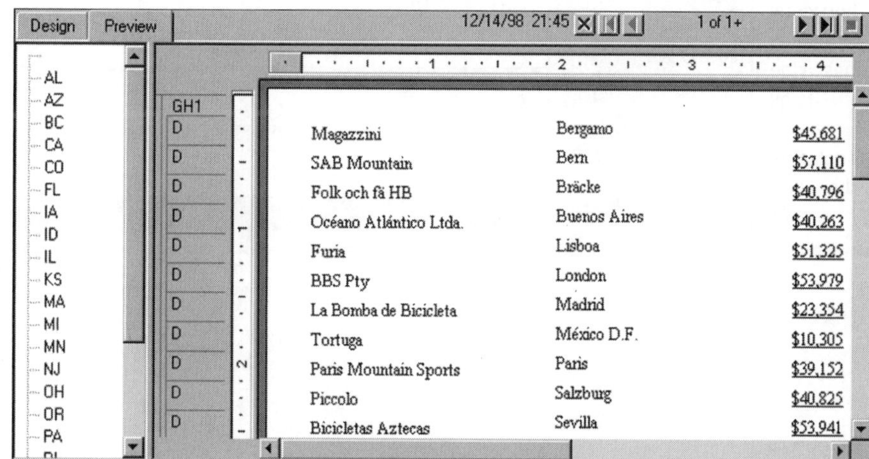

Figure 10-10: The Report header suppressed in Preview.

- If you want the section to grow by a single line, you choose the Insert Line option.
- If you want to make the section smaller by a single line, you can do so by right-clicking and choosing Delete Last Line.
- Use the Arrange Lines option to insert a series of horizontal lines in the section or to re-arrange the lines so that they are equally separated within the section.
- The final option on this menu is the Insert Section Below option. When you select this option, a subsection is inserted under the section that you clicked upon. You use a *subsection* when you want a report that has distinct information included in the report that is a subset of the section. You may never need to use this concept in your dealings with Crystal Reports, but if you do, at least you'll know how.

The best way to understand the Insert Line feature is to click a section and insert the lines themselves. Here's how:

1. **Right-click a section of the report.**

   In this example, I chose the Page Header section.

2. **Choose the Arrange Lines option.**

   Horizontal lines are inserted into the section, as shown in Figure 10-11.

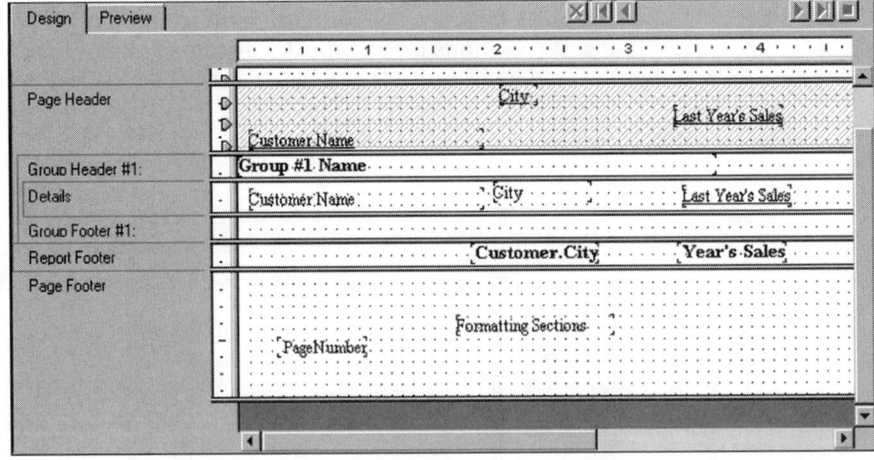

Figure 10-11: A series of horizontal formatting lines in the Page Header section of the report design.

Cool stuff about subsections

You can do all the work with subsections by just using the mouse, too. Subsections are used for multisection or multidetail reports, which are very popular in Crystal Reports. When necessary, subsections allow you to create very powerful tools.

Suppose that you want the Detail section to print each record with more space between each record. You would follow these steps:

1. **Right-click in the left margin on the Detail section of the report.**
2. **Choose Insert Line.**
3. **Repeat the procedure two more times.**

   The Details section now looks like the one shown in Figure 10-12.

Of course, you could have added the space simply by dragging the line between the Details section and the Group Footer section, but the foregoing method is more exact. Figure 10-13 shows the results (in the Preview tab) of adding lines to the Details section, resulting in more room between each record.

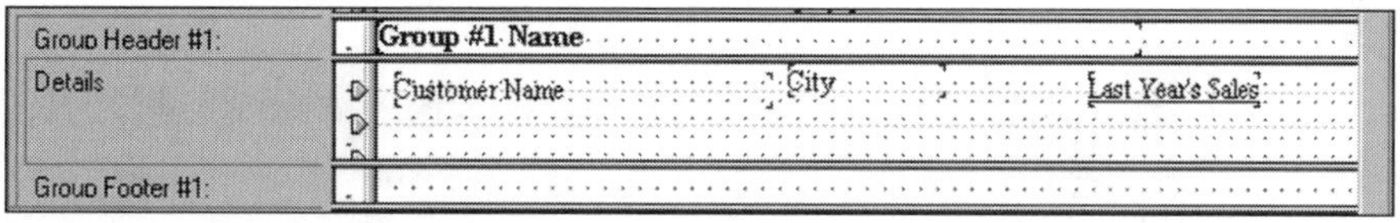

Group Header #1:	Group #1 Name
Details	Customer Name · City · Last Year's Sales
Group Footer #1:	

Figure 10-12: Lines added to the Details section.

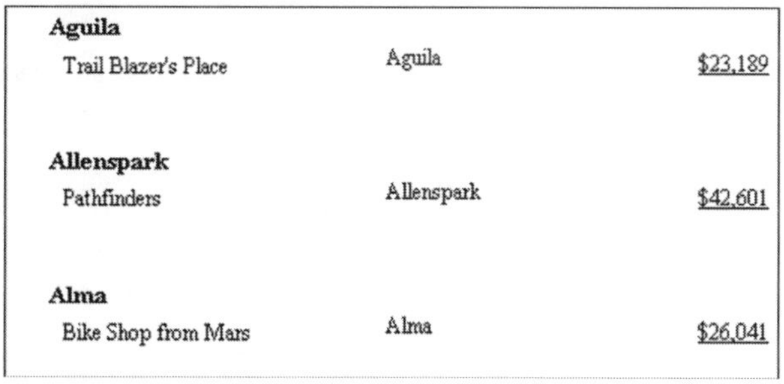

Aguila		
Trail Blazer's Place	Aguila	$23,189
Allenspark		
Pathfinders	Allenspark	$42,601
Alma		
Bike Shop from Mars	Alma	$26,041

Figure 10-13: A preview with spaces added between records.

Formatting Sections with the Section Expert

Because so many options exist in terms of formatting sections, Crystal Reports includes a handy Section Expert to show you the way.

You can open the Section Expert in three ways:

- Right-click the section that you want to format and choose Format Section.
- Click the Section Expert button.
- Choose Format⇨Section.

Figure 10-14 shows the Section Expert dialog box.

This dialog box is a busy one! You can make several choices, so I'm going to take the dialog box a bit at a time to help you better understand your options.

On the left side of the dialog box is a listing of all the sections in your report. At the bottom of the Section list is a horizontal scroll bar that enables you to move left and right so as to read the entire section name if necessary. When you open this dialog box, the highlight is automatically positioned on the name of the section where your mouse pointer was when you opened the dialog box.

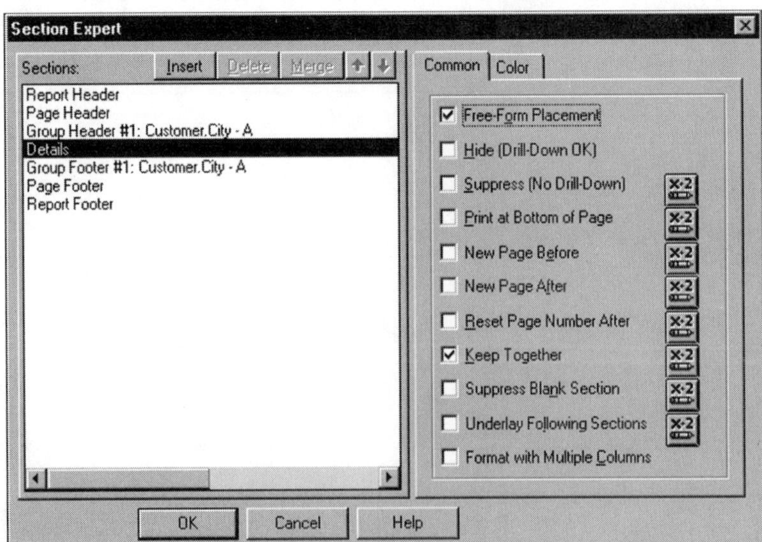

Figure 10-14: The Section Expert dialog box.

The top of the dialog box contains a series of buttons. The Insert button is used to insert subsections in the report. For example, Crystal Reports allows for several Page Footer sections, enabling you to print different page footers at certain pages of the report. These added sections can be formatted so that they are conditional, in the same way as the standard section, and therefore print based on a formula you have entered into this dialog box, as I explain in a moment. In Figure 10-15, a subdetail section has been added by clicking the Details Section listing and then clicking the Insert button.

When you click OK to close the dialog box, the new section is inserted into the report, as shown in Figure 10-16.

The section can be deleted as easily as it was added. Open the Section Expert, click the section you want to delete, and click the Delete button.

Note: The Delete button was not active — it was grayed out — when this dialog box was opened because you cannot delete the five basic components of a report design, the Report Header and Footer, the Details, and so on.

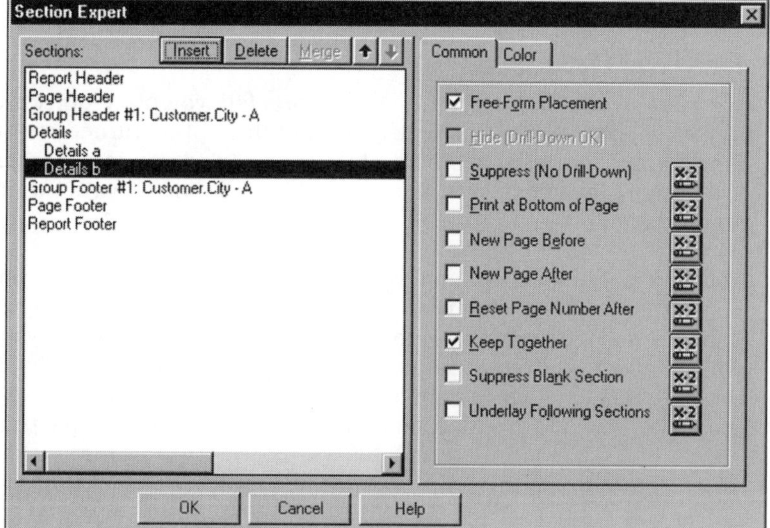

Figure 10-15: The Section expert with a new Detail section inserted.

Figure 10-16: The Details b section added to the report design.

You cannot delete sections from the Section Expert if only one section is left, even if that includes a Group Header or Footer.

The other two buttons at the top of the Sections box are for promoting or demoting sections that you have added. By clicking a subsection, you can move it up or down in the report layout. You are unlikely to ever use this feature unless you become the Crystal Reports maven for your company and need to keep a few tricks up your sleeve to justify your bonus, but it never hurts to know what these features do.

Using the Common tab

The Common tab deals with options that are generalized to most sections. If you need to set something related to labels or colors, you use the other tabs. Basically, the Common tab combines all the options that don't fit the other tabs — the Common tab is a catch-all tab.

The list of formatting options on the right side of the dialog box corresponds to the section selected in the left side.

Free-Form Placement

With Free-Form Placement, Crystal Reports lets you place objects anywhere in your report. Most of the time, you want this option turned on. Turning off Free-Form Placement causes Crystal Reports to create an underlying grid in the Design tab, which, in turn, causes objects to line up with the grid as you insert them.

You may make an exception if you have a paper form that you are trying to match in a report, and you can use the grid lines to align the objects to the paper form. Free-Form Placement only goes so far, however; Crystal Reports will not allow you to place a graph or a cross-tab object (see Chapter 12) in the Page Header, Page Footer, or the Details section because cross-tabs and graphs represent a grouped set of data that may span multiple pages.

Hide (Drill-Down OK)

This option is designed to stop the section from printing but not stop drilling down. So, you can still double-click a summary field and get a drill-down tab in Preview.

Suppress (No Drill-Down)

This option stops the section from being printed and stops a summary field from being drilled down. You can enter a formula to make this option conditional. That is, in some cases the drill-down would be available, and in others it wouldn't. This feature is also formula driven, offering different detail sections in different situations.

Print at Bottom of Page

You can use this option to print sections as far down a page as possible. The genesis for this alternative is the good old invoice. Obviously, you want the total to an invoice to print at the very bottom of the page, leaving the rest of the page for the invoice details. This option can be turned on or off by using a formula.

New Page Before

If you want a new page to begin before the section starts printing, click this option. You may use this feature when you have inserted groups into the reports (listings by state, for example) and you want each group to print on a separate page. You can use a formula to turn this option on or off.

New Page After

Select this option if you want a new page to start after the section is printed. This option is most often used with groups and can be turned off or on by a formula. The ideal use of this option is for a report's cover page. You can put all the information you need in the Report Header section and then force a new page to print after the header, ensuring that just the information you want is on the cover page.

Reset Page Number After

If you are using page numbering in your report, and you should be, you can adjust the count by turning this option on. A good example of using this option is groups. A group may very well span several pages of a report; if the pages are numbered by group, the report is easier to read. To achieve this numbering, you would set the option to on and insert the special field page numbering into the Group Footer section. Again, you can switch this option off or on by using a formula.

Keep Together

This option prevents Crystal Reports from printing a record on more than one page. If a full record with multiple lines does not fit at the bottom of a page, none of that record will print on that page — the entire record will be written on the next page.

Say that a page can show 64 lines. Each detail record is three lines long, so 21 full records ($21 \times 3 = 63$) will print on the first page. The last record (line 64) would print without its counterparts if it could, but Crystal Reports has told the section to stay together. So instead of the first line of record 22 printing on the first page, all three lines are printed at the top of the second page. This feature avoids having records split across pages, which is known as *widow/orphan protection.* (When used with a group section, this option keeps the group together.)

Suppress Blank Section

If a section contains no objects, this option prevents Crystal Reports from printing white space. Have you ever created mailing labels from a database where some addresses have a suite number and others do not? The labels without the suite numbers have a gap when printed. This option prevents that from happening and can be turned on or off by using a formula.

Underlay Following Sections

This option creates a special effect in the report. The option's purpose is to print graphic objects such as a logo underneath the sections that follow.

Format Groups with Multiple Column

This option is only available in the Details section, which you get to by highlighting it in the dialog box. You use this option when you want the report to print in a multicolumn format. Instead of having the data print straight down the page, you can set up multiple columns and have the data flow from column to column. You can also have your data print across and then down the page, printing one record in each column, and then printing a second record in the next column, then a third, and so on.

Click this option, and a new tab called Layout appears at the top right of the dialog box. This tab is divided into four smaller boxes: Width, Height, Horizontal, and Vertical. The Layout tab is selected in Figure 10-17.

The measurements in the smaller boxes determine the position and spacing of each of the record details. At a minimum, you must enter a width measurement. Most likely, you would use this option for name- and address-type reports (like mailing labels).

Using the Color tab

After formatting each of the sections with the settings I mention in the previous section, you can add color to the section as an absolute format or as a conditional format. If you have skipped all the other chapters in this book in order to figure out how to use conditional formatting, your best bet is to read Chapter 7 on formulas and Chapter 8 on conditional formatting. You do not have to be expert on either, but these chapters give you some ideas as to how to construct formulas for this purpose.

In Figure 10-18, the Section Expert is open, and I have clicked the Color tab.

The colors work in conjunction with the section you have highlighted. In other words, to set the background color for the Report Header, click Report Header in the Sections list and then click the Color tab.

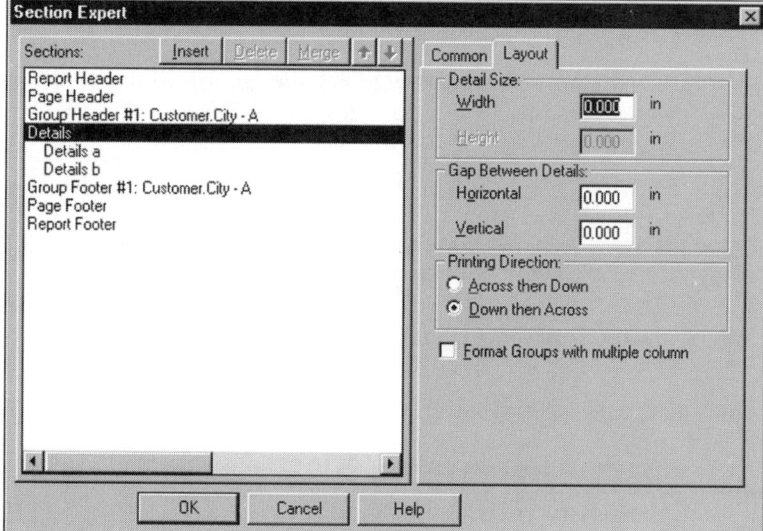

Figure 10-17: The Layout tab in the Section Expert dialog box.

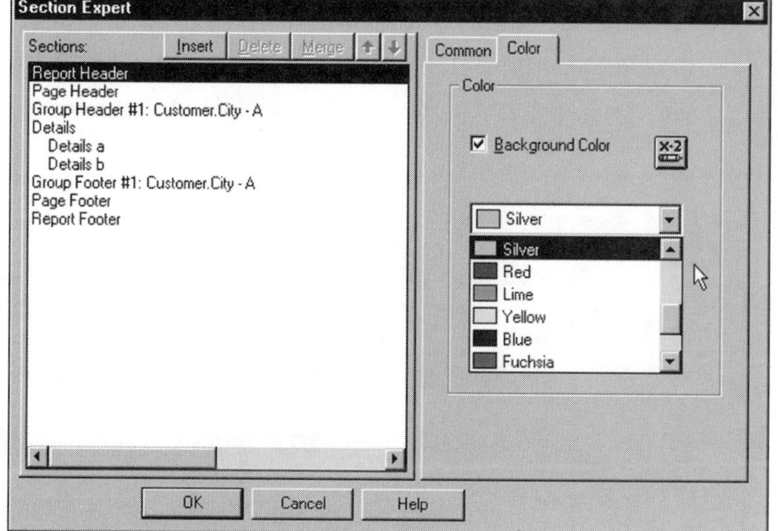

Figure 10-18: The Section Expert dialog box with the Color tab selected.

To add an absolute color to any section, follow these steps:

1. **Choose Format⇨Section (or click the Section Expert button).**

   The Section Expert dialog box appears.

2. **Click the section you want to format with a background color.**
3. **Click the Color tab.**

4. **Click the Background Color setting so that a Check mark appears in the box.**
5. **Click the pull-down arrow to see the color options, and then click the color you want.**
6. **Click OK.**

In Figure 10-19, the Details section has been colored red, so the records' backgrounds are in a darker hue than the rest of the report. I know the background may look gray to you, but trust me, it's red.

An example of a conditional format formula

Suppose that you want to color every other record in the Details section, making the report easier to read. Here are the steps to creating this formula:

1. **Open the report that you wish to format.**
2. **Choose Format⇨Section.**
3. **Click the Details section of the report.**
4. **Click the Color tab.**
5. **Click the Background Color box.**
6. **Click the Conditional Format button.**

   When you click this button, the Format Formula Editor dialog box appears, as shown in Figure 10-20.

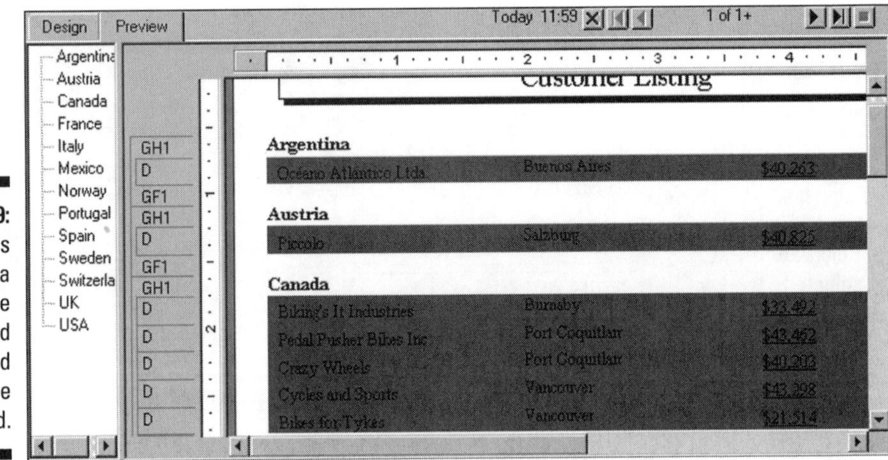

Figure 10-19: The Details section is a darker hue because red is applied in the background.

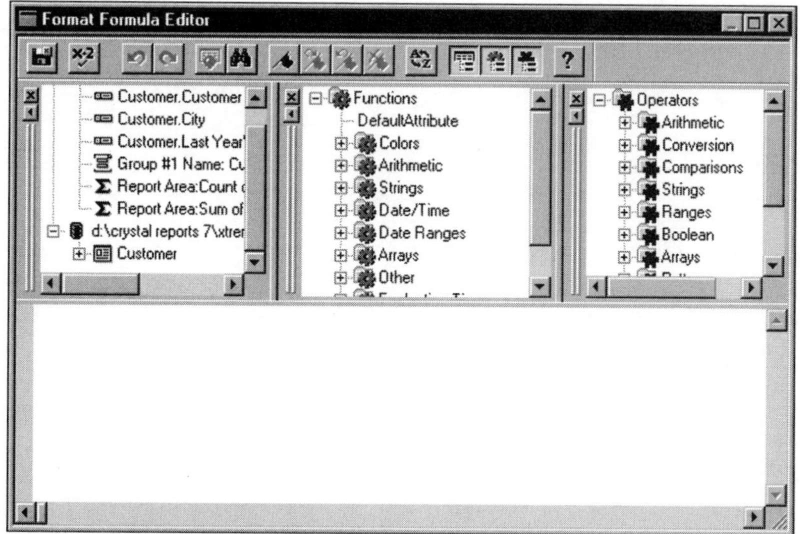

Figure 10-20: The Format Formula dialog box.

I could go into all the details on entering a formula, but I won't here. See Chapter 7 for more information.

Enter the formula exactly as follows:

```
if Remainder (RecordNumber,2) <> 0 then red else white
```

How does this formula work, you ask? The remainder `(RecordNumber, 2)` takes the record number and divides it by two. If a remainder other than zero is present, then the row prints in red (`then red`). Otherwise, the row color is white (`else white`). Figure 10-21 shows the formula properly entered in the Format Formula Editor text box.

For a complete tutorial that explains this whole effect, look up Green Bar Paper Effect in the Crystal Reports User's Guide.

7. **Click the Save and Close button to enter the formula.**
8. **Click OK to close the dialog box.**

To see the results of using the formula, click the Preview tab. The records are colored in every other fashion, as shown in Figure 10-22. Very cool.

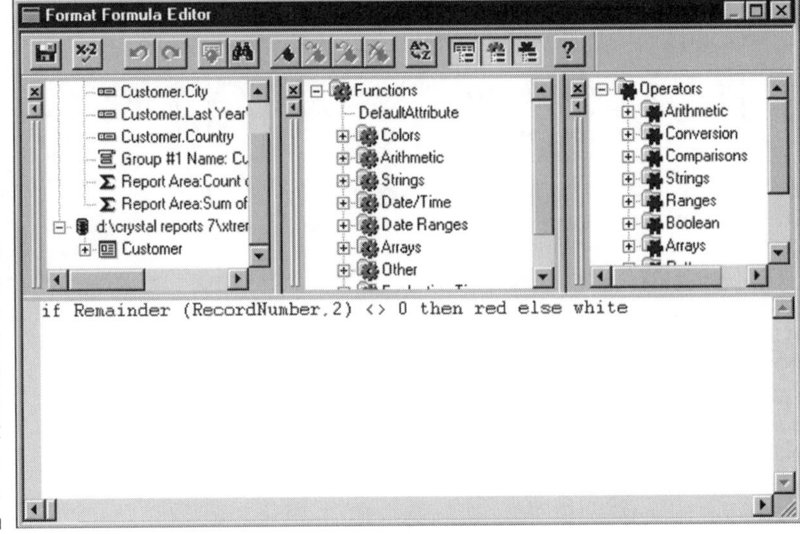

Figure 10-21: The every other record coloring formula in the Format Formula Editor box.

Argentina		
Océano Atlántico Ltda.	Buenos Aires	$40,263
Austria		
Piccolo	Salzburg	$40,825
Canada		
Biking's It Industries	Burnaby	$33,492
Pedal Pusher Bikes Inc.	Port Coquitlam	$43,462
Crazy Wheels	Port Coquitlam	$40,203
Cycles and Sports	Vancouver	$43,298
Bikes for Tykes	Vancouver	$21,514

Figure 10-22: Every other record colored in the Preview tab.

A conditional formula to color group results

Another use of color is to format certain group totals in a distinguishing color from other totals based on a conditional formula. If you have grouped your records by state or region and have added a subtotal by group, you can enter a formula that changes the color based on the value in the sum.

To add a conditional coloring formula to a group total:

1. **Open the report to which you want to add a conditional color.**

   In this example, I use the CUSTLIST report I created.

   The report has been grouped by country, and a sum has been added to each group by using the field Last Year's Sales.

2. **In the Design tab, choose Format⇨Section.**

   The Section Expert dialog box appears.

3. **Click the Group Footer section of the report.**
4. **Click the Color tab.**
5. **Click the Background Color option.**
6. **Click the Conditional Formula icon.**

   When you do, the Format Formula Editor dialog box appears.

7. **Enter** if.
8. **Go to the Fields list.**
9. **Find the Sum of Last Year's Sales under the Group Footer on Country and double-click it.**

   The following text is inserted:

   ```
   Sum ({Customer.Last Year's Sales}, Customer.Country
   ```

10. **Then type** > 90000 then Red else White.

    The result looks like the formula shown in Figure 10-23.

    In plain English, what this formula says is that if the total of the values in the Last Year's Sales field by Country is greater than 90000, the total will be printed in red. If not, then the total will be printed in white.

11. **Click the Save and Close button.**
12. **Click the Preview tab to see the results, as shown in Figure 10-24.**

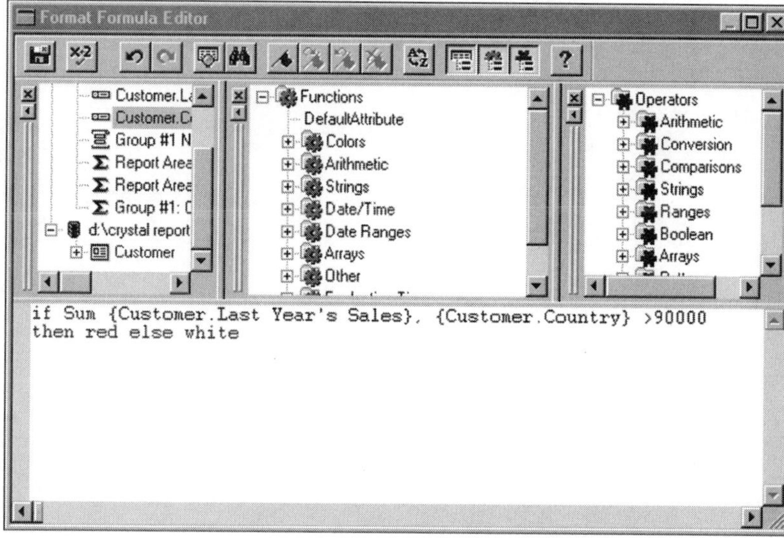

Figure 10-23: The Conditional Format Formula is entered into the Format Formula Editor dialog box to change the color of specified group totals.

Océano Atlántico Ltda.	Buenos Aires	$40,263
		$40,262.67
Austria		
Piccolo	Salzburg	$40,825
		$40,825.22
Canada		
Biking's It Industries	Burnaby	$33,492
Pedal Pusher Bikes Inc.	Port Coquitlam	$43,462
Crazy Wheels	Port Coquitlam	$40,203
Cycles and Sports	Vancouver	$43,298
Bikes for Tykes	Vancouver	$21,514
		$181,969.33
France		

Figure 10-24: A Group with sales greater than 90,000 printed in a different color.

The coloring options are limited only by your imagination. However, if you get too wild with colors, you distract from the report itself. I suggest that you set a color scheme for your company so that every report has identifiable qualities, such as coloring groups sums that fall below the company average and/or a color for those groups with negative values.

Chapter 11

Creating Presentation-Quality Reports

In This Chapter

- Using quick format options
- Adding Special fields
- Inserting lines and boxes
- Inserting a picture file
- Using the Can Grow feature
- Inserting an OLE object
- Using Auto Arrange

If you're not a creative person when it comes to formatting and designing report layouts, never fear! Seagate Crystal Reports includes ten predefined formats you can apply to your report for eye-pleasing effects. If none of these formats turns you on, you can read the rest of this chapter to find out how to apply formats.

Quickly Formatting a Report

Your report is done, complete with groups (refer to Chapter 5) and totals (refer to Chapter 7). Now that the substance is finished, you're ready to add some veneer to your report.

With a report open and ready, follow these steps to apply a quick format:

1. **Open a report you want to format using the Style Expert.**

   Figure 11-1 shows a report with little formatting.

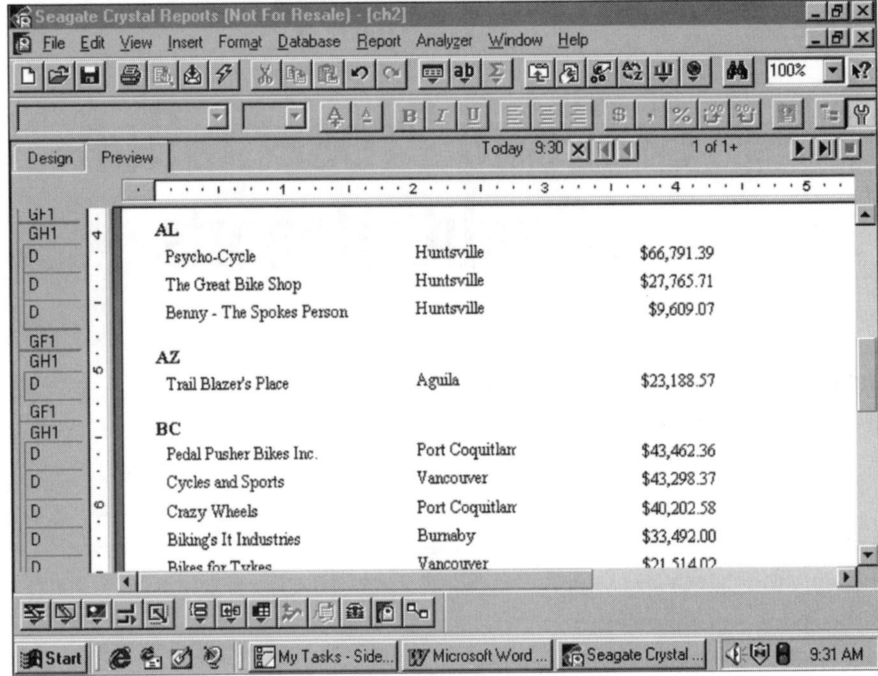

Figure 11-1: A report without much formatting.

2. **Choose Format⇨Report Style Expert.**

   Before the dialog box opens, Crystal Reports displays a warning dialog box alerting you to the fact that applying a style is not reversible with the Undo command. Don't worry — you can always remove on a case-by-case basis any format that is not what you want. The Report Style Expert dialog box is shown in Figure 11-2.

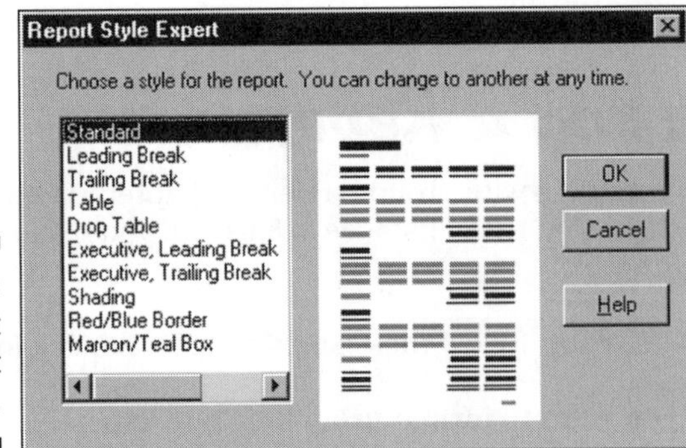

Figure 11-2: The Report Style Expert dialog box.

You can choose a style from this dialog box, apply it, and, if you don't like it, reopen the Report Style Expert and apply a new format. You don't have to worry about removing the previously applied format; the new format replaces it. As a preview of the format, click the format name; Crystal Reports shows you a representation of the format on the right side of the dialog box.

3. **Select a style you want to apply to your report.**

   Figure 11-3 shows the result of applying the Standard report style.

4. **If you want to try another style, choose Format⇨Report Style Expert.**

   In Figure 11-4, the Leading Break style has been applied to the report.

   One more time! The next style is named Drop Table, as shown in Figure 11-5.

Try the rest of the formats in a report and see which appeals to you. If you try them all without satisfaction, you can return to the original formatting by choosing File⇨Close. Crystal Reports asks whether you want to save the report with the changes. When you select No, the report closes without making any changes from the time you first opened it.

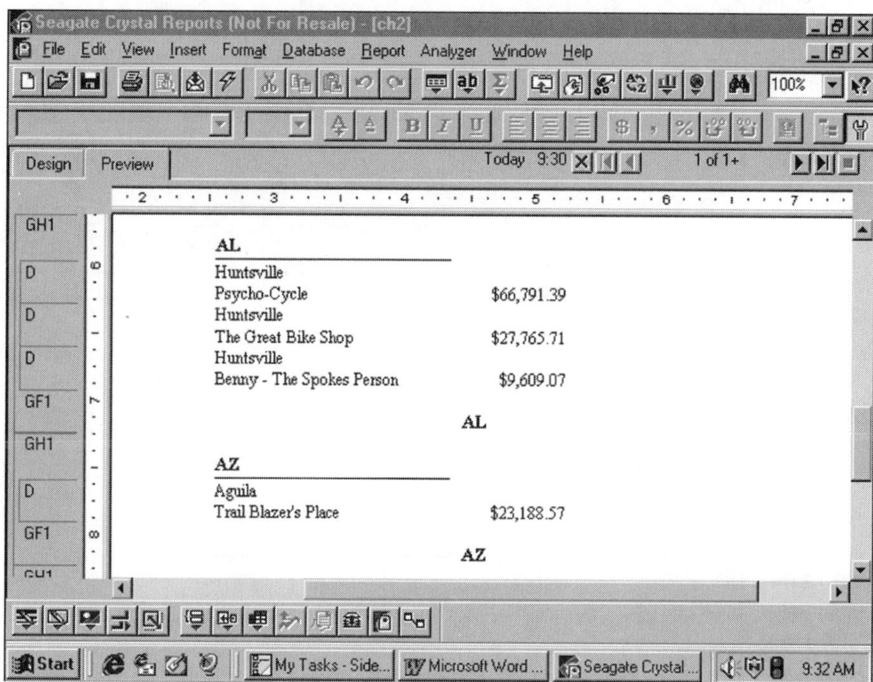

Figure 11-3: The Standard report style added to a report.

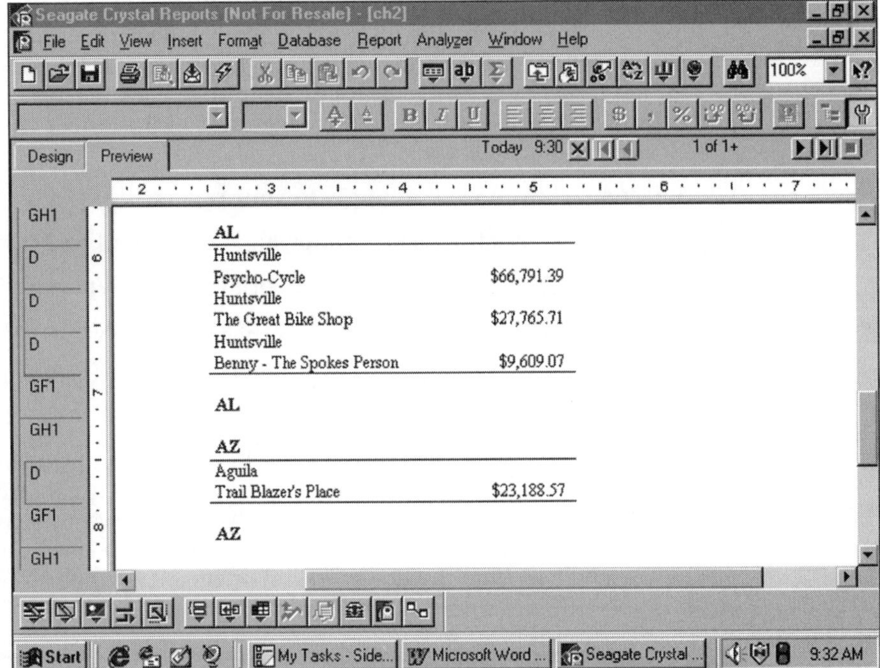

Figure 11-4: The leading Break style applied to a report.

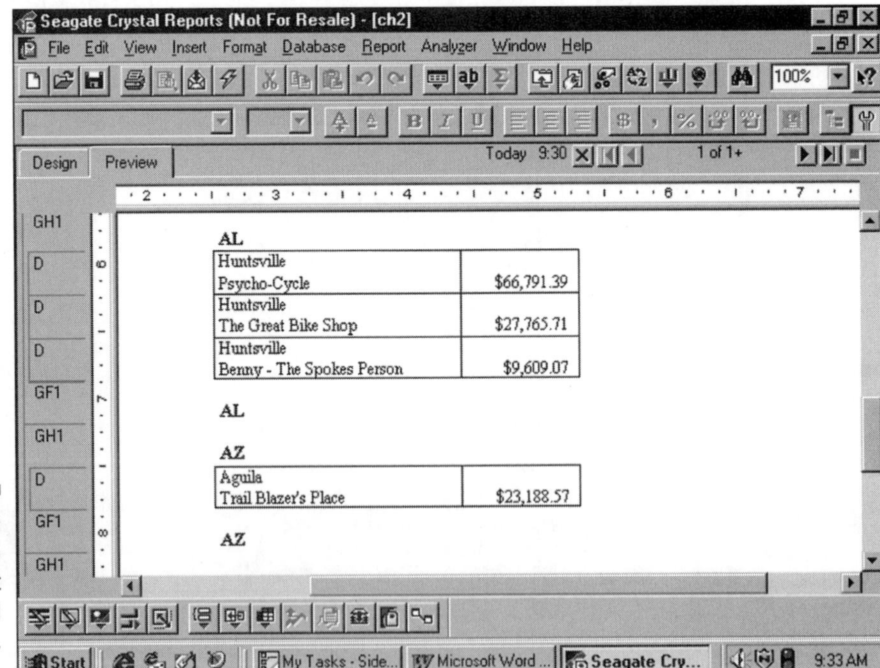

Figure 11-5: The Drop Table report style applied to a report.

Zooming In on the Report

When you're working hard to get a report to look just right, Crystal Reports gives you a tool to save your eyes from straining. The Zoom function enables you to take a close-up look at the formatting you have applied and to zoom out to see how the report looks in full-page view.

The Zoom feature works best on the Preview tab, because you're looking at live data. If you're working to get the spacing just right, however, the Design tab, when it's zoomed, gives you an easy way to see exactly where an object is on the layout. Formatting on the Design tab is easier because every time you make a change, the screen does not have to be refreshed, as it does on the Preview tab.

You can adjust the zoom factor in two ways:

- Choose View⇨Zoom.
- Click the downward-pointing arrow near the right end of the toolbar to use the Zoom Control drop-down list.

In the first case, the Magnification Factor dialog box appears, as shown in Figure 11-6. If you use the drop-down list, you choose from several predetermined percentages.

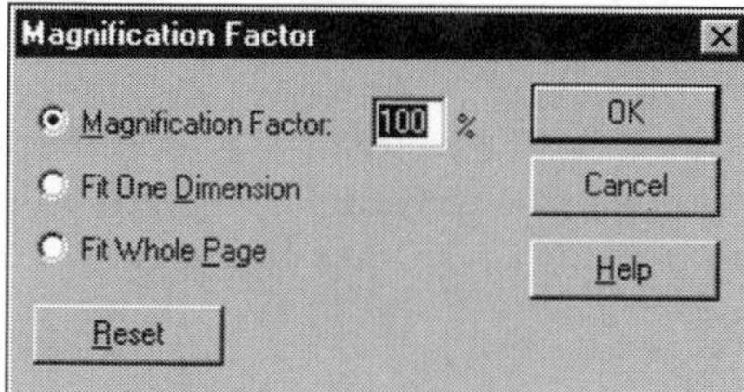

Figure 11-6: The Magnification Factor dialog box.

The first setting you can adjust in the Magnification Factor dialog box is the magnification factor, by typing a new value in the box. The valid zoom range is 25 percent through 400 percent. To see the report at twice the default magnification, type **200** in the box, which is exactly what has been done in Figure 11-7.

You may suppose that if you change the magnification factor in one window, the magnification carries over when you switch to the other window. It does not. Crystal Reports does not assume that you want the preview magnified. This approach makes sense because you may be changing the formatting on the Design tab and then want to see the change on the Preview tab at a static magnification. In this way, you can more easily compare apples to apples, so to speak.

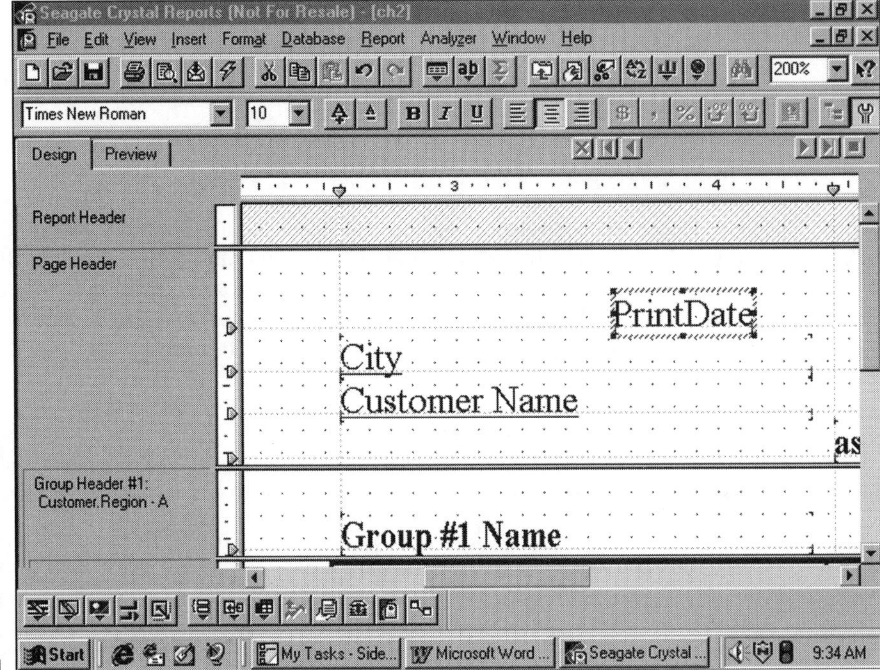

Figure 11-7: The Design tab zoomed by a factor of 200 percent.

The other options are Fit One Dimension and Fit Whole Page. When you toggle on the Fit One Dimension option, Crystal Reports fits the page according to the width of the report on the Design or Preview tabs. In other words, the report dimensions are controlled by the report objects and not by margin settings. The Fit Whole Page option causes Crystal Reports to adjust the report so that all the objects can be seen on-screen. In Preview mode, it shows one whole page.

In Figure 11-8, the Fit Whole Page option has been selected on the Preview tab. (If you use this option on the Design tab, the effect is not very noticeable.)

To return the report view to the default setting, click the Reset button. The 100 percent magnification factor returns. Now that you know how to adjust the view of the report to better judge the effect of formatting, a discussion of the Special fields is in order.

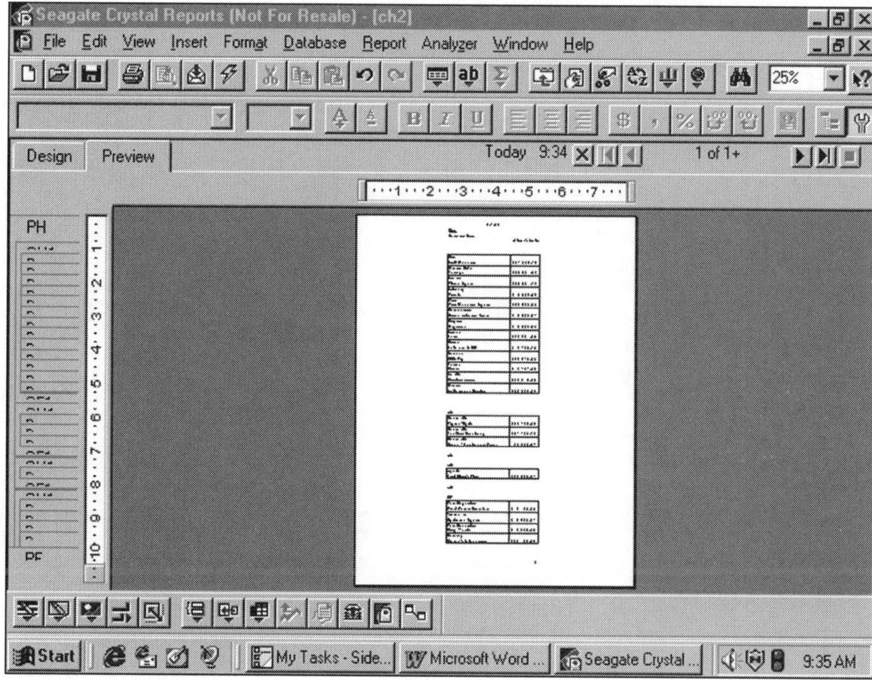

Figure 11-8: The Fit Whole Page option selected on the Preview tab.

Working with Special Fields

A presentation-quality report requires types of information that are not automatically part of a report. The reason is that not every report requires the same Special fields, and you need to decide what fields to include. *Special fields* are used to insert into a report information that is not derived from an underlying database table or from a report formula.

To insert a Special field, follow these steps:

1. **Choose Insert⇨Special field.**

   The Insert Fields dialog box appears.

2. **Click the Others tab, if it is not selected.**
3. **Double-click the Special Fields label to display the entire list of fields, as shown in Figure 11-9.**

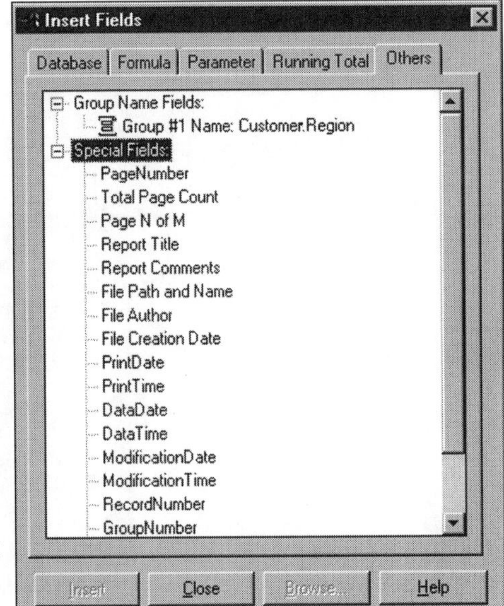

Figure 11-9: The Insert Fields dialog box with the Special Fields list expanded.

4. **Click the Special field you want to insert in the report.**
5. **Click the Insert button.**

   The frame cursor is attached to the mouse pointer. When you move the mouse to a position where the field can be properly inserted, the placeholder appears as a grayed rectangle; if the field cannot be inserted at the location of the mouse, the placeholder appears as a circle with a line drawn through it.

6. **Position the mouse pointer in the section of the report where you want the Special field information to be displayed.**
7. **Click the left mouse button to insert the field.**

Undo command

With any format you add (except those applied by the Style Expert), you can always revert to the original report status by choosing Edit⇨Undo. The Undo command is dynamic in that it reflects the last action taken. If you want to revert back, you must execute this command immediately after adding a noxious format. In fact, the Undo command works for multiple levels — pretty cool, huh?

Special fields defined

To help you decide which of the Special fields you would like to include in a report, each of the Special fields is described in Table 11-1.

Table 11-1 How Special Fields Operate

Field	*What It Does*
Page Number	Prints the current page number of the report.
Total Page Count	Prints the total number of pages in the report. This field is usually inserted in the report footer.
Page N of M	Displays the current page number of the total in the report, such as "3 of 15."
Report Title	Prints the contents of the Title field in the Document Properties dialog box. You can use this dialog box to enter summary information, such as the title of the report, the subject, and the author. Chapter 18 covers the file options and this topic.
Report Comments	Prints the contents of the Comments field from the Document Properties dialog box. You can use this dialog box to enter summary information, such as the title of the report, the subject, and the author. Chapter 18 covers the file options and this topic.
File Path and Name	As computer users enter the era of the terabyte drive, determining the location of stored files becomes more of a problem. Inserting this field in your report ensures that you know where the report is being stored.
File Author	This field prints the name of the person who created the report, as long as the information was entered by using the File menu and the Summary Info option. Because this information is document specific, several users can create reports and have their own names attached.
File Creation Date	Prints the date the report was created.
Print Date	Prints the current date based on the clock in your computer. (You can change the date by choosing Report⇨Set Print Date.)
Print Time	Prints the current time based on the clock in your computer when the report was last refreshed.
Data Date	Prints the date when the data in the report was last refreshed. This field works only with a report that has saved data.

(continued)

Table 11-1 *(continued)*

Field	*What It Does*
Data Time	Prints the time when the data in the report was last refreshed. This field works only with a report that has saved data.
Modification Date	Prints the date on which the report was last modified.
Modification Time	Prints the time at which the report was last modified.
Record Number	Prints the current record number. This field is usually used in the Details section of a report.
Group Number	Prints the current group number. This feature can be used in the group header or group footer.
Record Selection Formula	Prints the criteria used to select records included in the report.
Group Selection Formula	Prints the criteria used to select records included in the report.

Inserting a Special Field

Before you insert a Special field into a report, consider where you want the information generated by the Special field to print. For example, the Date field probably belongs in the Report Header section or perhaps in the Page Footer section. Report information such as the last modification date, report comments, and report title (not of the report itself, but of the computer filename) may belong in the Report Footer. As with most formatting in Crystal Reports, trying different locations and combinations is the best way to determine what works for your reports.

An additional consideration is that you can condition the printing of the Special field information and the way it's displayed by using a formula. (See Chapter 5 for more information about formulas.)

Follow these steps to insert the current date:

1. **Open the report in which you want a Date field inserted.**
2. **Click the Design tab if you're looking at the Preview tab.**
3. **Choose Insert➪Special Field.**

4. **From the Insert Fields dialog box, click Other. From the list of Special fields that appears, double-click the Print Date field.**

   The mouse pointer is transformed so that a gray box is attached to it. This box indicates that the field placeholder is ready for insertion, as shown in Figure 11-10.

5. **Move the pointer to the section of the report in which you want the Special field to print.**

   In this case, the pointer is positioned in the Report Header section.

   TIP: If you move the pointer over an existing text field, the placeholder may disappear for a moment. Be patient, move the pointer to another area of the report, and wait for the pointer to reappear.

6. **Click the left mouse button.**

   The field is inserted at that spot. Figure 11-11 shows the Date field inserted above the report title in the Report Header section of the report.

Previewing the report with the new field inserted yields the result shown in Figure 11-12.

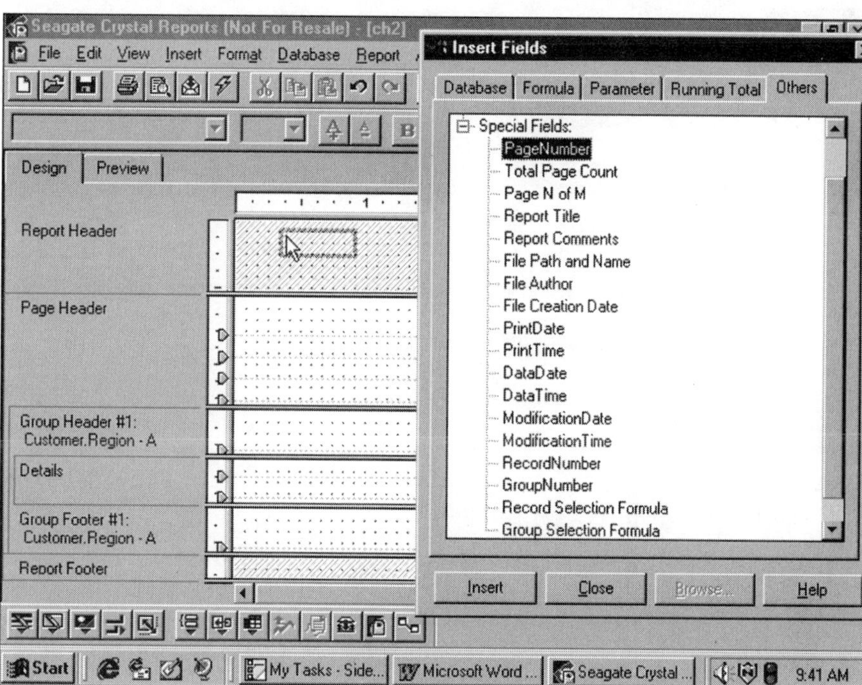

Figure 11-10: The mouse pointer with a Special Field box attached.

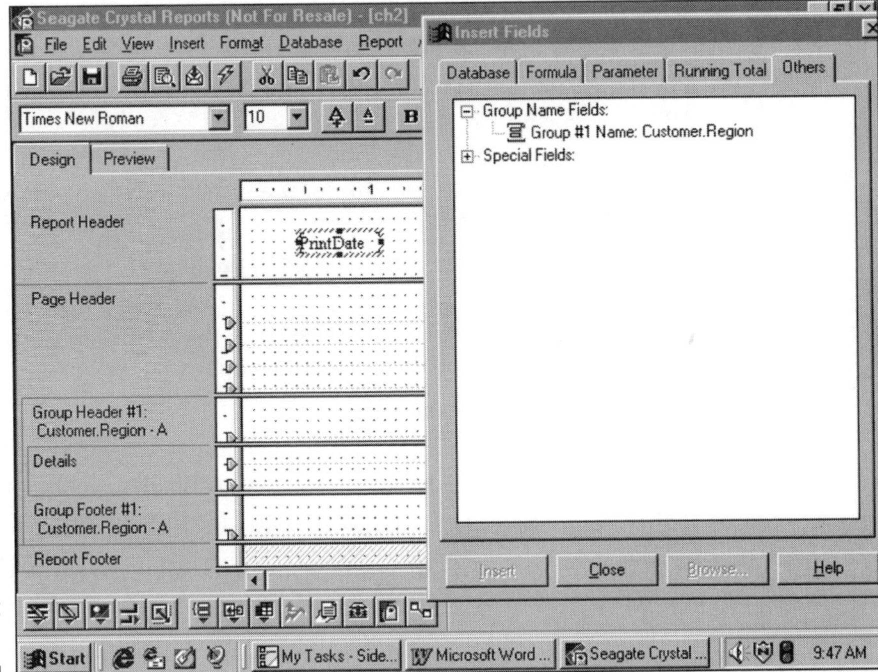

Figure 11-11: A Date field inserted in the Report Header.

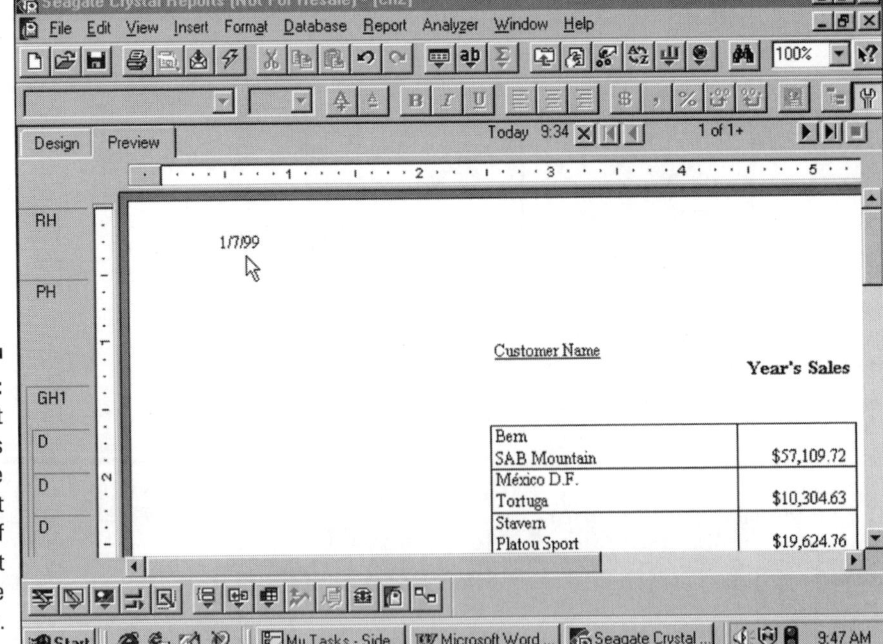

Figure 11-12: The Print Date field is visible in the top-left corner of the report on the Preview tab.

Adding a Record Number field

The *Record Number field* simply lists the number of the record in sequential order as it is printed in the report. Because this field generates a number for each record, the best place to insert this field is in the Details section of the report. In Figure 11-13, the field has been inserted to the right of the Last Year's Sales field. This feature is used quite often in legacy reports (mainframe-style reports), usually in control breaks. That way, even though the records have been split across many groups, the record numbering remains the same.

The *Record Number Special field* counts the number of records in the report and prints the number where you specify, as shown in Figure 11-14. The first record printed in the report, for example, is record Number 1, the second is Number 2, and so on.

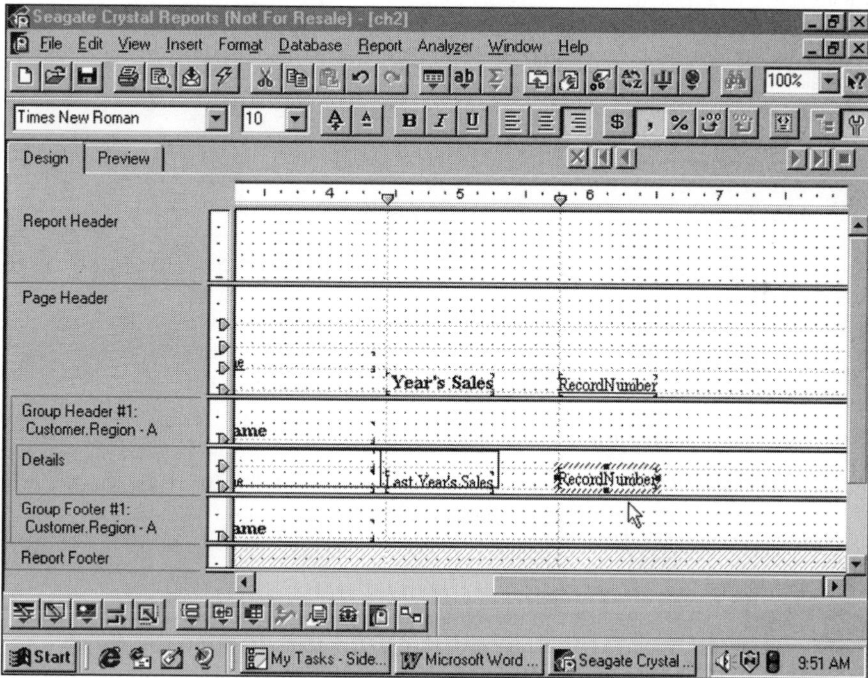

Figure 11-13: The Record Number field inserted to the right of the Last Year's Sales field.

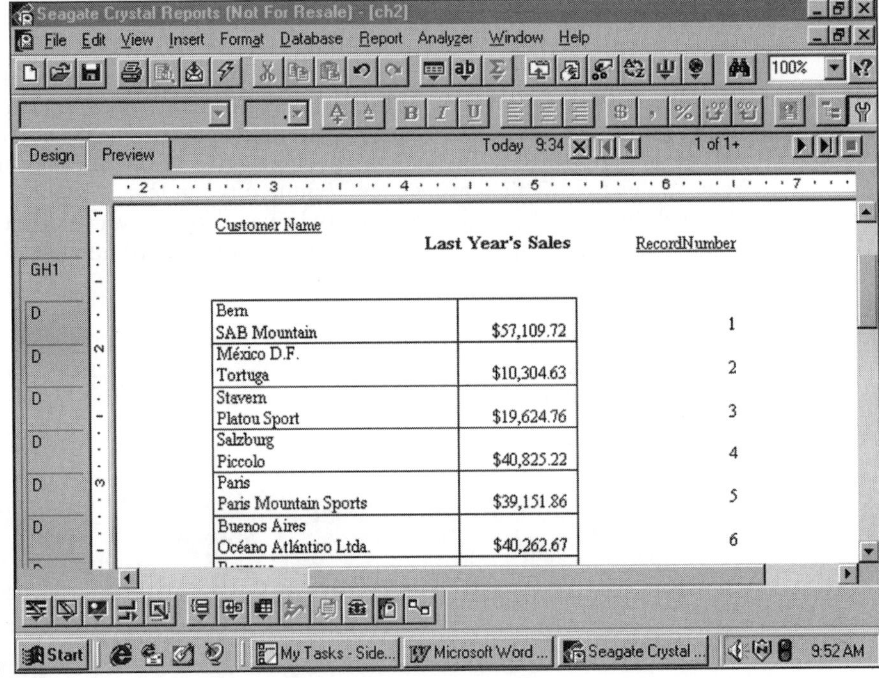

Figure 11-14: The Record Number field has been inserted.

Adding information to the Report Footer

As I mention earlier in this chapter, the placement of the Special field is as important as the information itself. Adding several pertinent pieces of information to the Report Footer makes identifying the report an easy task:

1. **Click the Design tab.**

   Because the sample report, as shown in Figure 11-15, has little room for the Report Footer, your first step is to increase the space allotted to the footer by clicking the horizontal line and dragging it toward the bottom of the report.

2. **To see the formatting better, move the mouse pointer to the left margin of the report and right-click to open the shortcut menu.**

3. **Choose the Arrange Lines option from the shortcut menu to insert horizontal guidelines, as shown in Figure 11-16.**

   Now you add the Special fields.

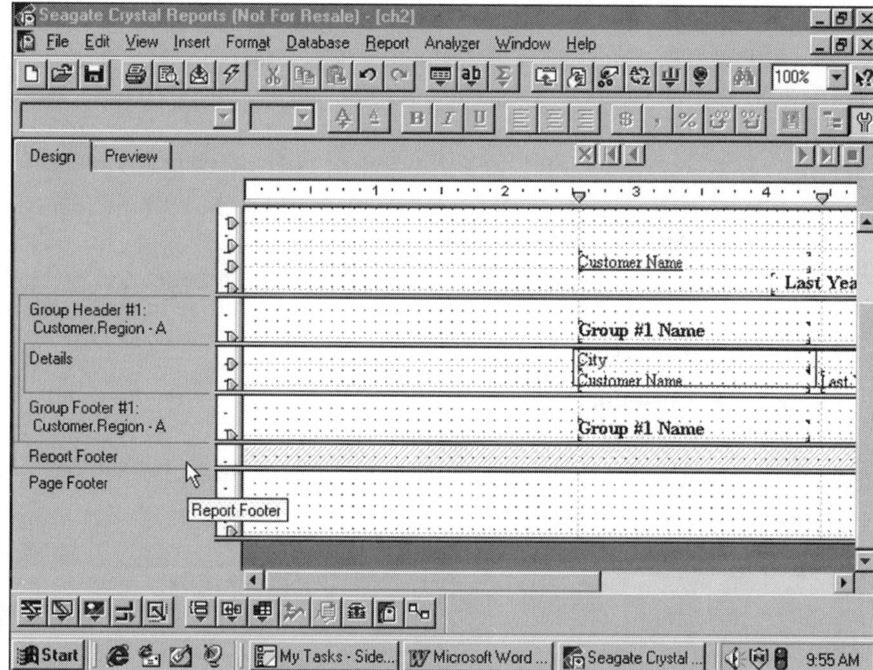

Figure 11-15: The Report Footer with little space available.

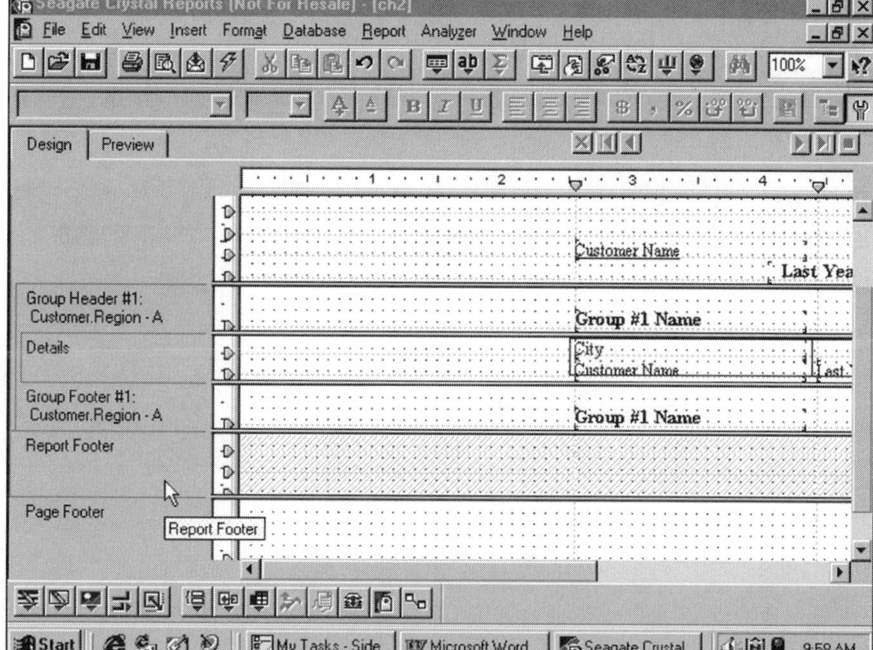

Figure 11-16: Horizontal lines inserted into the Report Footer section of the report.

4. **Choose Insert⇨Special field.**
5. **From the Insert Fields dialog box, select the Total Page Count field. (If the list of special fields doesn't appear, click the plus sign (+) to reveal the list.)**
6. **Press and hold the Ctrl (Control) key on your keyboard.**
7. **Select the Modification Date field. If you have done this step properly, both fields should be highlighted.**
8. **Insert the placeholders in the Report Footer section by clicking the Insert button and clicking the mouse pointer in that section.**

   The results are shown in Figure 11-17.
9. **Click the Preview tab, and click the Page Movement button that takes you to the last page of the report.**

   The inserted fields appear, as shown in Figure 11-18.

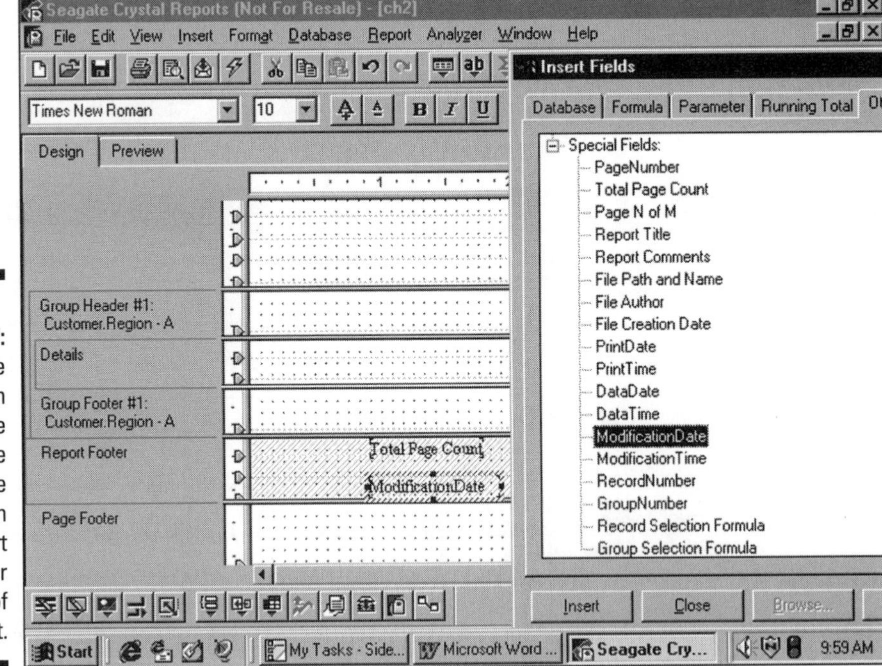

Figure 11-17: The modification date and the total page count are inserted in the Report Footer section of the report.

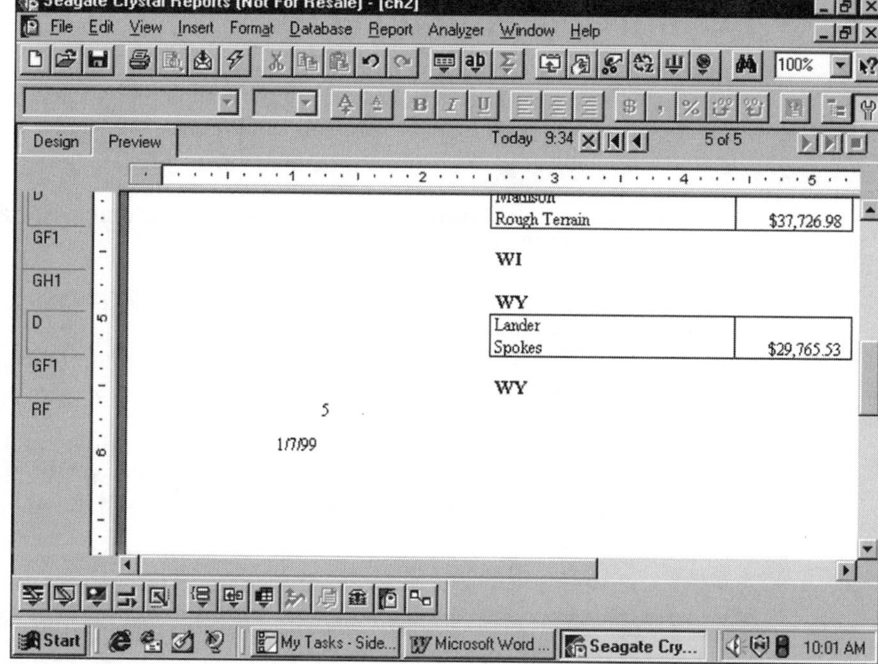

Figure 11-18: The Total Page Count field(5) and the modification date are inserted in the report footer.

The Group Number special field in action

Joe is the manager of the Craze Mountain Bikes Sales Force. He has a report that lists all the sales reps sorted by their regions (NE, SE, and West) and then sorted by descending order on their sales so that the top sellers are at the top. This report is *pages* long because Joe has a sales force of 1,000 people. Yikes. What he is really interested in is giving a bonus to the top five reps in each region. So Joe opens the report and chooses Report⇨TopN/Sort Group Expert. After he gets in there, he chooses the grouping related to their sales figures. Where the Sort All is selected from the drop-down list, Joe selects TopN. Crystal Reports automatically grabs the most logical summarized field. In this case, Joe is looking for Sum of the Sales Forces Last Year's Sales. Then he realizes that he wants a descending order because he wants to reward his hard-working staff. (Of course, if he wants more than five records for this group, he would just change the N from 5 to any other number.) So he presses the OK button and then clicks the Refresh button. Wow! A potentially 32-page report to get 15 names has been reduced to a page or two. And now Joe realizes that with the change from TopN to BottomN, he can find out who his delinquent reps are. What a product!

Formatting Special fields

Although you may find that the default font, color, and other format attributes are fine as presented, that's not likely. To make changes, simply right-click the particular field or value on the Preview tab. Figure 11-19 shows the shortcut menu.

Choose the Format Field option, and the Format Editor dialog box appears, as shown in Figure 11-20.

Note: If your mouse pointer is on a String field or a Date field when the Format Field option is chosen, the tab that is highlighted is named String or Date, respectively. The information on the tab is slightly different because Crystal Reports displays relevant information in the field.

The formatting possibilities are seemingly endless! The abundance of adjustments you can make to a field makes exposing them all nearly impossible. Just for the fun of it, click the Font tab to adjust the size of the number, as shown in Figure 11-21.

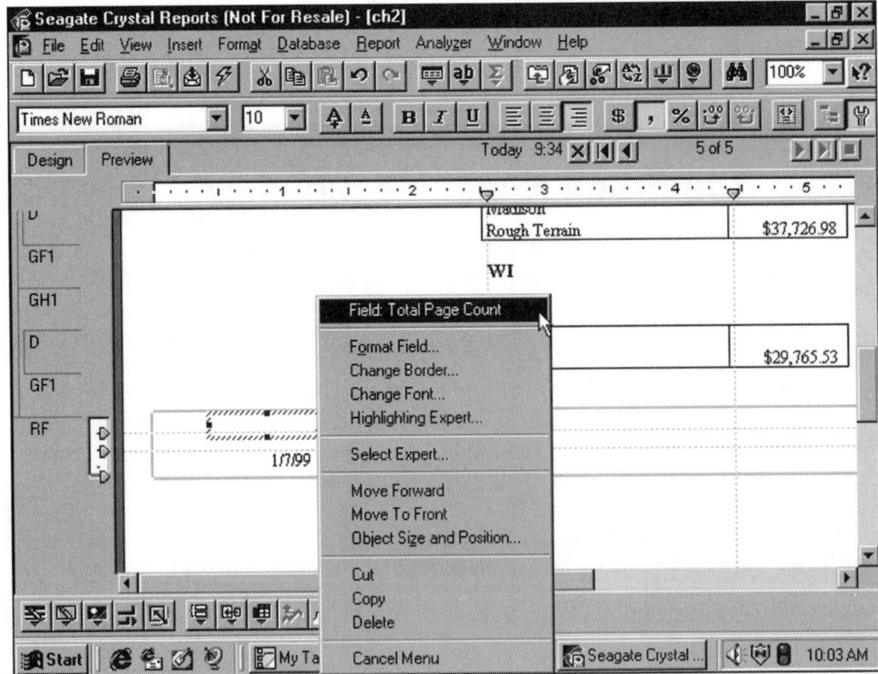

Figure 11-19: Right-click to open the Format Field shortcut menu.

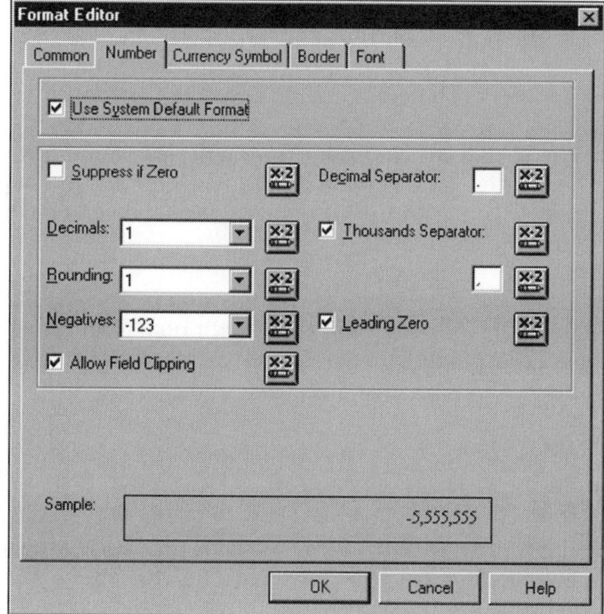

Figure 11-20: The Format Editor dialog box, with the Number tab selected.

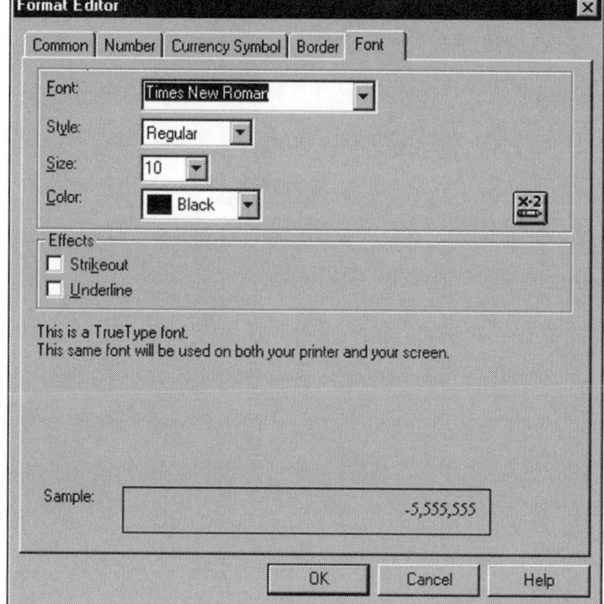

Figure 11-21: The Font tab selected in the Format Editor dialog box.

When you adjust the size in the box, Crystal Reports shows you the effect in the Sample box at the bottom of the dialog box. If you increase the size too much for the space allotted in the Sample box, the numbers look like they're cut off. But, not to worry: The numbers look okay in the report.

A point to consider is that the Underline option in this dialog box works together with the Border options (which I discuss later in this chapter, in the section "Boxing records in a group"). In other words, you can have an underline and a border at the same time.

As is true with most format settings, the application of a particular format can be conditioned by a formula. Click the Conditional Formatting button to open the Formula Editor dialog box and enter the conditions. (For more on formulas, see Chapter 5.)

Formatting a Date field

A Date field can be formatted in a variety of ways, too. To see the formatting options, right-click the Date field you have inserted, the Design tab, or the date itself on the Preview tab. Figure 11-22 shows the date after it has been right-clicked and the Format Field option has been selected.

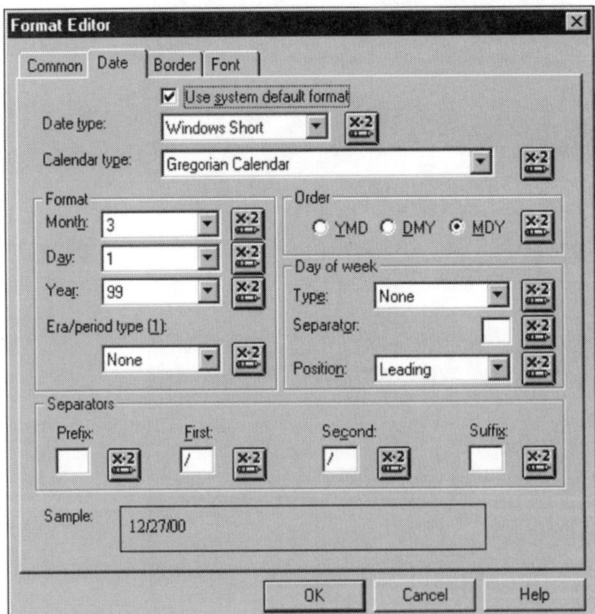

Figure 11-22: The Format Editor dialog box for a Date field.

This dialog box includes a sample box at the bottom that reflects the changes you make as you make them. The default setting that Crystal Reports uses is derived from the date setting established by the Windows operating system, as indicated by the check mark. If you prefer to have your own format, however, you can certainly do so. An easy change is to select the Windows Long format, which changes the date to something like Tuesday, March 16, 1999, rather than to a numerical format. To choose this format, click the drop-down arrow in the Date Type box and select the format, or go wild and select Custom. With Custom as the selection, you can change the order of the date numbers, the exact format of each of the components — Month, Day, and Year — and so on.

If you change the date format from short to long, you must reformat the field in the report by stretching it so that the entire date can be displayed.

All the special fields you insert in a report can be formatted. When you right-click, the menu that appears is specific to the field you selected. Experiment with the different formats until you're satisfied with the results.

Combining a text object with a Special field

Knowing how to execute the formatting in this section sets you apart from novice Crystal Reports users. You may know how easy popping a Special field into a report is, as described earlier in this chapter, but what if the person reading the report does not know what the Special field numbers represent? For example, because the Total Page number field can be mistaken for just about anything, you, the report creator, have the duty to include explanatory text for each Special field entry.

When the Record Number field was added, Crystal Reports included the name of the field because the field was added by itself in an open column. The other Special field you added to the report did not have the luxury of the space to include a field name. Yet, knowing the identity of each object is crucial for everyone dealing with the report.

You may be thinking that you can simply add a text object preceding or following the Special field and enter the description of the field. Crystal Reports has a much more elegant solution: Combine the Special field and a text object.

To demonstrate this technique with the sample report, the Page Number must be deleted and reinserted. You cannot drag a Special field into a text object and get the correct result, so starting over is easier.

1. **On the Design tab, right-click the Total Page field and choose Delete from the shortcut menu.**

2. **Click the Text Object button on the toolbar, and insert a text box in the Report Footer section of the report.**

   The best location is where the Total Page Number field used to be, before being deleted. The Text Object Edit field appears with a ruler line, as shown in Figure 11-23.

3. **Type** Total Number of Pages: **.**

   Don't forget to add a space after the colon! Now, the pièce de résistance. . . .

4. **With the text object still open, choose Insert⇨Special Field.**

5. **From the Insert Fields dialog box, select Other and then choose the Total Page Count field. If the list of special fields doesn't appear, double-click the words *Special Fields* or click the plus sign (+).**

6. **Click the Insert button and then click the mouse pointer inside the text object.**

   The Special field is inserted in the Text Object box, as shown in Figure 11-24.

7. **To see this esoteric formatting trick in action, click the Preview tab.**

   The report appears, as shown in Figure 11-25. The Preview tab has been zoomed to 200 percent to better see the result.

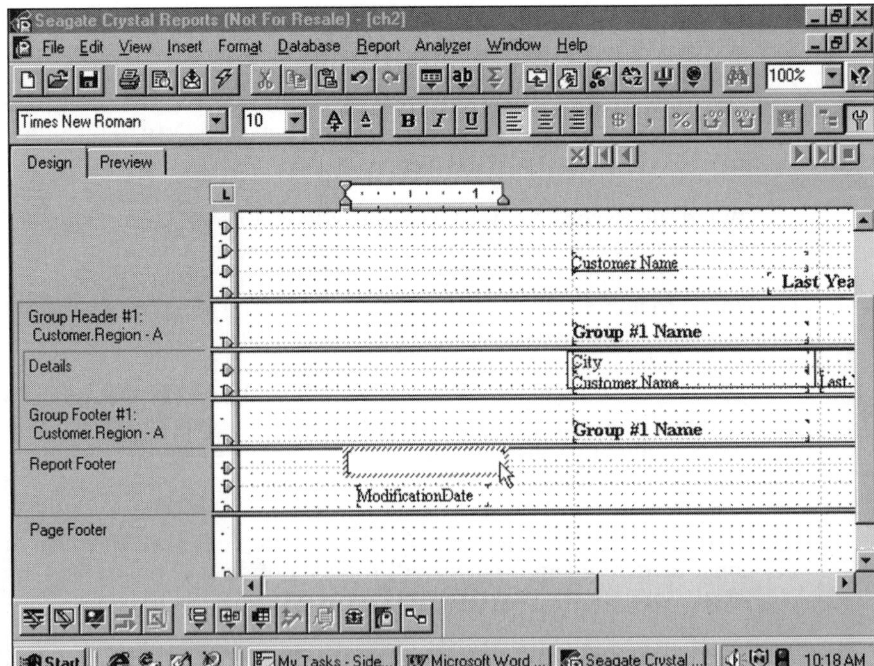

Figure 11-23: Inserting a new text object.

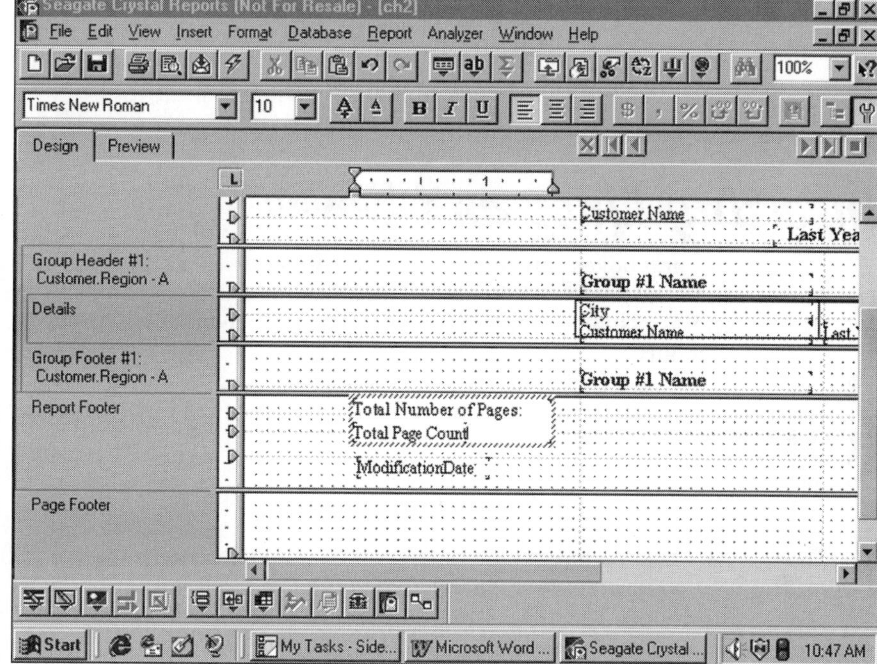

Figure 11-24: The Total Page Count Special field is inserted in the Text Object box.

Figure 11-25: A text box combined with a Special field on the Preview tab, zoomed to 200 percent.

This combination of a Special field and a text box gives you much more flexibility in terms of options than creating two separate objects ever could. You can even combine two database fields rather painlessly. Just drag and drop them into a text object and off you go.

Inserting Lines and Boxes

Lines and boxes can enhance particular values in a report and are a snap to add to the layout. If you add a line object in a group summary, Crystal Reports assumes that you want the line inserted in every group summary in the report.

If you're really looking to underline the contents of just *one* field, click the Underline button.

You can insert a line in one of three ways:

- Click the Insert Line button on the supplementary toolbar. If the supplementary toolbar isn't visible in the lower-left corner of the window, choose View⇨Toolbars. In the dialog box, click Supplementary Tools and then click OK.
- Choose Insert⇨Line.
- Highlight the object you want underlined, and then click the Underline button.

In either case, the mouse pointer is transformed to look like a small pencil on the screen. You then use your mouse to draw the line by holding down the left mouse button and dragging the mouse. Use the Design tab to add these formats.

To add a line to a group summary, follow these steps:

1. **Click the Design tab.**
2. **Increase the magnification to 200 percent by choosing View⇨Zoom.**

3. **Click the Insert Line button on the toolbar.**

   The mouse is transformed into a pencil.
4. **Position the pencil tip underneath and to the left of the object you want to underline.**

   In this example, the placeholder for the Last Year's Sales Group Total is the target.

5. **Click the left mouse button, and drag the pencil to the right so that the placeholder is underlined, as shown in Figure 11-26.**
6. **To appreciate the beauty of this format, click the Preview tab.**

   In Figure 11-27, the Preview is shown and the magnification is 200 percent.

The advantage of adding a line in this way is that you can choose exactly what you want to emphasize, whereas the Field Format options for borders are drawn wherever Crystal Reports thinks they should be drawn. You can also draw the line so that more space appears between the line and the object, making it easier to select just a line when you're formatting.

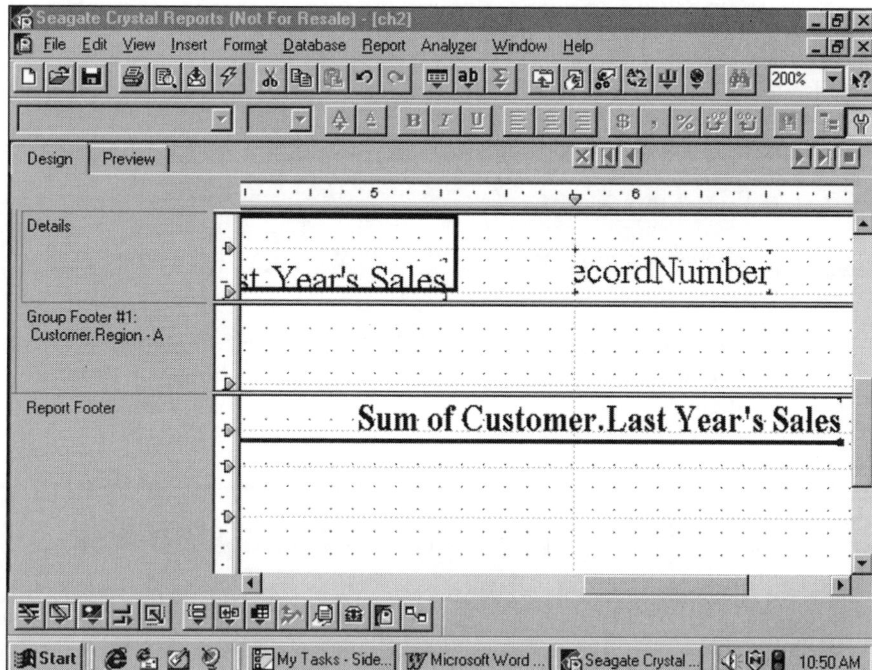

Figure 11-26: Underlining the Group Total placeholder.

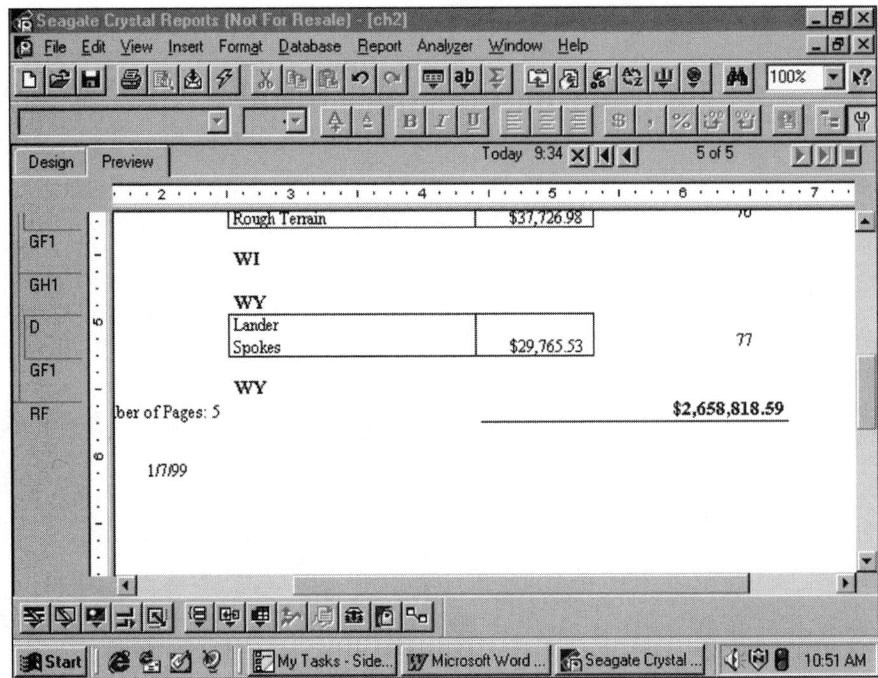

Figure 11-27: A preview of an underline added to the Group Total for Last Year's Sales.

A drawn line can be only horizontal or vertical. Angled lines are not possible. The benefit is that you can be certain that any lines you draw are perfectly aligned.

Using the Supplementary toolbar

Users of Version 6.0 and later have an additional toolbar just for adding enhancements to reports. To see the new toolbar, click the icon at the far right of the second toolbar from the top of the screen. The toolbar is directly under the Zoom button, and the icon has a yellow wrenchlike figure on it. With the mouse on the icon, the pop-up text reads *Toggle Supplementary Toolbar.* Clicking the icon displays the toolbar in the lower-left corner of the screen, just above the Windows Start button. Move your mouse pointer over each of the icons, and Crystal Reports displays the pop-up description of each.

All the toolbars are at your command. Choosing View⇨Toolbars opens a dialog box from which you can toggle off and on any or all of the three toolbars.

Formatting a line

Lines can be adjusted after they are in place. You begin any line object with the original line, as demonstrated in the preceding example, and then build from there.

To change the format of a line in a report:

1. **Right-click the line to open the shortcut menu, as shown in Figure 11-28.**

   Opening this menu is a bit tricky. The best approach is to move the mouse pointer beneath the line and then right-click. Otherwise, Crystal Reports thinks that you want to format the group summary. You may also want to choose Format⇨Line.

2. **Choose the Format Line option.**

   When you do, the Format Editor dialog box appears, as shown in Figure 11-29.

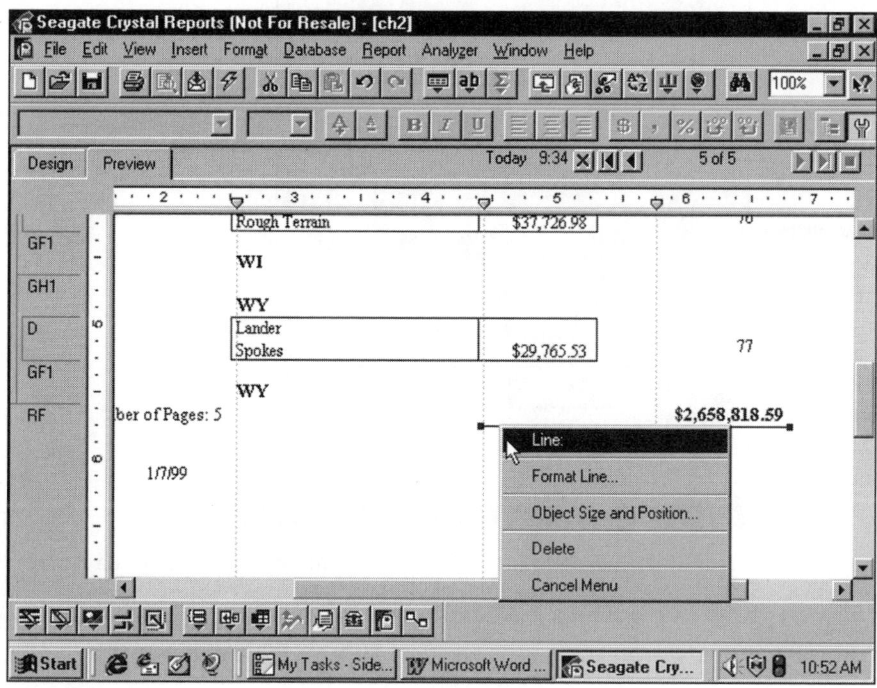

Figure 11-28: The shortcut menu for line formatting.

This dialog box is one of the few in which you have no sample field to gauge the format you select before applying it to the report — the buttons show you the width.

3. **To check the line density, you click the line size you want, and the number (in points) is displayed to the right.**
4. **Add a color preference by clicking the drop-down arrow in the Color box, and, if you want the line to print at the bottom of the section (like an accounting statement), you can have it do that.**
5. **Click OK to close the dialog box.**

One other thing you can do, and the magnification feature makes it easy, is grab the handles at either end of the line and lengthen or shorten the line to match the length of the field if you have misdrawn the line.

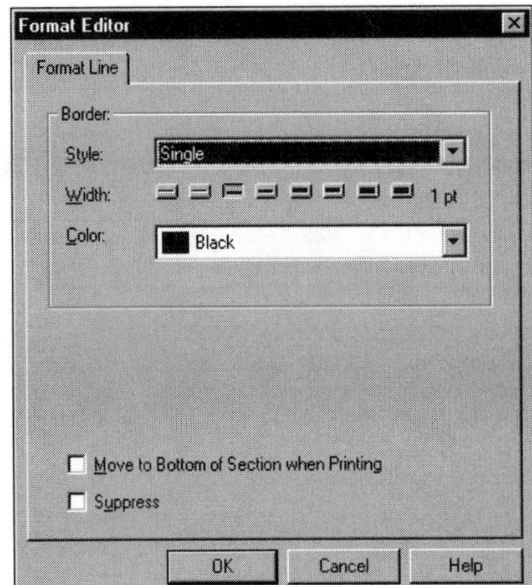

Figure 11-29: The Format Editor dialog box for line formatting.

Boxing records in a group

What if you want to add a border around every record in a report?

Simply follow these steps to add a border around individual records in a report:

1. **Click the Design tab in your report.**
2. **Click the field name in the Details section of the report.**
3. **Right-click to open the shortcut menu.**

   The shortcut menu is shown in Figure 11-30.

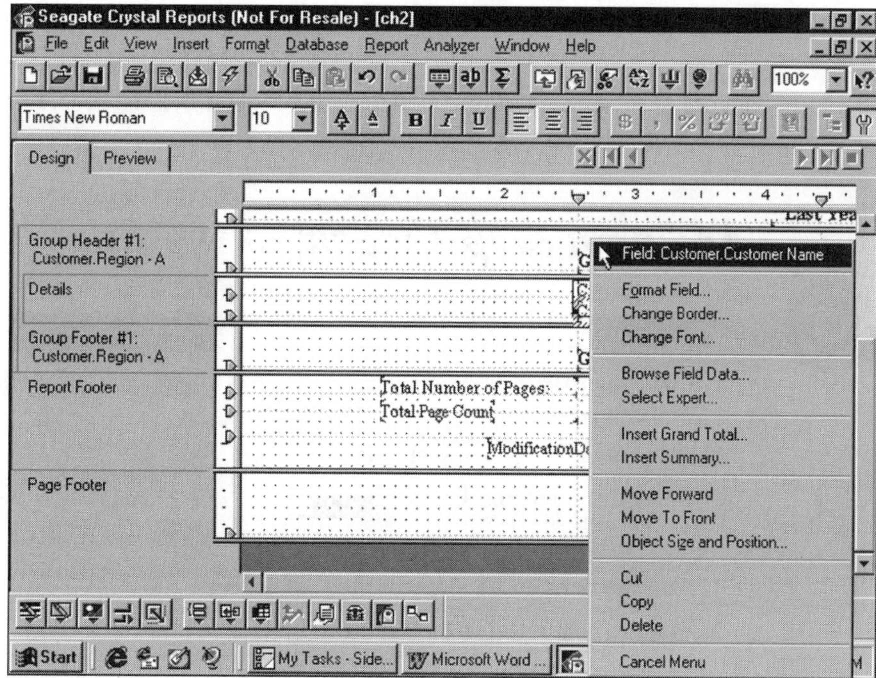

Figure 11-30: The shortcut menu for formatting a field.

4. **Choose Change Border.**

   The Format Editor dialog box appears.

   Crystal Reports, flexible tool that it is, gives you a choice of exactly which lines should be included in the border: top, left, right, bottom, all, or some. On top of that, each of the border lines can be conditional! Set a formula to determine which line prints and when — a little much in my opinion, but some folks undoubtedly will use this feature.

5. **Click the drop-down arrow next to the border you want to include and select the type of line you want to use.**
6. **Click OK to close the dialog box and apply the new format.**

The Tight Horizontal option trims the border to the size of the field. When this check box is toggled off, the border is the same size for each record. When this check box is toggled on, the border is trimmed to the size of each individual record.

The Drop Shadow option adds a façade of depth to the border. Check this box if you want that effect. In this case, where the border is going around each individual record, the shadow would be an over-format — all it would do is add clutter.

You can select the color of the border lines as well as a background color inside the border lines.

Figure 11-31 shows the report with each of the individual records with a border drawn.

Adding a drop shadow to the title

TIP

A great place to use the drop shadow effect is in the report title. This effect is easy to create and adds a classy, professional look to your report:

1. **Click the title of your report, or any text object, so that the border is outlined.**
2. **Right-click to open the shortcut menu.**
3. **Choose the Format Border option.**

   The Format Editor dialog box appears.
4. **Add borders on all sides of the text object.**
5. **Click to select the Drop Shadow check box and click OK.**

   The title is displayed, as shown in Figure 11-32.

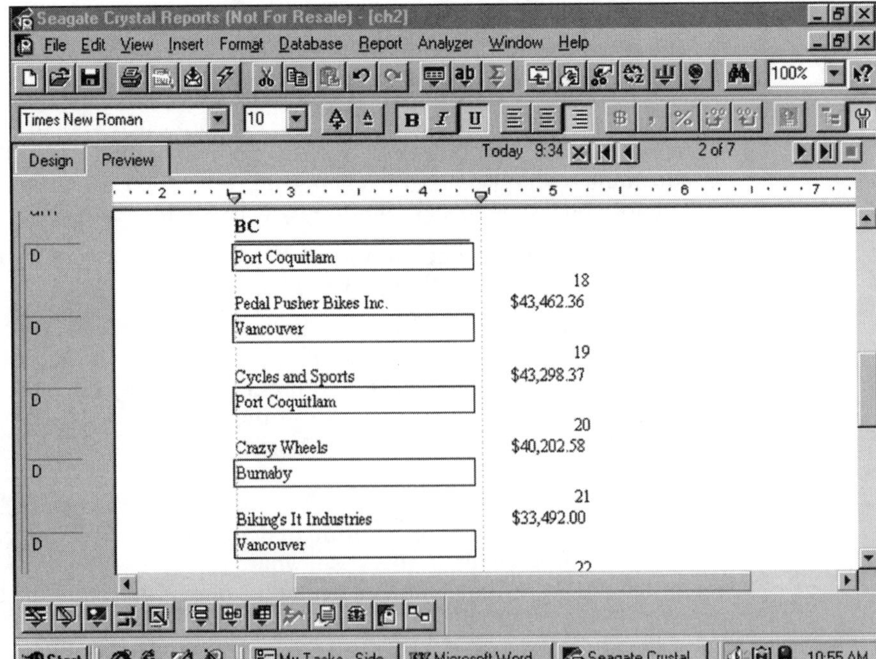

Figure 11-31: A border drawn on individual records.

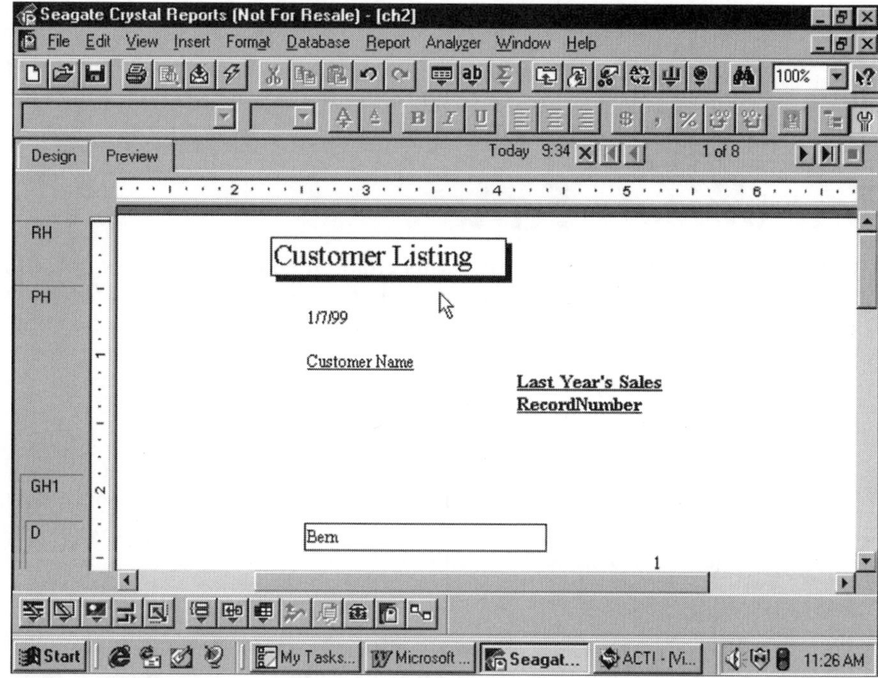

Figure 11-32: A border and drop shadow added to the title of the report.

Drawing a Box around an Object

Drawing a box around a group of records can be especially tricky if you try to draw a box that crosses sections of the report. Drawing a box involves a little planning. The best way to draw it is to select the point where you want the upper-left corner and then draw the box by dragging the lines across and down to the point where you want the lower-right corner.

To draw a box around an object or objects, follow these steps:

1. **Open the report in the Design window because it's easier to see the lines that define sections in the report.**
2. **Click the Insert Box tool button, or choose Insert⇨Box.**

   The mouse pointer is transformed into a pencil shape.
3. **At the point where the upper-left corner of the box will start, click the left mouse button and hold it.**
4. **Drag the mouse across and to the right to the point where you want the lower-right corner to be drawn.**
5. **Release the mouse button.**

You may format the box by clicking it to show the handles and then right-clicking to open the shortcut menu. Choose Format Box to select the line type, color, and thickness. You may even add a drop shadow. In Figure 11-33, a box has been drawn around the Group Header section, which includes the names of the fields in the report.

Text Objects Extra

If you have read the rest of this chapter, you already know how to insert a text object and then type the text you want in the object. You know how to right-click to add formatting. You know how to combine a text object with a Special field. The following example shows you how to insert database fields into a text object and then to format the field so that no matter how long the information in the database is, it prints properly.

The sample report file has a list of customers, their respective cities, and their last year's sales. For this example, adding the name of the owner enhances the report. You can create a text object of your own and then insert a database field, as I describe in this section.

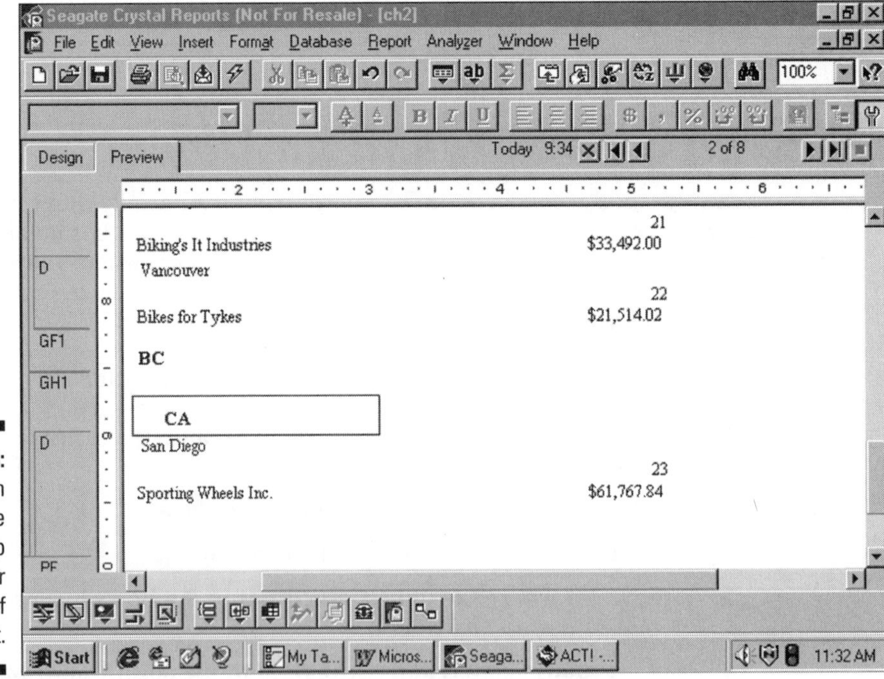

Figure 11-33: A box drawn around the Group Header section of the report.

To create a text object, follow these steps:

1. **From the Design tab, choose Insert⇨Text object.**
2. **Insert the text object above the field name in the Details section.**

   You may have to resize the section to fit the new field.
3. **Type some explanatory text, such as** Owner's name: **.**

   Add a space after the colon.
4. **Choose Insert⇨Database field.**

   The field placeholder is attached to the mouse pointer. In this example, the first field to insert is Contact First Name.
5. **Position the mouse pointer right behind the text you just typed in the text object box.**

   The field placeholder becomes a small insertion point when it is inside the text box.
6. **Left-click the mouse button to insert the Database field.**

   The text box appears, as shown in Figure 11-34.

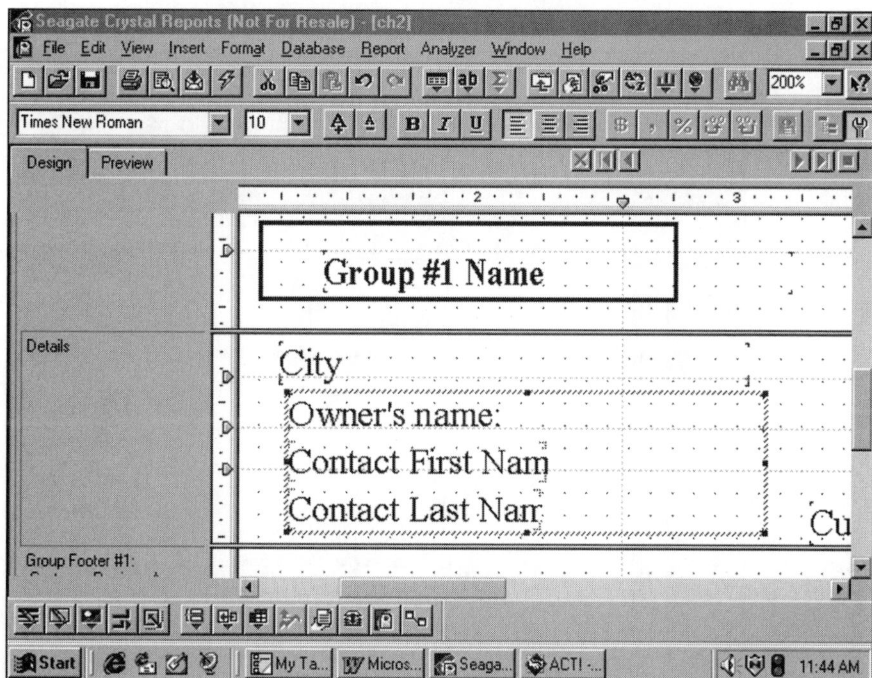

Figure 11-34: The text box with a Database field inserted and shown at 200 percent zoom.

7. **Choose Insert⇨Database field.**

   Don't forget to add a space before adding the second field.

8. **In this example, the next field to insert is Contact Last Name, so that field is selected.**

The great thing about this process is that Crystal Reports automatically trims the field information so that the format is correct, as you can see in Figure 11-35. Without this capability, your report would have significant gaps between the first and last names.

Adding the Can Grow option

Although the report prints properly in the preceding section, you can take another step to make sure that the text box is the correct size to contain the fields you insert:

1. **Right-click the text object.**

   The shortcut menu appears.

2. **Choose the Format Text menu item.**

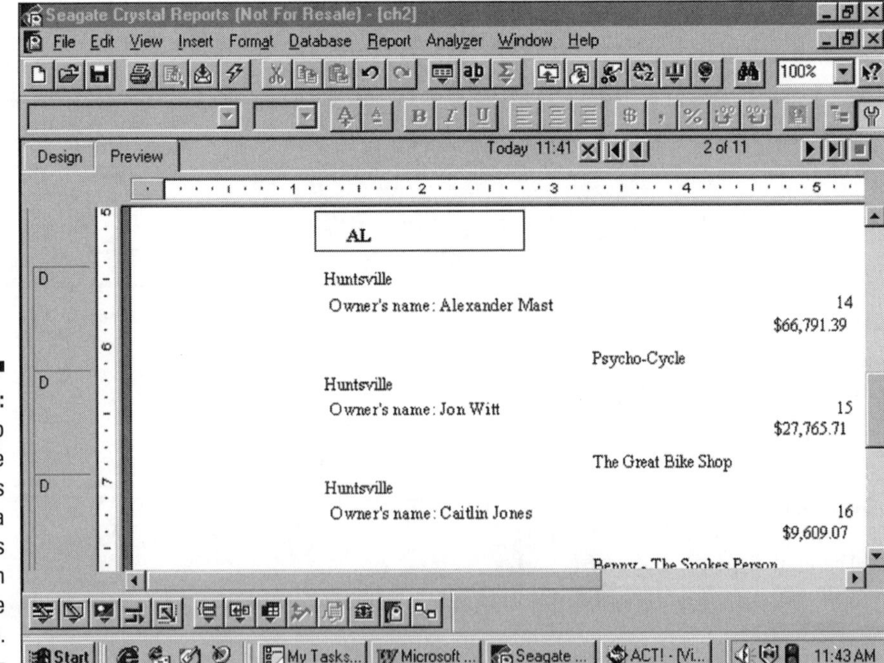

Figure 11-35: Two Database fields inserted in a text box, as shown on the Preview tab.

3. **In the Format Editor dialog box, click the check box in front of the Can Grow option, if it is not already checked.**

   With this option on, the text object grows vertically, not horizontally. That is, the text object gets taller, not longer.

As soon as a field (of any type) is dropped into a text object, Can Grow is automatically turned on (so you don't have to go and find it). Cool, huh?

Editing text within a text object

Because a text object may not be perfect after you insert it in a report, you may have to make some changes. Follow these steps:

1. **Double-click the text object you want to edit.**

   The text editor ruler appears above the object, and you can edit the text inside the box.

2. **If you want to change options for the entire text object, choose the appropriate option (such as Font, Border, or Format Text) to open the Format Editor dialog box by right-clicking the text object.**

Inserting a Picture or Logo into the Report

As soon as your boss sees the other nifty formats you can add to your reports, she'll certainly ask you to insert a picture or logo. By the time you have added all the other attributes, that finishing touch is the company graphic. And why not? The big deal with Windows is its capability to read bitmapped files throughout all applications. Before you can insert a picture or logo, it must exist in a format Crystal Reports can accept, such as .BMP (a bitmap), .PCX, .TIF, .JPG, or .TGA. The Paint program included with Windows creates files in .BMP format.

To insert your company logo in a report, follow these steps:

1. **Open the report in which you want to insert a picture or logo.**
2. **Click the Design tab.**

   Depending on where you want the picture inserted, you may have to resize the section to accommodate the new picture object. Crystal Reports adjusts the size of the section for you, however, if you position the picture beneath an existing object and the section border. For example, if you want the picture to be in the Report Header, beneath the title, position the pointer just underneath the title and click. Figure 11-36 shows the picture outline at the point where Crystal Reports adjusts the section size to make the fit.

3. **Choose Insert⇨Picture (or press the Insert Picture button on the toolbar).**

   The Open dialog box appears. You may have to switch folders or drivers to locate the file you want to insert. Crystal Reports includes a bitmap of the Xtreme Mountain Bike Company logo in the Crystal Reports folder named Xtreme, making this file easy to use as an example.

4. **Click the file you want to insert.**
5. **Click the Open button.**

   The Open dialog box closes, and the mouse pointer has a gray outlined box attached, indicating the size of the picture or logo. The outline of the logo is shown in Figure 11-36.

6. **Position the box at the point where you want the logo inserted.**
7. **Click the left mouse button to insert the picture, as shown in Figure 11-37.**

   Notice that Crystal Reports has pushed the page header down to make room for the logo.

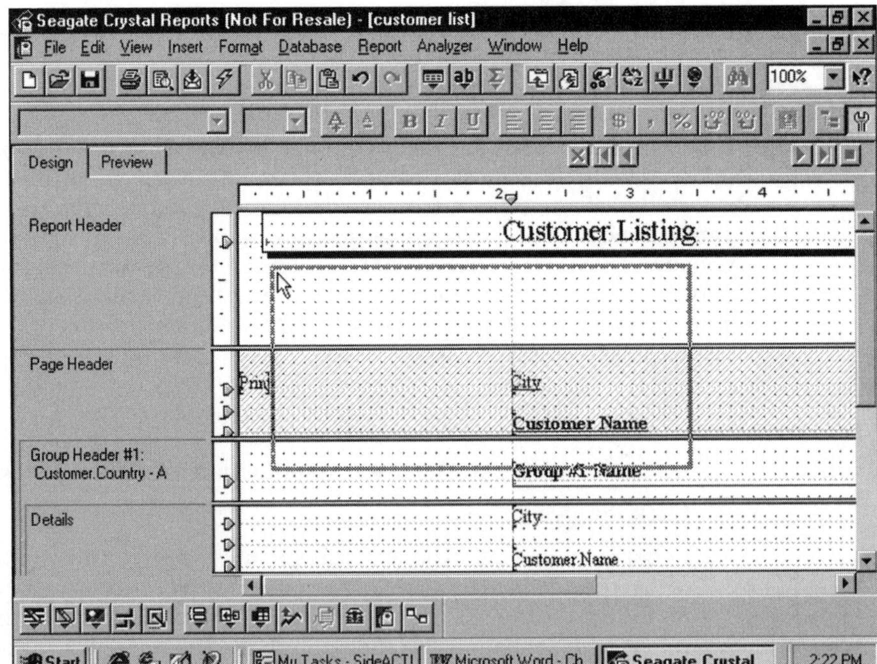

Figure 11-36: A picture outline before being inserted.

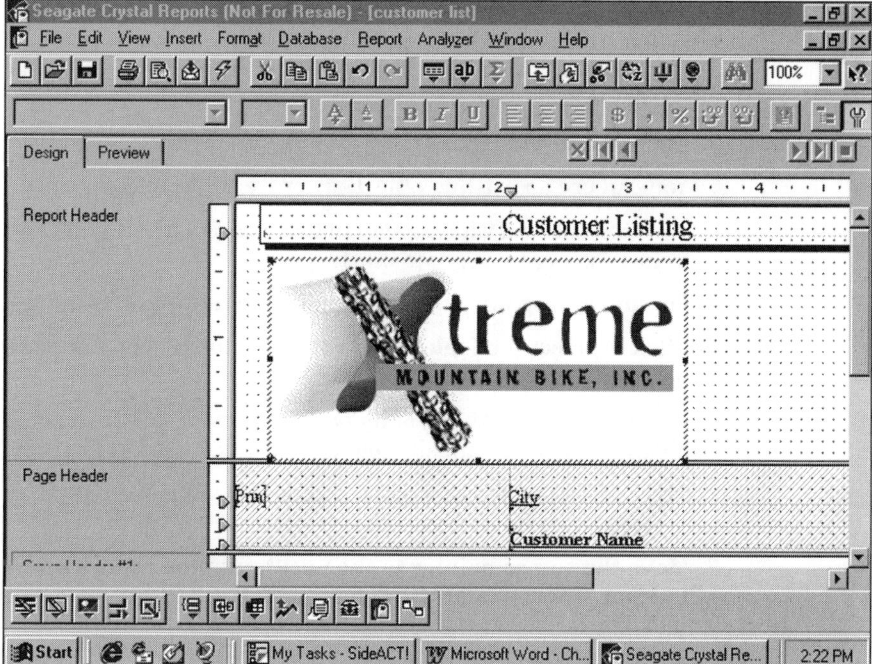

Figure 11-37: Additional space is automatically provided for the logo.

Inserting an OLE Object

An OLE (Greek — or is it geekspeak? — for Object Linking and Embedding) object is different from any ordinary picture or logo file in that it is an active file. That is, an OLE object is usually a file that was created in another application, such as Microsoft Paint. If the object needs editing, you normally have to go to the trouble of making the edit in Paint, deleting the old object from your report, and then reinserting it. Whew! Too much like work. To make life easier, using OLE, you can click the object, and the application that created the object starts up so that you can make changes directly.

Linking versus embedding

If the logo changes when a *linked* object (a company logo, for example) is added to a report, the *new* logo is in the report the next time the report is run.

When an *embedded* object is added to a report, even if the object (file) changes) if someone nukes the logo file, for example), those changes are not made in the refreshed report.

To insert an OLE object, follow these steps:

1. **Open the report in which you want to insert the OLE, and click the Design tab.**
2. **Choose Insert⇨OLE.**

   You can use an existing object or create a new one.

   You can embed a wide variety of OLE objects in a report. The range is from a picture to a spreadsheet.
3. **For an existing object, click the Browse button to locate the file.**
4. **Click to select the Link box if you want the object automatically updated.**

   If you change the object in its native program, such as Excel, the changes are automatically reflected in Crystal Reports.

   The OLE can be identified in the report by an icon created by Crystal Reports or by an icon you select.
5. **Move the mouse pointer to the position in the report where you want the OLE inserted and then click.**

To activate the OLE, double-click it. If you have inserted a spreadsheet, Excel starts within Crystal Reports. Very cool.

Using Auto Arrange to Format Reports

When you place a field from a database in your report, Crystal Reports allocates space in the report based on the length of the field as designated in the database table. If the designer of the database allocated 50 character spaces for the Product Name field, for example, that's the length of the field set aside in Crystal Reports. The space that's allocated is often much too long. The Auto Arrange command resizes the field length by finding the longest entry in the Database field and adjusting the length in the report based on that.

The second thing Auto Arrange does is to reposition the field to better use the space freed up by the resizing. Auto Arrange also centers the report on the page.

To use the Auto Arrange command, follow these steps:

1. **Insert the fields you want in the report, and add groups and other formatting.**

2. **Choose Format➪Auto Arrange.**

   Crystal Reports warns you that this command cannot be undone.

It seems that every aspect of Crystal Reports can be modified in some way. The key idea may be that you should be careful not to overdo the formatting. If the report is too "busy," it takes away the message you're trying to convey. If *obfuscation* is your goal, of course, you can accomplish it easily with the formatting options.

Part V

Creating Specific Types of Reports

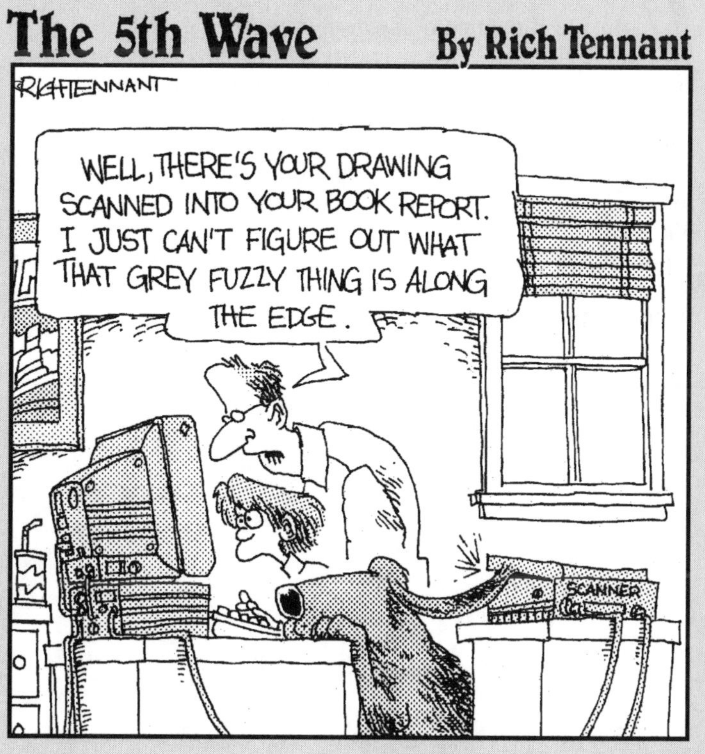

The 5th Wave
By Rich Tennant
RICH TENNANT
WELL, THERE'S YOUR DRAWING SCANNED INTO YOUR BOOK REPORT. I JUST CAN'T FIGURE OUT WHAT THAT GREY FUZZY THING IS ALONG THE EDGE.
SCANNER

In this part . . .

Variety is the spice of life, and in reporting, it is no different. So, in this part, the thyme, sage, saffron, curry, and fenugreek all become a part of your flavorful report repertoire — metaphorically, at least. Seagate Crystal Reports has a wide variety of report types from which you can choose. This part is devoted to helping you cook a report that will cure the common cold and land you that corner office with a key to the executive washroom. By matching the report type with the needs of those in your organization, you will gain the reputation of a master report chef. Stand aside, Wolfgang Puck, there is a new report maker in town.

Chapter 12

Creating a Cross-Tab Report

In This Chapter

- Creating a cross-tab
- Inserting a cross-tab into an existing report
- Using the Cross-Tab Expert
- Checking out the Advanced button

A cross-tab object turns fields on their side, so to speak, so that you can see different relationships between and among fields, much like you can in a spreadsheet. A cross-tab report can be a great analytical tool and a way to identify trends. In this chapter, I help you create a simple one.

Identifying the "By" Word

A *cross-tab* is an arrangement of fields in which the data in the fields can be compared in order to identify trends. Pollsters, those best friends of politicians, use cross tabulations of voter interviews to see which issues are creating a response *by* age, *by* location, or *by* whatever demographic or psychographic category the respondent fits. Campaign directors then design TV and direct-mail ads to target those respondents in such a way that their candidate's image is acceptable to those respondents. If the directors are good at reading cross-tabs, they get their candidate elected.

When you're using cross-tabs, the operative word is *by* because the genesis of a cross-tab is sales *by* region, products *by* customer, votes *by* precinct, or *by* whatever. Whenever you think that a report would be more valuable if it included a set of data that can be defined as something *by* something else, you are in Cross-Tab Land.

In business, the same principle applies. With an existing or new product, the survey research can be cross-tabulated to determine which customer profile is most likely to purchase the product. You can even determine the price range acceptable to the customer. In the example in this chapter, I create a cross-tab to determine which suppliers sold products in which regions.

A cross-tab is hard for people to handle conceptually. Think of something like this:

	Beer	*Wine*	*Total*
Males	100	20	120
Females	15	75	90
Total	115	95	210

This table is a cross-tab that analyzes sales by sex and alcohol type. You can learn a great deal by taking a quick look at a cross-tab.

In Crystal Reports, a cross-tab is an object, not the entire report, so a cross-tab can be inserted at a particular place in the report or combined with a summary report (see Chapter 13). The cross-tab can be inserted into the report header or report footer or the group header or group footer. Where you place the cross-tab object is crucial in this respect: If you insert the cross-tab in the report header or report footer, the cross-tab object is displayed only once and includes every record in the report. The other option, inserting the cross-tab in the group header or group footer, causes the cross-tab to consider only the records in that particular group, and the cross-tab is displayed before or after every group of records.

Creating a Cross-Tab Object in a New Report

A cross-tab object is arranged by rows and columns. If you have worked with a spreadsheet, you have seen this concept at work. When you select a Database field for inclusion in a cross-tab, each value in the Database field is given its own row or column. The column header or row header is the name of the field.

Before discussing how to add a cross-tab to an existing report, start with a new report to see the entire process. In this example, the xtreme database is used.

1. **Choose File⇨New.**
2. **From the Report Gallery dialog box, select Custom.**
3. **At the bottom of the dialog box, click Data File.**
4. **In the Choose Database File dialog box, click Xtreme.**
5. **Click OK.**

   The Select Tables dialog box appears, as shown in Figure 12-1.

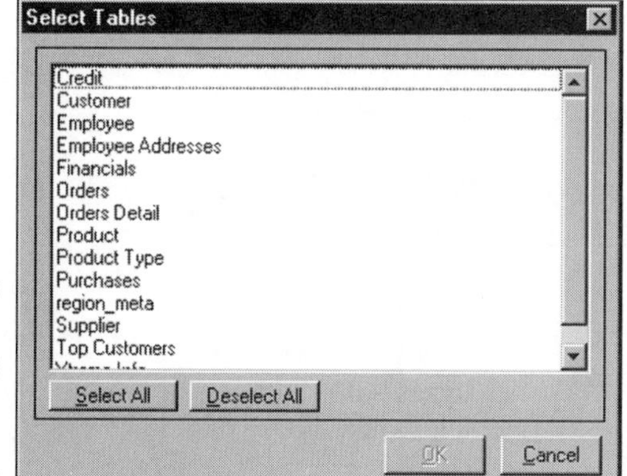

Figure 12-1: The Select Tables dialog box.

6. **Click OK.**

   The Visual Linking Expert dialog box opens, as shown in Figure 12-2.

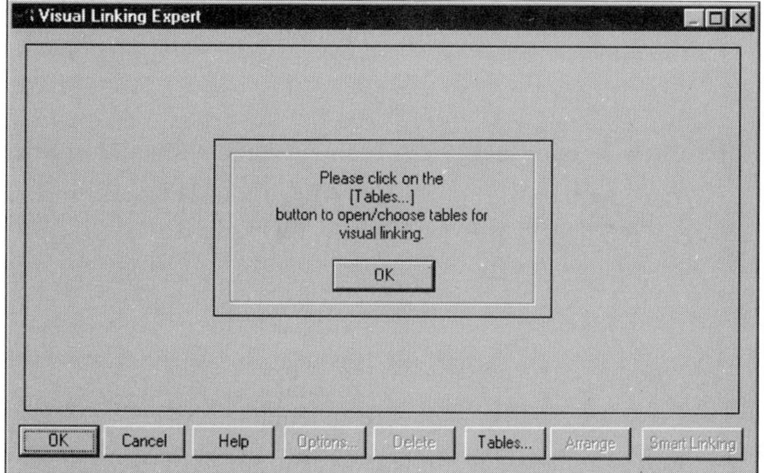

Figure 12-2: The Visual Linking Expert dialog box.

7. **Click the Tables button.**

   The Choose Tables to Use in Visual Linking dialog box appears, as shown in Figure 12-3. The dialog box lets you manipulate linking among different tables based on like fields. Ninety-nine percent of the time, you do not have to do anything more than complete this set of steps to get your reports to work. (Chapter 14 covers linking in more detail.)

8. **Click the All button, which causes Crystal Reports to include every table.**

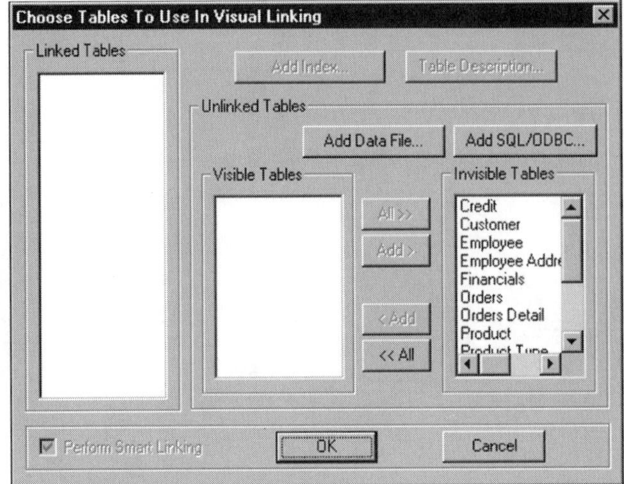

Figure 12-3: The Choose Tables to Use in Visual Linking dialog box.

This dialog box has in its lower-left corner a check box labeled Perform Smart Linking that is set to on. This switch enables Crystal Reports to determine which fields should be linked, making your life easy.

9. **Click OK.**
10. **Click OK once more to close the Visual Linking dialog box.**

    You now have the opportunity to insert fields into the report. The Insert Fields dialog box appears in the Design window.

To follow this example, insert the following fields in the Details section of the report:

- Product Name from the Product table
- Customer Name from the Customer table
- Region from the Customer table

1. **From the Insert Fields dialog box, click the field name Customer Name, and then click the Insert button.**
2. **Position the mouse pointer so that the field is inserted in the Details section of the report.**
3. **Repeat Steps 1 and 2 to insert the remaining fields: Region and Product Name.**

   You may want to shorten the Customer Name field.

   Figure 12-4 shows the report with the fields inserted.
4. **Click Close to close the Insert Fields dialog box.**

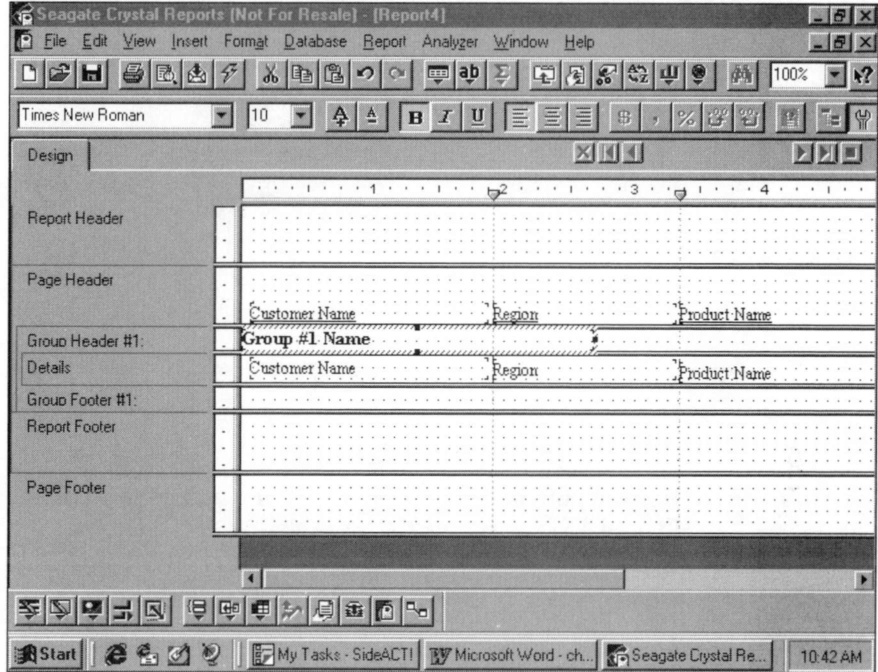

Figure 12-4: Fields inserted in the Report Design.

Group the report by Product Name by following these formatting steps:

1. **Choose Insert➪Group.**

   The Insert Group dialog box opens.

2. **In the Insert Group dialog box, select Region from the Customer table.**
3. **Click OK to close the dialog box.**

Because this sample database contains many records, the next step is to use the Select Record Expert to select records from the regions of Iowa (IA), Minnesota (MN), and Texas (TX). (Because Crystal Reports is a Canadian product, the generic term *region* is used for states and provinces.) For more detailed information about creating a record selection, see Chapter 4.

1. **Click the Select Expert button on the toolbar.**
2. **From the Choose Field dialog box, select the Region field from the Customer table (as shown in Figure 12-5) and click OK.**

   The Select Expert dialog box appears.

3. **From the second box in the Select Expert dialog box, select the One Of option.**

   A third box appears to the right.

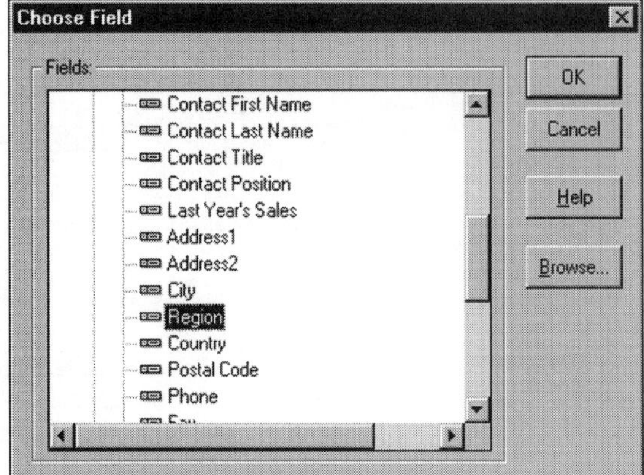

Figure 12-5: The Choose Field dialog box.

4. **Click the pull-down list from the third box, and individually select IA, MN, and TX.**
5. **Click OK.**
6. **Click the Preview button to see the report. It's shown in Figure 12-6.**

The purpose of these steps is to show you how to look at sales of products in different ways. The Xtreme Bike Company sells many different products, as you can see in the figure.

In this set of steps, because I am interested in seeing the sales of only three products (Xtreme Mountain Lock, Xtreme Rhino Lock, and Xtreme Titan lock), I have to add to the record selection only these three products.

Follow these steps to add to the record selection:

1. **Click the Select Records button on the toolbar.**
2. **In the dialog box, click New.**
3. **From the Choose Field dialog box, browse to the Product table and select the Product Name field, and click OK.**
4. **Use the same logic as in the preceding selection, by using the words *is* and *one of.***

   From the drop-down list, select the three products: Xtreme Mtn Lock, Xtreme Rhino Lock, and Xtreme Titan lock.
5. **Click OK.**

   You are asked to refresh the data or use saved data. Because the report includes all records, the Saved Data option works. Select Saved Data. The newly refined report appears, as shown in Figure 12-7.

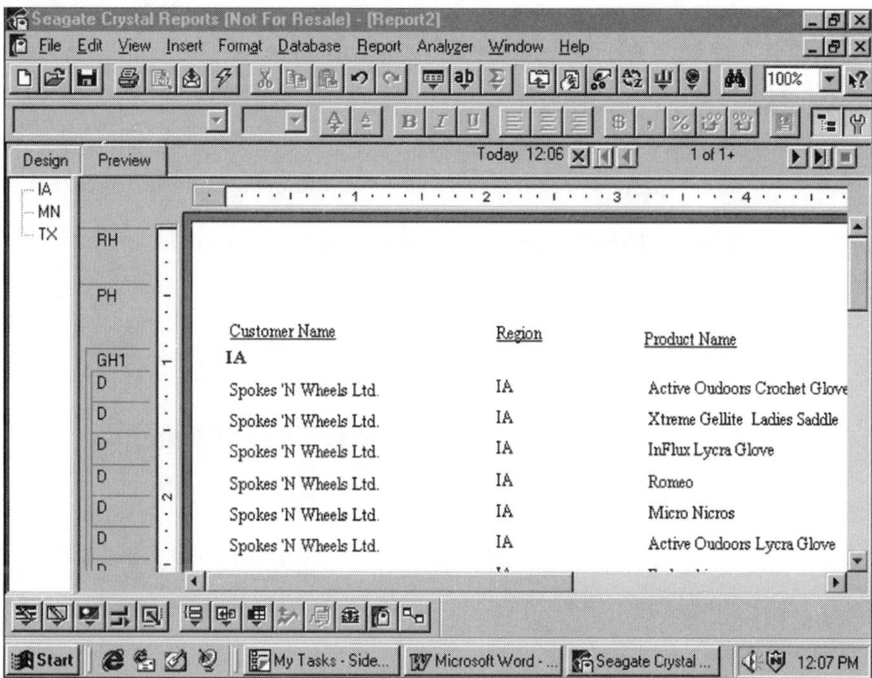

Figure 12-6: Previewing the report.

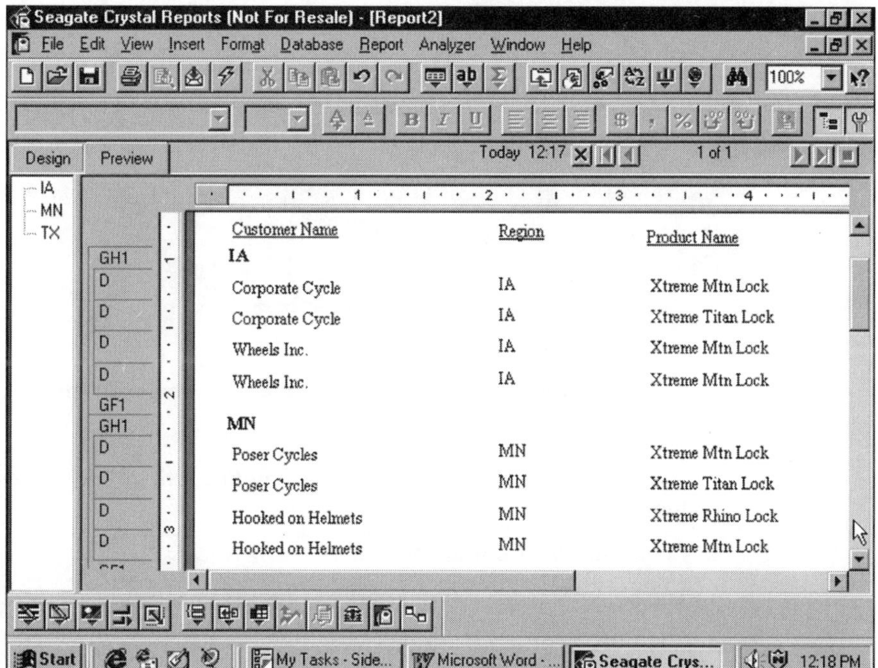

Figure 12-7: Only three products are now included in the report.

Inserting a Cross-Tab into an Existing Report

After your report is ready for the cross-tab object (and it is, if you've followed along in this chapter), you can open the Cross-Tab dialog box in two ways:

- Click the Insert Cross-Tab button on the toolbar.
- Choose Insert⇨Cross-Tab.

Take a look at the Cross-Tab dialog box, as shown in Figure 12-8.

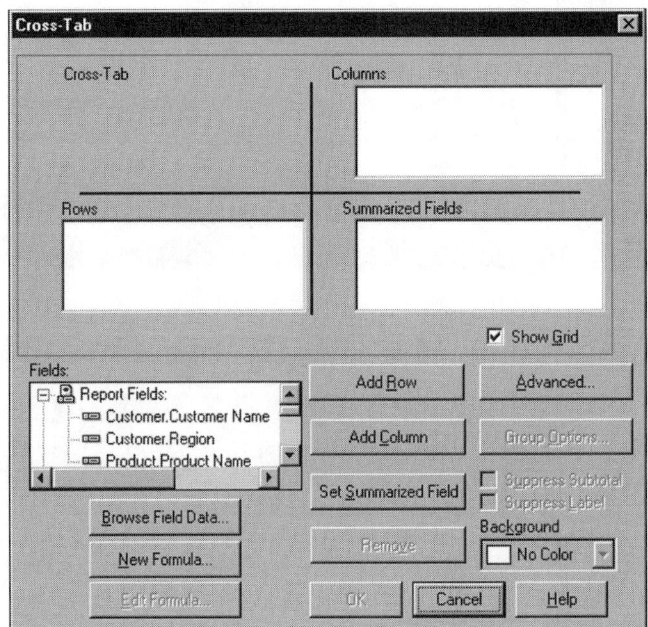

Figure 12-8: The Cross-Tab dialog box.

This cross-tab is designed to show the quantity of sales of three products by region:

1. **From the Fields box within this dialog box, click the Customer.Region field.**
2. **Click the Add Column button.**

   The field name is inserted in the Columns box. Next, you need a row.
3. **Click the Product.Product Name field name.**

4. **Click the Add Row button.**

   The field name is inserted in the Rows field.

   Although you can use the Add Column, Add Row, or Set Summarized Fields button to add fields to a cross-tab, a shortcut is to just drag-and-drop the field from the Fields list to the Rows, Columns, or Summarized Fields boxes.

   The final step is to add a summarized field so that you can see the quantity of each product ordered by region.

5. **Click the Product.Product Name field.**
6. **Click the Set Summarized Field button.**

   The completed Cross-Tab dialog box is shown in Figure 12-9.

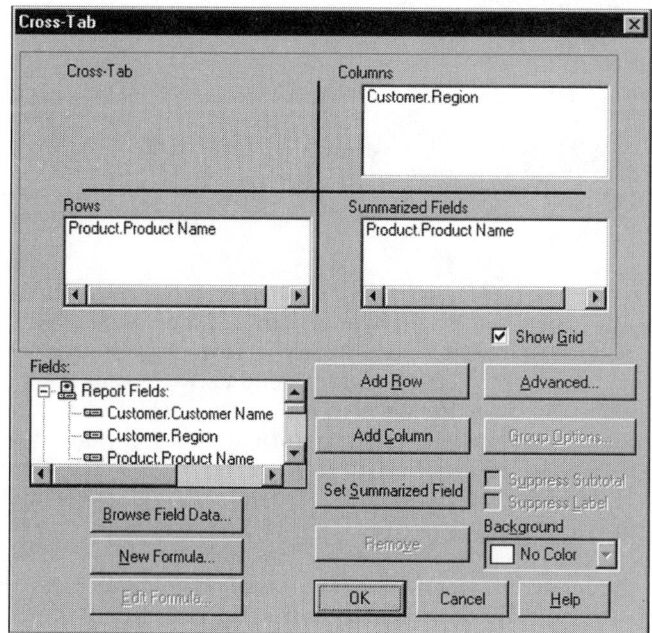

Figure 12-9: The completed Cross-Tab dialog box.

7. **Click OK.**

   The cross-tab is attached to the mouse pointer as a rectangle; you insert the cross-tab in the same way as you insert a field.

8. **Insert the cross-tab object into the Report Header section of the report by moving the mouse pointer to that section and clicking the left mouse button.**
9. **Click the Preview tab to see the report.**

   In Figure 12-10, the cross-tab object appears on the Preview tab.

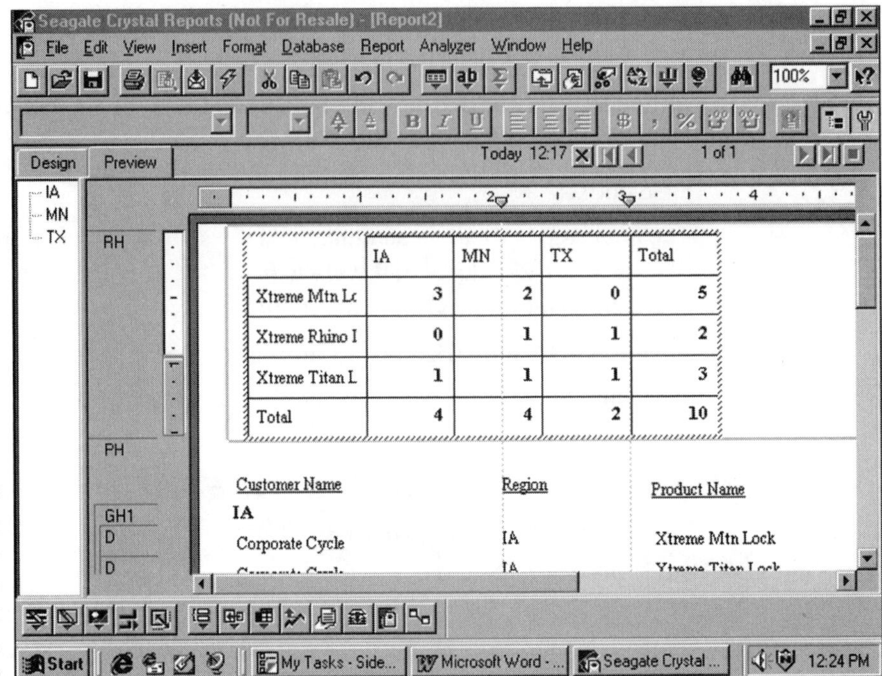

Figure 12-10: The cross-tab object in the report header.

Crystal Reports is quite smart when it comes to cross-tabs. The program automatically generates the appropriate rows and columns. In this example, you see one column for each region and one row for each product. If you have incomplete data, however, you may end up with blank rows or columns. If that happens, you have to fine-tune your record selection so that the report does not contain records with partial information, by clicking the Advanced button in the Cross-Tab Report dialog box. (The Advanced options are discussed at the end of this chapter, in the section "An Advanced Idea!") Look at the results of a cross-tab (refer to Figure 12-10). On the left side of the cross-tab is a list of the three products; at the top of each column is the region location; and in the intersections of the rows and columns is the number that represents the quantity of product purchased by each region.

Reformatting the layout

You can reformat the layout of the Cross-Tab tab by clicking and dragging. To resize a column, simply resize any field in the column. By shortening the intersection cells, you obscure the column headings, so you have to adjust prudently. You can reformat the numbers by right-clicking them and choosing a format option from the shortcut menu. If you refer to Figure 12-10, you see that the names of the products are shortened because of the length of the field. Figure 12-11 shows the table with the Product Name field lengthened.

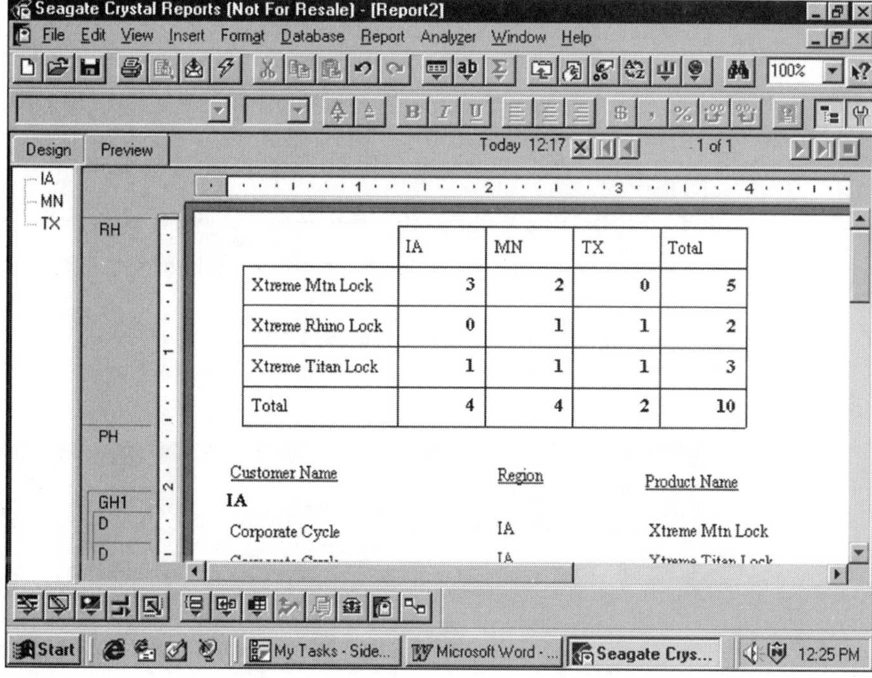

Figure 12-11: The Product Name field is lengthened to reveal the entire name.

Removing the grid

In addition to being able to format individual numbers and resize the columns in a table, you can turn off the grid outline that defines the table.

Follow these steps to remove the table grid:

1. **Right-click the table to open the shortcut menu.**

   The shortcut menu should be headed by the Cross-Tab command.

   Note: When you right-click over the cross-tab, Crystal Reports may think that you are trying to modify a single field rather than the entire cross-tab. To select the entire cross-tab for editing, try right-clicking over the top-left corner of the cross-tab.

2. **From the menu, choose Format Cross-Tab.**

   The Cross-Tab dialog box appears, with the Show Grid option checked.

3. **Click the Show Grid option to turn off the grid around the cross-tab, and then click OK to close the dialog box.**

Pivoting the cross-tab table

New to Version 7 of Crystal Reports is the capability to pivot the rows with the columns in order to quickly provide a different view of the data.

To pivot the table, follow these steps:

1. **Right-click the table so that the entire object is selected.**

   I recommend that you click in the upper-left corner of the table, above the first row.

2. **From the menu shown in Figure 12-12, choose Pivot Cross-Tab. The rows and columns change places, as shown in Figure 12-13.**

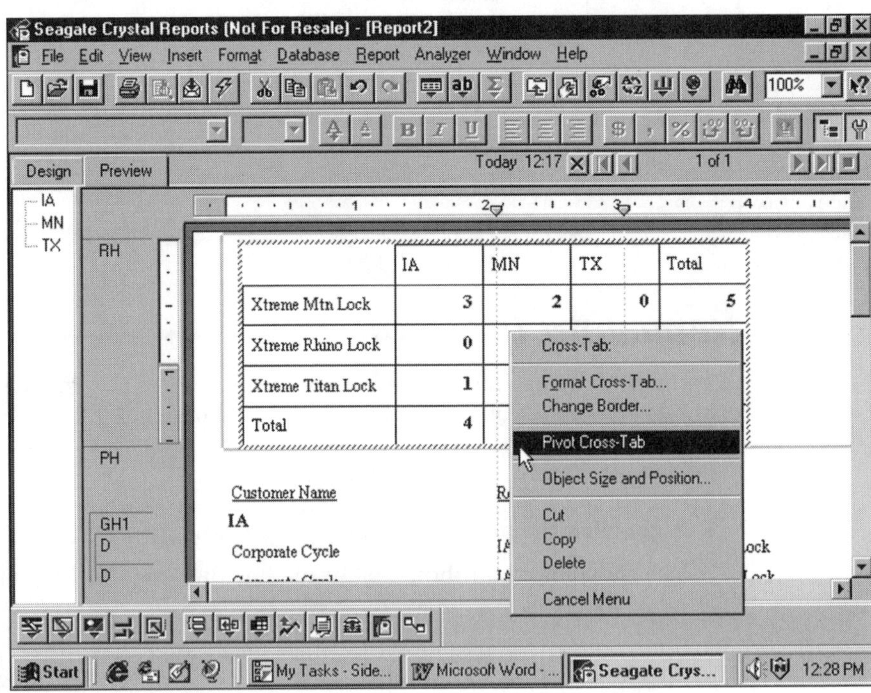

Figure 12-12: The pop-up menu for the cross-tab object.

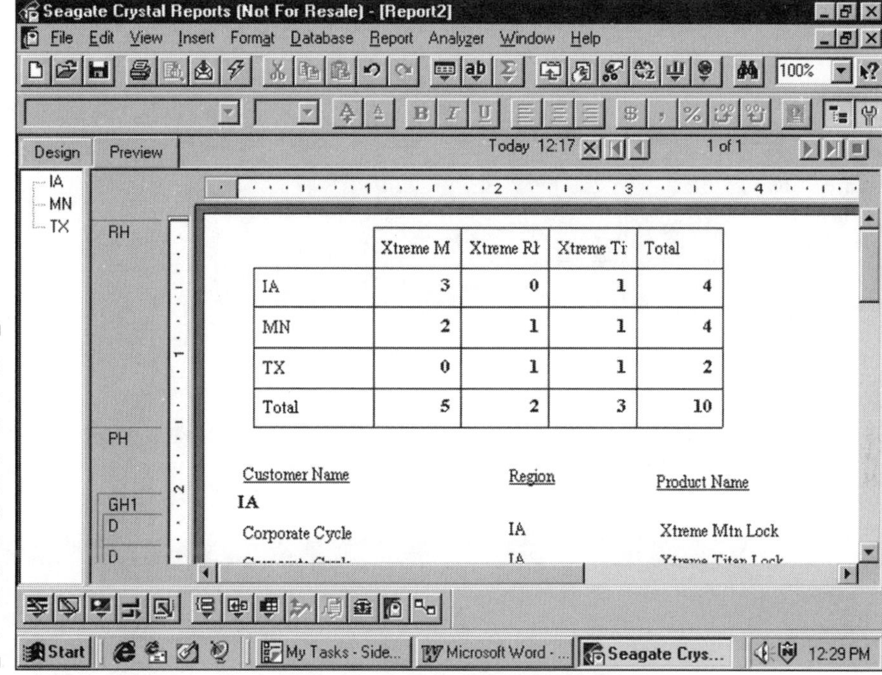

Figure 12-13: The cross-tab object is pivoted, changing the positions of the rows and columns.

Creating a Cross-Tab by Using the Cross-Tab Expert

Earlier in this chapter, in the section "Inserting a Cross-Tab into an Existing Report," I show you how to add a cross-tab object to an existing report. You may want to have a report, however, that only contains a cross-tab. The easiest way to do that is to create a cross-tab by using the Cross-Tab Expert and then follow the prompts to complete the cross-tab. When you create a cross-tab this way, the report starts out with only a cross-tab object. You can then go back and add other data to the report.

In the example in this section, you walk through the steps of using a cross-tab Expert to create a cross-tab by using the Xtreme database. (For a brief introduction to using the Experts, refer to Chapter 2.)

1. **Choose File⇨New.**

   The Report Gallery dialog box appears, as shown in Figure 12-14. Because you want to use a Report Expert to create your report, find the Expert that most closely matches the type of report you want to create — in this case, the Cross-Tab option.

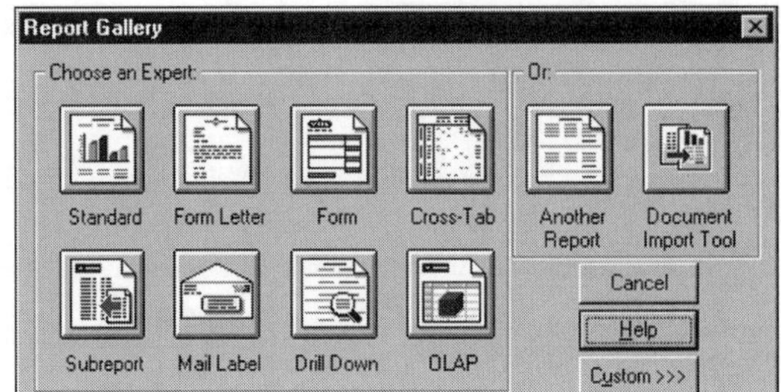

Figure 12-14: The Report Gallery dialog box.

2. **Click the Cross-Tab icon.**

   The Cross-Tab Report Expert dialog box appears, as shown in Figure 12-15.

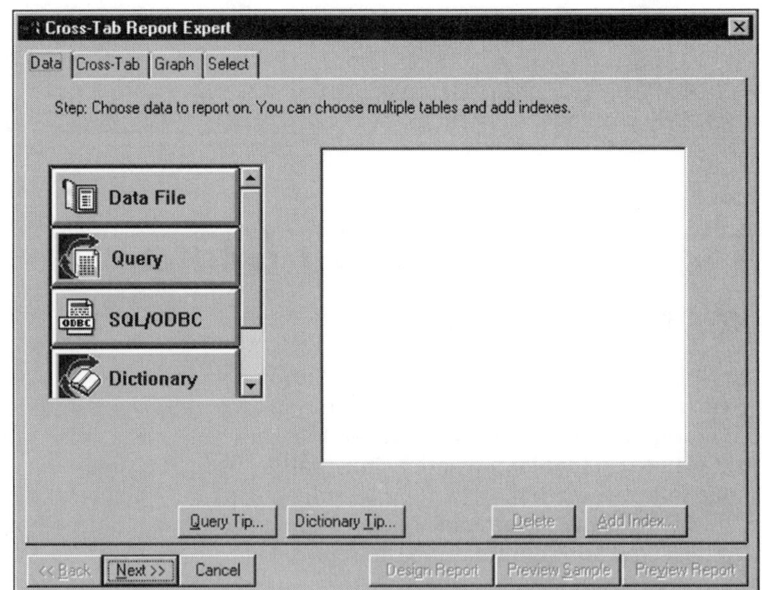

Figure 11-15: The Cross-Tab Report Expert dialog box.

3. **Your first step is to tell the program what data you want to use for your report: Click the Data File button on the left side of the screen.**

   The Choose Database File dialog box opens, as shown in Figure 12-16.

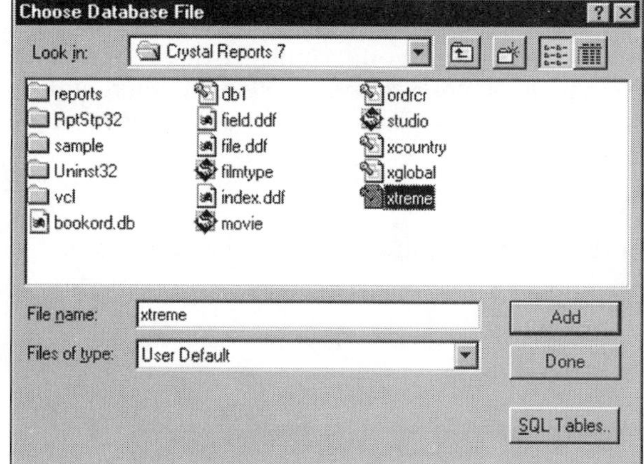

Figure 12-16: The Choose Database File dialog box.

4. **Click Select All to include all tables in the Xtreme database, and then click OK.**
5. **Close the Choose Database Files dialog box by clicking Done.**

   The Cross-Tab Report Expert dialog box appears, with the Links tab selected, as shown in Figure 12-17.

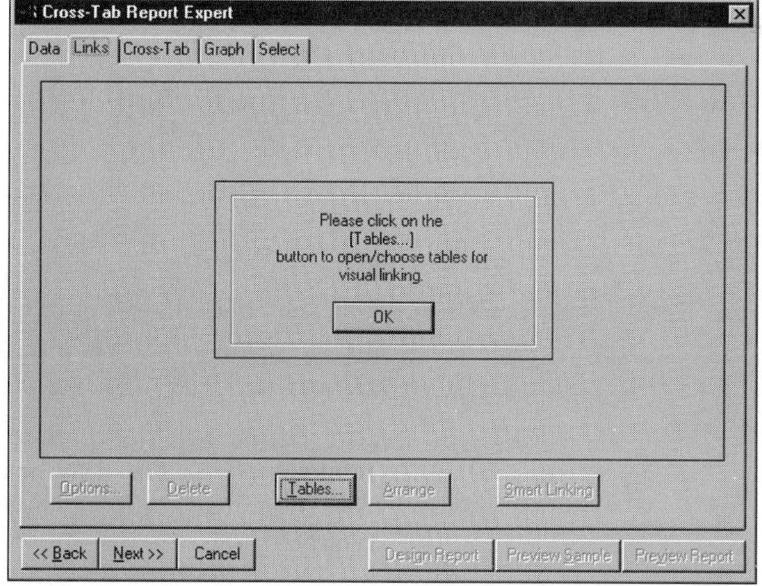

Figure 12-17: The Cross-Tab Report Expert dialog box with the Links tab selected.

6. **Click OK.**

   Crystal Reports gives you an opportunity to select another database to add to the cross-tab. If you want to use several different databases, you can continue adding the databases you need. In this example, the xtreme database is enough.

7. **Click Done.**

8. **Click the Tables button at the bottom of the dialog box.**

   The Choose Tables To Use In Visual Linking dialog box appears, as shown in Figure 12-18.

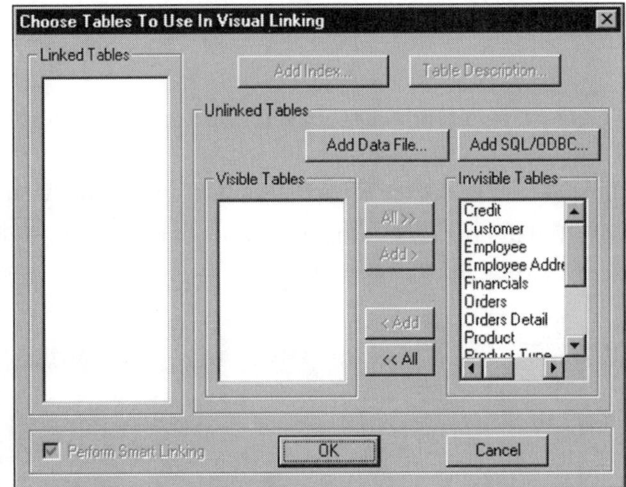

Figure 12-18: The Cross-Tab Tables To Use In Visual Linking dialog box.

9. **Click the All button.**

10. **Click OK.**

    The field links are represented graphically in the dialog box.

11. **Click the Next button, unless you want to add or delete links now.**

    See Chapter 14 for more information about linking.

    After you click Next, the Cross-Tab Report Expert dialog box appears with the Cross-Tab tab selected. The layout of this dialog box is slightly different from the Cross-Tab dialog box you see when you create a cross-tab from inside a report. It works in exactly the same way, however. Figure 12-19 shows the new arrangement.

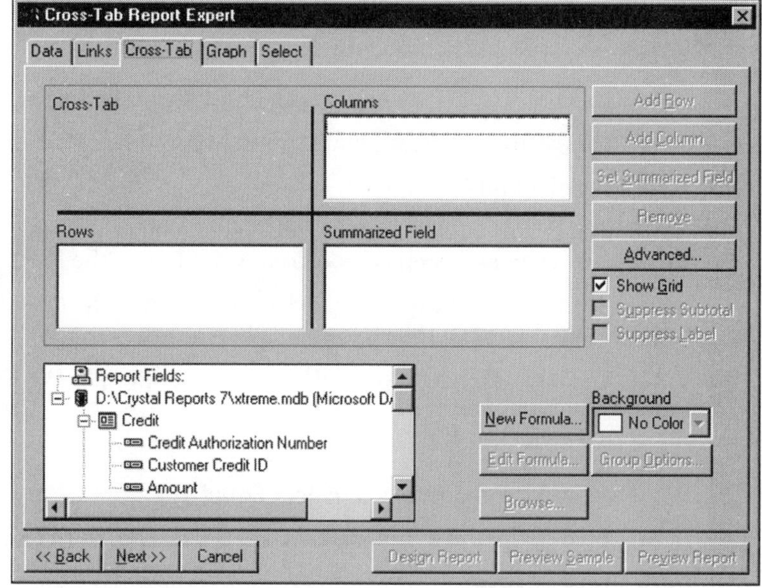

Figure 12-19: The Cross-Tab Report Expert dialog box, with the Cross-Tab tab selected.

12. **Insert the rows, columns, and summary operations you want (see Figure 12-20).**

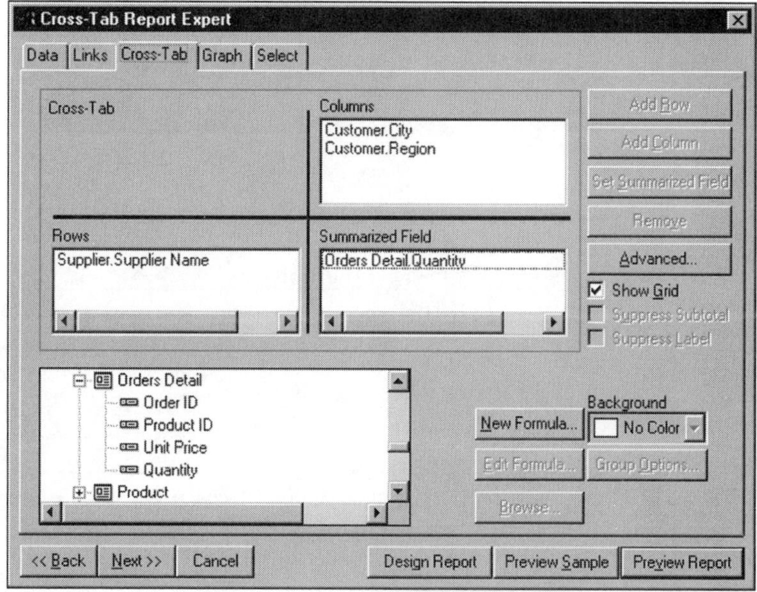

Figure 12-20: The Cross-Tab Report Expert dialog box filled with fields.

To follow the example, insert the following fields:

- Supplier Name from the Supplier Table As Row
- Region and then City As Column (both from the Customer table)
- Quantity from Orders Detail As Summarized Field

13. **Click the Select tab.**

    Notice that I skipped the graphing tab. When you're working with Experts, you can skip steps if you don't want to use the functionality.

    In this step, you build the record selection by using the Select Expert to include only records if the customer is Canadian.

14. **In the Available Fields box, scroll down and highlight the Country field in the Customer table.**
15. **Click Add.**
16. **In the second drop-down box, select Equal To.**
17. **In the third drop-down box, select Canada, as shown in Figure 12-21.**
18. **Click Preview Report.**

    The cross-tab appears, as shown in Figure 12-22.

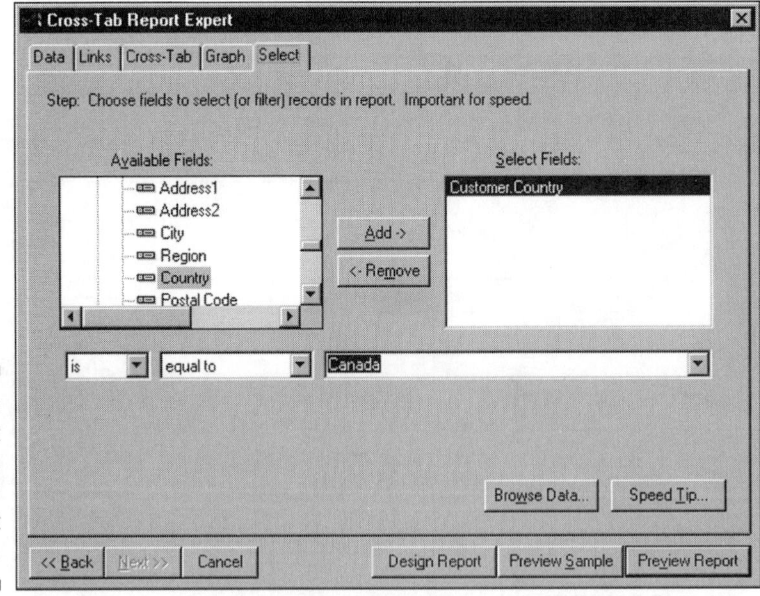

Figure 12-21: The Select step of the Cross-Tab Report Expert.

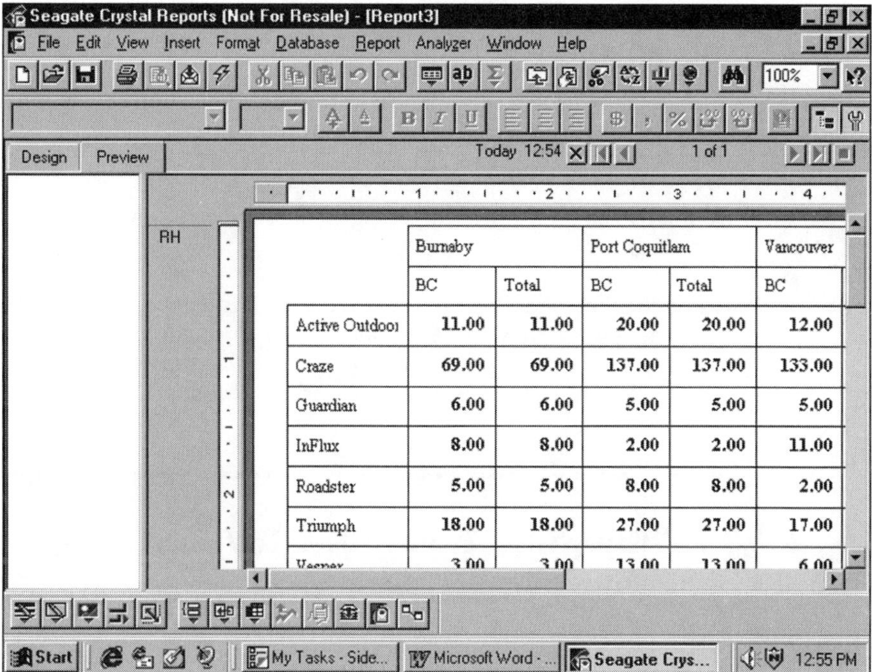

Figure 12-22: A cross-tab object created by using the Expert.

An Advanced Idea!

Although this book is targeted to beginners, you should check out the Advanced button in the Cross-Tab dialog box anyway. To see the Advanced options, open the Cross-Tab dialog box and click the Advanced button. The Advanced Cross-Tab Options dialog box appears, as shown in Figure 12-23.

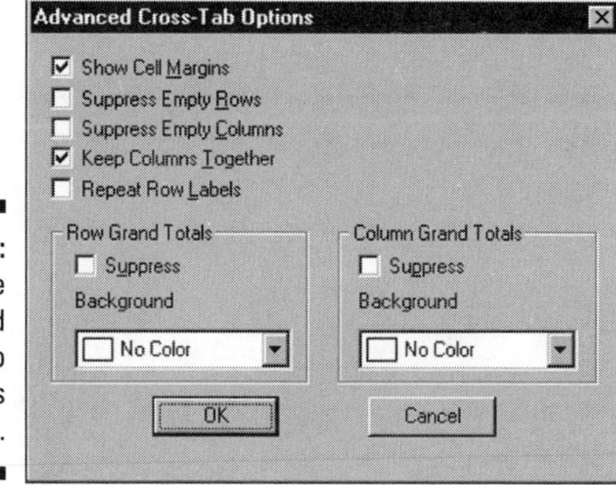

Figure 12-23: The Advanced Cross-Tab Options dialog box.

The options you should be most concerned with are Suppress Empty Rows and Suppress Empty Columns. When these two options are turned on, Crystal Reports removes any columns or rows that have no entries. If you don't take the time to create a record-selection formula to eliminate records that don't have any data, use these options to remove the blanks from your cross-tab object.

To modify the cross-tab, simply right-click the cross-tab and choose Format Cross-Tab.

Although a cross-tab is one of the more obscure aspects of Crystal Reports, it's extremely useful when you identify the kind of information you want to compare with other information in a report. Remember it and what it can do, and you'll wow and amaze your co-workers, friends, and bosses alike.

Preview Report versus Preview Sample

What's the difference between Preview Report and Preview Sample in the Expert? Preview Report generates the report, including all data that meets your record selection. Preview Sample enables you to tell Crystal how much data to include in the report. Do you want to show, for example, 100 records, 500 records, or 1,000 records?

Preview Sample is great to use when you're creating a report that includes tons of data. Maybe it's a quarterly transaction report of all orders that easily contains 100,000 records. You can speed up the report design process by using Preview Sample and designing the report against a smaller number of records.

If you want to use this feature, click Preview Sample.

If you want to preview the report with all records, click OK. If you want to limit the number of records, click the First 100 Records radio button, enter the sample number you want, and click OK.

After you have finished designing the report and want to show all records, simply click the Refresh Report Data button on the toolbar or choose Report➪Refresh Report Data.

Chapter 13

Creating a Summary Report

In This Chapter

- Creating a summary report
- Suppressing data

After you complete a report, you sometimes want to condense its information. For example, if you have hundreds of records in the Details section, the individual records may not be as important as the summary operations you have created — although someone else may want to delve in and see the individual records. No need to create two reports; all you have to do is use drill-down on the summary information to get the details. In this chapter, I show you the best ways to present the report in a summarized manner.

Looking at a Summary Report

You cannot create a summary report without first having a, for lack of a better word, full report that includes records in the Details section and (this is important) a group and a Summary field.

You can consider a *summary report* to be the opposite of the drill-down, in which you double-click a summary operation to see the underlying individual records.

To create a summary report, follow these steps:

1. **Open the report you want to modify.**

   Make sure that the report has at least one group already created. If not, you must create one, as I describe in Chapters 2 and 5.

2. **Click the Design tab and open the Section Expert in one of these three ways:**
   - Click the Section Expert button.
   - Choose Format⇨Section.
   - Move the mouse pointer to the left margin, right-click to open the shortcut menu, and then choose Format Section. The Section Expert dialog box appears, as shown in Figure 13-1.

   If you have read Chapter 9, about formatting sections, you have some familiarity with the options in this dialog box.
3. **Click the Details section, listed on the left side of the dialog box.**

   The options listed on the right side of the dialog box, on the Common tab, pertain to the section selected on the left. Now that you've selected Details, your next step is to choose the option.
4. **Choose the Hide (Drill-Down OK) option.**
5. **Click OK.**
6. **Click the Refresh button.**
7. **Click the Preview tab to see the result of choosing this option, as shown in Figure 13-2.**

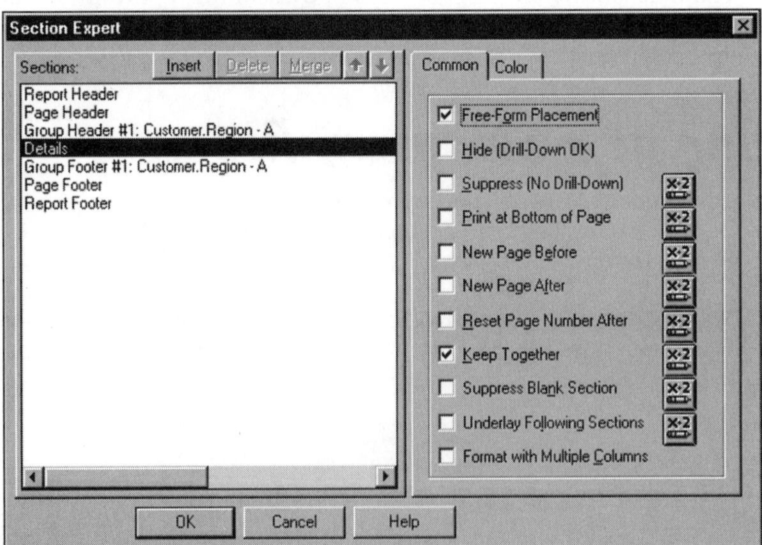

Figure 13-1: The Section Expert dialog box.

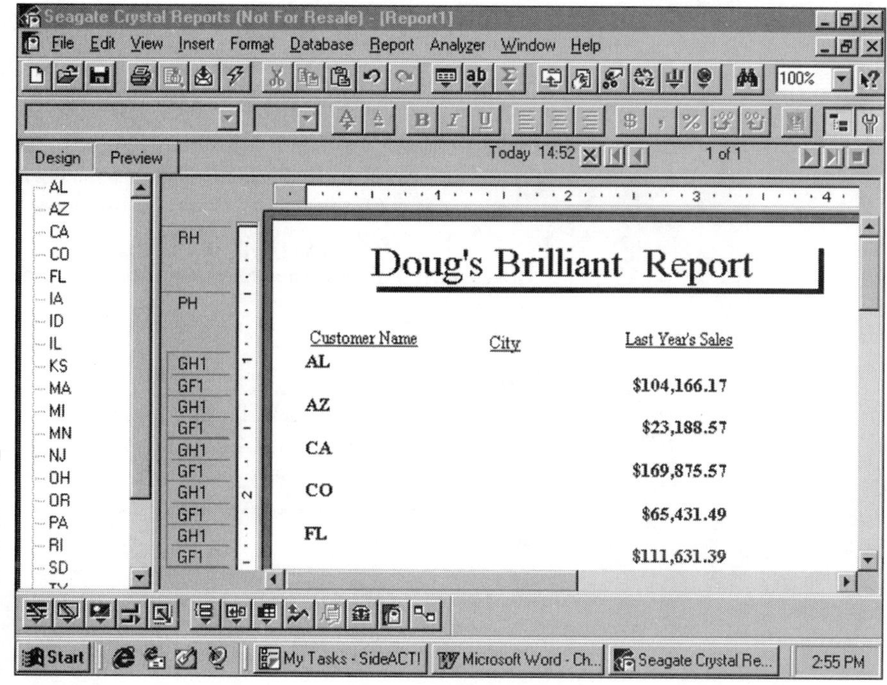

Figure 13-2: A report with the Details section hidden.

You can also hide sections of the report by moving the mouse to the left margin in the section you want to change and right-clicking the mouse. The pop-up menu appears, as shown in Figure 13-3. Choose Hide to achieve the same effect.

The report has only two reappearing entries: the group name, which in this example is the name of the state (or *region,* in Crystal Reports jargon), and the summary fields for each group. The first thing I noticed was that identifying the correct group name field with its respective total may be difficult.

One solution is to move the group header closer to the totals:

1. **Click the left mouse button and hold it down on the group name field.**

   A box appears around the text.

2. **Move the group name field by moving the mouse to the position in the report where you want the group name field to appear.**
3. **Release the mouse button.**

Figure 13-4 shows the report with the group name field moved.

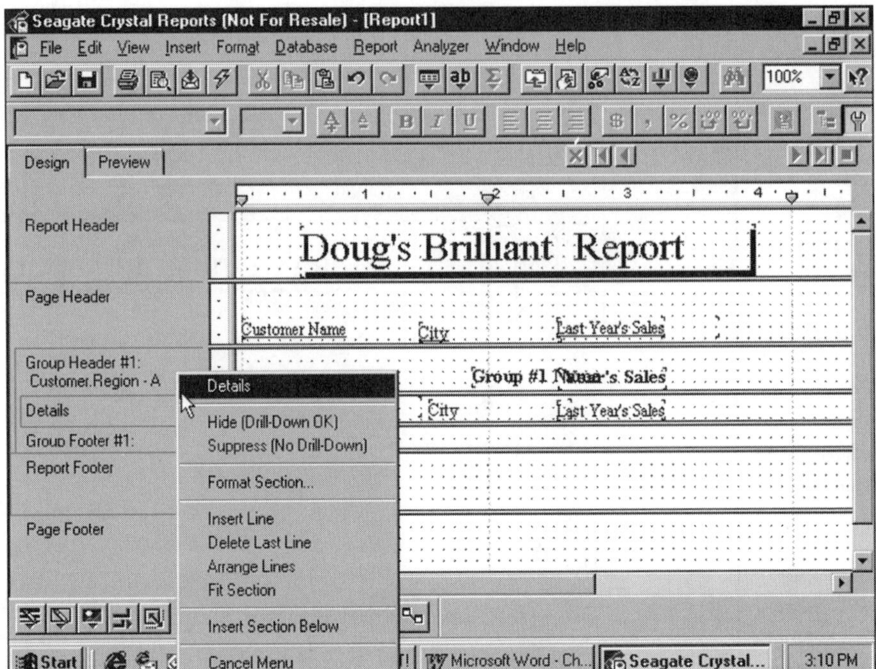

Figure 13-3: Hiding sections of the report.

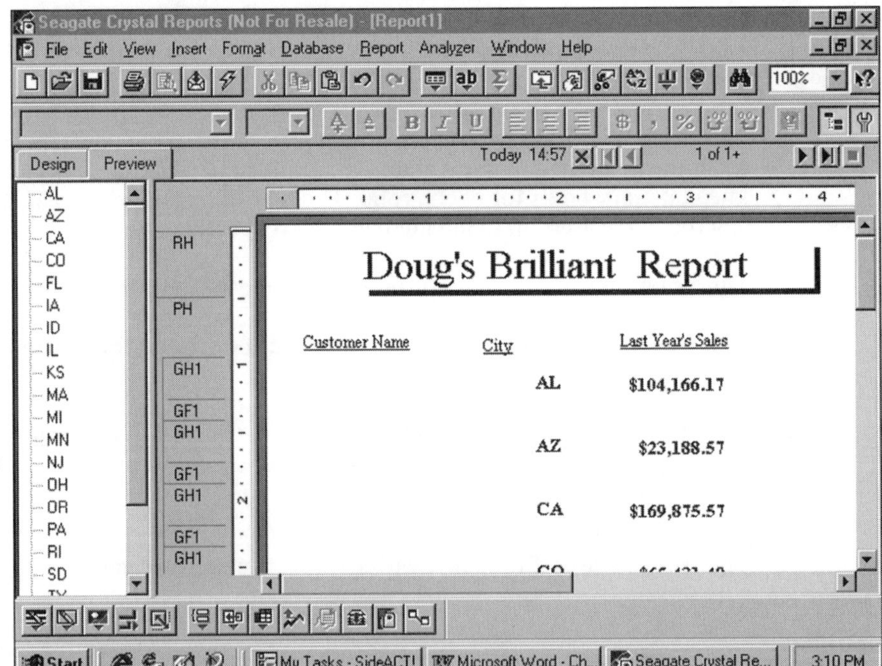

Figure 13-4: The group name field moved closer to the totals.

To Drill or Not to Drill, That Is the Question

Forgive the bad allusion to Shakespeare — I just cannot resist showing off my liberal arts education. When you open the Section Expert dialog box, as I describe in the first set of steps in this chapter, you have two options regarding the way Crystal Reports should format the section. In the example in the preceding section, you choose the Hide (Drill-Down OK) option. Using that method, anyone looking at the summary report can double-click the summary number and get the underlying records to display in a new Preview window. Try this trick yourself.

Double-click a total in your report. The new Preview tab appears, as shown in Figure 13-5. With the Summary set to Hide, and allowing drill-down, you can see the underlying records the way you want.

If you do not want anyone to see the underlying records, you can select the Suppress (No Drill-Down) option in the Section Expert dialog box. This option could come in handy on a report with payroll, for example, in which each record lists the salary of employees. Other people may need the summary data but not the individual record data. Using this option, you can hide the information and make it somewhat inaccessible.

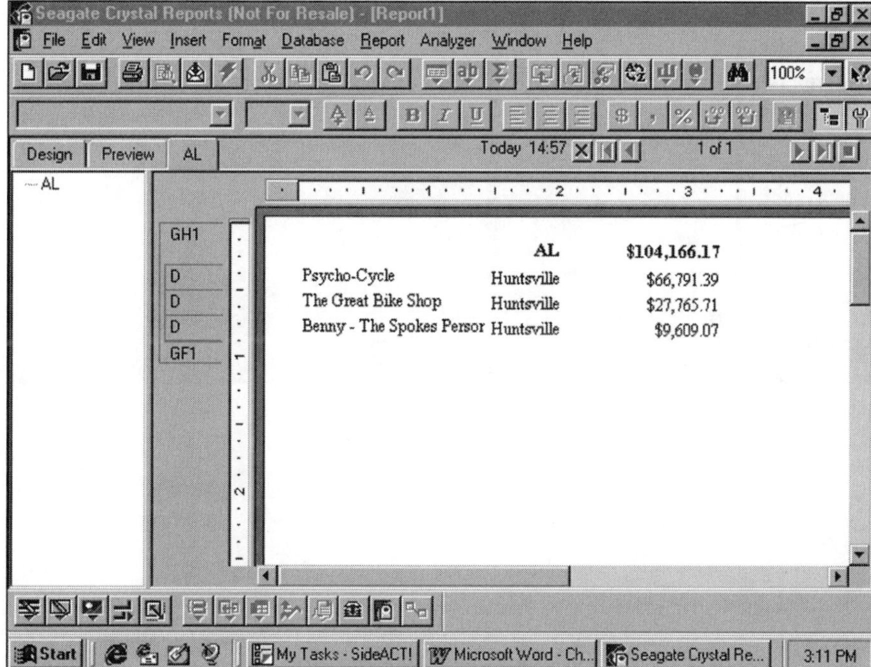

Figure 13-5: Double-click a summary, and the drill-down tab appears.

The Suppress option overrides the Hide option, so if you mistakenly have them both turned on, the Suppress option is in charge.

Figure 13-6 shows an example of what happens when you try to drill down with suppression turned on.

Crystal Reports gives you the same summary information, on a new tab.

As you move the mouse pointer over the various components in a previewed report, the mouse pointer may be transformed into a magnifying glass. That's your clue that the object underneath the pointer can be drilled down.

If you're planning to create run-time reports, the drill-down feature works on graphs.

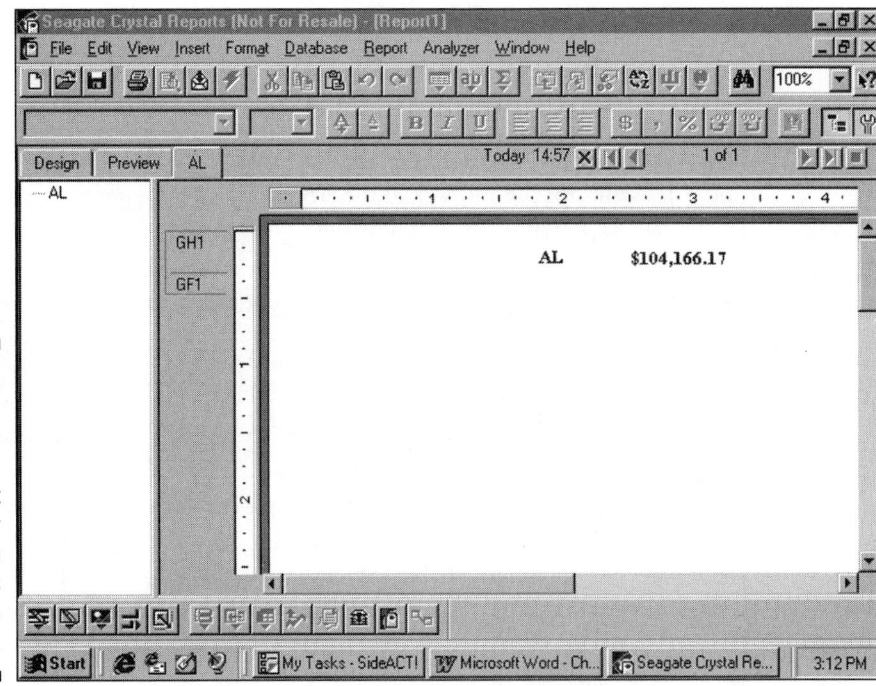

Figure 13-6: An attempted drill-down on a report summary with the Suppress option turned on.

Chapter 14

Linking to Other Databases

In This Chapter

- Understanding linking concepts
- Working with links
- Using SQL joins

In the esoteric world of database design, one table does not a database make. (*Esoteric,* in this case, means "understood by a chosen few," which now includes you!) Although you can create a database with just one table, most databases are made from collections of tables that have links between them. The links are made from fields in one table that are similar, perhaps even identical, to fields in another table. In this chapter, I explore the ins and outs of linking database tables and files.

Linking Concepts

The simple linking concept is that if you don't link, your reports don't work. Much more is involved in linking, however, than that simple statement implies. As an example, Tables 14-1 and 14-2 show an order table and a customer table, respectively.

Table 14-1 An Order Table

Order #	*Customer #*	*Product*
055	467	Pupas
056	258	Butterflies
057	333	Pupas
058	258	Caterpillars
059	467	Moths

Table 14-2 A Customer Table

Customer #	*Address*	*City*
258	5050 Parkland Road	Indianapolis
333	657 Maple Plain	Pittsburgh
467	95443 High Hills Plaza	Tucson

If customer number 258 places an order, you could enter all that customer's information in the order table. For example, you could take an order, complete the customer's address, and add the phone number. By using links, however, you save yourself unnecessary steps by simply inserting the customer number. The database then goes to the customer table, finds the matching number 258, and finds the address for you. You enter 258, and the database finds the address, 5050 Parkland Road. By using this technique, you type the address only one time — not on every order, every invoice, or every letter.

Normalizing a database

The process of making a database as efficient as possible, by not storing redundant data, is called *normalizing.* A well-designed database is normal. (Our only hope is that we all can be somewhat normal.)

By having a normalized database, the person who enters certain types of data enters that type only one time, in one table. When that data is needed in conjunction with other information, the database goes out and looks up the data. That's where the links come in.

Tables 14-1 and 14-2, the Order table and the Customer table, are linked by a common field: the customer number. The linking field usually has the same kind of data in it — in this case, a number. The data is usually the same length — in this case, three digits. The linking field usually is a primary key in a table, as I describe in the following section.

Keying primarily

A *primary key* is a field in a database that serves as a unique identifier for each record. You have a primary key. Someone wanting to find information about you, for example, may look up your Social Security number, which is a unique number for each individual. (Hopefully, no two people have the same Social Security number.) In the sample tables shown in the section "Linking Concepts," a little earlier in this chapter, you would look up a customer based on the customer number. The customer number is the primary key for the customer table.

A primary key usually has an *index* or is an *indexed field,* which means that a database, by using a number of techniques, can quickly look up a record on an indexed field. Using primary keys to link tables with indexed fields makes your database fast and efficient.

How does an index work? Its name gives the secret away. Just as an index in a book makes looking up specific information easier, a database index makes looking up data faster and easier. An index may organize the same data in several different ways, enabling you to easily find matches among hundreds of records.

Some of the databases on which you do reports automatically index a primary key. Other databases don't have indexing capabilities. If you can, make sure that each database table has an index. Doing so not only improves the performance of your database but also improves the speed at which you can generate reports.

Why should you link tables? The answer is that links make data in one table accessible to data in another table. If you don't link the customer number from the Order table to the customer number in the Customer table, you cannot find the customer address. When you later create a report, you cannot print the customer address on the report if the tables aren't linked via the customer number. When you design a database, you create the links between fields so that you can easily find the data you're looking for.

Linking not only makes finding the data you want easier, but it's also crucial to finding the correct data. Suppose that you want to find all the orders for a single customer — in this case, customer number 258. Because number 258 is the lowest customer number in the table, you figure that you can get all the beginning orders and they will be the orders for customer 258. Does that method work? No, because the orders are listed in order of the order number. Linking matches the order to the correct customer number.

Suppose that you *query* (ask) the database to find all the orders for customer number 258. The computer looks at order number 055 in the order table and then asks whether that's an order number for 258. Because the answer is No, that order isn't included in the answer to your query. The computer moves on to the next record. Is order number 056 an order for customer 258? Yes. That record is included in the answer. The computer matches the orders to customer number 258. Those orders are 056 and 058. Even though the orders aren't in any sequence related to customer number, the computer finds the records matching your request by using the links between the tables.

What Crystal Reports calls "links" between tables are sometimes referred to by other names. Some of the other names you may hear are *keys,* including primary keys and foreign keys, and *pointers.*

Working with Links

To view the links already established in a report in the Xtreme database, follow these steps:

1. **Begin by opening a report.**

2. **Click the Open button on the toolbar.**

   The Open dialog box is displayed.

3. **Double-click the reports folder.**
4. **Double-click the Xtreme folder.**
5. **Double-click the Invent file, or click the Invent file to highlight it and then click the Open button.**

   The report's Design tab opens.

6. **Click the Link Expert button on the Supplementary toolbar or choose Database⇨Visual Linking Expert.**

   If the supplementary toolbar isn't visible at the bottom of the window, click the tool button that looks like a wrench at the far right end of the toolbar.

   The Visual Linking Expert dialog box opens.

In the Visual Linking Expert dialog box, you see the underlying tables from which this report collects its data. The tables are shown in the dialog box with the indexed fields highlighted by a colored symbol next to the field name and the links drawn between the tables, as shown in Figure 14-1.

The tables (Product, Purchases, and Product Type) from the database used for this report are displayed in the Visual Linking Expert dialog box. Arrows indicate the links in the tables. For example, you can see that the Product ID field in the Product table is linked to the Product ID field in the Purchases table. By using these links, you can navigate through the tables to collect and match information from any of the linked tables.

A colored arrow head with a number sign (#) inside it indicates that the field is part of more than one index.

Click the scroll bars at the bottom and side of the Visual Linking Expert dialog box to view tables not shown in the window.

You may have noticed a pattern with linked fields: All the linked fields in this example have identical names; they just appear in different tables. If you take a closer look, you see that the linked fields also have the same characteristics. The data length is the same, as is the data type. That's why smart linking works!

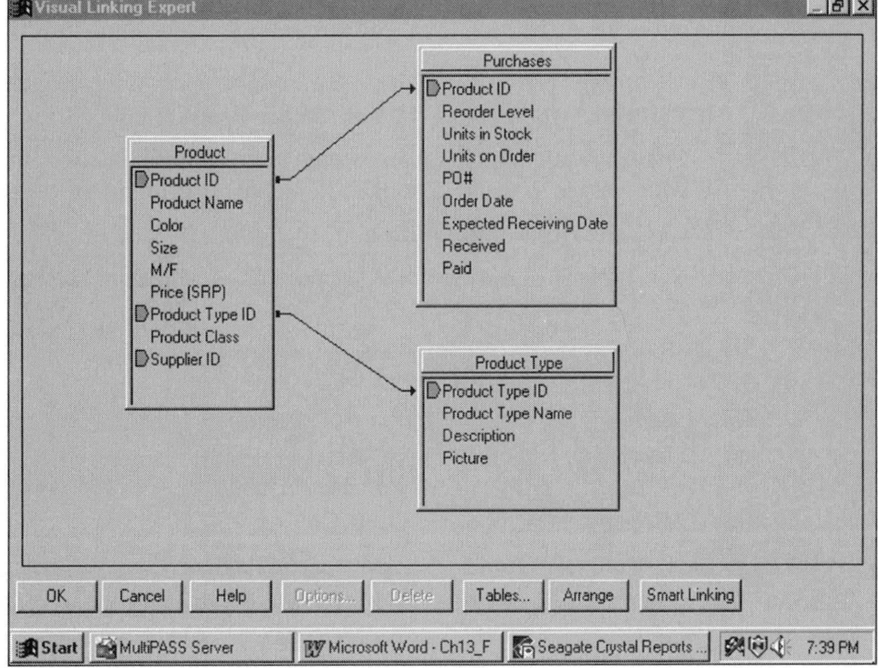

Figure 14-1: The Visual Linking Expert dialog box with Invent tables and links displayed.

Moving a table

Little black arrows show you precisely where links appear. You can click in any table and drag it to a different position. When you do, the links remain to connect the linked fields. This feature is especially valuable when the database on which you are reporting is complicated.

Follow these steps to rearrange the tables while keeping the links intact:

1. **Click the title bar of a table and hold down the mouse button.**
2. **Drag the table to a new location in the Visual Linking Expert dialog box.**
3. **Release the mouse button.**

   The table is displayed in the new location with the link still attached.

Looking at field properties

If you look at the Product table shown earlier in this chapter, in Figure 14-1, you see that it has two fields linked to other tables. Each field that is linked to or from has an arrow head pointing to or from it. Each arrow head may be a different color.

In the Visual Linking Expert dialog box, you can look at the properties of the indexed fields with the arrow heads to help you determine how the fields are connected:

1. **Right-click the Product ID field in the Product table.**

   The Field menu appears. From this menu, you can browse the field to see what data is in the field, look at the table description, or cancel the menu.

2. **Click the Description option.**

   The Table Description dialog box opens, as shown in Figure 14-2.

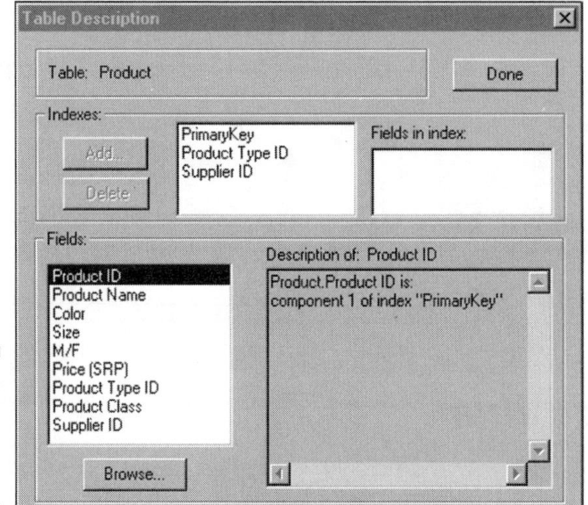

Figure 14-2: The Table Description dialog box.

At the top of the Table Description dialog box is the name of the table (Product, in this example). Underneath that is a list of the indexed fields. In the lower-left corner is a list of all the fields in the table. You can click the scroll buttons to move up and down to see all the fields, and you can even add new indexes (files).

If you click any of the indexed fields in the list, the Description box to the right shows a description of that field. (The description is generated by Crystal Reports.) When you select an indexed field, the Description box shows index information.

Browsing through fields

As in other table boxes in Crystal Reports, if you click a field in the Fields list in the Table Description dialog box and then click the Browse button, the data in the field is displayed in a separate dialog box. Something else for linking is also displayed; this important information includes a field definition with the type of data and the size of the field.

Follow these steps to view details about each field in a table:

1. **With the Table Description dialog box open, click the Product Name field in the Fields box to highlight the field.**
2. **Click the Browse button.**

   The Product Name dialog box opens, as shown in Figure 14-3.

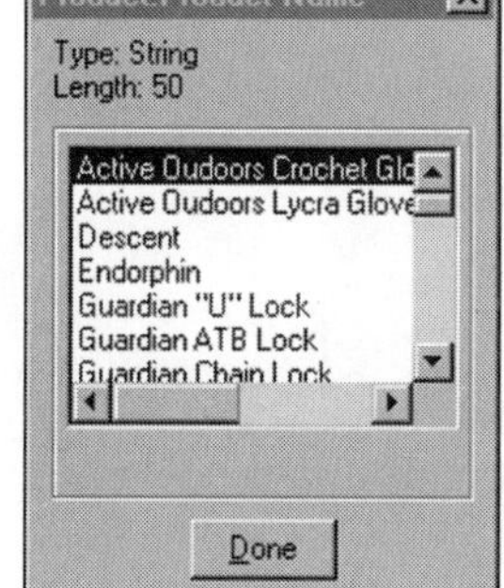

Figure 14-3: The Product Name browsing dialog box.

The Product Name box shows important information. At the top, you can see the type of data in the field; in this example, the data type is a string. A *string* is composed of alphanumeric characters. Underneath that is the length of the string; in this example, the product name contains no more than 50 characters. For example, a string may include "1888 Production Blvd." Although this address includes numbers, the database doesn't treat it as a number. Rather, it's treated as part of the address.

This information is useful if you want to create links between tables. You can link between two fields where the string consists of 50 characters in both fields and where they contain identical information and one field has an index. In some circumstances, you may be able to link when one field has a string of 20 characters and another has a string of 50 characters (for example, when you want to link an address field from one database in which the field is defined as 20 characters with the address field from a different database that allows 50 characters).

You cannot link numeric data with string data. *Numeric* data can be used in a mathematical calculation; for example, a date field, a value, a measurement, or currency. *String* data, although it may include numbers, isn't used as part of a mathematical calculation.

Crystal Reports can link two records based on a partial match of a string of data, called a *partial link.* To turn this option on, open the Link Options dialog box, as shown in Figure 14-4, by clicking the link and then clicking the Options button. Click to select the Allow Partial Text Matches check box. Partial linking works only when the string in the lookup table (see the section "Looking at links," later in this chapter) is longer than the string in the primary table (see the section "Keying primarily," earlier in this chapter).

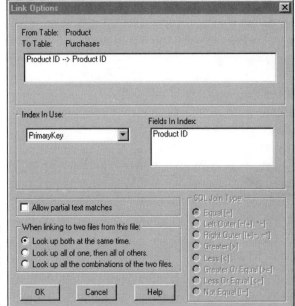

Figure 14-4: The Link Options dialog box.

Closing the Table Description dialog box

When you finish perusing the Table Description dialog box, simply click the Done button. After clicking the Done button, you're ready to start creating your report.

Looking at links

The arrow heads in the tables in the Visual Linking Expert show you the indexed fields. The black lines between tables show you the link between tables. When you click a link line to select it, the line changes color to show that it is selected.

When you select a link and the link changes colors, the text in the linked tables is highlighted. You can then easily see the linked fields.

When you link tables in Crystal Reports, you have to know a few important concepts. One is that you have a primary table and a lookup table. The primary table has a link to a field in the lookup table. Using that link, a query of the primary table goes to the matching record in the lookup table to find the correct data. The *primary* table is the table you link *from;* the *lookup* table is the table you link *to.*

In the Visual Linking Expert dialog box, the Product table is a primary table. From this table, you link to the Product Type table via the Product Type ID field. The Product Type table is the lookup table.

Exploring the Visual Linking Expert buttons

The buttons along the bottom of the Visual Linking Expert dialog box enable you to initiate different activities. Table 14-3 describes these buttons, which you use to complete a report.

Table 14-3 Buttons in the Visual Linking Expert Dialog Box

Button	*What It Does*
OK	Accepts the links you have created. Click this button when you have all your links set up the way you want and you are ready to create a report.
Cancel	Cancels your activity in the Visual Linking Expert dialog box.
Help	Accesses context-sensitive help. When you click this button, Help information is displayed in the Visual Linking dialog box.
Options	Specifies options for the link. When you select a link line and click Options, the Link Options dialog box opens. You can then choose which type of index you want to use and select other options about the selected link.
Delete	Deletes a link after you select a link line.
Tables	Opens the Table to Use in Visual Linking dialog box. You can then select the tables you want to link to create your report.
Arrange	Arranges all the tables in the Visual Linking dialog box. Click this button to arrange tables after you have added several tables and want them automatically arranged.
Smart Linking	After you have added several tables to the Linking box in the Visual Linking dialog box, automatically creates logical links between those tables. If Crystal Reports can't create links, a message appears, telling you that links are not possible.

Using link options

When you link two fields from two tables, more than one index may be on the link. Crystal Reports selects one of the indexes available to use for the link. You may want to change the index to improve the report performance or to make indexes consistent for one report.

If you want to adjust the index used for the link, open the Link Options dialog box by following one of these methods:

- Click the link line and click the Options button.
- Right-click a link line. When the menu appears, click Options.
- Double-click the link line.

The Link Options dialog box opens (refer to Figure 14-4).

The top box in the dialog box provides a description of the link. The description shows the direction of the link by indicating the table the link travels from and the table the link travels to.

The middle section tells you the index that's in use. In this figure, the primary key (see the section "Keying primarily," earlier in this chapter) is the index in use. Click the drop-down arrow to see any other options. If you choose the No Specific Index option, Crystal Reports selects an index for you when you display the report in the preview window. To the right of the Index In Use information is a list of the fields in the index.

Below the middle section is a check box that lets you make partial text matches. This feature can be useful when you try to link, for example, one field with 50 characters and another with 20 characters and with similar data in the fields. Click this box to allow a match on the partial text in the fields rather than an exact match of the text: for example, when you have an address field from one database defined as 20 characters and an address field from a different database defined as 50 characters. Allowing a partial text match enables you to match "10789 Rancho Pen. Bv" with "10789 Rancho Penasquitos Boulevard."

Note: A partial text match works only when the string in the lookup table is longer than the string in the primary table.

In the lower-left corner of the Link Options dialog box are three options that enable you to determine how you want to link two records from these tables. Click the radio buttons (the circles next to the text — they look like old-fashioned car radio buttons) for these options to choose the one you want. Table 14-4 lists the three options and briefly describes how they work. These options are available only on data files (non-SQL data sources).

Table 14-4 Options for Linking Records

Look Up Option	*What It Does*
Look up both at the same time	Looks up one record in the primary table (Table A) and a matching record in the lookup table (Table B). Crystal Reports looks for the next matching record in one lookup table and then for the next matching record in the next lookup table (Table C) until it finds all the matching records. This process is repeated for every record in the primary table (Table A).
Look up all of one and then all the others	Directs Crystal Reports to look up each record in the primary table (Table A) and then all the matching records in the lookup table (Table B). After all the matching records are found in Table B, Crystal Reports looks for all the matching records in the second lookup table (Table C). The program goes back to the primary table and repeats this process with each record in the primary table. In other words, it links first from Table A to Table B, and then from Table A to Table C.
Look up all combinations of the two files	For each record in the primary table (Table A), looks for a matching record in the lookup table (Table B), after which it finds all the matching records in the next lookup table (Table C). After all the matching records in Table C are found, the process is repeated with the next record in the first lookup table (Table B). After all the matches are found for that record in the first lookup table (Table B), the process is repeated on to the next record in the primary table (Table A).

In the lower-right corner of the Link Options dialog box are the SQL join options, addressed at the end of this chapter, in the section "Using SQL Joins."

Creating a new report when you open Crystal Reports

When you open Crystal Reports, you're asked whether you want to create a new report or open a report that has already been created.

Follow these steps to create a new report:

1. **Either click the New Report button on the opening screen or click the New button on the toolbar.**

   The Report Gallery dialog box opens.

2. **Click the Custom button in the Report Gallery dialog box.**
3. **Click the Data File button to choose the Data File option.**

   The Choose Data File dialog box opens. From this dialog box, you navigate through the file to select a database to use for the source data.
4. **Select the database you want by clicking it and then clicking OK.**

   When you select a database, the Select Tables dialog box is displayed.
5. **Select all the tables by clicking the Select All button. Then click OK.**

   The Visual Linking Expert dialog box opens, showing all the tables in the selected database (see Figure 14-5).

   Note: In some cases, you may have to add the tables manually. If no tables are displayed in the Visual Linking window, click the Tables button at the bottom of the window. All the tables are listed in the lower-right corner of the dialog box. You can select some or all of the tables to display in the Visual Linking window. To select some of the tables, click the tables you want while holding down the Shift key. Then click the Add button. If you want to display all the tables, click the All button.
6. **Click the Orders, Orders Detail, Product, and Product Type tables while holding down the Shift key. Click the Add button to include just those tables.**

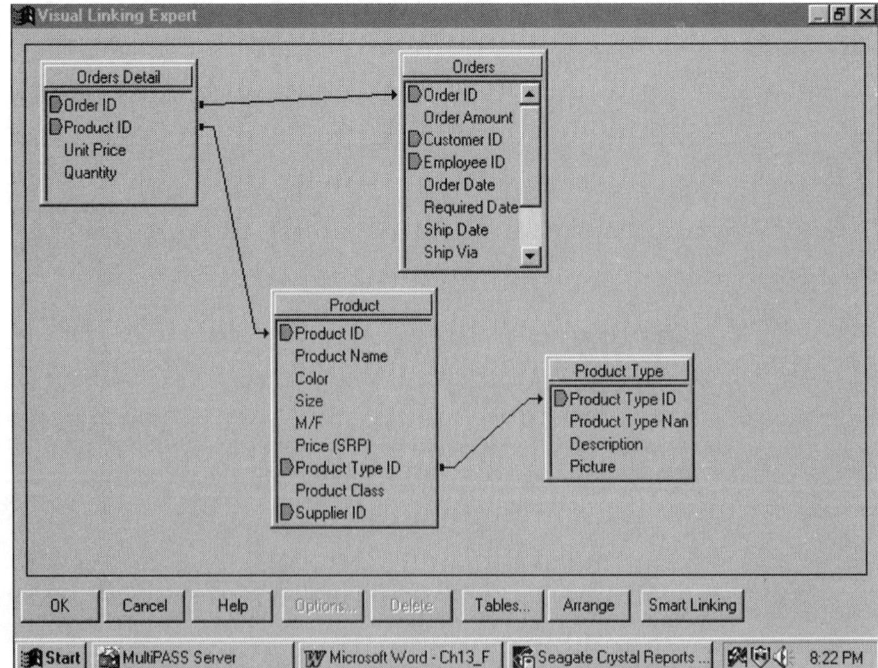

Figure 14-5: The Visual Linking Expert dialog box with four tables displayed.

In this example, you see the Xtreme database, with the Orders Detail, Product, and Product Type tables. The following section looks at the Order ID, Product, and Product Type associated with that Order ID.

Creating links

Suppose that you have added to the Visual Linking Expert dialog box a table that wasn't linked. You can create a link to the new table in two ways: Manually draw a link, or press the Smart Linking button.

With the same Visual Linking Expert dialog box open, follow these steps to delete all the links and then re-create them:

1. **Click a link between two tables so that the link changes color.**
2. **Click the Delete button at the bottom of the Visual Linking Expert dialog box.**

   Continue selecting and deleting links until all links are deleted.
3. **In this example, move the mouse pointer to the Orders Detail table, click the Product ID field, and hold the mouse button down.**
4. **Drag the mouse pointer to the Product ID field in the Product table.**

   A linking pointer appears that looks like a zig-zagged line with an arrow on one end.
5. **Release the mouse button.**

   A link is created between the Product ID fields in the two tables.
6. **Click the Smart Linking button at the bottom of the Visual Linking Expert dialog box.**

   All the fields you would expect to link now have a link between them.

Deleting a linked table

In this section, I show you how to delete the Orders table because it's not necessary for the report.

While you're in the Visual Linking Expert, follow these steps to delete first a link and then a table:

1. **Click the link between the Orders Detail table and the Orders table.**
2. **Click the Delete button at the bottom of the Visual Linking Expert dialog box.**

   Figure 14-6 shows that the link between the two tables has been deleted.

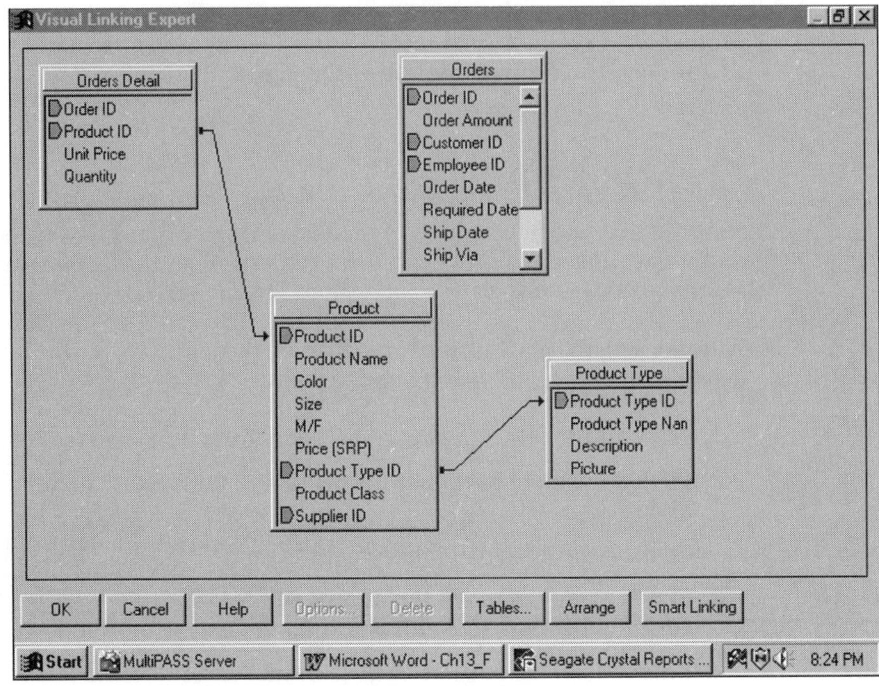

Figure 14-6: The link between two tables has been removed.

3. **Click the Tables button at the bottom of the Visual Linking Expert dialog box.**

   The Choose Tables to Use in Visual Linking dialog box opens, with the Linked Tables listed on the left. Unlinked tables are listed on the right. The Orders table is now an unlinked table located in the Visible Tables box. To remove the table, move it to the Invisible Tables box.

4. **Click Orders in the Visible Tables box.**

   Orders is highlighted.

5. **Click the Add button.**

   This step moves Orders from the Visible Tables box to the Invisible Tables box.

6. **Click OK.**

   The Choose Tables to Use in Visual Linking Expert dialog box closes. As you can see in Figure 14-7, the Orders table is no longer visible.

To delete tables and links at the same time, follow these easy steps:

1. **Choose Database⇨Remove from Report.**
2. **Select the table you want to remove from the report.**

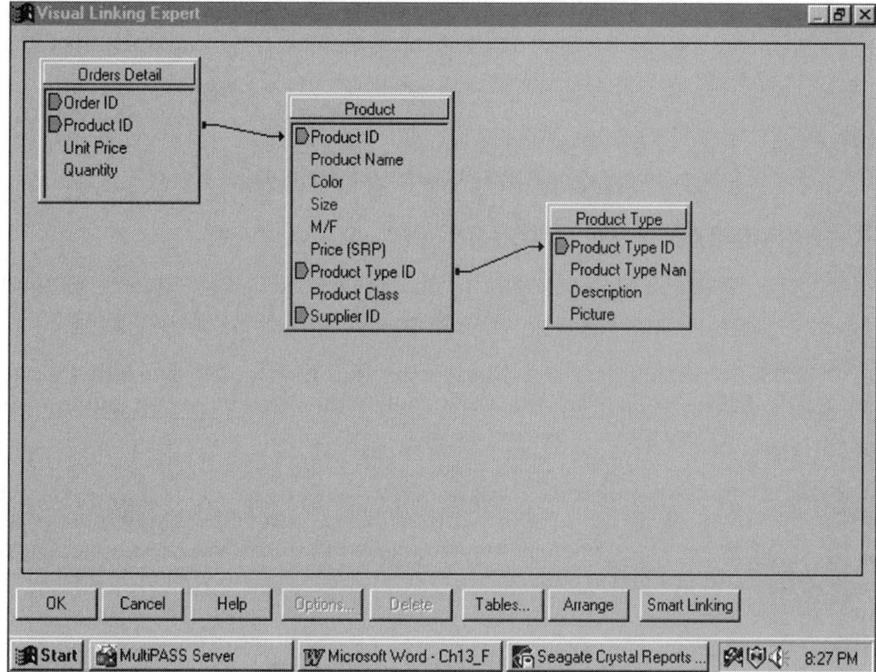

Figure 14-7: Poof! The Orders table is gone.

3. **Click the Remove button.**
4. **Repeat Steps 2 and 3 for each table you want to remove.**

These steps automatically remove any links you had.

Adding tables in the Visual Linking Expert dialog box

You can add tables from the Visual Linking Expert dialog box. In the opposite way from the way you made a visible table invisible, you can make an invisible table visible:

1. **Click the Tables button in the Visual Linking Expert dialog box.**
2. **Click the name of the tables in the Invisible section so that they're highlighted.**
3. **Click the Add button.**

   This step moves the selected table from the invisible side to the visible side.

After the table is visible, you can choose to either smart-link the table or draw a link by clicking the field in the new table and dragging to the field you want to link it with.

Creating a report after you've selected tables

After you have selected all the tables you want for your report and removed any you don't want, click OK in the Visual Linking Expert dialog box.

Return to the Design window for your new report. The Insert Fields dialog box is open, ready for you to select the fields you want and to insert them in the Design window (see Figure 14-8).

Because the three tables are linked in the Visual Linking Expert dialog box, you can create a report with fields from any of the three tables. Using these three tables, you can create a report that lists the orders detail, products, and product types.

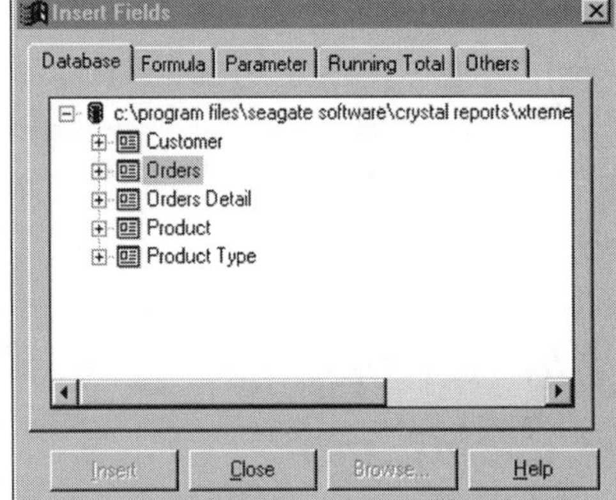

Figure 14-8: The Insert Fields dialog box.

Using SQL Joins

The information in this section is important because, according to the creators of Crystal Reports, 60 percent of their customers use SQL databases. Don't worry — you don't have to be an expert in SQL to be able to use SQL joins. Some of this information is handy reference material if you're making an SQL connection.

SQL, or Structured Query Language, is the underlying language used in many databases. (Some people just say "S-Q-L," and others pronounce it "sequel." Either way, they're referring to Structured Query Language.) Although the language is fairly easy to learn, a discussion of it is beyond the scope of this book. For a more in-depth discussion, you can buy one of the many available books about the SQL language, including *SQL For Dummies,* 3rd Edition, by Allen Taylor (IDG Books Worldwide, Inc.). In addition, many colleges and technical schools offer classes in the subject. If you're familiar with working with databases in Access, you know that you can create a query and then view the SQL language written to produce that query.

Crystal Reports enables you to link SQL tables to create reports and to specify the kind of join you want to use to link them. The type of join you specify determines in what order the lookup is made between tables. SQL join types are listed in the Link Options dialog box. To be able to use these join types, you must add a table via *Open Database Connectivity (ODBC),* the Microsoft standard for connecting client/server systems.

Adding tables via ODBC

When you create a new table in Crystal Reports, the Report Gallery window opens. If you select Custom, the database options open at the bottom of the window. On the right side, you can select Data File, SQL/ODBC, or Dictionary. You add tables via ODBC just as you would if you were using tables from a data file.

When you select ODBC, you're using the Microsoft ODBC connection to reach the tables:

1. **Click the Tables button in the Visual Linking Expert dialog box.**

   The Choose Tables to Use in Visual Linking dialog box opens.

2. **Click the Add SQL/ODBC button on the right side of the dialog box.**

   The Log On Server dialog box opens, as shown in Figure 14-9.

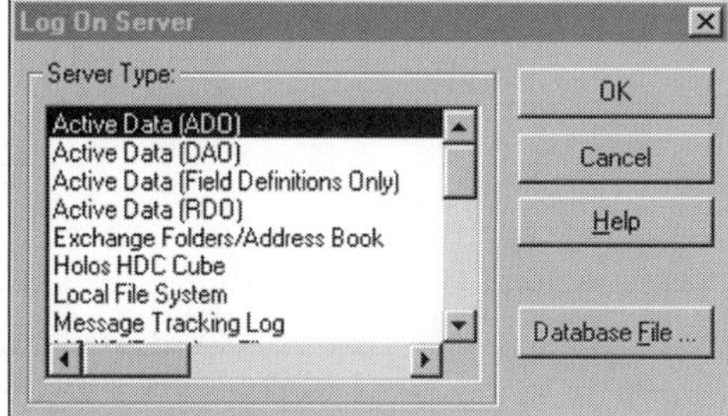

Figure 14-9: The Log On Server dialog box.

Crystal Reports and SQL

Although SQL is primarily a query language, it also has capabilities for creating, managing, and organizing tables in a database. Usually used in a client/server application, SQL sends statements to an SQL database server. The statements ask (or *query*) the database to return certain information. The SQL database server receives the SQL request for information, analyzes the request, finds the requested information, and then returns that data to the source of the query statement.

Because Crystal Reports provides a graphical user interface (GUI, pronounced "gooey") with which to query an SQL database, the program creates the actual SQL statement with the information you provide in the various dialog boxes. With Crystal Reports, you don't have to be a programmer to get results. It's one of many SQL-compliant application products that use SQL for querying a database.

From the Log On Server dialog box, you can either select the ODBC server type you want to use to select a database table or select different database files. Here are a couple of options:

- Click the Database File button to open any other database (.mdb) files on your system or network.
- In the Server Type box, click the ODBC server type for the database to which you are connecting, and then click OK.

When you connect to an ODBC server, you have to know which library files to use. Table 14-5 shows the database name in the first column and the ODBC data source in the second column. Use this table as a guide when you're deciding which library file to use in your ODBC connection.

Table 14-5 ODBC Drivers

Database	*ODBC Data Source*
IBM DB2/2	CRDB2
Microsoft SQL Server	CRSS
Oracle 7	CRORA7
Informix 7	CRINF7
SQLBase	CRGUP
Sybase System 10/11	CRSYB

Note: Check with your ODBC administrator if you're connecting to a different database. Other databases are supported by other drivers.

If you're connecting to a database by using ODBC, Crystal Reports uses ODBC syntax in the SQL statement. If you're connecting to an SQL database without using ODBC, Crystal Reports uses a syntax recognized by the SQL database.

Using SQL join types

A description of how to delve into the nitty-gritty of SQL is beyond the scope of this book. You can use Table 14-6, however, as a guide to help you select the SQL join type you want to use. If you're experienced with SQL, the table already makes sense; if you're not, however, take this table to your nearest SQL guru to help you make sense of the various SQL join types.

(The symbol used for the SQL join type is included in the SQL Where clause.)

Table 14-6 Defining the SQL Join Types

SQL Join Type	*Symbol*	*What It Includes*
Equal join	=	All records in which the linked field value is an exact match
Left outer join	*=	All records in which the linked field value is an exact match, plus a row for every record in the primary table whose linked field has no match in the lookup table
Right outer join	=*	All records in which the linked field value is an exact match, plus a row for every record in the lookup table whose linked field has no match in the primary table
Greater join	>	All records in which the linked field value in the primary table is greater than the linked field value in the lookup table
Less join	<	All records in which the linked field value from the primary table is less than the linked field value in the lookup table
Greater-or-equal join	>=	All records in which the linked field value from the primary table is greater than or equal to the linked field value in the lookup table

(continued)

Table 14-6 *(continued)*

SQL Join Type	*Symbol*	*What It Includes*
Less-or-equal join	<=	All records in which the linked field value from the primary table is less than or equal to the linked field value in the lookup table
Not-equal join	!=	All records in which the linked field from the primary table is not equal to the linked field value in the lookup table

If you're connecting to an ORACLE database, the syntax is different for left and right outer joins. For a left outer join, use =(+); for a right outer join, use (+)=. If you're connecting to an Access database, the syntax is also different for left and right outer joins. In Access, you use the words *left outer join* and *right outer join*. Place this syntax in the SQL From clause rather than in the SQL Where clause.

Equal join

You use the equal join option when you want to find all instances in one table that match with another table. For example, in a table that lists the ID number of a product that was ordered, you want to find every matching product name that goes with that ID number. Doing so helps you find any errors in data entry. If you have two products that have the same ID number, you know that you have to change the number for one of the products.

At the bicycle shop used in the Crystal Reports examples, you can use the equal join to find every product ID and the product name that goes with it. You may find a helmet with two different ID numbers, for example, which could lead to confusion in ordering or selling that product. Using the equal join helps you find these types of problems.

Left outer join

Using the same idea as in the preceding section, using a left outer join gives you a list of the ID number of a product that was ordered and every matching product name. This join also lists all the ID numbers for which no product name is listed. Your data-processing folks have to return to the database to make sure that each product ID has an associated product name.

In the bicycle shop example, you may find several ID numbers with no product names. You have to look through your hard copies or a source database to find the products that correspond with the ID number. This process helps you keep track of your inventory by making sure that every number has an associated product.

Right outer join

Using a right outer join gives you a list of the ID number of a product that was ordered and every matching product name. In addition, it lists all the product names that have no ID number. How can a customer order a product if the product has no number? You can easily correct this omission by going back and adding a product ID number for each product.

Greater join or greater-or-equal join

Suppose that you sell bicycles, as shown in the Xtreme database, and you also sell many bicycle accessories. You want to make sure that no accessory for a bicycle costs more than the bicycle itself. The greater join helps you verify that information. First, you determine the cost of the most expensive bicycle. By using a greater join, you can generate a list of all accessories where the cost is *greater than* the cost of that bicycle. You enter a single value into your query. In this type of join, every record greater than that value is listed. If your pricing strategy works according to plan, you have no accessories listed that cost more than the price of the most expensive bicycle.

Using a greater-or-equal join results in a list of accessories that are equal to the cost of the most expensive bicycle or that cost more than the most expensive bicycle.

Less join or a less-or-equal join

Using the opposite idea of a greater join or greater-or-equal join, you use a less-than join to list all accessories that cost less than the price of the most expensive bicycle. If your pricing strategy works, all the accessories listed are included because they cost less than the bicycle. In this example, using the greater join is better for answering this type of query because the result is a much smaller list.

Using a less-or-equal join results in a list of accessories that are equal to the cost of the most expensive bicycle or that cost less than the most expensive bicycle.

Not-equal join

The most common use for a not-equal join is to compare a table to itself. Suppose that in your bicycle business, you decide to hold a buy-one-accessory-get-the-second-one-for-half-price sale. Using your Product table, you run a query to list just the accessories (excluding all bicycles). Call this table the Accessory1 table, and make a duplicate of it called Accessory2.

Now use a not-equal join to list all the possible combinations of products. Because each accessory table has a distinct name, Crystal Reports considers them to be two separate tables. The not-equal join links the accessories by name. One column lists all the accessories from the Accessory1 table. The second column lists all the accessories from the Accessory2 table that are not equal to the accessories listed in the first column. Using the not-equal join, you don't get any helmets matched with helmets — you get helmets matched with gloves or water bottles.

If you have complex query needs, the SQL Designer may be useful to you.

Part VI

Disseminating Reports without a Hitch

"The new technology has really helped me get organized. I keep my project reports under the PC, budgets under my laptop and memos under my pager."

In this part . . .

Would you rather be rich or famous? No, "both" is not an option in answer to this question. Seagate Crystal Reports has the capability to take your reporting *masterpieces* and share them with the world! Herein lies the ticket to fame. Imagine . . . your report is distributed to every salesperson in the company. Or, better yet, it's posted to that new Orwellian device known innocently as the World Wide Web. (In numerology, World Wide Web translates to the number 666.) Undoubtedly, the end is near. Better get that report done before Armageddon, or there will be heck to pay. Your report is spreading everywhere at the speed of light! Supplicants are sending you e-mail from all over the world acknowledging your greatness. This is your moment in time! *Music up, lights fade to a single spotlight on a lone worker at a computer terminal. On the desk, a copy of the IDG Books catalog and* Seagate Crystal Reports 7 For Dummies. *The look on the face of the worker resembles Caesar crossing the Rubicon. . . .*

Chapter 15

Distributing Reports

In This Chapter

- Exporting a report
- Mailing a report
- Faxing a report
- Compiling a Crystal Reports report
- Using the Report Distribution Expert
- Sending a report to your Web site

In this chapter, I show you how to share your reports with a variety of software programs other than Seagate Crystal Reports. After you have created a magnificent report, you naturally want to share it with the world! You can share your handiwork with other people in three general ways:

- Send a Crystal Reports file so that they can open the file in their copy of Crystal Reports.
- Export the report to a specific format, such as Microsoft Word or Microsoft Excel.
- Create a *run-time version* of the report, which enables others to see the report in a Crystal Reports-like environment without having to have a copy of Crystal Reports on their computer.

What Is an Export File?

All computer programs are composed of files, and computer programs create files. Crystal Reports creates report files. Underlying all files is a common data structure that other programs with the proper settings can understand. An *export file,* therefore, is simply a Crystal Reports file that has been translated into a structure other programs can read and interpret. Some programs can interpret all the aspects of Crystal Reports files, and others cannot.

When you export a report file, you can retain some or all of the fancy formatting you have created, depending on the program to which you are exporting the report file.

Exporting Reports

Exporting a report file requires similar steps each time. You always select the *file format* (the data structure) into which you want to export the report file, and then you choose the physical destination for the translated report.

Follow these steps to export a report:

1. **Open the report you want to export from Crystal Reports.**
2. **Click the Export button on the toolbar.**
3. **Choose the format for exporting the report.**
4. **Choose the destination for the report and click the OK button.**

   Crystal Reports exports your report to the specified location and in the specified format.

Choosing a file format

Every time you export a report file, you must specify a report format. Table 15-1 lists some of the formats you can use. It gives you information to help you decide which file format to choose. The main thing you have to know for this process to work is what type of software the other person has.

Table 15-1 Export Formats

Software Application	*Format*	*File Can Be Read By*
Crystal Reports	.RPT	Crystal Reports or Crystal Info
Word processing	.DOC, .RTF	A word processing program (Word for Windows reads .DOC files; almost all word processing programs read Rich Text Format (.RTF) files)
Spreadsheet	.XLS, .WKS	Spreadsheet programs (Excel reads .XLS files; Lotus reads .WKS files)
Lotus Notes	Any format	Lotus Notes
Exchange	Any format	Microsoft Exchange

Software Application	Format	File Can Be Read By
ODBC	Data	An ODBC data source set up through an ODBC administrator
HTML	HTML	Netscape, Internet Explorer, and other Web browsers

For example, if all the employees in your office have Crystal Reports on their systems, export the file in Crystal Reports format. This format is sometimes called *native format* (it refers to the product you're using to distribute the report, not to aborigines).

If your office uses Microsoft Exchange and all your co-workers have Microsoft Office (but not Crystal Reports), you can export the report in one of the Microsoft formats. Choose either Excel (XLS) or Word (DOC).

Choosing the report destination

Another decision you have to make is the destination of the report you're exporting. Table 15-2 lists the export destination options and where the report goes if you select that option.

Table 15-2 Export Destination Options

Export Destination	What It Does
Disk file	Saves the report to a disk file. When you select this option, a dialog box opens in which you can select the destination file. The file can be exported to a hard disk on your system or to a disk in drive A (or any other drive).
Mail application	Attaches the report to an electronic-mail application document. Crystal Reports supports *MAPI,* the Microsoft Mail format used for either Exchange or Microsoft Mail. (For more information about MAPI, see the section "Mailing a Report," later in this chapter.)
Exchange folder	Stores the report in a Microsoft Exchange folder. A dialog box opens, in which you select the destination folder.
Lotus Notes database	Exports the report to a Lotus Notes database. This option is displayed if you're on a network.

If you're exporting a report file to Excel (XLS), for example, you select Disk File as your destination. When the dialog box opens so that you can select the destination file, choose the filename you want, such as Dougrpt, and click OK.

If you work in a company that uses Microsoft Exchange, select Exchange Folder as the export destination. A dialog box opens in which you designate which Exchange folder is the destination folder.

Exporting a report with saved data

You can either save a report definition layout or save data with a report. The difference is that when you save a *report definition,* you save the sorting, grouping, summaries, and other elements and characteristics, but no data. If you save the *report with data,* you save the definition plus all the records that make up the report. The saved data does not include the source tables or the databases from which you selected individual records.

If you're the sales manager for a company, for example, you may want your salespeople to have just the report definition in which they can insert their own records. Or you may decide to give them the reports with the records so that they can work with only the records you select. Either way, this feature is a powerful one for any business.

If you export only the report definition:

- Your report requires less disk space.
- The program you use to open the report has to retrieve data before it prints the report. In other words, the person receiving the definition must have access to the database.

If you save data with the report:

- Your report requires more disk space.
- The program you use to open the report does not have to retrieve data before it prints the report, because that data is already part of the report.

Note: Along with the preceding options, you have to know that when Crystal Reports saves data with a report, the data is compressed so that it takes up less disk space. When you open the report, Crystal Reports decompresses the data.

To change the options in Crystal Reports to save the data with the report or just the report definition, follow these steps:

1. **Choose File⇨Options.**

   Figure 15-1 shows the File menu with the Options option highlighted. Notice that the menu is different when no report file is open.

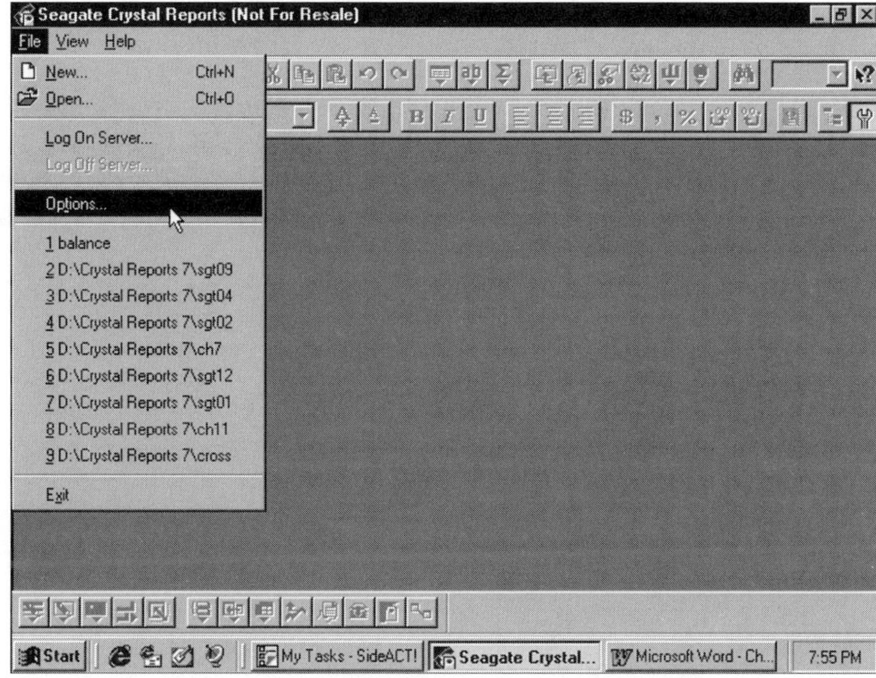

Figure 15-1: The File menu with Options highlighted.

2. **From the File Options dialog box, click the Reporting tab, as shown in Figure 15-2.**

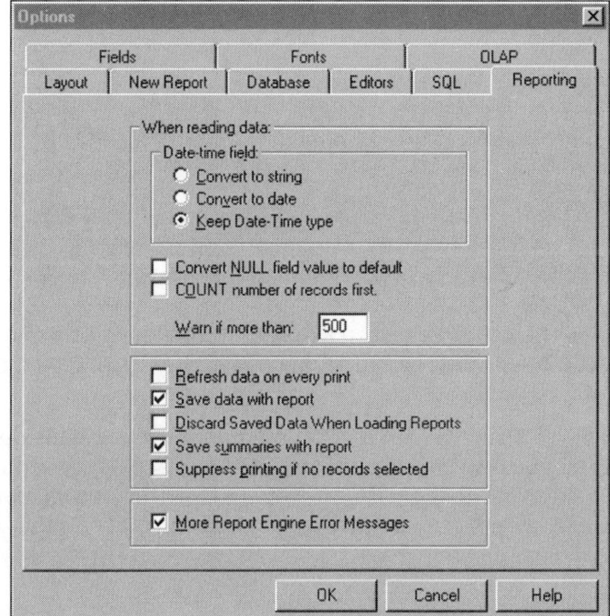

Figure 15-2: The Reporting tab in the Options dialog box.

In the third section of the Reporting tab is the option Save Data with Report. The check mark in the check box (the default setting) means that the option is selected and that the data will be saved with the report. To save just the report definition, you have to deselect the option (click to remove the check mark).

3. **Click the check box to select the Save Data with Report option.**

   The check mark is removed. Crystal Reports now saves only the report definition when you save a report.

4. **With a report file open, click to open the File menu (see Figure 15-3).**

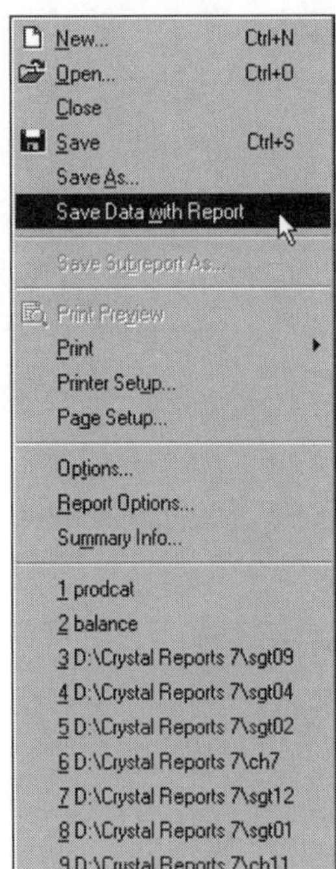

Figure 15-3: The File menu.

You can use this menu to save a file in one of three ways:

- **Save:** Saves the active report to a disk under its current name. All changes you have made to the report overwrite the preceding version of the report.
- **Save As:** Saves the report to a disk under a new name. This option is handy when you want to save an original copy separately from the copy to which you make changes. When you choose this option, you have two files (under different names): the untouched original and the report to which you've made changes.

- **Save Data with Report:** Saves the underlying data that accompanies the report. The data saved with the report is sort of a snapshot of how the data looked when you ran the report. You still have to use Save or Save As to create a saved report file, however.

Opening a saved report

Crystal Reports includes a series of sample reports. In this section, I show you how to open one of these reports so that you can use it for exporting practice. (You must open a report before you can export it.)

Follow these steps to open a report file to export:

1. **Choose File⇨Open (or click the Open button on the toolbar).**

   The Open dialog box is displayed with the Crystal Reports 7 folder opened.

2. **Double-click the Reports folder.**
3. **Double-click the Xtreme folder.**
4. **Click the filename (Income).**

   Figure 15-4 shows the highlighted file in the Open dialog box.

5. **Click the Open button.**

   The Income report file opens.

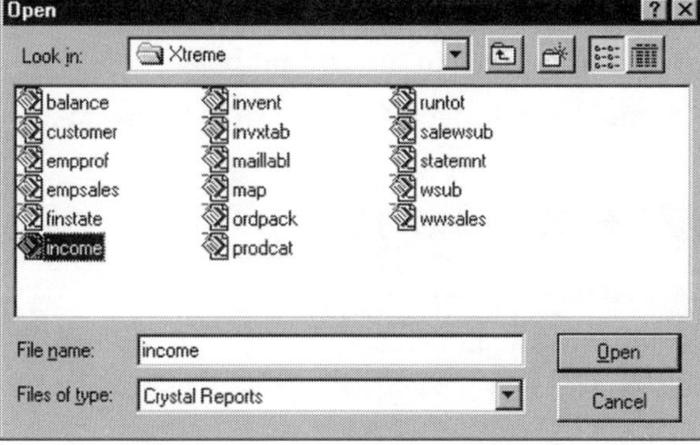

Figure 15-4: Selecting the Income file in the Open dialog box.

In this example, you can use any report file you want to experiment with. Because the report is not changed in any way, you can safely export any report you want.

Exporting to a Lotus Notes database

The Lotus Notes database is a *groupware* application, often used in an organization to provide information-sharing between departments. The steps in this section tell you how to export a Crystal Reports report file to the Notes environment.

Note: You must have Version 3.0 or later of the Lotus Notes Windows client; Crystal Reports does not export to previous Lotus Notes clients or OS/2 clients.

Lotus Notes is displayed as a destination option only when your computer has the Lotus Notes client installed.

Open the file you want to export, and then follow these steps:

1. **Click the Export button on the toolbar.**

   The Export dialog box is displayed, as shown in Figure 15-5.

Figure 15-5: The Export dialog box.

2. **Click the drop-down arrow in the Format box.**

   The export formats are displayed, as shown in Figure 15-6.

Figure 15-6: The Export dialog box shows some formatting options.

3. **For this example, choose the Excel 5.0 (XLS) format.**
4. **Click the drop-down arrow in the Destination box.**

   The possible report destinations are displayed.

5. **For this example, select Lotus Notes Database and click OK.**

   The Select Database dialog box is displayed.

6. **Select the Lotus Notes Database server on the Servers list.**

7. **Select the name of the database to which you want to export the report, and then click OK.**

   The Comments dialog box opens.

8. **Type any comments you want associated with the report.**

   You may want to add a brief description of the report.

9. **Click OK.**

   Crystal Reports exports the report.

Any users who log on to Lotus Notes with access to the Lotus Notes database you specified can view your report if they have Excel software. Users double-click the report filename to display your comments and can double-click the report icon to view the report.

Exporting to Excel format

In a situation in which you're networked and other users don't have Crystal Reports, you can export reports in other file formats directly to their machines. If you're in a small shop, for example, you may have to use *sneaker net* (the system of physically carrying a disk to another computer, otherwise known as *troglodyte net*) to get a file from your machine to another. Or, you may attend a meeting and need to bring the report with you on a disk. Export the report to an Excel file on a floppy disk.

Begin with a report open in Crystal Reports, and then follow these steps:

1. **Click the Export button on the toolbar.**

   The Export dialog box opens.

2. **Click the drop-down arrow in the Format box.**

   The export format choices are displayed.

3. **Select Excel 5.0 (XLS).**

4. **Click the drop-down arrow in the Destination box.**

   The destination choices are displayed.

5. **Select Disk File.**

   Figure 15-7 shows what the Export dialog box looks like after you complete these selections.

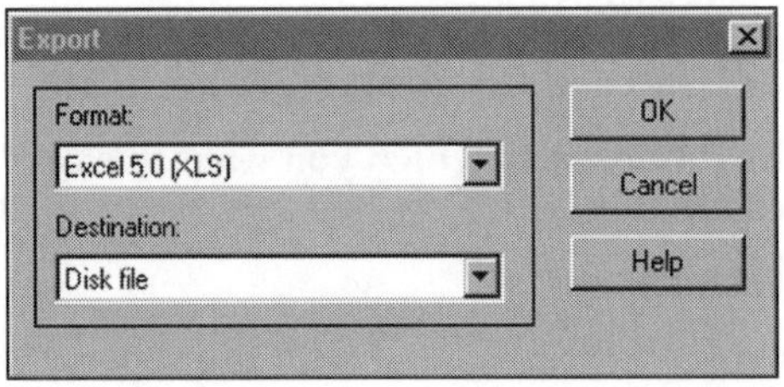

Figure 15-7: The Export dialog box, with the Excel 5.0 format and the Disk File destination selected.

6. **Click OK.**

   The Choose Export File dialog box is displayed. Your next step is to choose the destination for the report file.

7. **Click the button with the folder with the up-arrow on it.**

   Continue clicking that button until My Computer shows up in the Save In box. Figure 15-8 shows what the Choose Export File dialog box looks like now.

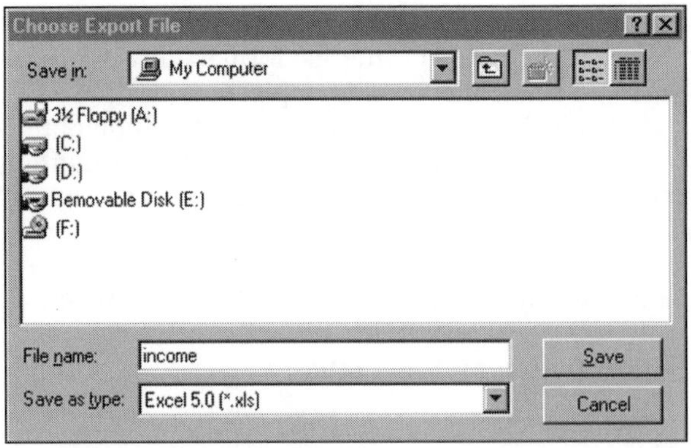

Figure 15-8: My Computer in the Choose Export File dialog box.

8. **Before you take another step, make sure that a 3½-inch floppy disk is in drive A.**

9. **Select the 3½ Floppy (A:) option.**

10. **Click the Open button.**

    The Choose Export File dialog box remains on-screen with a few minor changes.

11. **Click the Save button.**

    The Exporting box is displayed. It's not a dialog box; it's just displayed during the exporting process.

You can easily tell whether the export worked. Follow these steps to see whether the file is on drive A:

1. **Click the Start button.**
2. **Choose Programs, and then choose Windows Explorer.**

   Windows Explorer opens.
3. **Select the 3½ Floppy (A:) option.**

The file you exported (Income, in this example) is displayed on the right side of the Explorer window. Figure 15-9 shows that this file is a Microsoft Excel worksheet.

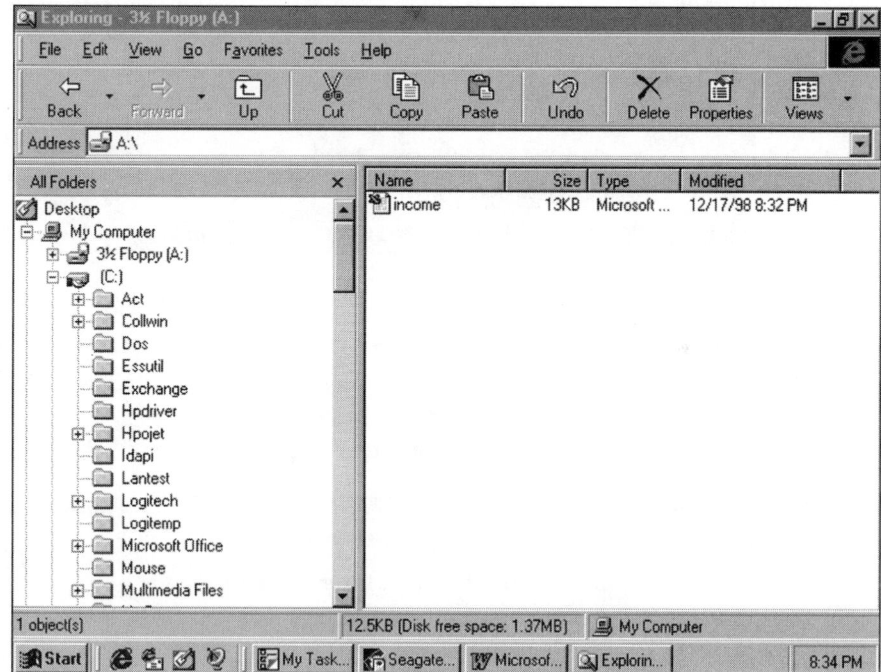

Figure 15-9: The Income file is saved on drive A in Microsoft Excel Worksheet format.

You can compare the formatting differences in the exported Excel file with the original Crystal Reports file. In Figure 15-10, you see the open Income report in Crystal Reports. Figure 15-11 shows the open Income file in Excel. You can see that some of the formatting is lost in the export process. Excel does not support all the features in Crystal Reports; therefore, the displayed report is different.

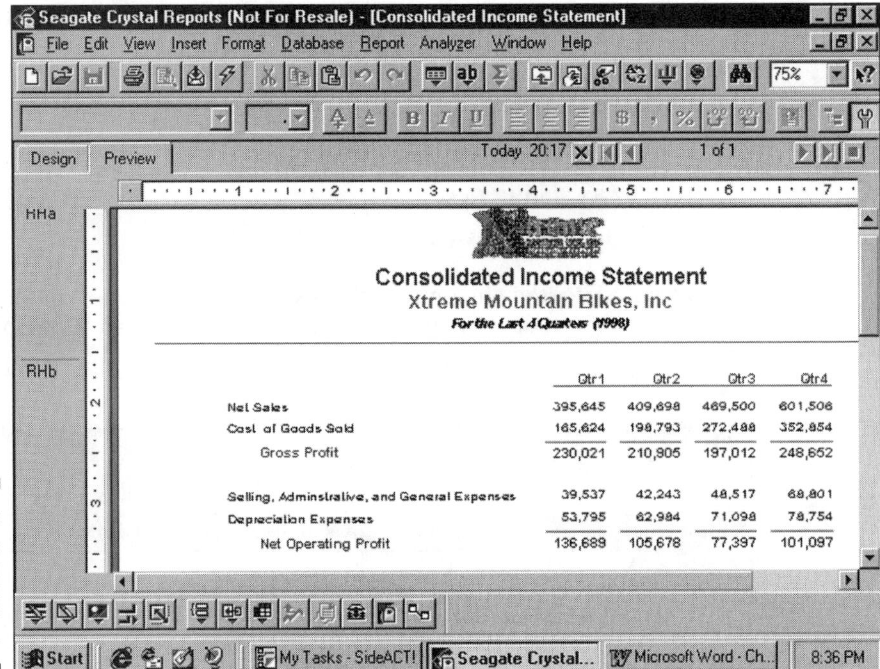

Figure 15-10: The Income file, opened in Crystal Reports.

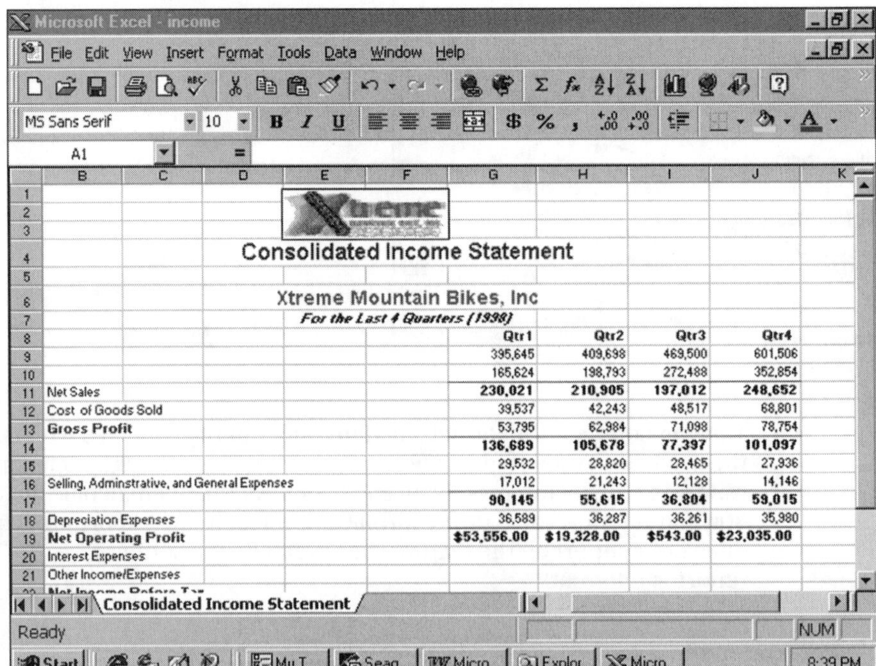

Figure 15-11: The Income file, opened in Excel.

Exporting to Microsoft Word format

Export your Crystal Reports report to a Microsoft Word file to convert the file to a .DOC document. All Word users will have ready access to your report. You can export a report to a file that already exists.

If you want to export a report into a Word document file, and you're working in Word, follow these steps:

1. **Choose File⇨New (or click the New button).**
2. **Select a new, blank document as the new file.**

   A blank document opens in Word.

3. **Choose File⇨Save (or click the Save button).**

   The Save File dialog box opens.
4. **Enter a name, such as** cr example**, in the Save File dialog box.**
5. **Close this blank document by choosing File⇨Close.**

Go back to Crystal Reports, open a report, and then follow these steps:

1. **Click the Export button on the toolbar.**

   The Export dialog box is displayed.
2. **Click the drop-down arrow in the Format box.**

   The export format choices are displayed.
3. **Select the Word for Windows document format.**

   You have to click the scroll buttons to move to the bottom of the list.
4. **Click the drop-down arrow in the Destination box.**

   The destination choices are displayed.
5. **Select Disk File and click OK.**

   The Choose Export File dialog box is displayed, as shown in Figure 15-12. Your next step is to choose the destination for the report file.

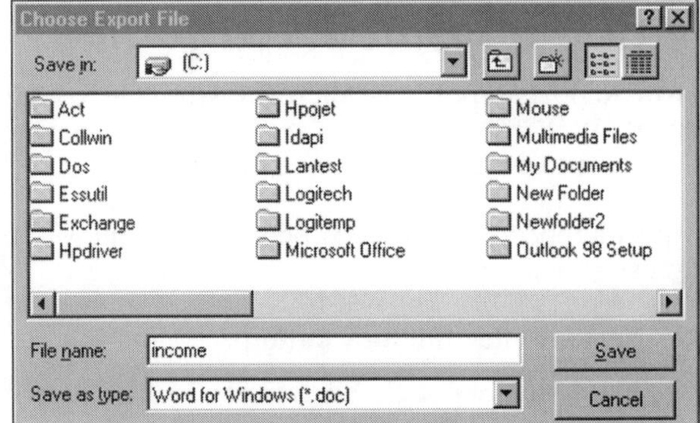

Figure 15-12: The Choose Export File dialog box with drive C selected.

6. **Locate the folder you want to export to and double-click it.**

   The files in that folder are displayed.

7. **For this example, click the CR Example file to highlight it.**

   Figure 15-13 shows the CR Example file highlighted.

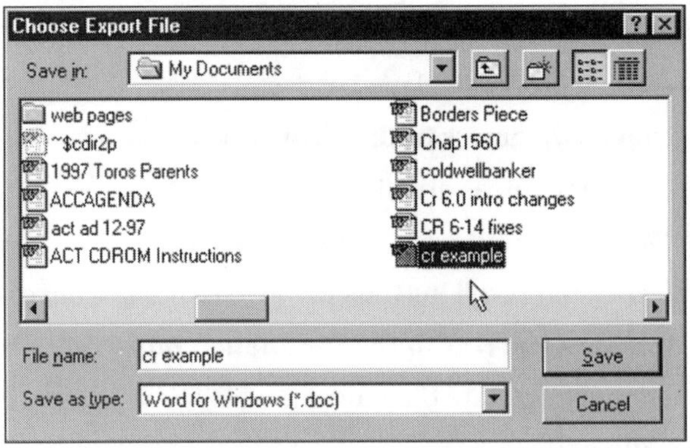

Figure 15-13: Selecting the CR Example file.

8. **Click the Save button.**

   The File Already Exists dialog box opens.

9. **Click Yes when Crystal Reports asks whether you want to overwrite the existing file.**

   The Exporting box is displayed. Crystal Reports is running the report again against the database. The box alerts you to the program's progress in reading the source database. This way, you get the latest information in your exported report.

Canceling an export

When the Exporting box is displayed, you can cancel the export by clicking the Cancel button (except for very short reports). Doing so stops the export in progress.

Comparing a Word document with a Crystal Reports report

Figures 15-11 and 15-12, shown earlier in this chapter, compare the exported Excel file with the Crystal Reports report file. You can also open a Word document to see how much of the formatting is displayed in the Word document:

1. **With Microsoft Word open, click the Open button on the toolbar.**
2. **Highlight a Word file and click the Open button in the Open dialog box.**

   Figure 14-14 shows a typical report open in a Word document.

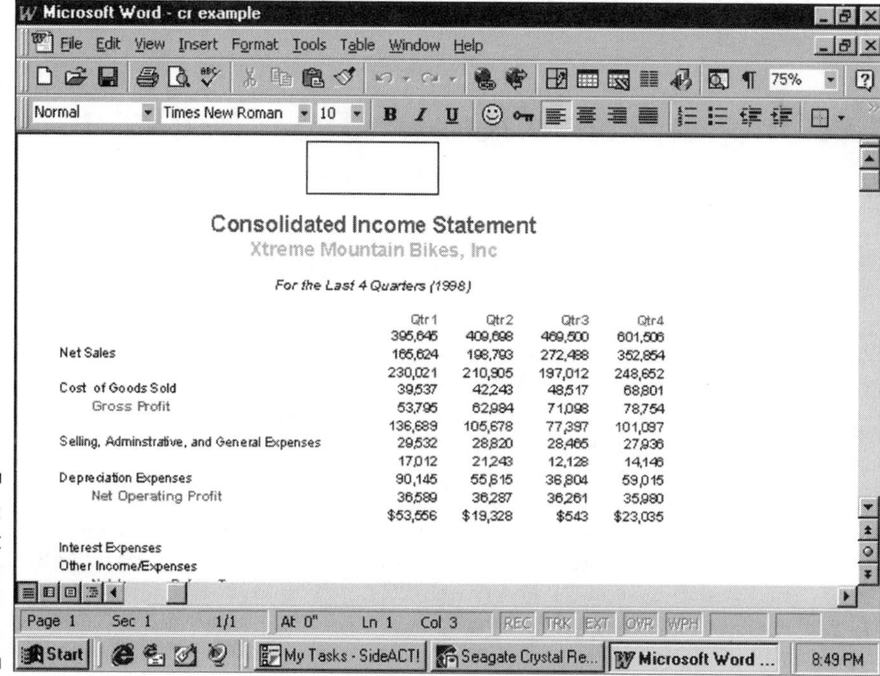

Figure 15-14: A report opened as a Word document.

Exporting to an ODBC data source

With Crystal Reports, you can export reports to any ODBC data source. *ODBC,* or Open Data Base Connectivity, is a Microsoft standard for network communications between databases. (You may think that it stands for Obfuscation Daily By Computer.) You may ask yourself why you would want to export reports to an ODBC data source, anyway. Here are a few reasons:

- You can change data from a centralized database into a format you can use in a local database. For example, you can change data from a Microsoft SQL Server to data you can use with Microsoft Access on your local database.
- Conversely, you can change data from a local database to data compatible with a centralized database. For example, you can change data from a Paradox database on your machine to data you can use with Oracle on a centralized database.
- You can convert a report to a new database table that can be used as a separate data set. Then you can create reports from that set of data.

When you're exporting to ODBC, the following assumption is made: You have an ODBC data source set up through ODBC Administrator for Crystal Reports. If not, follow the steps in the following section.

Setting Up an ODBC Data Source

Each database you work with has specific libraries for the database. For example, Crystal Reports can read a database created by the Microsoft SQL Server. Crystal Reports has a library file installed with the program that translates requests to the SQL Server and then returns data from it.

The PDSSQL.DLL library file in Crystal Reports talks to the MSDBLIB.DLL file on the Microsoft SQL Server. Each application has its own language. The library files enable one application to talk to another via ODBC. (By the way, *DLL* stands for *d*ynamic *l*inking *l*ibrary. Drop that one at your next party, and you will have established your dynamic link to Geekville!)

Files with the .DLL extension are library files used for translating between application programs. When you export a report by using ODBC, you have to know which library files to use for the destination database. Table 15-3 shows the database name and the ODBC data source as it is shown in the Export dialog box. Selecting the correct data source ensures that you're using the correct libraries.

Table 15-3 Library Files

Database	*ODBC Data Source*
IBM DB2/2	CRDB2
Microsoft SQL Server 6.x	CRSS
Oracle 7	CROR7
Informix 7	CRINF7
SQLBase	CRGUP
Sybase System 10/11	CRSYB

Use this table as a guide when you're deciding which library file to use in your ODBC connection.

Begin with a report open in Crystal Reports, and then follow these steps to export to an ODBC data source:

1. **Click the Export button on the toolbar.**

   The Export dialog box is displayed.

2. **Click the drop-down arrow in the Format box.**

   The export format choices are displayed.

3. **Select an ODBC format.**

   You have to click the scroll buttons to move to the ODBC options. Table 15-3 can help you select the correct ODBC format. In this example, select ODBC-CRSS for SQL Server.

   Note: When you're working with ODBC, disregard the Destination section.

4. **Click OK.**

5. **If your ODBC data source specifies a particular database, the report is exported to that database. If not, the Select Database dialog box is displayed.**

6. **Select the database to which this report will be added as a new table.**

   The database name is highlighted.

7. **Click OK.**

   If the ODBC data source you highlighted requires a logon ID and password, the Log On dialog box is displayed.

8. **Enter your ID and password, and click OK.**

   The ODBC Table Name dialog box is displayed.

9. **Type the name for the new table in the database, and click OK.**

   Crystal Reports exports the report as a new table in the destination database.

Mailing a Report

Each electronic-mail system is unique. Because of the differences in how mail systems work, I give you generic exporting instructions in this section. The figures shown in this section are from a real-life example, although you have to use your own mail application program.

Whenever you combine the activities of one program with another, things get a little more complicated. You have to know about some caveats and assumptions about exporting to e-mail. Both Microsoft Mail and Microsoft Exchange use MAPI. Crystal Reports supports exporting to MAPI and to Lotus Notes.

MAPI is just a standard for e-mail; it's the Microsoft Mail API (application programming interface), which many companies use. VIM, another standard for getting mail, has a different format. It was created and is maintained by Lotus.

Follow these steps to mail a report:

1. **Click the Export button on the toolbar.**

   The Export dialog box is displayed.

2. **Click the drop-down arrow in the Format box.**

   The export format choices are displayed.

3. **Select Crystal Reports (RPT).**

   You have to click the scroll buttons to move to this selection.

4. **Click the drop-down arrow in the Destination box.**

   The destination choices are displayed.

5. **Select Microsoft Mail (MAPI).**

   Figure 15-15 shows these selections in the Export dialog box.

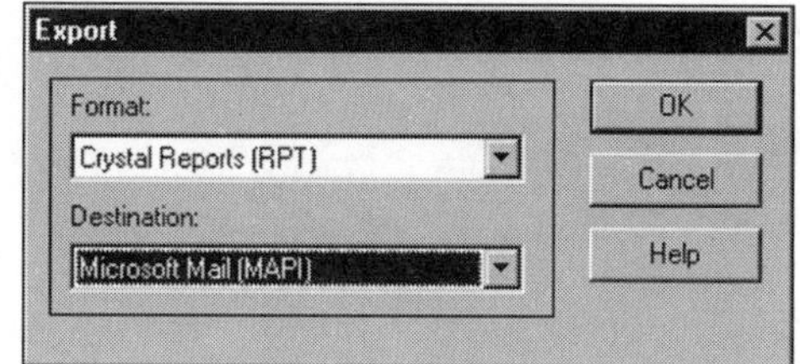

Figure 15-15: The Export dialog box, with Crystal Reports and Microsoft Mail selected.

When you export a report to e-mail, one of two things may happen: Crystal Reports may ask you to log on to your e-mail application in the normal way, or your e-mail application may automatically open. Continue sending mail as you normally do in your e-mail application.

Faxing a Report

You can fax a Crystal Reports report directly to a fax machine if you have a fax application, such as Microsoft Fax or Delrina WinFax, installed on your system. You must have installed a fax application before you can use this Crystal Reports feature.

Follow these generic steps to fax directly from Crystal Reports:

1. **Choose Crystal Reports, and open the report you want to fax.**
2. **In Crystal Reports, choose File⇨Printer Setup.**

   The Print Setup dialog box is displayed.
3. **Click the drop-down arrow next to the name of the printer.**

   All available printers are listed.
4. **From the list of available printers, select the fax driver and click OK.**

   Figure 15-16 shows the screen with a fax printer driver selected.
5. **Choose File⇨Print⇨Printer.**

   The Print dialog box opens, as shown in Figure 15-17.

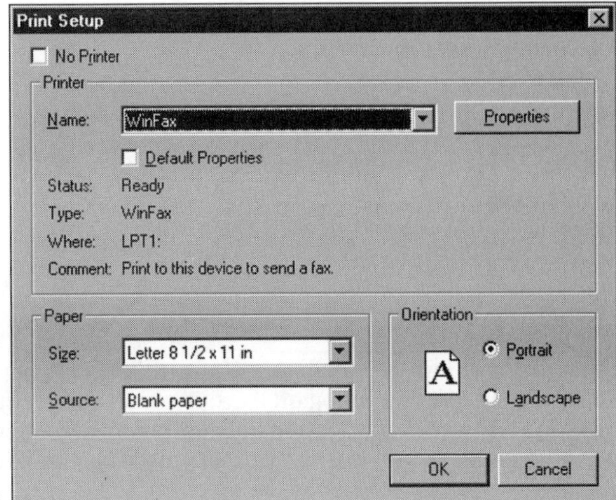

Figure 15-16: Selecting a fax printer driver.

Figure 15-17: The Print dialog box.

6. **Click OK.**

   The fax application is displayed. From the fax application, you can select a cover page and fill in the number to which you are faxing and other required information.

7. **Select the option that lets you send the fax from your fax application.**

Compiling a Crystal Reports Report

Compiling a report creates an *executable version* of the report, which means that you can create a report that can be printed on demand. You simply click an icon. You don't have to open Crystal Reports first to print the report.

By compiling a report, you can create a report and share it with others. If those people don't know how to use Crystal Reports, they can still print the report. They don't even have to have Crystal Reports on their system to be able to take advantage of a compiled report.

When you want to create reports that someone can print regardless of whether he has Crystal Reports or widely distribute a report without regard to the recipients' application products, use a compiled report. Keeping a compiled report on your own desktop means that you can open the report with the click of a button. The report is displayed instantly because you don't have to open Crystal Reports.

Here are some more things you can do with a compiled report:

- Print a compiled report to a window, a printer, or a file.
- Print a report immediately.
- Print a report later, such as after hours, when the printers are more available.
- Tailor a compiled report to individual needs.

Creating a compiled report is a six-step snap:

1. **Choose Report⇨Compile Report.**

   The Compile Report dialog box is displayed, showing the name of the report file you have open.

2. **You can compile this report, type a new name, or click the Browse button to find the report you want to compile.**
3. **Click the Yes radio button to create a program item for the report in the program.**

   Creating a program item means that this item is displayed in a program window after the report is compiled.

4. **Click the Yes button to be able to distribute the report after you compile it.**

   Figure 15-18 shows the Compile Report dialog box with these selections.

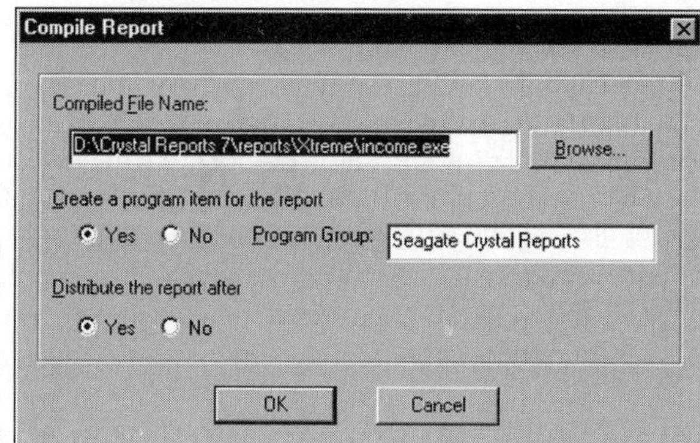

Figure 15-18: The Compile Report dialog box.

5. **Click OK.**

   Crystal Reports creates a report icon in the Crystal Reports Professional window. Next, the Report Distribution Expert is displayed. From the Report Distribution dialog box, you can control the distribution of the report. This dialog box also helps you identify and gather the required files to make the executable compiled report run. Figure 15-19 shows the Report Distribution dialog box.

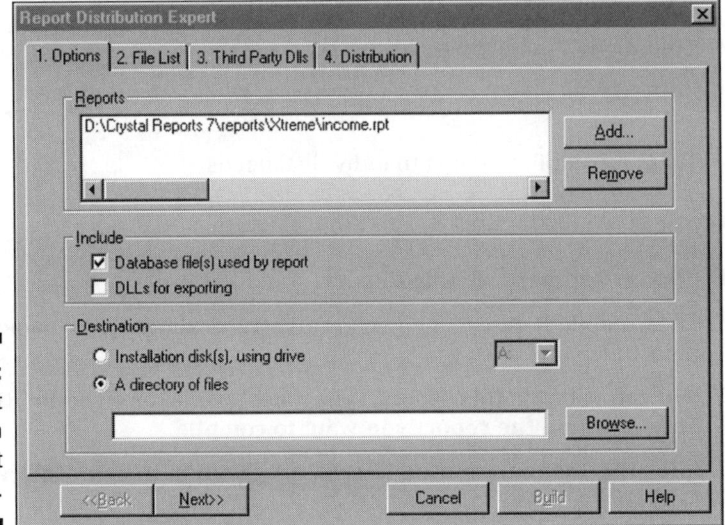

Figure 15-19: The Report Distribution Expert dialog box.

Using the Report Distribution Expert

After you compile a report by choosing the Compile Report command from the Report menu, Crystal Reports asks whether you want to distribute the report. In the steps shown in the preceding section, the option to distribute the report is selected. When you select that option, the Report Distribution Expert dialog box is displayed.

You use the Report Distribution Expert when you compile reports, save reports to a disk for mass distribution, send a report to a network drive so that others can use it, or ship reports with an application you develop by using the Crystal Reports engine. (In other words, you have reached a higher plane when you start doing these sorts of tasks, and you become a much more valuable employee.)

For now, close the Report Distribution Expert by clicking the Cancel button.

Before you can distribute a report, you have to make several minor adjustments to keep from having to make a call to the helpful people at Seagate.

Opening the file you want to distribute

To open the file you want to distribute, select the file. In this example, the Income report from the Xtreme folder is selected.

1. **Choose File⇨Open (or click the Open button on the toolbar).**

   The Open dialog box is displayed with the Crystal Reports 7 folder open.
2. **Double-click the Reports folder.**
3. **Double-click the Xtreme folder.**
4. **Click the filename (Income).**
5. **Click the Open button.**

   The Income report file opens.

Saving the file you want to distribute

To distribute the report, you have to save it in the same folder as the database. In this example, the income file is in the Xtreme folder. I show you how to save the file to the Crystal Reports folder, where the Xtreme database, the .Mdb file, is located. A copy of this report is put in the Crystal Reports folder. The income report file is also in the original location, the Xtreme folder.

Follow these steps to save the file to distribute:

1. **Choose File⇨Save As.**

   The Save As dialog box is displayed with the Xtreme folder open.
2. **Click the up-arrow folder button until the Crystal Reports folder is highlighted.**

   Figure 15-20 shows the Save As dialog box. You can see the Xtreme file listed there.
3. **Click the Save button.**

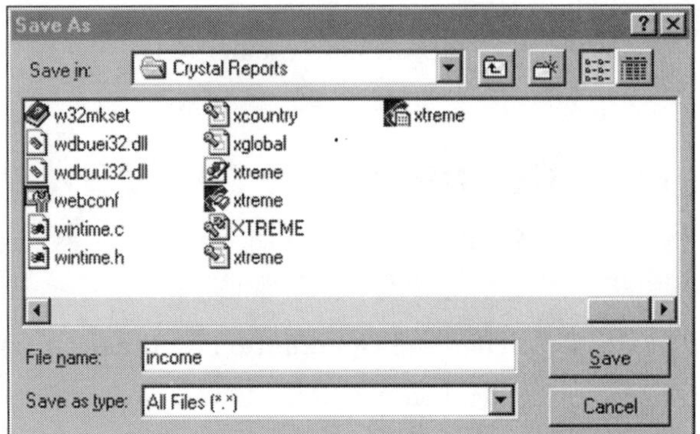

Figure 15-20: The Save As dialog box.

Close the Income file, and reopen it from the Crystal Reports folder. Now you're working in that report file from the Crystal Reports folder, not in the report file that's in the Xtreme folder. ***Important:*** To distribute a compiled report, the report and the database must be in the same folder.

4. **To close the file, click the X button in the upper-right corner of the Income report file, and then choose File⇨Open.**

5. **From the Crystal Reports folder, select the Income file and click the Open button.**

The next phase is to set the location of the Income report. Because you copied this report file to a new folder, you have to set the location of the report to the folder it's in.

Follow these steps to set the location:

1. **Choose Database⇨Set Location.**

   The Set Location dialog box opens, as shown in Figure 15-21. Crystal Reports looks for any tables on which the income report is based. In this example, only the Financials table is shown because it's the only table in the Xtreme database used for this report.

2. **Click the Same As Report button.**

   This step enables Crystal Reports to locate the records used to create the report. If more than one table is listed in this dialog box, you select each table and click the Same As Report button for each one.

3. **Click Done.**

4. **Choose File⇨Save.**

   Be sure to do Step 4 — it's crucial! If you leave it out, you cannot distribute the report.

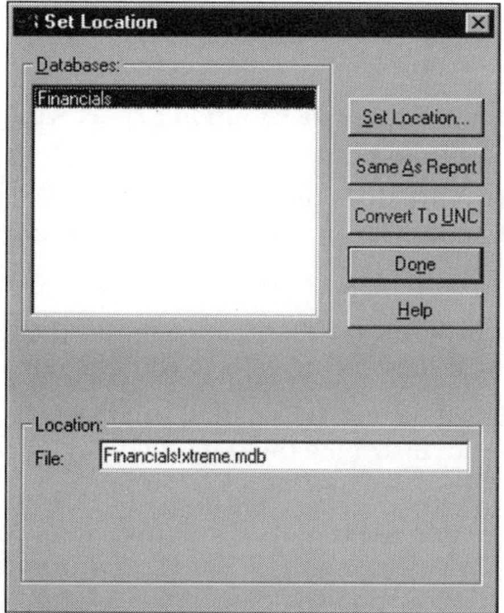

Figure 15-21: The Set Location dialog box.

After you complete the preceding steps, start the Report Distribution Expert by following these steps:

1. **Choose Report⇨Report Distribution Expert.**

   The Report Distribution Expert dialog box helps you gather the required files to distribute a report. From this dialog box, you can also ship data with the report, compress the component files, and build an executable file. This file, which is really a small computer program, is the one created in this process so that the person receiving the report can install it on his computer. Any user can run the executable file to install the report you are distributing. When the user runs the file, Crystal Reports decompresses the files, installs the files where the user designates, and then creates an icon for calling up the report.

   You can identify an executable file in two ways. Because the file has an .Exe extension, it's called an *application* file when it's listed in Windows Explorer or in an Open File dialog box. Later, after you have built the .Exe file, you look for this file and open it. Crystal Reports names the .Exe file with the name of the report you're compiling. In this example, the name of the compiled report is Income.Exe.

   The options on the Report Distribution Expert Options tab are listed in Table 15-4.

2. **Click the Browse button to determine the destination of the report you want to distribute.**

   The Choose Distribution Directory dialog box opens. The default folder is the Crystal Reports folder. Because your report file and database are in this folder, it's the one in which you want the compiled report to be built.

3. **Click OK.**

   The path for the Crystal Reports folder is now in the Destination box.

4. **Select the two boxes in the Report Distribution Expert window in the Include section.**

   This step tells Crystal Reports that you want to include the database files used by the report and the associated DLLs for exporting.

5. **Click the Next button.**

   Crystal Reports begins analyzing the files that comprise the report. The program then identifies the files you need to go with the report.

   Not every report you distribute has DAO files. If you receive a message asking whether you want to distribute the DAO engine and its related files, click Yes.

   Use the File List tab to add or delete files. The options for selecting files are listed in Table 15-5. You can use Tables 15-4 and 15-5 for more information as you become a more sophisticated Crystal Reports user. During the beginner's phase, however, just accept the defaults for the File List tab and the Third Party DLLs tab.

   Figure 15-22 shows the file list in the Report Distribution Expert.

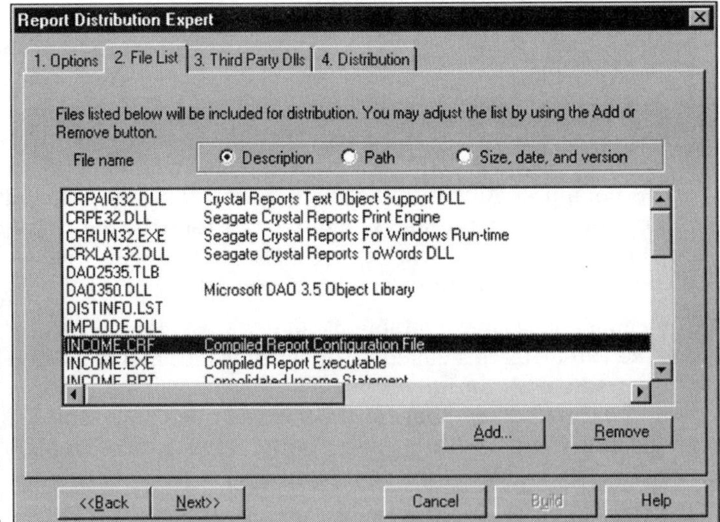

Figure 15-22: The File List tab in the Report Distribution Expert.

6. **Press the Next button until you get to the Distribution tab, and then click the Build button.**

   Crystal Reports begins building your compiled report for distribution. Figure 15-23 shows what the screen looks like after you press the Build button. The speed of your computer and the number of records in the report determine the amount of time it takes to create the file. If you have more than 500 records in the report, for example, it's time for a long lunch — with dessert.

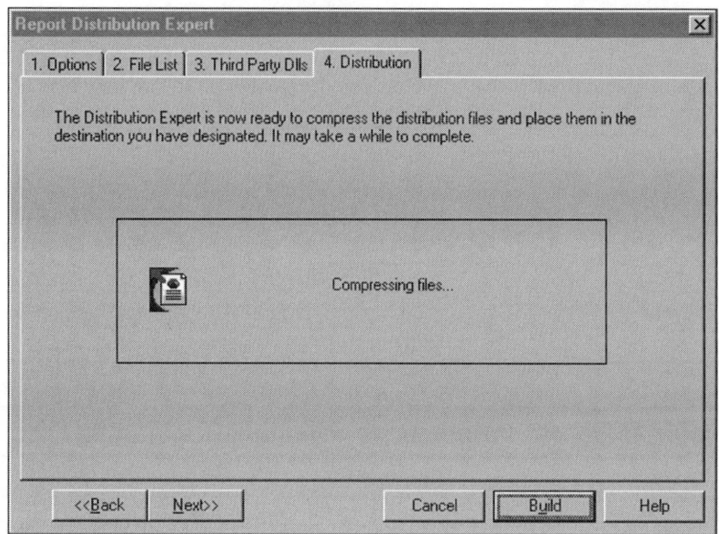

Figure 15-23: Compiling the report.

After the report is built, a dialog box pops up, announcing that the file distribution has succeeded.

7. **Click OK.**

Table 15-4 Options on the Report Distribution Expert Options Tab

Option	*What It Does*
Reports	Displays the list of files you want in your report distribution file.
Add	Adds files to the Reports to Be Distributed box.
Remove	Removes highlighted files from the Reports to Be Distributed box.
Include Database Files Used By Report	Lets you decide whether you want to include data files with your report. This option ties into the steps you take to alert Crystal Reports to set the location of the underlying database used in the report. Without that location, Crystal Reports cannot include the records with the distributed report.

(continued)

Table 15-4 *(continued)*

Option	*What It Does*
Include DLLs for Exporting	Lets you decide whether you want to include the DLLs for exporting.
Destination — Installation Disk(s), Using Drive	Chooses the destination of the report distribution file after you create it (with this option, files are saved to a floppy disk).
Destination — a Directory of Files	Directs the destination of the report distribution file after you create it (with this option, files are saved to a directory on the hard disk; you can either enter the directory path or click the Browse button and select a directory).
Browse	Lets you browse the folders and files on the hard drives.

Table 15-5 Options for Selecting Distribution Files

Option	*What It Does*
File Name	Lists the names of the files to be included in the distribution file. (You can choose from the three radio buttons in the following three table entries.)
Description	Shows the type of file being included.
Path	Shows the DOS path for the file location.
Size, Date, and Version	Shows size, date, and version details.
Add	Opens the Choose Distribution File dialog box and adds the current report to an existing report.
Remove	After you've highlighted a file, prevents the file from being distributed with the report. The file is added to the Don't Copy box.

If you develop reports for another program, such as an accounting program, you may need to include DLLs in order for the report to work. Select them on the Third Party DLLs tab.

Printing the Distributed Report

A compiled report opens without Crystal Reports. Close Crystal Reports now, and then locate the compiled report. The Income.Exe file should be in the Crystal Reports folder, which is the location specified as the destination for the report.

To print a distributed report (an .Exe file), follow these steps:

1. **Open Windows Explorer.**

   Locate the Income.Exe file. Figure 15-24 shows the location of this file on my system. On your system, it may be in a different location. Notice that the Income file has an executable icon that's different from the Income.Rpt icon. When you look in the Type column, it says that the file is an application.

2. **Double-click the Income application file.**

   The Consolidated Income Statement window opens. From this window, the person who receives your executable file can determine when she wants to print the report (see Figure 15-25).

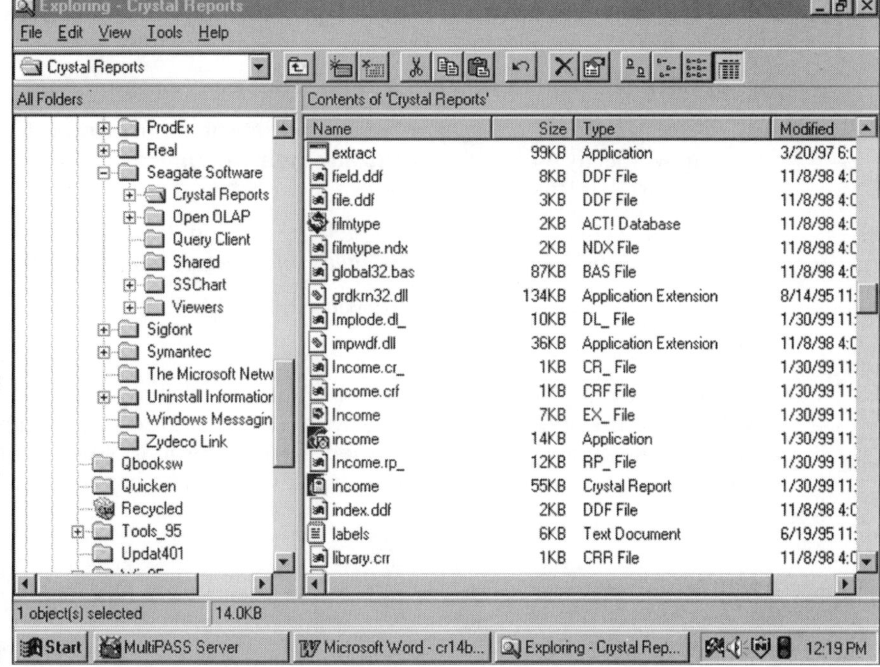

Figure 15-24: Windows Explorer with the Income application program highlighted.

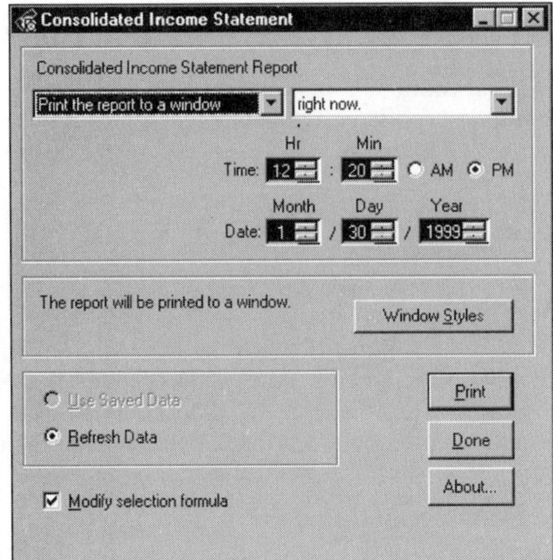

Figure 15-25: The Consolidated Income Statement dialog box.

3. **Click the drop-down arrow in the Print box (on the left).**

   You have three choices: Print the report to a printer, print the report to a window, or export the report. For this example, print the report to a window.

4. **Click the drop-down arrow in the Time box (on the right).**

   You have many choices for when to print the report. You can print it now, specify a time, or specify an amount of time from now to print the report. For this example, choose Right Now.

   If you elect to specify a time, click the up- and down-arrow buttons next to the time values to specify the exact time you want the report to print.

5. **Click the Print button in the Consolidated Income Statement dialog box.**

The income report opens to a window. Figure 15-26 shows how the window will look to the person who receives your distributed report. From this window, the person who receives the report can print it or export it. He can then view the pages of the report almost as though he has Crystal Reports on his machine.

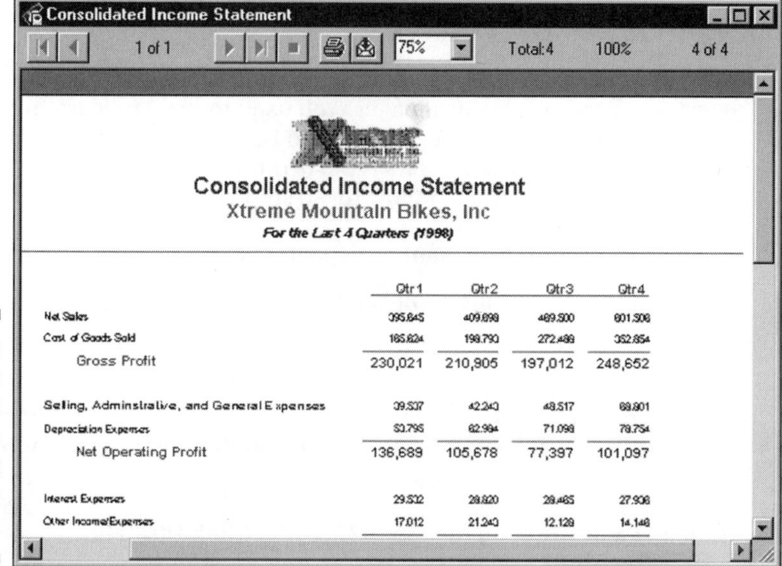

Figure 15-26: The Consolidated Income Statement report dialog box.

Web Reporting

The *World Wide Web* is the graphical portion of the Internet. The Web is the newest way of spreading information to many people at a very low cost. By posting your reports to the Web, you provide access to information that until now has required human attention to receive. No more faxing or mailing reports; simply tell your salespeople or customers to point their browser to your Web site.

The Internet is a collection of high-powered computers all connected by telephone lines. A standard system for addressing a computer and then a site on the computer have been established, making it easy for people to locate your Web site.

To post your reports to the Web, you have to have an Internet Web site. To get one, you or your company must have either an internal computer system that is an Internet host or an account with an ISP (Internet Service Provider).

After you have established your account, your ISP gives you the information about how to access your account.

Exporting to HTML

The World Wide Web uses a standard language — HTML (HyperText Markup Language) to create graphical pages. You used to have to learn to rewrite your reports in HTML in order for them to be usable on the Web. Not so anymore. Crystal Reports exports its reports directly to HTML format! To export a report to an HTML format, follow these steps:

1. **Open the report you want to export.**

2. **Click the Export button on the toolbar.**

   The Export dialog box appears. The Export dialog box enables you to select two things: the format and the destination for the report file.

3. **Click the drop-down arrow in the Format box, and scroll through the list until you see the format that's compatible with your Web browser.**

   In this example, select HTML 3.2 Extended.

4. **Select a destination for the .HTML file. Click Disk File.**

   The Export to Directory window is displayed. Accept the default, which in this case is the Crystal Reports folder.

5. **Click OK.**

   The Export to Directory dialog box appears. The reason a *directory* (a folder) is being created is that a report may contain several elements that, for HTML purposes, must be separated into individual files. For example, all graphics in the report are translated into individual JPEG files, which is a graphical file type acceptable to HTML.

Checking your Web page

The main page (or *home page,* in Web jargon) is named Default.Htm by default. It's the file you open by using your Web browser — which, by the way, is a good way to check the layout and readability of your report in HTML. You don't have to post your report to the Web before you can view the report. Follow these steps to view an exported HTML report:

1. **Start Netscape (or the browser that matches your export format).**

2. **Choose File⇨Open.**

   In the Open dialog box, locate the directory (folder) in which you have exported the report.

3. **In the directory, locate the Default.Htm file and select it.**

   If everything has gone according to plan, the report opens inside your browser. After checking the layout, you can then follow the directions of your ISP to post the report to your Web site.

Chapter 16

Setting Your File Options

In This Chapter

- Field formats
- Font formats
- The default report dictionary

If you have worked with computers, you may recognize the term *default*. It's not your fault if you don't; it refers to an automatic setting in computer software, such as the size of text you add to a Crystal Reports report. With a default setting, every time you add a text object to a report, for example, you can direct Crystal Reports to make the text 18 points high. That way, you don't have to format every piece of text every time you add one to a report. In this chapter, I show you a variety of default settings that make your report creation much easier.

The Crystal Reports environment consists of settings that determine how every report is formatted. You can enter a setting, for example, that formats all numbers with two decimal places. You can override the setting, of course, if necessary; you can always change the format to whatever you need. The point is that when you create a report, you can have most of the settings you want already in place rather than have to add them for every new report.

These settings work only for reports you create in the future. An existing report is not affected by these settings. If you add a new object to an old report, however, the new settings are in effect for that object. It's time to take a look at the Options dialog box and the accompanying report environment settings.

With any report open, check out the default options in Crystal Reports by choosing File⇨Options. The Options dialog box appears, as shown in Figure 16-1.

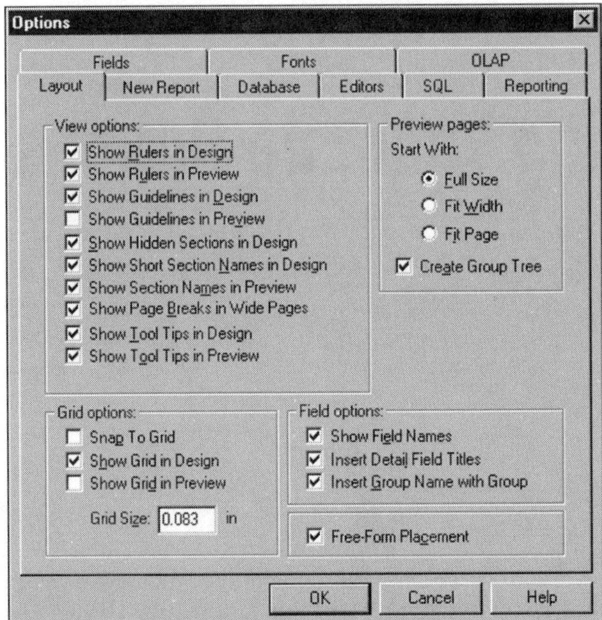

Figure 16-1: The Options dialog box.

Note: If a setting is on, the box next to the option has a check mark in it. Click the setting to remove or add the check mark.

The Layout Tab

In Figure 16-1, you can see that the Options dialog box is open and the Layout tab is selected. Use these options to set the layout defaults you want to use when you create new reports.

View options

The View options are settings you can customize. The default settings include rulers and guidelines on both the Design tab and the Preview tab. The section names are similar to the group tree in that each of the sections is listed to the left of the report body. Figures 16-2 and 16-3 show the difference in the way the section names are displayed. Figure 16-2 shows the full name, and Figure 16-3 shows the abbreviated name. New in Version 7 are the Show Page Breaks in Wide Pages setting and the Tool Tips setting on both the Design tab and the Preview tab.

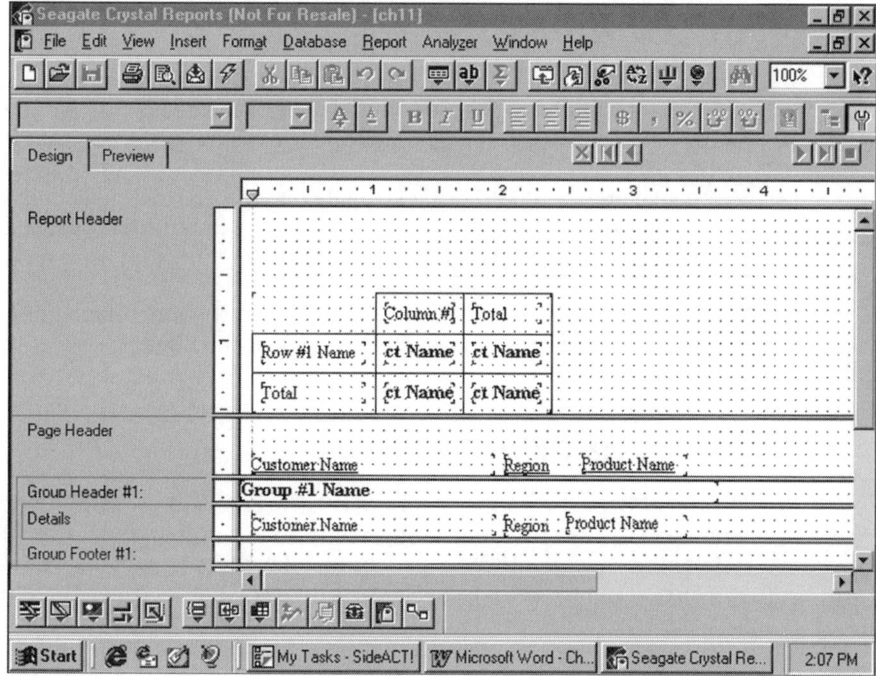

Figure 16-2: A long section name on the Design tab.

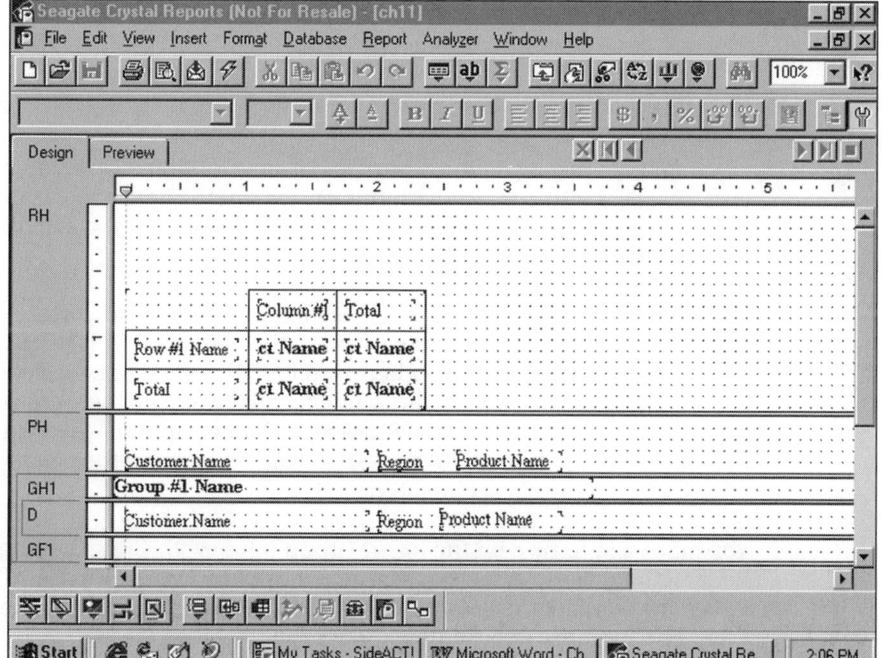

Figure 16-3: An abbreviated section name on the Design tab.

Grid options

Crystal Reports automatically turns on the Snap to Grid option, and — in my opinion — that's where you should leave it. The idea is that when you insert an object into a report, Crystal Reports moves the object so that it is in alignment with a grid of horizontal and vertical lines. This feature gives the report a well-spaced layout without a struggle on your part with each object. If you want, you can have the underlying grid visible in both the Design and Preview windows.

The grid size determines the spacing between the individual lines. The smaller the number, the more closely packed the lines.

Preview Pages

In Crystal Reports, you can work in the Design window or the Preview window. The Preview window gives you a view of the report that includes live data and, consequently, is as close as you can get to seeing how the report will look without printing it. Use the Preview Pages settings to determine the way the report is viewed in the Preview window.

A default setting introduced in Version 6.0 and continued in Version 7 creates the group tree. If you find it annoying, you can click to turn it off and keep it from being created automatically. You can still add it to an existing or new report, if you want. See Chapter 5 for more details about groups.

Field options

I recommend turning on the Show Field Names option. When you insert a database field into a report with this option on, the field name is inserted in place of a series of *XXX*s. If seeing the space allotted for the field is important to you, leave this setting off.

The Insert Detail Field Titles option is already on when you create a new report. When you insert a database field, the field name is inserted as a heading above the Details section where you inserted the database field. The idea is that you can easily determine which field is where in your report. If you use this setting in concert with the Show Field Names option, when you insert a database field the field name appears as the header and the field name appears in the Details section, too.

You may want to turn on the Insert Group Name with Group setting too because it adds the name of the group within the Design window. The default in Version 7 is that the group name is not automatically added. (Refer to Chapter 5 for more information about group names.)

Free-form placement

The Snap to Grid option always decides whether free-form placement is used. If you have the Free-Form Placement option turned on and you have numerous guidelines, you can place fields between guidelines. If this option is turned off, you can move fields only from one guideline to another. Check out the Free-Form Placement option and play with it.

The New Report Tab

The New Report tab is used to determine two things: where new reports are saved and where reports you're mailing are sent by default. To get to the Choose Directory dialog box, as shown in Figure 16-4, you click the Browse button for the report directory to display the folders.

The Mail Destination setting on the New Report tab determines where a report is sent by default when you want to use electronic mail to send it.

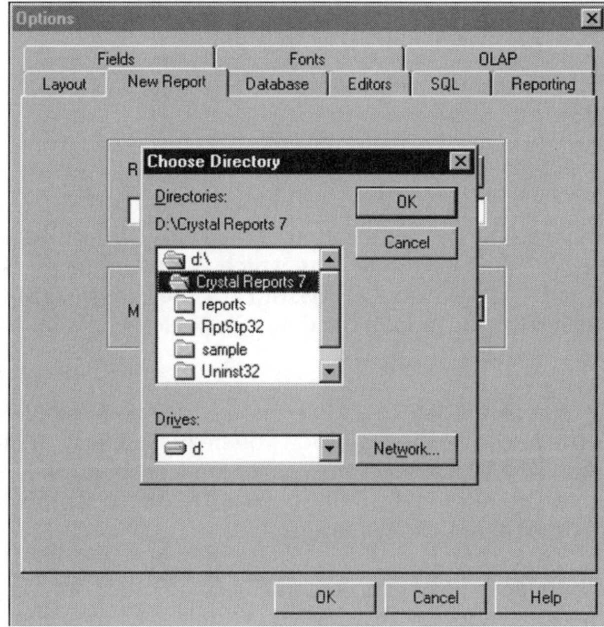

Figure 16-4: Selecting the New Report tab and clicking the Browse button.

The Database Tab

Clicking the Database tab opens the dialog box shown in Figure 16-5.

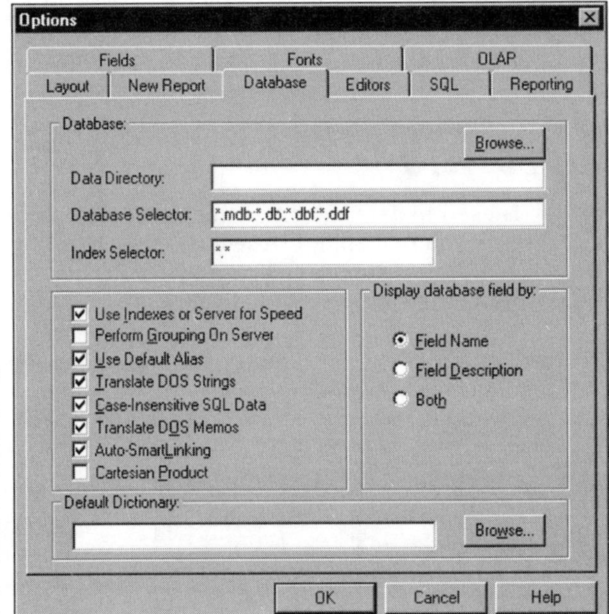

Figure 16-5: The Options dialog box with the Database tab selected.

If you need to change the default location of the source of your databases, either enter the *path* (an old DOS term to which all computer users are wedded), such as C:\MSACCESS\DOUGS, or click the Browse button (the easy way) and click the location of the database tables you want to use to create reports.

If you're trying to access a database that has an extension not listed in the Database Selector field, add the extension you need. Similarly, add the index extension if necessary. Don't forget the semicolon (;) separator. Get a copy of *DOS For Dummies,* 3rd Edition, by Dan Gookin (IDG Books Worldwide, Inc.), for more information about extensions.

The default setting for indexes, the default alias, and other options are best left alone unless you know exactly what you're doing. An exception is Auto-SmartLinking, which is used to link tables, as I describe in Chapter 14.

Another setting you need to think about is the Display Database Fields By area. The automatic setting is Field Name. You can select Field Description, which provides more information about the type of data in the field, or you can have Crystal Reports display both.

Version 7 has two new options:

- **Perform Grouping on Server:** Added for SQL users just so that more of the work involved in sorting and grouping can be done on a server rather than at a desktop. To get this setting correct, read the Help information Crystal Reports provides.
- **Cartesian Product:** The Cartesian Product setting enables you to work with data in unlimited ways — so unlimited that I cannot describe them all.

The SQL Tab

If you're working with SQL databases, you can manipulate the settings on the SQL tab to make Crystal Reports work with your system (see Figure 16-6). *SQL* databases are large databases, as mentioned in Chapters 14 and 15. If you're a beginner, you should ask your company's system administrator to assist you in entering the settings in this dialog box.

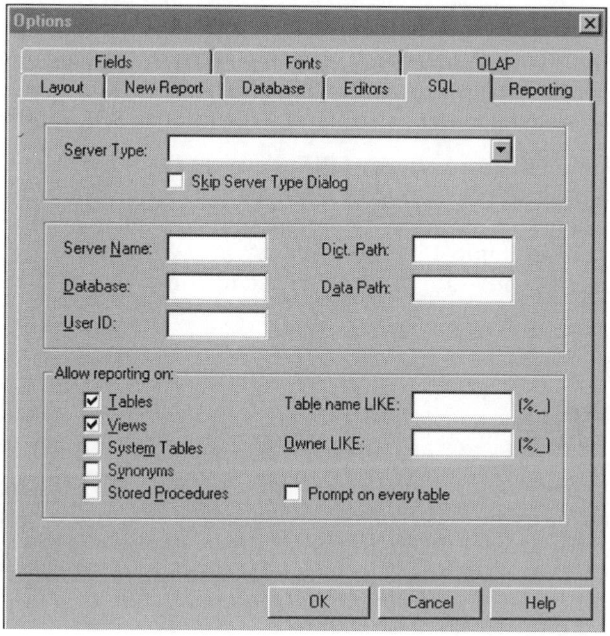

Figure 16-6: The SQL tab in the Options dialog box.

Here's a quick rundown of what each edit box does:

- **Server Type:** Sets the default data source for you.
- **Skip Server Type Dialog Option:** Forces the server type (specified in the Server Type edit box) to be used with no chance for the user to change it. That way, you don't have to hunt down the server type every time you create a new report.
- **Server Name:** Indicates the name of your database server.
- **Database:** Indicates the name of the database on the server.
- **User ID:** Shows the personal code necessary to log on to the database (it's sort of like your network logon ID).
- **Dictionary Path:** Specifies a default dictionary if your database supports dictionaries. That way, you don't have to keep choosing one every time you create a new report.
- **Data Path:** Shows where the data is on the database server.
- **Allow Reporting On:** Enables you to show only the objects you need. If you don't want to see the *views* (a virtual table), for example, don't check this box. With this option turned off, only physical tables are available to you for reporting.
- **Prompt on Every Table:** Gives you the opportunity to specify the data types you want to appear in the Choose SQL Table dialog box. If the box isn't checked, you aren't prompted by the Choose SQL Table dialog box.
- **Table Name LIKE and Owner LIKE:** Narrows the number of tables listed on a database server by finding something generic. (Because a server sometimes has *thousands* of tables, getting them all in a list would take forever.) For example, DAV% returns DAVE, DAVID, DAVIDO, and so on. It's sort of like the * and ? notation used in Windows and DOS to find files.

The Editors Tab

In Crystal Reports Version 7, you can set the default view of the text in the Formula Editor or in the SQL Expression Editor. It's simply a way to make reading the entries easier on your eyes. I increase the size of the font for the Formula Editor to at least 14 points. Figure 16-7 shows the Editors tab.

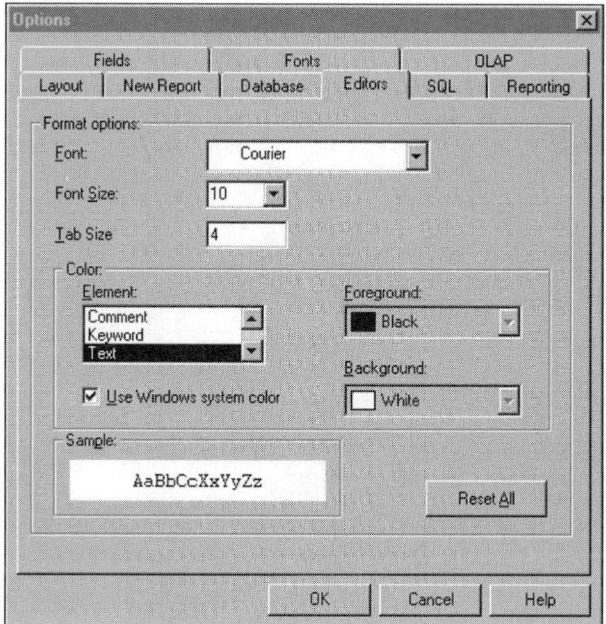

Figure 16-7: The Editors tab.

The Reporting Tab

The Reporting tab, as shown in Figure 16-8, has some more-sophisticated settings that you probably won't need until you have used Crystal Reports awhile.

The options in the Date-Time Field box are specific to Microsoft Access. You can choose to convert the date-time field to a string or to a date or keep it exactly as it is in the original. If you select the Convert to String option, for example, fields in Access that are combined date-time fields are converted to string fields.

The first check box (Convert NULL Field Value to Default) in the next part of the dialog box handles the conversion of NULL-value data in a field (usually zero, or an empty field) to a specific value as determined by the source database.

The other check box in that area, Count Number of Records First, is important if you work with extremely large SQL databases. Why? Because when you're in the process of designing or previewing a report, you don't have to have a multitude of records in the report to determine whether the design is giving you the report you want. Crystal Reports gives you the opportunity to retrieve only a portion of the records.

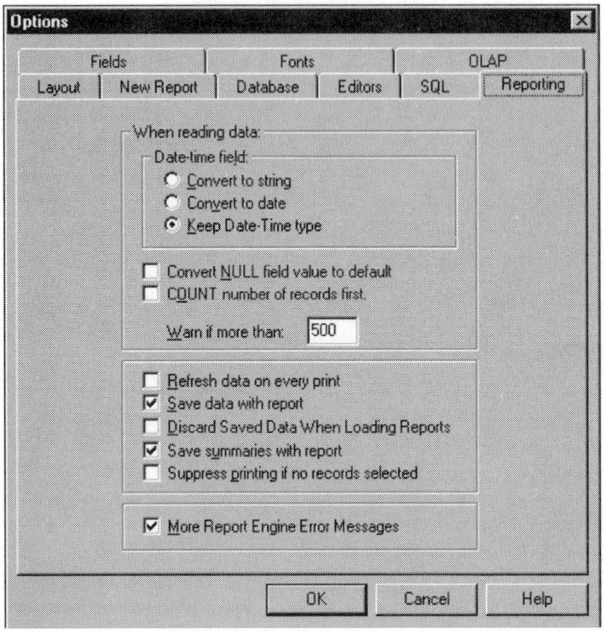

Options

Fields | Fonts | OLAP
Layout | New Report | Database | Editors | SQL | Reporting

When reading data:
Date-time field:
( ) Convert to string
( ) Convert to date
(•) Keep Date-Time type

[ ] Convert NULL field value to default
[ ] COUNT number of records first.
Warn if more than: 500

[ ] Refresh data on every print
[x] Save data with report
[ ] Discard Saved Data When Loading Reports
[x] Save summaries with report
[ ] Suppress printing if no records selected

[x] More Report Engine Error Messages

OK | Cancel | Help

Figure 16-8: The Options dialog box, with the Reporting tab displayed.

The Count option works in concert with the next field, Warn If More Than. Enter a number in this field to set the maximum number of records you want to retrieve during the design phase.

Here are a few more options on the Reporting tab:

- **Refresh Data on Every Print:** When you have made changes to the report and are going to print or preview the report, Crystal Reports prompts you with a dialog box asking whether you want to use the saved data or refresh the data. When you click the check box to select the Refresh Data on Every Print option, the dialog box does not appear and Crystal Reports refreshes the data automatically.
- **Save Data with Report:** I recommend that you click to select this option because most of the time you want the data included with your report. If you don't, you can simply choose File⇨Save Data with Report to toggle the command off. For more information about saving or not saving data with a report, refer to Chapter 15.
- **Discard Saved Data When Loading Reports:** When you open a Crystal Reports report, you usually want the underlying data to accompany it, although you may want the data not to be part of the report. If you select this option, the formatting and other settings remain.

- **Save Summaries with Report:** I don't know why you would deselect this option, but you can!
- **Suppress Printing If No Records Selected:** The default setting is that Crystal Reports prints the report whether or not any records are present. You can change that with this option.

The More Report Engine Error Messages check box is for techie types who need to know why the special code they added to a report by using the Report Engine doesn't work. This option opens the floodgates on the Crystal Reports messages for run-time reports. Rather than hold back any errors, *all* the errors are shown. The option to display all error messages is already selected when you see the Crystal Reports Design tab, but you get to decide what the run-time user sees by using this option.

The Fields Tab

The Fields tab, as shown in Figure 16-9, lists all the types of fields you can insert in a report. This tab enables you to set up the format of fields you insert.

Each of the field types has its own particular formatting attributes; therefore, when you click one of the field type buttons, a dialog box specific to that field appears. For example, clicking the String field type button opens the dialog box shown in Figure 16-10.

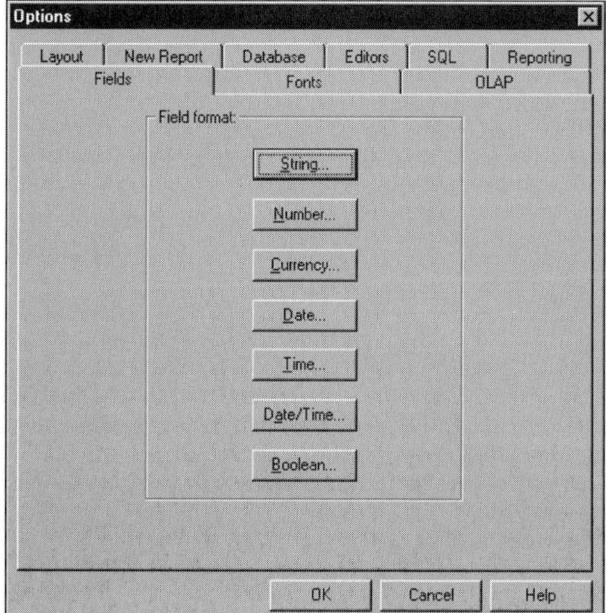

Figure 16-9: The Fields tab, with field type buttons.

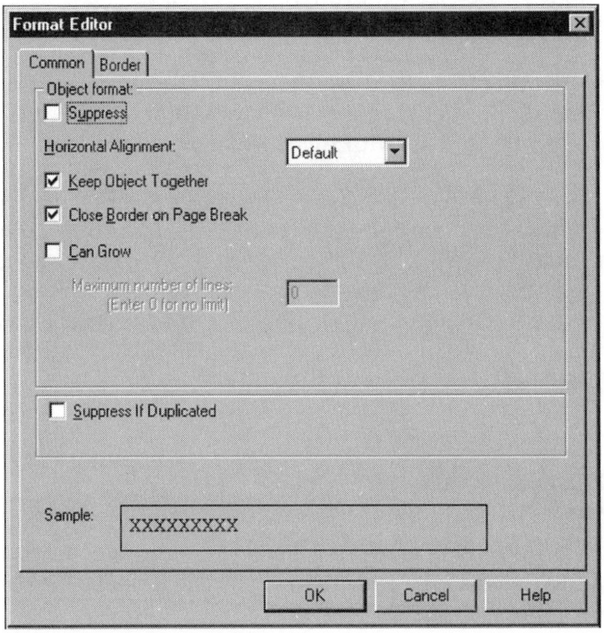

Figure 16-10: The dialog box for the String field type.

A *string field* is made up of characters not considered numbers or dates. That doesn't mean that the field can't have numbers or dates — it's just that Crystal Reports treats as character strings any characters not specifically formatted as dates or numbers. Crystal Reports doesn't make this decision, however. The data type comes from the database itself.

On the Border tab in this dialog box, you can automatically add elements, such as drop shadows or single- or double-line borders, every time you insert text objects. If you have established a consistent style for every text object you insert, you use this tab to make those settings automatic.

To open the Format Editor dialog box, as shown in Figure 16-11, you select the Number field format. The dialog box has four more tabs: Common, Number, Currency Symbol, and Border.

In the Format Editor dialog box, you can click the Number tab to determine such settings as the number of decimal places to display, the degree of rounding that occurs, and the way negative numbers are displayed. Click the Currency Symbol tab to set the manner in which numbers are displayed relative to the type of currency symbol that is included. When you make a change in the format, it is reflected immediately in the preview box at the bottom of the dialog box.

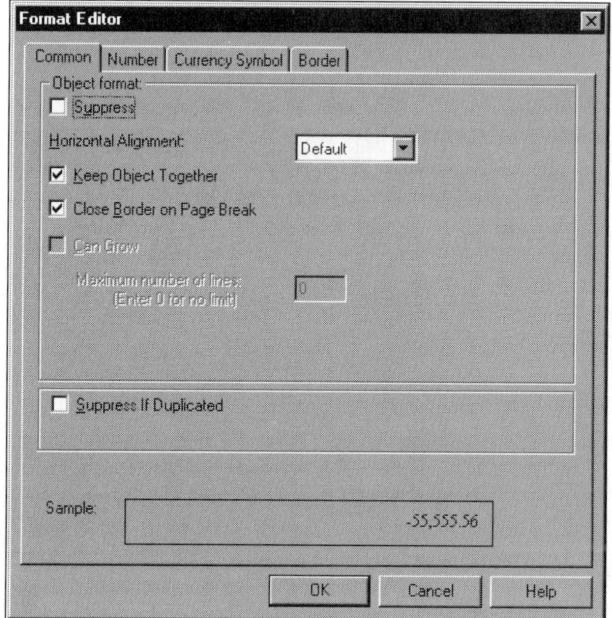

Figure 16-11: The Format Editor dialog box, with the Common tab selected.

The remaining buttons on the Fields tab are of the same nature: You use them to set the automatic format for the type of field associated with the button.

The Fonts Tab

The Fonts tab gives you the tools to set the automatic (or *default*) font sizes and types for each of the fields listed in the Options dialog box. You should use this tab in conjunction with the Fields tab to develop the look you want in your reports. Clicking a Fields button on this tab opens the Font dialog box, as shown in Figure 16-12.

In the Font dialog box, you can select the preferred font and size for each of the fields you insert into a report. As you try different fonts and sizes, the change is reflected in the Sample preview box.

Clicking any of the Fields buttons on the Fonts tab opens the Font dialog box. Click each button in succession and make the settings you want for each field.

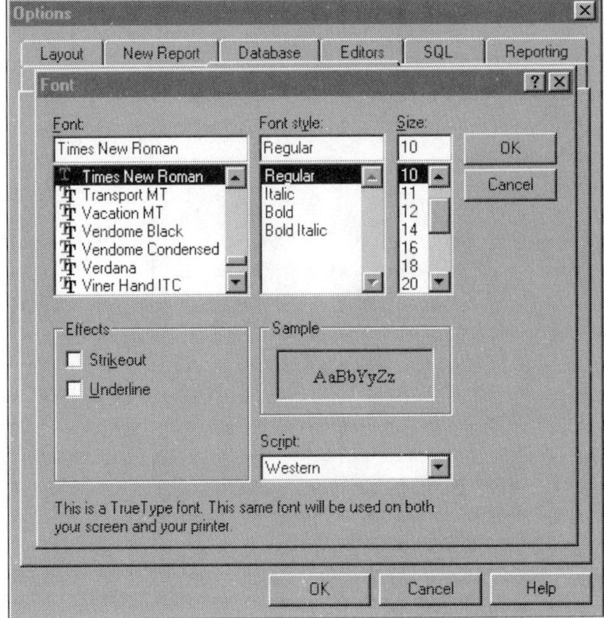

Figure 16-12: The Font dialog box opens after you click any of the Fields buttons.

The OLAP Tab

The OLAP tab is specific to OLAP reports based on OLAP databases, which, as far as I can tell, are from Arbor Essbase. If you know what OLAP is (I don't), you know what you want from these options.

Part VII
The Part of Tens

"I'm sure there will be a good job market when I graduate. I created a virus that will go off that year."

In this part . . .

In April 1990, I happened to be at a writers' conference where another unknown, relatively poor author, Dan Gookin, was in attendance. He told me of the idea he had of writing a real beginner's book on DOS, including humor, with the cover name *DOS For Dummies.* I told him that it was a great idea and that I bet no publisher would do it — their groupthink was that no person would self-identify as a *Dummy.* He replied that the title had indeed been sniffed at by several major publishers. Well, history agrees with Dan and me — over 3.5 million copies of *DOS For Dummies* have been sold. Dan is no longer worrying about paying the rent.

So the Part of Tens, a Gookin original, lives on. In this Part of Tens, I try to convey some of the more important concepts regarding planning and executing your reports. Hand the Ten Questions to Ask Before You Create a Report to your boss the next time she demands a report but does not convey any guidance. Ask for the answers before starting. Then, with the report under construction, look at the enhancement ideas to create a dynamic report.

Chapter 17

Ten Questions to Ask Before You Create a Report

In This Chapter

- Finding the special purpose for your report
- Determining what to include in your report
- Getting your report out to the audience

Your boss comes in to your office in a rush stating that she needs a sales by salesperson report right away! Now what do you do? Remain calm. You need to ask the person, boss or not, requesting a report the following ten questions.

How sensitive is the information in the report?

Is the person requesting this report allowed to access the data? Does the report contain any confidential information?

Although writing down the purpose of the report may seem like a useless exercise, it is very important. Doing so allows you to focus on what should or shouldn't be in the report and how the information should be displayed. This question also allows report recipients to know if this is the report that they want to see or if they should go look for another one.

More and more, companies and institutions are careful about security issues, such as who sees what data. In a hospital, a corrections facility, a school, or a business, some information may not be available to all people. In a company, a person may have to have a security clearance to see certain data. Some financial data may only be distributed to certain people. Some information may be company private or proprietary. Keep these security issues in mind when you create a report.

From what databases, views, or tables do you need to include information in this report, and what fields do you want to include in the report?

Data for a report may come from different sources. Record the databases, tables, or views that hold that data you need. You may need to know the exact directories that hold information. You may need to know what network to access. You may need a password to obtain access to some data.

If you have more than one table involved, you need to link them. The Visual Linking Expert can be helpful to you.

Do you want all the records in the report or a subset?

Women only? Over 60 years old? Transactions for March?

Many reports are run on a monthly, quarterly, or yearly basis. You need to know this information before you create your report. If you don't know, you may be in a position where you are waiting for 15 minutes for a report preview to display because you are looking at data for the last ten years. Whether you are looking for data from a certain region, a certain gender, or a certain time period, you're better off if you can reduce the number of records in your report. The Select Expert can be helpful to you.

How do you want the data grouped?

Find out if the data should be grouped by region, by date, or by alphabet. Some reports may have several groups. A report could be grouped by state, then by gender, and then by age.

How do you want the data sorted?

Usually the two choices are ascending order or descending order. In addition, you will want to know if the data should be sorted in ascending or descending order by amount, alphabetically, or some other criteria. As with groups, you may sort alphabetically by state and then sort by amount within those groups.

What summary calculations do you want in the report?

Monthly totals? Grand totals? Averages? Find out if you need to count the records in the report, get a running total, add summaries at the end of the groups, and other information. Consider whether you want summaries after every group.

What text do you want to appear in the

- Report Header?
- Page Header?
- Page Footer?
- Report Footer?
- Other Text?

Record the text you want to display in each of these report sections. Decide on which pages you want this text to display. You may want to display some text on the first page, but not on the others. Find out if any other text is required. You may need to describe some of the summary calculations. You may need to add some quotes or expressions.

Do you want certain data to stand out?

You can make data stand out by using flags, special formatting, or conditional formatting. If the person for whom you're creating the report wants the data to stand out, find out how.

This step is for the more sophisticated presentation quality report. Will the report be printed? Will the report be distributed on a network? Do you have a color printer? You can make totals greater than 10,000 appear in red. If you are presenting in black-and-white, then you want to make totals greater than 10,000 appear in reverse image. Based on the report's purpose you can make the critical data stand out.

How should the report be distributed and to whom?

You may have a network, where all the reports are distributed to an Exchange folder or to Lotus Notes. You may want reports uploaded automatically to a company intranet page. Perhaps you are distributing a report to a group who does not have access to Crystal Reports. Find out if you want to send them a compiled report or if you need to export the report so it can be read by another software product.

Again, the security issue raises its head. Can anybody see the information in this report, or is it company private, proprietary, or confidential? You're better off to find this information out before you distribute the report.

When do you need to see this report, and when should it be distributed?

You should get into the habit of finding out the due date for activities assigned to you. The person requesting the report may want to see and approve the report before you send it out. Find out if the report has a critical deadline.

Is this how the report should look?

Before you start creating the new report, draw a picture of the report with all the titles, columns, groups, and so on. Get the drawing approved. Then you will have a guideline made for creating the report. Here is how you might make the report look:

Title		
Header		
Group		
Field	Field	Field
XXXXXXXXXX	XXXXXXXXXX	XXXXXXX
	Summary Data	XXXXXXX
Footer		

If you follow these steps, even in an oblique way, the stress and strain of creating reports is greatly reduced.

Chapter 18

Ten Tricks to Enhance Reports

In This Chapter

- Remaining consistent
- Adding enhancements appropriately
- Using pictures to convey data

The purpose of a report often is to summarize and identify key information necessary to manage your enterprise. (Unless you work in government, then your purpose is to obfuscate and befuddle, thereby guaranteeing the need for more reports and securing your job!) So the following ideas are not tricks really, just some guidelines that will make your reports easier to understand and interpret.

Use a predictable format

Being predictable does not mean being boring. Life is simpler for everyone if you and your readers can identify a report with a glance.

- Be clear and consistent.
- Note selection conditions in the Report Footer.

By using standard formats for specific reports, you engender consistency for all concerned. At a glance, anyone can then identify the kind of report by its format. Adding the selection conditions in the Report Footer tells the reader what data has been used to generate the report.

Another way to record information regarding the report is to enter the information into the Document Properties dialog box. To do so:

1. **Open the report.**
2. **Choose File⇨Summary Info.**

3. **Add the comments you want and close the dialog box.**
4. **Add the Comments field in the report by choosing Insert⇨Special Field and selecting Report Comments.**

   Insert the Report Comments field in the Report Footer or wherever you feel appropriate.

Another labeling aspect is to use the same labeling format for the same type of report object — subtotals, summaries, and grand totals.

Allow generous white space

The acronym used to describe reports that are too busy and number laden is MEGO, meaning My Eyes Glaze Over. Keep this fact in mind when you start adding detail to the report. Your report is only as good as the information that is easily conveyed to the reader.

Another way to add readability is to format every other line of the Details section in a different color. See Chapter 10 for the formula to do so.

Position report headings and page numbers in the same place for every report

Many reports are generated on a regular basis. Therefore the design should remain the same to avoid the need to re-create and edit the look of a report with each generation.

- Your report reader can easily locate crucial information.
- Display data in a predictable order.

Consistently paying attention to format makes the information in your report accessible. To do this easily, create a report template with all the major formatting in place, save the report, and then use the Another Report button from the Report Gallery dialog box to select the saved template.

Make data easy to understand

Insider terms and jargon should always be avoided. If your report includes calculations, you should have a key to how they were constructed.

- Wrap or use abbreviations rather than truncate data.
- Use standard terminology.

All the field headings in a report are editable. If the field name that is copied from the database is cryptic, change the field heading to something that everyone can understand. Wrap field headings, that is, carry the full heading to a second line, rather than truncate, which means to shorten, because not all readers will be able to interpret the truncation properly.

Place and align columns appropriately

Readers can easily become confused if the data is not correctly labeled. Keeping the headings with the proper data and positioning data in a consistent, logical order is very important. See the steps in Chapter 3 for help with this.

- List fields from left to right, consistent with the sort specification.
- Use ascending order, or note descending order in a header or footer.
- Align data.

Keeping the data aligned with the accompanying headers and using a logical order is another way to make the report more understandable.

Keep columns consistent

The following may be difficult, but arrange your report columns of data so that readers can easily determine where one set of data ends and another begins. Carrying over headings from page to page relieves the reader from moving back and forth to confirm the heading for the data. See Chapter 9 for more on formatting.

- Space columns evenly to make boundaries obvious.
- Keep columns near enough so a reader can scan a line.
- Repeat column headings on each page.

Use column headers strategically

Any numeric columns must have a clear heading that defines what the column contains. Chapter 10 shows you how to combine a field with explanatory text.

- Use meaningful column headers above each field space.
- Specify units (meters, units, millions of dollars) when not clear.
- Use abbreviations in field labels that the reader will understand.

Visually group data

Reading a report that resembles a dictionary is quite tiring to the eye. Effective use of white space relieves eye fatigue.

- When record information is on more than one line, separate each record with a blank line.
- Leave a blank line between groups of data.

Crystal Reports does leave space between groups, but you may want to increase the distance for added clarity. Or you may choose to draw a box around the individual groups.

Add graphs and/or maps to make your reports more descriptive

Graphs and maps are far superior to numbers when it comes to relating relationships or trends. The graphing and mapping capabilities of Crystal Reports make including the right kind of graph or map in the right place an easy task.

Add graphics to your report to make it visually interesting

You want to avoid graphic clutter, but keep in mind that a photograph, designs, or a logo can convey a great deal of information.

What company report is complete without your photo adorning the title page? Maybe you should save that idea for when you become company president.